Margaret Morris

D1611856

The General Strike

Radical Men, Movements and Ideas

GENERAL EDITOR: A. F. THOMPSON,

WADHAM COLLEGE, OXFORD

Already published:

RESPECTABLE RADICAL

George Howell and Victorian Working Class Politics

F. M. LEVENTHAL

KEIR HARDIE

Radical and Socialist

KENNETH O. MORGAN

The General Strike

The Politics of Industrial Conflict

G. A. Phillips

Weidenfeld and Nicolson
London

© 1976 G. A. Phillips

All rights reserved. No part of this publication may be reproduced, stored in a retrieval system, or transmitted, in any form or by any means, electronic, mechanical, photocopying, recording or otherwise, without the prior permission of the Copyright owner.

Weidenfeld and Nicolson
11 St John's Hill London SW11

ISBN 0 297 77063 2

Printed and bound in Great Britain by
Morrison & Gibb Ltd, London and Edinburgh

Contents

Tables

Abbreviations

AEU	Amalgamated Engineering Union
ASLEF	Associated Society of Locomotive Engineers and Firemen
ASRS	Amalgamated Society of Railway Servants
ETU	Electrical Trades Union
IFTU	International Federation of Trade Unions
ILP	Independent Labour Party
LM&S	London, Midland and Scottish Railway
MFGB	Miners' Federation of Great Britain
MM	Minority Movement
MMM	Miners' Minority Movement
NUR	National Union of Railwaymen
OMS	Organisation for the Maintenance of Supplies
RCA	Railway Clerks' Association
SIC	Special Industrial Committee
SOC	Strike Organisation Committee
T&GWU	Transport and General Workers' Union
TUC	Trades Union Congress

Editor's Introduction

The aim of this series is to bring together a variety of studies by historians and others of the development of the Left in recent times. Its eventual purpose is to provide a general survey of the impact of radical men, movements, and ideas on both sides of the Atlantic. The first volumes, however, are concerned with the Left in Britain, and in particular with the evolution of the Labour Movement, whose chequered history throws so much light on problems which face the would-be reformer in any advanced society.

The main objective of the Left is always a 'radical reform' of the existing order in the interests of 'the people'; but the meaning of the term 'radical' varies with time, place, and circumstance. The history of the British Labour Movement illustrates this fluctuating relationship between constant and variable, ends and means. If it is to be understood, the Movement has to be set against the background of nineteenth-century Radicalism from which it emerged, and its activities in the twentieth century must be related to the changing conditions which have modified its beliefs and governed its destinies.

The immediate need is for scholarly but readable studies of those aspects and phases of the Movement which are of increasing interest both to students and to the general reader. In part, this means filling the more important gaps in our existing knowledge; but it also means adding new dimensions to what is familiar and opening up new perspectives in the light of changes in the historian's methods and the range of research in allied disciplines upon which he can now draw.

The reader must also be offered a choice of approach. The projected studies will therefore consist of four main types: the biographical, covering intellectuals as well as men of action; the structural, analysing the organization of the Movement and setting its activities in their economic and social context; the ideological, exploring the role of ideas and their promoters in these activities; and the episodic, dealing with the interaction of men, movements, and ideas in moments of crisis or in areas of crucial importance for the Left.

A. F. Thompson

Acknowledgements

For help in writing this book my chief thanks are due to my editor and former tutor, Mr A. F. Thompson, who has influenced my outlook on history for too long a period and in too many ways for me adequately to acknowledge, and who again on this occasion offered constant encouragement and counsel. I am also indebted to my friends, Bob Bliss and Dai Smith, for their comments on earlier drafts of chapters I and III and their efforts to elicit my sympathies for the miners and for the general reader. If what follows remains deficient from these points of view, it is no fault of theirs. Benjamin Buchan, of Weidenfeld and Nicolson Ltd, was responsible for correcting many stylistic blemishes.

I have benefited from the courtesy and assistance of a number of trade unions and union officers in the process of gathering material, in particular the Transport and General Workers' Union, the National Union of Railwaymen, the National Union of Mineworkers and the Iron and Steel Trades Confederation. The Amalgamated Union of Engineering Workers allowed me to read their journal, but not their executive minutes. I am also, above all, grateful to the Trades Union Congress Library and Records Section for giving me access to their holdings and providing me with working facilities over many weeks.

I acknowledge with thanks the opportunity to consult Lord Gainford's papers, by permission of the Hon. Joseph Pease, and Ramsay MacDonald's papers, which were made available to me by the kindness of David Marquand MP. Adrian Scheps, whose unpublished doctoral thesis was of considerable use to me, also gave me advice about possible sources at the outset of my research. I am grateful, too, to Mike Woodhouse for allowing me to see his thesis on the South Wales miners. I profited from a friendly discussion with Patrick Renshaw, whose own book on the General Strike appeared when my manuscript was on the point of final delivery.

The following libraries and depositories have afforded me valuable services, and in some cases provided important unpublished materials: The British Library of Economic and Political Science; Nuffield College, Oxford; the Cambridge University Library; the Beaverbrook Library; Durham County Record Office; the House of Lords Record Office; the Public Record Office; Colindale Newspaper Library; the British Museum.

This work may not prove easily digestible, and I should, perhaps, in the manner of past writers conscious of their humble status ask for the indulgence of my readers. Those students of recent British history who may be required to use it for the purpose of answering essay questions conventionally addressed to matters of cause and consequence will find the framework of its argument in the first sections of chapters I and XII and in the concluding chapter; the account of the immediate antecedents of the strike in chapter V is summarized in pages 127–33.

I Anticipations

To almost all those who passed judgement on it, then or later, the British General Strike was remarkable on the one hand for the scale of working-class support which it received, on the other for an almost total absence of revolutionary attributes. Although 'general strikes' in various forms had occurred elsewhere in Europe and America since the beginning of the century, nowhere had proletarian forces been mobilized so effectively as they were during the nine days of May 1926. If well-organized, these earlier offensives had involved smaller numbers, usually within narrower industrial or geographical confines; alternatively, they had assumed the spasmodic and uncoordinated character of spontaneous revolutionary outbreaks. The problem which first presents itself in a history of the General Strike in Britain, therefore, is the coincidence of exceptional union solidarity and comparatively modest objectives.

In the make-up of this compound, a number of elements are readily discernible. British trade-union membership was high – it had, since the mid-nineteenth century, been almost unrivalled elsewhere in the world. It had grown particularly rapidly, from about two and a half to over eight millions, in the decade 1910–20 and even after five years of economic depression remained at some five and a half millions in 1926. The period of most rapid expansion had been accompanied by a consolidation of union resources, the creation through amalgamation of a handful of pre-eminent organizations, notably among workers in transport, local government, metal and engineering and building. The movement as a whole had also acquired a central representative body, in the General Council of the TUC, with wider responsibilities and greater pretensions than its predecessor. It had not, on the other hand, acquired a revolutionary ideology. The unions' fairly gradual progress towards political independence and collectivist principles since the 1880s had been accommodated by the establishment of a Labour Party which accepted almost without reserve the national institutions of parliamentary democracy.

These factors explain, in broad terms, the disciplined and moderate lineaments of the General Strike; they scarcely explain its outbreak. The union movement clearly had the *capacity* to undertake a stoppage of this kind for some years prior to 1926 – perhaps as early as 1914; where the political will to employ it came from remains, however, obscure. Three more difficult lines of inquiry need to be followed in order to answer this problem. The first traces the mental distinction which the union leadership came to make, consistently after about 1918, between 'industrial' and 'political' strikes – the former supposedly safeguarded by law and usage, the latter extraordinary and justified only *in extremis*. It was this contrived antithesis which made it possible to conceive of a concerted sympathetic stoppage that was devoid of revolutionary implications. The second is the relationship which had been formed between that same leadership and their rank and file, which even before the 1920s had helped to foster a popular belief in the efficacy of the general strike tactic, and was then to weaken official resistance to it. The third follows the policies of industrialists and governments from the onset of the post-war slump in 1921, in the perspective of which the mining crisis of the mid-1920s was seen as demanding so drastic a response on labour's part.

Union organization and the tactic of the general strike, 1889–1920

By the end of the first decade of the twentieth century the general strike was already a familiar aspect of the theoretical debates, and in some cases part of the historical experience, of the labour and socialist movements of Continental Europe and the United States. It was a revolutionary tactic expounded by syndicalists in France and anarchists in Spain and Russia, left-wing marxists in Germany and industrial unionists in America.[1] And it had been enacted, on a larger or smaller scale and with differing objectives, in Belgium in 1893 and 1902, in the Russian revolution of 1905 and in Sweden in 1909. Though remaining a focus of dispute, from both an ideological and practical point of view, it was a subject to which socialists and trade unionists alike had been compelled to give serious and regular attention.

Three principal uses had been conceived for this class weapon. It was seen firstly as an instrument of revolutionary social change – self-sufficient in the eyes of anarchists and syndicalists, complementary to other forms of political activity in the view of some marxists. It was regarded, too, as a means of securing particular and limited political goals: the extension of the suffrage, the defence of civil liberties or rights of combination. From either perspective the general strike could also be advocated as a preventative of war, revolutionary or otherwise depending on whether or not wars were regarded as an unavoidable product of modern capitalist society. Finally, though only in Sweden, the general strike had been used by trade unions to prosecute an ordinary industrial dispute with national bodies of employers.[2]

In Britain, on the other hand, interest in this method of class warfare had hitherto been marginal. The absence of a tradition of revolutionary political activity, a relatively liberal system of government and a trade-union movement apparently securely established at least among more skilled workers, tended to confine discussion of the general strike, as of other imported elements of socialist thought and policy, to minority radical sects: the Socialist League, the Socialist Labour Party and its offshoots, and the anarchist groups associated with the magazine *Freedom*.[3] Though it had been more widely canvassed in the 1830s and '40s, and again less energetically in 1867, as a means of obtaining working-class enfranchisement, it no longer had, as it did in Belgium or Russia, apparent relevance to causes of democratic reform. And the main socialist organizations which emerged in late-nineteenth century Britain – the Social Democratic Federation, the Fabians and the ILP – never considered it as a viable method of bringing about social change. It was true that, after 1905, the members of the ILP had embraced the proposal of a general strike for the particular purpose of preventing war, and thereby gave a lead which a few trade unions were to follow prior to 1914.[4] In the Second International this created an incongruous alliance between British socialists and the spokesman of French anarcho-syndicalism. But the ILP's motives were pacifist, not revolutionary; and in terms of its actual or prospective power to execute such a policy, its commitment was nominal. Though enthusiasm for using industrial action as an anti-war measure was to persist, and to gain a more significant expression after 1918, its advocacy was, even then, an extraordinary response to a short-lived crisis, with relatively slight consequences.[4a]

The general strike entered the consciousness of British labour leaders, therefore, not as the result of ideological influence or intellectual argument, but through the slowly changing character of trade-union organization and tactics. It can be understood, accordingly, only in the light of structural developments in the movement since the late 1880s, well before the term became current or the phenomenon recognizable. It was, firstly, the formation of national unions of unskilled and other unapprenticed workers, and secondly the evolution by them of the tactic of the industry-wide and the sympathetic strike, which created the preconditions, and determined the form, of the 'general strike' which took place in 1926.

Though national recruitment had been undertaken amongst craftsmen, in some cases, by the New Model Unions of the 1850s and 1860s, it was the organizations established (or renovated) in the late-1880s which first adopted it as a basic geopolitical principle. They did so initially as a condition of survival in face of hostile employers and of volatile and undependable members. In the case of the miners, who came together in a federation of county unions in 1889, the association of the men of various coalfields had been regarded since the 1840s as a necessary response to the power of employers at a local level, to intense inter-regional competition within the industry, and to the severe economic fluctuations to which the industry was liable. Attempts had already been made on two previous occasions to establish such a broad combination of workers.[5] On the railways the Amalgamated Society of Railway Servants was founded in 1871, but it adopted a national all-grades programme for the first time only in 1889, as a method of combating the strong and intensely anti-union companies and to defeat the divisive effects which the elaborate system of promotion had upon their employees.[6] For a variety of labourers' unions in transport, building and manufacturing, national organization seemed imperative, as in many cases did coverage of several industrial groups, in order to offset the effects which casual employment, seasonal migration and cyclical recession had upon unskilled and supposedly footloose workers and to increase their resistance to the use of free labour.[7] Among this category, even the most local and sectionally based unions adopted the title 'national' as a mark of their aspirations to grow and colonize.

The desire to operate on a larger scale led these and similar unions to adopt organizational ideals and models which rationalized and popularized their growth. 'Organization by Industry' was already a familiar slogan before 1910, taken up by the miners, the ASRS and by elements of the engineers, builders and transport workers.[8] It was an ideal, however, incompatible with and even inimical to 'general' unionism, with its amorphous patterns of recruitment and its tendency to absorb neglected minorities in any industry. The leaders of this type of combination therefore propounded, though less consistently, the even more grandiose goal of 'one big nation'.[9] For the most part, however, the immediate purposes of 'industrial' and 'general' unionists were the same: to combat union sectionalism by amalgamation or federation; to establish closed shops and exclusive bargaining arrangements; to pool funds and centralize decision-making. The use of contrasting arguments of a more abstract, rhetorical kind in commending these objectives created an impression, always somewhat unreal, that the movement was at odds; and at the same time, because such slogans were the invention of a distinguishable 'left wing' they suggested, again only with a partial validity, that trade unionism was attracted towards a new ideological pole.

If national organization was seen as enhancing the bargaining power of particular groups of workers it was because it conferred the potential capacity to conduct large-scale industrial stoppages. The use of the wisely extended strike was required by the ambitious industrial objectives of the unions; national programmes, standardizing conditions of work, were unlikely to be enforced by piecemeal action. Both miners and railwaymen had formulated demands by the late 1880s which were ultimately to lead to national strikes. The resultant collaboration among employers on an industry-wide basis to resist union aggression increased the probability of large-scale conflict, not only on the railways but also in shipping, and in some of the traditional provinces of the craftsmen: engineering, building and printing. The Amalgamated Society of Engineers had already experienced a general lock-out of its members in 1898.[10]

For the general and unskilled unions the problems of conducting successful stoppages were especially acute. Though those labourers employed in public utilities, local government or port and road transport were not particularly affected by the growth of market competition which prevailed in manufacturing and mining, they suffered comparatively more from the fact of a disorganized labour market. Strikes, in consequence, could usually succeed only in conditions of full employment – and even then the threat of free labour was rarely absent. Seeking means to increase their strike power, these unions soon recognized the advantages of the simultaneous withdrawal of men in contiguous and interdependent occupations; a form of warfare, effective even in a local context, for which their miscegenous industrial composition was particularly suited. It was this tactic which came to be known, often misleadingly, as the 'sympathetic' strike. The parallel stoppage of various unions in the London docks in 1889 and the strategy which those organizations subsequently sought to apply through the Federation of Trade and Labour Unions provided the classic prototypes.[11] And the creation of the National Transport Workers' Federation in 1910 was an attempt, by much the same group of union leaders, to revive their earlier practices of collaboration.

The widespread industrial disputes of the 1890s were followed by a period of relative quiescence; but in the years immediately before the first world war conflict revived, affecting many of the same trades. Though widely regarded as a novel phenomenon, the labour unrest of 1910–14 did not differ in its main features from the phase of warfare experienced after the *annus mirabilis* of 1889. It occurred at this juncture simply because economic conditions now became more favourable to the use of the strike weapon.[12] Marked violence and intensity were almost certainly not the result of radical political influences, but rather of the accumulated discontents and successive reverses suffered in the long interlude of persistent unemployment and union weakness which had gone before.

The chief importance of the industrial conflict of 1910–14 in the evolution of union tactics was to bring about, unforeseen, an association of those two forms of strike action, 'national' and 'sympathetic', hitherto separately used in different industries. During the summer of 1911 strikes took place among railway employees, seamen, dockers, carters and others throughout the country. This movement was contagious, unplanned and largely uncoordinated.[13] But its temporary success served to demonstrate the apparent potency of simultaneous large-scale stoppages in different industries. Once they had witnessed it, union leaders were quick to set out the lessons. If stoppages had ceased to observe industrial boundaries, this was because capitalism had ceased to do so. Railway companies numbered dockers, carters and canal workers among their employees, for example; the Shipping Federation, most hostile of all employers' associations to union organization since the 1890s, hired dock labourers as well as seamen. Moreover the impact of almost any sectional strike could be partially neutralized if transport services remained unaffected – an observation confirmed by the continued importation and distribution of coal during the mining stoppage of 1912. It was in coal and transport first of all, therefore, that workers and unions embraced cooperation against their mutual enemies, partly a natural reflex and partly a tactical principle.

During these years, too, an unfamiliar left-wing current of ideas appeared within the union movement, lending the prevailing unrest an apparently more profound significance. The syndicalists of the pre-war period were the first such group to give widespread publicity to the general strike as an aspect of a social theory and strategy. Though many divergent opinions flourished under this *nom de guerre*, almost all those connected with the Industrial Syndicalist Education League advocated the systematic use of the national and sympathetic stoppage in the prosecution of industrial movements; and an ultimate resort to the general strike for the purpose of transforming the social order. Their Manchester Conference in November 1912 called upon workers 'to prepare for the expropriation of the capitalist class . . . by means of the Revolutionary General Strike'.[14] The expression of such opinions mesmerized press and politicians, convincing them and some later historians that new forces were at work beneath the industrial troubles of the time.

In fact the real impact of syndicalism, measured in terms of ideological conversions, was small. In its efforts to gain approval, at the TUC or elsewhere, for an anti-parliamantary standpoint and union isolation from the Labour Party, it was easily defeated.[15] And its attitude to the general strike was rarely taken seriously in the movement. The syndicalists gained prominence because they were, unlike their revolutionary predecessors, activists within the unions, directly engaged in sectional strikes and campaigns for reorganization.[16] But their contribution to the occurrence of unrest was slight, and the schemes of amalgamation with which they were closely associated were unsuccessful. The importance of left-wing opinion in the unions may be less than fully gauged by such clinical tests; syndicalist slogans retained their appeal down to 1926. But it is clear that though the General Strike owed much to the practical effects of the militancy of the pre-war period, it owed little directly to syndicalist propaganda.

The conclusions which union leaders drew from the stoppages of this period, on the other hand, were most fully expressed in the Triple Industrial Alliance – the coalition of miners, railwaymen and transport workers whose constitution was drafted in the spring of 1914. It was this body which, envisaging a concerted withdrawal of labour by several national union organizations, first signified an explicit conversion of senior union officials to the policy of the general strike. But their conception of this weapon, though confused by alarmed statesmen and employers with that of the syndicalists, was in reality very different. The Alliance was to be an instrument firmly in their own control, not at the disposal of a militant rank and file. Its purpose was confined to securing the conventional industrial objectives of improved working conditions. Though the architects of the Alliance expected to prompt the government to take a prominent part in industrial disputes, its intervention was desired simply to assist in realizing the demands made of employers. And although they were contemplating joint action on a vast scale they hoped that, for this very reason, the frequency of conflict would be reduced and gains obtained by the exercise of an enhanced bargaining power. In short, the miners and transport workers regarded a general strike simply as a way of applying more effectively and in the last resort methods of warfare previously employed in a narrower compass in their respective industries. The Alliance had, for them, no revolutionary import; the consequences of collective action under its auspices were, indeed, only superficially considered.[17]

The General Strike was in origin, therefore, the tactical product of a pattern of industrial conflict and union organization which had developed over the past twenty-five years or so in industries where unionism had been introduced only with difficulty, among rapidly expanding labour forces traditionally resistant to organization, or against strong opposition from employers. It was, in labour's view, not a major innovation, but an extrapolation from kinds of militancy relatively familiar before 1914, intended to augment their effectiveness. Hence the immediate economic and political repercussions of such a strike were not thought to differ to any significant extent from those of other widely-extended stoppages. This assumption was to be preserved in the years down to 1926; indeed, post-war events were to strengthen the feeling that a distinction could be made between general strikes for political and for industrial ends, and that the former but not the latter were *sui generis*. To suggest that union leaders were wholly uninfluenced by radical ideology would be an exaggeration, but the nature of that influence was not such as to dislodge the view that their own practical commitment to joint industrial action was without revolutionary undertones.

For a short time after the war, it is true, the difference had been obscured. As early as 1916 the Triple Alliance threatened to organize a strike against any attempt by the wartime government to introduce industrial conscription in the trades for which it provided. In 1919 it again proposed, though did not manage to execute, a joint stoppage against the continuance of military conscription and British intervention against the Bolshevik regime in Russia. In March 1920 the miners expressed a special Trades Union Congress to approve a stoppage to enforce the nationalization of their industry.[18] And the following summer the TUC and the Labour Party joined forces in a Council of Action which was authorized, if necessary, to bring about a general strike to prevent British participation in the war between

Russia and Poland.[19] The rapid numerical growth of the union movement during the post-war boom, in conjunction with the weakness of the Labour Party in parliament after the 1918 election, created an evident temptation to use industrial action for purposes hitherto unconsidered.

The appeal of direct action was, however, transitory. It arose, in the first place, from a confusion of industrial and political spheres brought about by the peculiar wartime circumstances, when state controls on the economy and the repercussions of conscription widened the perspectives of trade unionists on what were their responsibilities and interests. The uncertainty persisted during the slow dismantling of the government war machine, but did not outlast it. Furthermore, attempts to use industrial force to gain manifestly political ends usually created dissension within the movement. The Triple Alliance's initiative in 1919 led to divisions within its ranks which made a repetition unthinkable.[20] The miners themselves disagreed about the advisability of a general strike over nationalization and their proposal received scarcely any support from other unions[21] Both episodes indicated the difficulty of obtaining a sense of corporate interest on issues of this kind. The Council of Action did not encounter such opposition, since the possibility of a renewal of war provided an emotive moral rallying point; but for this reason it constituted an exceptional case. The anticipation of a general strike in 1920 did stimulate the creation of local rank-and-file organizations which set the pattern followed in 1926.[22] And to an extent obviously incalculable the impact which the threat of a collective stoppage *seemed* to have upon the government must have increased the faith of ordinary union members in the potency of this weapon, encouraging an inclination to put it to other uses. But it cannot reasonably be argued that the campaign of 1920 was a necessary condition, either psychologically or organizationally, of the events of 1926. As for the national labour leadership, many of them were by no means anxious to see a repetition of this venture. Their bravado during the crisis had concealed a continued sense of vulnerability to the charge of endangering the parliamentary system, and they were accordingly relieved that no such accusation had been seriously pressed by the government. The chief significance of this episode was thus, perhaps, to foster a false sense of immunity to any indictment for unconstitutional behaviour when they projected similar action, on a question far less overtly political, six years later.

The propaganda of syndicalists before the war and the arguments over direct action afterwards had both questioned the validity of separating political and industrial objectives of union policy. But even at the height of the post-war unrest most union leaders still adhered to this conceptual antithesis. The conventional terms of the dichotomy – political *versus* industrial – were, however, misleading: the distinction being made was essentially between the prosecution of trade movements (which might in fact implicate the government as employer, conciliator or even legislator, but which were confined to questions of working conditions) and on the other hand the use of coercive means to cause elected administrations to change policies or institute laws which had no reference to any current industrial dispute. Action of the former kind was deemed legally and constitutionally unexceptionable even when it threatened to lead to stoppages on an unprecedented scale. It was only union initiatives on the latter basis that were held, strictly speaking, *ultra vires* – potentially revolutionary even if on occasion morally justifiable. It is true that during the ten years or so before 1926 some prominent labour spokesmen suggested from time to time that eventually the unions must prepare to attack the capitalist system in entirety. But these predictions, visionary or rhetorical, were not relevant to any immediate objectives. Nor, what is more important, did they cast doubt on the assumed legitimacy of concerted stoppages directed to more practical and restricted goals.

The lessons of Black Friday

From the end of 1920 to 1926 the prospects of coordinated union action were discussed almost entirely in relation to industrial issues. This preoccupation reflected, first and foremost, the rapid change in economic circumstances and union fortunes brought about by the collapse of the post-war boom. Throughout the previous decade a general strike had been considered against a background of rising membership and full employment. Its primary industrial purpose, therefore, had been seen as the realization of demands for recognition or bargaining rights and for establishing or improving national standards of pay or hours. No such general stoppage had occurred prior to 1920, however, partly because considerable gains had been made in these directions by sectional stoppages or simply by successful collective bargaining through the mechanism of Joint Industrial Councils and the like. During the trade boom such claims and stoppages had usually not required sympathetic support. The first signs of a climatic change occurred in October 1920, when the miners, still seeking for wage increases by means of strike action, and resisted by a government now preparing for decontrol, failed to win the backing of their partners in the Triple Alliance. The following April, they appealed to the Alliance to fulfil a specifically defensive role, by helping them resist the wage reductions and district settlements demanded on the return of the industry to private enterprise. The débâcle of Black Friday, when the railwaymen and transport workers withdrew their promise of industrial support, led to their eventual abandonment of the struggle some eleven weeks later.[23] In the next two years similar unaided attempts to resist a down-grading of their standards were made by, among others, engineers, builders, printers and footplatemen. All ended in defeat. Concerted stoppages came to seem the more urgent, as the only alternative to further reverses and abject surrender. The general strike was thus viewed by the unions almost wholly as a means of resistance to attack, on matters of basic material interest which had traditionally been their main concern.

The defeat of Black Friday was, then, to be of far greater importance in shaping the events of 1925 and 1926, than the alleged victory of the Council of Action the year before. Far from discrediting the efficacy of the national sympathetic strike, it served in retrospect to provide a stronger rationale for that very strategy. The threat of a combined withdrawal of labour in 1921 had momentarily brought both employers and government to the point of suggesting terms better than anything the MFGB could subsequently extract.[24] The miners' effort to continue their struggle in isolation was weakened because other unions continued to transport British and foreign coal (attempting only a brief and ineffective boycott). Above all, the Federation's capitulation was followed by heavy wage reductions in almost all other industries as well as in coal – opposed, if at all, to no avail, and amply fulfilling the prediction which Robert Williams, the NTWF Secretary, had made in the TUC of 1920: 'unless we can act in the mass we shall be broken in detail'. The widespread belief in the superior organization and strategy of the employers was also confirmed. Looking back in the aftermath of Black Friday a year later the TUC's Assistant Secretary, Fred Bramley, wrote:[25]

> The Trade Union Movement is not yet fully equipped to deal effectively with economic tendencies of this kind or the operations of employers' federations who attempt to take full advantage of the opportunities created.... The Federation of British Industries represents a much more perfect form of organization than anything we can show on the labour side. Against powerful

combinations of this kind the individual union is as useless as a pop-gun on the modern battlefield, or a cockle-boat against a dreadnought.

This explanation of the failure of trade unionism in face of the post-war depression was widely believed. And its currency helped to give the movement an appearance of having united upon a distinctively 'left-wing' platform. How deep this unity was remains open to question; but an interpretation which presents the unions *as a whole* as having adopted a more radical posture, at least on certain issues, is probably more revealing than one which analyzes their behaviour in this period in terms of a rivalry between distinguishable left- and right-wing factions. Though such dissensions had been a feature of the direct action controversy, and though some individual union leaders (above all, J. H. Thomas of the railwaymen) had earned the undying hatred of many militants for their conduct on Black Friday, the economic adversities and industrial setbacks of the following years encouraged a greater public accord; whilst the divisions on issues of policy which occurred after 1921 often defied simple political classification, and reflected rather the special circumstances and organizational characteristics of particular industries and unions.

The attitudes of union leaders are the more resistant to generalization because of the complex relationship between them and their rank and file, vocally represented by a left-wing movement that was itself diverse and amorphous. In so far as 'unofficial' radicalism had a clear political identity, whether syndicalist or Communist, it was held in some suspicion. But, as has been mentioned, even these organized minorities stood for certain policies – in particular, union concentration – which were also advocated by many of the official leadership. Nor were the latter unsympathetic to the ideal of workers' control, at least in the post-war years when the original and revolutionary definition of the syndicalists had been somewhat softened by the influence of Guild Socialism.[26] After 1921, besides, the Communist Party stressed its identification with a defensive industrial strategy, and neglected its revolutionary principles in pursuit of a united working-class front. In a more imprecise sense the unofficial left consisted simply of the militant activists of the unions' rank and file, troublesome at times but also essential to the local vitality and administration of any large-scale organization. The maintenance of their morale and loyalty was a task which no union leader could afford to neglect.

It was partly for this reason that union officers found it requisite to employ a radical style of rhetoric in addressing both their own membership, and that of the movement as a whole. But, more fundamentally, that rhetoric had been a product, since the 1880s, of the very process of union growth. Originally an indispensable means of recruitment, it remained a necessary medium for the statement of common goals to a vastly enlarged body of supporters, geographically scattered, situated in different trades or subject to varied conditions of work, lacking any natural sense of group interest and identity. The emphasis on the importance of class and movement was designed to foster a unity which other, more visible, factors obstructed. Similarly, the association of union activity with democratic social objectives served to disguise or even justify the increasingly centralist and bureaucratic tendencies of union government. Though a rhetoric of this kind came more easily to some than to others, it was still part of the qualifications of almost every labour spokesman. Without the myths of an all-powerful capitalist enemy and the ultimate ideals of a socialist commonwealth, union leaders in the years before 1926 could have offered only the most halting and makeshift defence for the vast size, elaborate structure and diverse composition of their organizations.

This left-wing vocabulary and propagandist tone created its own imprisoning ideals and the guards to patrol them. During the depression years after 1921, the general strike came to be seen not just as the sole remaining means by which wage cuts might be resisted, but also as the prime expression of the movement's moral standards. The less the opportunity for short-term gains and sectional action, the more it became the decisive test of solidarity. But a rank and file susceptible to such an appeal naturally demanded of its leaders that they abided by their own professions of principle. This was in fact another lesson of Black Friday, whose perpetrators, try as they might, could never repeal the popular verdict of betrayal. It was not as a policy-making but as a disciplinary force that the unofficial left acted with most effect. For this reason the events of 1926 were to be, in large measure, a kind of expiation for 1921.

The general strike could be regarded, therefore, as both a symbolic representation of the ideals of the movement, and a specific answer to immediate industrial problems. Neither perspective, however, solved the practical difficulty of carrying it out. In the aftermath of Black Friday three very different views had been expressed about the causes of the Triple Alliance's collapse. The miners themselves saw the explanation in terms of the absence of a natural desire for unity on the part of their associates, and of the conditions which would induce it.[27] Some of the other leaders concerned, notably Ernest Bevin, attributed the fault to the organizational defects of the Alliance itself and in particular to the autonomy preserved by its many constituent bodies.[28] The Communist Party and its sympathizers argued that the Alliance lacked sufficient internal democracy to ensure the control of the rank and file over pusillanimous officials.[29]

In the next four years or so, much energy was spent in an attempt to design a more satisfactory instrument for the purpose of coordinating union action. The discussion continued to focus on the same three arguments here outlined. As has been suggested, however, the debate did not reflect clear-cut political allegiances, and there were, in fact, some significant shifts of opinion both in the Communist Party and in individual unions. In the end those who advocated a greater degree of centralization and consolidation in the union movement were never able fully to overcome the suspicions which their proposal for an overriding collegial authority aroused. Of the two organizations designed to frame collective policies and conduct collective strikes, the General Council remained constitutionally straitjacketed and the Industrial Alliance was stillborn.

The establishment of the General Council

The proposal to create a more authoritative executive for the Trades Union Congress was the natural outcome of union expansion between 1910 and 1920 and of the advent of industrial bargaining with government and employers at national level during and after the war. The old Parliamentary Committee was too small in size and functioned too exclusively as lobbyist and pressure group to act as the representative organ of the movement. Its political responsibilities had, besides, been largely appropriated by the Labour Party. It was the *industrial* functions of the General Council, the body which replaced it in 1921, which were from the outset the focus of attention and argument, and which remained so throughout the first five years of its existence.

The origins of the General Council lay in the national railway dispute of October 1919, when an *ad hoc* committee of officials from the unions primarily affected by the stoppage was formed to attempt to mediate with the government. The members of this committee subsequently urged upon the Parliamentary Committee the desirability of establishing an organ of Congress which could fulfil such industrial purposes on a more regular basis. The Parliamentary Committee itself had already been considering the possibility of such reform, in a desultory fashion; it now set up a 'coordination committee', including spokesmen from those unions who had interested themselves in the matter of its reconstruction, together with other representatives of the movement.[30]

The intention of some of those who participated in the planning of the General Council was to create what they termed a labour 'general staff', capable of initiating common policies and collective action for the whole union movement.[31] And the proposals eventually endorsed by the Congress of 1921 did confer wide responsibilities on the new body: not only to adjudicate inter-union disputes, to assist organizational activity and to watch legislation of interest to labour, but also 'where possible' to coordinate industrial movements, to 'promote common action . . . on . . . any matter of general concern' and 'to assist any union which is attacked on any vital question of Trade Union principle'.[32] These obligations were obviously imprecisely expressed, however – and as its officers were quick to point out the General Council was vested with no constitutional powers and guided by no agreed procedure in fulfilling them. The affiliated unions were expressing a faith in the idea of a concerted strategy for the movement but no particular commitment to its practical accomplishment.

Those who drafted the original scheme of 1920 undoubtedly hoped that such an accord might develop in time. They saw the General Council as a medium through which the possibility of more effective cooperation might be explored, but not as a means of imposing it. The collapse of the Triple Alliance, however, helped to destroy this faith in organic and evolutionary processes, and by 1922 the members of the Council, encouraged by its assistant secretary, Fred Bramley, were already seeking an increase in their statutory powers. They asked the TUC to instruct its affiliates to supply in advance information on all industrial movements, and to allow them to 'take the initiative' in a large-scale dispute. Where negotiations within an industry broke down the Council was to be authorized to consult the unions directly and indirectly involved, to offer the former 'its considered opinion and advice', and – if a stoppage nonetheless occurred – to organize 'all such moral and material support as the circumstances of the dispute may appear to justify'. Financial aid was to be made possible by empowering the Council to levy the constituent organizations in proportion to their membership.[33]

These recommendations were strongly opposed by the miners, the railwaymen and the T&GWU, among others. Fears were expressed that a stronger Council would restrain affiliated unions wanting to pursue militant policies on a sectional basis; but a more widely accepted criticism was voiced by the industrial secretary of the NUR, C. T. Cramp, who argued (not for the last time) that it was the spontaneous feeling of solidarity among the workers, rather than the creation of a more authoritative central body, which made possible sympathetic strike action:[34]

The general assumption underlying all proposals which make for mass action is that there is always virtue and certain success in a general strike. . . . My own view is that only under certain given circumstances, at certain times, can the greatest mass action be effected. . . . You cannot get mass industrial action by any paper constitution or Standing Orders which you choose to frame. You can only do this when the minds of men and women who are concerned are thoroughly in unison with the objects sought to be achieved. . . . The possibility of attaining those things . . . cannot be definitely fixed long beforehand.

This was not a viewpoint which can accurately be described as 'right-wing'. In the case of the railwaymen it owed less to the conspicuous moderation of their political secretary, J. H. Thomas, than to the past experience of the union, the impact of whose stoppages had owed much to their unexpectedness. But it was not unlike the attitude adopted by the miners after Black Friday; and, still further to the left, the old syndicalist Tom Mann conveyed an idea of the general strike similar to, though more facile than, that of Cramp:[35]

. . . there is . . . one way that beyond any question, if resorted to, will enable the workers to absolutely stop the retreat, and to turn about and march forward. . . .

This is by resorting to a General Strike – by the War of Folded Arms – by refusing to function as workers except under conditions we as workers approve of. . . .

It is not necessary to have a prolonged stoppage – one week would be enough – and no strike pay would be wanted or should be asked for; each family must now make its own preparations, men and women alike doing their best. The women must begin at once to get in a little extra week by week, flour one week, sugar the next, and so on. Already the matter has been widely discussed and unanimously endorsed at typical meetings of workers.

Not until the formation of the Minority Movement in 1924, in fact, did the Communist Party adopt the slogan, 'All Power to the General Council', and even then many left-wingers in the union movement remained, like A. J. Cook, disposed to search for the sources of militant action in working-class enthusiasm untempered by bureaucracy.[36]

Despite these prejudices, the advocates of a strengthened General Council persisted. A resolution similar to that of 1922 was again defeated at the 1923 Congress.[37] But by the following year significant improvements in the Council's position had been achieved by administrative initiative. Fred Bramley was promoted to the office of full-time secretary (compensating, in part, for the TUC's refusal to appoint a permanent chairman at its inauguration). Walter Citrine became in turn the new assistant secretary and did much to raise the efficiency of the Council's routine services. Contacts were established with the Trades Councils through a Joint Consultative Committee, with the object of converting them into local publicity agencies. And for the first time the Council acted in the capacity of mediator in industrial disputes involving shipbuilding workers, dockers, builders and railwaymen.[38]

Finally, at the Hull Congress of 1924, the Council managed to secure the passage of an amended resolution on joint industrial action. Its eventual success in this regard has been widely attributed to the increasing strength of left-wing opinion in the movement since 1921; and in other contexts, evidence for such a current is not lacking. In 1924 the TUC adopted a series of controversial and boldly-worded resolutions on sympathetic strikes, cooperation with Russian trade unions and union amalgamation with scarcely any opposition. As far as the reform of the Council itself was concerned, it has been seen that the advent of the Minority Movement had provided fresh backing for this cause. And the fact that two known left-wingers, George Hicks and A. J. Cook, moved the motion amending the Standing Orders appears to lend further force to this interpretation. Professor Roberts and Mr Lovell argue, accordingly, that the principal reason for the success of the proposal was the readiness of left-inclined unions like the miners to assume that the Council would no longer exercise a consistently inhibiting influence upon the policies of its electors, but would actually be prepared to organize 'moral and material support' for those involved in disputes. The complexion of the Council itself, which was about to replace one left-wing chairman, Alf Purcell, by another, Alonzo Swales – and from which prominent moderates like J. H. Thomas and Harry Gosling had been removed by service in the Labour government – allegedly buttressed this assumption.[39]

Plausible as it appears, however, this argument remains unconvincing. In the first place more than three and a half million votes had been cast against the Council's constitutional recommendations in 1922 and almost three million in 1923, as against a mere 259,000 in

1924. This is a far larger movement of opinion than can be explained by the accession of left-wing support. Secondly, there is no evidence that the miners or any other union had any immediate intention of calling upon the General Council for industrial assistance in sectional movements. 1924 was a year of economic recovery, breaking the sequence of industrial reverses which had given 'coordinated action' its immediate appeal and allowing most large organizations to obtain wage increases by their own efforts. The absence of Thomas and the elevation of Purcell and Swales were not, in this connection, factors of much significance. Thomas had taken no part in previous debates on the powers of the General Council – his fellow-secretary, C. T. Cramp, having voiced the railwaymen's negative views. Left-wing chairmen had not reflected any *general* change in the balance of forces on the Council, where the right remained predominant throughout the whole of this period. There were however no signs of its elected officers disagreeing on important issues of TUC policy in 1923–4, either with its other members or with the permanent staff.

The 1924 resolution passed with such ease because four major unions besides the miners, had switched their votes from opposition to support since 1922: the two leading general unions, the engineers and the railwaymen.[40] It seems unlikely that any of them were influenced by the more militant complexion of the General Council – though the AEU may perhaps have been won over by the accession of Swales, one of its officers, to the chairmanship. The T&GWU, and Bevin in particular, were probably impressed with the Council's improved administrative capabilities, and had already shown their willingness to cooperate with it during the dockers' and tramwaymen's disputes of that year. And the General and Municipal Workers (like many others) were likely to have welcomed the excision of the proposal made in 1922 and 1923 empowering the General Council to make financial levies upon its constituents.[41] But it is not evident that any of these organizations regarded the Council after the amendment of its Standing Orders as significantly more important to them than before; in 1924 three of the four were represented on it by subordinate officials.[42]

In the absence of more pressing considerations, it is still reasonable to assume that some other unions were prompted to change sides on this issue by the miners' conversion. But were the miners themselves moving on a left-wing tide? It was at least as likely that their attitude to the Council would have changed anyway with the emergence of new leaders and the passage of time. In 1920–1 Smillie and Hodges had little cause to be enamoured of the Parliamentary Committee, which had failed to assist them effectively in securing nationalization of the mines and had crossed swords with them over direct action. And they had seen the General Council, at that stage, as merely a new incorporation of the old guard. By 1924 the miners' chief officials were Herbert Smith and Arthur Cook, neither of whom had inherited the personal animosities which had shaped the opinions of their predecessors. But they, too, did not seem to value the Council very highly in practice. Cook himself was not to become a member until 1927; and Smith, having played an inconspicuous part in its activities since 1922, was to be replaced by Tom Richards in 1925.

If these fairly minor and personal considerations could bring about so large a reorientation, a more major conclusion seems to follow: the alteration of the Standing Orders secured such overwhelming approval in 1924 because it was not regarded as an issue of great moment. This impression is reinforced by the extremely abbreviated debates produced by the resolution both in 1923 and 1924. Initially, the proposals had aroused apprehension that the Council might interfere in disputes against the wishes of the protagonist; but the Council's own discretion (as well as the withdrawal of the objectionable financial recommendation) had removed this fear. The Council itself was at pains to point out, in discussing its diplomatic activities of the previous year, 'in any efforts of a mediatory character which [it] has undertaken it has always been a primary condition that the disputing union or unions should first have indicated their acceptance of the Council's assistance.'[43] Thus interpreted, the terms of the 1922 motion seemed harmless enough. Moreover, closely scrutinized, it was obvious that, excluding the levy, they gave the General Council no *powers* which it did not already possess, save the unenforceable one to require affiliates to supply information about impending trade movements. The resolution did no more than set up a procedure for use in the event of major industrial crises which the TUC's member bodies approved in advance but which they would have to consent to again on each separate occasion it was employed.

It seems fair to conclude that the TUC accepted these proposals, as they did most 'left-wing' resolutions in 1924, as an inexpensive gesture of solidarity. Not only had the General Council no experience of joint stoppages; it had given no serious thought to the problems of organization or policy which they would present. Nor had this been demanded of them by their constituents. Whilst the amendment of the standing orders was a further testament of faith in the ideal of the general strike, and whilst 'coordinated action' was a popular and inspiriting cry, most unions had scarcely considered it as a practical matter since 1921. In so far as they shared an idea of the *nature* of a general strike, it was as a larger replica of past national stoppages or an extended sympathetic strike. In so far as they had thought about its planning, probably the majority agreed with Cramp's contention that this should be left to the hour of crisis. And so far as its actual execution was concerned there remained, apparently, much doubt about whether the General Council was truly adequate for fulfilling this particular purpose. Smillie had said in 1922, even after the collapse of the Triple Alliance, that 'it is the great key industries like the miners, the railway people and the transport workers that we must depend upon to defend the general interests of the Trade Union movement in this country'.[44] For the performance of functions so central to their existence most unions were, not surprisingly, reluctant to place any substantial degree of reliance on an untried body composed of diverse interests and lacking any tangible resources. Those organizations most urgently concerned with the task of upholding working-class standards at the beginning of 1925, the miners in particular, turned away from the Council towards a more manageable and compact alternative.

Government counter-preparations: the Supply and Transport Committee

Although the Liberal government before 1914 had been faced with national strikes in basic industries and public services, leaving ministers to conjure with the spectre of a 'general strike', it was not until after the war that attempts were made, by the Coalition administration of 1918, to devise effective counter-measures to such disruption. The post-war administration was no doubt alarmed by the apparently revolutionary connotations of some of the stoppages declared or threatened in the spring and summer of 1919: by the Clyde workers over hours, by the miners demanding nationalization, by the Triple Alliance over conscription and intervention in Russia. In addition, however, the new government simply had less opportunity to adopt a position of neutrality in industrial disputes than had its predecessors. Both the mining and railway industries remained under state control until 1921, so that stoppages in these sectors involved the government directly. And its larger conception of economic policy, the acceptance of responsibility for industrial reconstruction and for restraining inflation, likewise compelled it to take a deeper interest in the effects of strikes and trade agreements.[45] At the same time the *possibility* of establishing emergency services to alleviate the impact of strikes was much larger, thanks to the increased range of official economic activity born of the war. The powers exercised under the Defence of the Realm Act, the skilled manpower retained in the armed forces, the machinery and personnel of the Ministry of Food and the reserves of transport built up by various departments since 1914 were all at the disposal of an administration wishing to curtail the repercussions of large-scale stoppages. A Cabinet committee on industrial unrest, with an interdepartmental staff, was thus set up in February 1919. It was extended and renamed the Strike Committee during the national railway strike in September. The following month it became the Supply and Transport Committee, and the minister in charge, Sir Eric Geddes, was given the title of Chief Civil Commissioner. It was with this apparatus that the Coalition sought to disarm or to deter the labour unrest of the period up to the mining lock-out of April 1921.[46]

This first exercise in the containment of strikes had two enduring results. Firstly, the administrative system worked out prior to 1921 was adhered to in the Supply and Transport Committee's second phase of life in 1923–6. The hierarchy of central departments of state subordinated to a Cabinet committee, of special divisional offices in the regions and a mixture of public and voluntary local organs, was retained subsequently with small modifications of boundaries and functions. Secondly, the legislative basis of both the earlier and later emergency plans was provided by the Emergency Powers Act of 1920. Passed on the occasion of the mining strike of October, this measure had in fact been under consideration by the government for some time before. It gave the executive power, on the declaration of a state of emergency, to introduce temporary but legally binding regulations by order-in-council to preserve the peace and to maintain essential supplies.[47] It became the *ultima ratio* of all governments, Conservative, Coalition and Labour, faced with large-scale stoppages in the next few years.[48]

The collapse of the Triple Alliance on Black Friday was at least in part a tribute to the formidable appearance of the first supply and transport machine. With the defeat of the miners in 1921, however, the organization was allowed to lapse, as the immediate threat of industrial conflict receded. The decontrol of mines and railway reduced the government's economic responsibilities, and the upkeep of an emergency cadre became more difficult as well as potentially more expensive after military vehicles and other wartime supplies had been sold or exhausted. In the financial year 1920–1 £750,000 was spent on anti-strike provisions; in August 1921 Geddes, as chairman of the Cabinet Economy Committee, reduced the annual budget of the organization over which he had presided to £2,000. The following May local authorities were told to 'make such arrangements for maintenance of local services as may be thought to be required in the event of need arising'. For a time the Supply and Transport Committee passed into obscurity.[49]

The decision to revive the machinery was taken in May 1923, when Baldwin appointed his private secretary, J. C. C. Davidson, as Chief Civil Commissioner (concealed behind the official facade of Chancellor of the Duchy of Lancaster). Davidson's chief assistant was the under-secretary of the Home Office, John Anderson. It was he who prepared a report for the Cabinet in July 1923 indicating the state of obsolesence of the post-war supply and transport organization and arguing the need for their replacement. Between then and the election of December Davidson claims that he 'laid the groundwork and created the nucleus of the organization' of a new scheme. The process of rebuilding was suspended during the term of the first Labour government, but resumed in the autumn of 1924, when the Postmaster General, Mitchell-Thomson, succeeded Davidson as Chief Civil Commissioner.[50]

These counter-strike measures, taken in secret and restricted in scope, were not evidence of official clairvoyance, but they did reveal the belief, shared by Baldwin himself, that the possibility of a general strike existed. Conservative ministers were always prone to see the forces of labour as divided into left- and right-wing camps – and to exaggerate the influence, actual or latent, of the former. The Prime Minister, on the eve of his most celebrated plea for industrial peace in connection with the Trade Union Levy bill early in 1925, had spoken of 'that subtle poison of hatred which is being preached in some quarters', and of 'signs of an industrial storm gathering' – and the call for 'peace in our time' arose from this sense of tension.[51] This sort of diagnosis, however, showed little appreciation of why essentially moderate union leaders might resort to the use of general or sympathetic strikes; or, therefore, of how to prevent them. If the TUC could be accused of failing to see the political implications of such an industrial weapon, the Conservatives were, more and more, to fail to see anything else.

II The Miners and their Industry

The depression of coal

The history of the coal industry in the years from 1880 to 1926 epitomized Britain's fall from world-wide industrial supremacy. Prior to the first world war coal mining had maintained an incomparable record of growth and prosperity. Its product was both the basis of Victorian industrial enterprise and by the twentieth century the second most valuable of Britain's exports. It employed by 1914 almost one in ten of the male labour force, and afforded them more job security and higher average wages than were enjoyed in any other important occupation.[1] It was also the subject of close political and legislative attention. By 1925, however, mining had become an indicator of all the problems and deficiencies of the national economy. Miners formed the largest single numerical group among the unemployed, though the rate of unemployment (excluding short time) was only just above the national average. Real wages fell more drastically between 1920 and 1924 than in most trades elsewhere, whether sheltered or depressed.[2] And coal had already become the centre of an embittered political and industrial conflict, in which the source of and the cure for its malaise were equally disputed.

The decline of the coal mining industry was not, however, a straightforward and continuous process. As the statistics in Table 1 reveal, movements in output, exports and profits after 1918 were erratic in the extreme. The war years were obviously a climacteric; production never thereafter regained the record level of 1913. But exports were higher in 1923 than ever before; and in that year, as well as in the post-war boom of 1919–20, the industry secured larger real returns than before the war.[3]

It was to the unpredictable variation of export volumes and values, however, that the vicissitudes of the industry after 1918 were mainly due. Foreign trade in coal was subject to temporary and fortuitous influences which obscured underlying industrial trends. For a brief period after the armistice, the devastation of the important French coalfields and the immobilization of the German allowed the British industry (still under state control) to exercise a near monopoly of the European market. Export prices rose, in some cases to ten times their pre-war figure.[4] With the world depression of 1920–1, these windfalls abruptly ceased. But two chance developments soon brought about an equally rapid recovery in the industry: the prolonged national mining strike in the USA in the summer of 1922; and more significantly the French occupation of the Ruhr in January 1923. Once again the British mine-owners were afforded largely uncontested access to a variety of overseas markets, new and old. The sharp decline in the fortunes of the coal trade which began late in 1924 could thus superficially be considered as no more likely to persist than any previous interlude of its post-war history.

TABLE I. *Coal Mining:*
Output, exports and labour productivity, 1909–25

	output (m. tons)	*exports*	*output per man year*
1909–13	269·59	88·37	257
1913	287·43	98·34	260
1919	229·75	n.a.	240 (1918)
1920	229·40	43·7	n.a.
1922	249·61	87·34	195 (1919–23)
1923	276·00	102·82	229
1924	267·12	81·75	220
1925	244·42	68·97	217

Source: Samuel Report, pp. 118, 127–8; Jones *et al.*, *The Coal Mining Industry*, pp. 27, 31; Redmayne, *The Coal Mining Industry during the War*, p. 284.

The fundamental causes of the slumps of 1921 and 1925 were, however, to endure now for the rest of the inter-war period. The most intractable problem of the industry was simply the declining rate of growth of the world's demand for coal, unaccompanied by any comparable decrease in the rate of supply. For fifty or sixty years before 1914 international coal consumption had risen on average by about four per cent a year; from 1918 to 1929 this increase fell to one per cent or less, and prior to 1926 world demand actually remained below its pre-war level.[5] The reasons for this retardation are fairly well established (although their relative importance is more debatable). Firstly, the development of new methods of fuel economy in industry was greatly encouraged, in the years 1914–20, both by the curtailment of foreign trade during the war and by the exorbitant price of coal subsequently. The slump of 1921 tended further to reduce industrial requirements. At the same time, new and competitive sources of energy became available – petroleum oil and hydro-electricity. In Britain, oil provided a substitute for coal especially in the fuelling of ships. Thirdly, consumption in some parts of the world – most notably in Russia – was reduced by political and economic disorganization.[6] On the other hand the exploitation of fresh resources of coal and lignite continued throughout the years 1914–20, so that from the beginning of the post-war depression all major coal-producing countries were raising larger outputs than they could hope to sell.[7]

The British coal industry was particularly vulnerable to these global disturbances because it had been so heavily dependent on international trade in earlier years. In addition Britain suffered peculiar – though secondary – problems of her own. The ability of her mine-owners and coal merchants to compete successfully in foreign markets was affected by the terms of the Versailles peace treaty, which required Germany to supply free reparations coal to her former enemies, Italy and France,[8] and which created a Polish nation whose economic welfare became crucially linked with its capacity to export coal. These provisions thus upset established patterns of trade upon which Britain had thrived before the war. Moreover the depreciation of the currencies of several western and central European nations in the early 1920s gave them a substantial, albeit temporary, advantage in disposing of exports of all kinds. This advantage was later gratuitously restored by the British government's decision to return to the gold standard on the pre-war rate of exchange in April 1925.

The difficulties which the British coal trade faced on the demand side may also have been magnified by deficiencies on the side of supply. How far the coal industry of this country could be fairly accused of inefficiency is a matter of dispute; but most disinterested contemporary observers (to say nothing of the Miners' Federation) held the performance of management to be in some measure unsatisfactory. The chief ground for this charge was the evidence provided by the figures for labour productivity (see Table 1). Ever since the early 1880s, output per man per year in the British coal industry had been falling.[9] The volume of production had increased prior to 1914 wholly by virtue of the enlargement of the labour force. During the years of public regulation in 1915–21 the decline in productivity accelerated. And although this downward movement was halted after 1921, no significant improvement was achieved before 1925. Meanwhile, at least until 1924 the numbers of men employed in the industry continued irregularly to increase, reaching a peak in that year of 1,213,700.[10]

The marked fall in labour productivity in the period of 1915–21 was largely attributable to the transitory impact of war – the absorption of skilled and experienced workers into the armed forces and the suspension of investment in development work – together with the reduction of miners' hours of work in 1919. But the long-term decline in the productivity index was clearly the result of other factors which more seriously called into question the enterprise of the industry's management. Before the war mine-owners had chosen to meet the rising demand for their product primarily by the introduction of labour into existing pits, in preference to the adoption of new mechanical techniques of coal cutting and conveyance, or even to the more energetic development of under-exploited fields. After 1921 the pace of technical innovation remained slow. The Ruhr coalfield, more backward than most British mining areas in this respect in 1913, obtained over eighty per cent of its coal by mechanical means in 1927, when the equivalent British proportion was only twenty-five per cent. Native industrialists had likewise fallen behind, since the turn of the century, in the adoption of the most economical underground layouts and the development of more concentrated ways of working the coal faces.[11]

The relative sluggishness of technical progress in coal-mining seems to indicate the reluctance or inability of British mine-owners to take the long view in making investment decisions.[12] Right up to the General Strike, in fact, the age and structure of the industry discouraged innovation. Coal production was in the hands of a multiplicity of undertakings, many of them long-established, operating in an atmosphere of fierce competition. In 1925 half the country's miners were employed in collieries which had started work before 1875. In 1923 about 1,400 companies were in existence, owning 2,481 mines. About three hundred of the largest concerns were responsible for the bulk of coal output, but the remainder, though often inefficient and financially precarious, managed to survive and obstruct further concentration through the generosity of the banks and in the hope of future harvests like those of 1913 and 1923.[13] Many contemporary commentators on the state of the coal industry thus drew the conclusion that its performance could be improved by the creation of more large amalgamations which would absorb, and where necessary liquidate, small and backward enterprises.

In fact this assumption was only partly valid.[14] Technical improvements in production had been secured without such large-scale operation in some cases, and were not likely to have been significantly facilitated by it in most others. No consolidation of companies, in any case, could have much effect on the geological and logistical characteristics of existing mines; and most developmental activity was probably already in the hands of the bigger combines. Even if the low level of mechanisation in mining had been due to lack of financial resources, it was not likely that higher investment in this direction could have been justified in terms of profits by any undertaking, large or small, suffering from conditions of languishing demand and low prices.

The atomistic structure of mining enterprise had perhaps been a more serious handicap to efficient selling. The Lewis Committee on cooperative trading concluded in 1926 that 'as yet the industry on its marketing side is probably less organized than any other important industry of the country against the effects of excessive internal competition in selling and of organized buying by its customers', and suggested that this deficiency would only be remedied if 'the industry can be consolidated by amalgamations into a much smaller number of units'. Though at the time the owners' representatives contested this point, that they afterwards became relatively willing participants in voluntary selling schemes and amalgamation projects seems to indicate a change of heart.[15] And it did prove possible, though only with legislative backing and after an interval of some ten years, to raise prices both at home and abroad by controlling competition.[16] The difficulty for the parties to the 1926 dispute was (and, for economic historians, still is) to calculate with any precision the extent to which by inhibiting commercial competition the management could have offset the operating losses of existing companies in either the short or long term. In the absence of such estimates cooperative selling remained a chimera.

As the evidence of structural contrasts would suggest, conditions in the coal industry were, in almost all aspects, extremely diverse. Both market situation and productive performance varied enormously, from coalfield to coalfield and even from pit to pit. During the 1920s the main burden of declining world demand fell naturally upon the exporting districts. As the data on profits in Table 2 show, it was

South Wales, Scotland, Northumberland and Durham which suffered most in the slumps of 1921–2 and 1924–5 – the same regions which had been most remunerative in the pre-war years. The midland coalfields of South Yorkshire, Nottinghamshire and Derbyshire, which chiefly supplied the home market and were, furthermore, an area of more recent colliery development, were relatively much less depressed. Judged in terms of productivity and unit costs, on the other hand, Scotland and Northumberland were no less efficient than the Midlands; whilst conversely Lancashire, sustaining smaller losses than the export areas, had fewer large undertakings and less power-driven equipment than many worse-hit districts. Durham and South Wales, finally, were afflicted both by adverse market conditions and by high costs of production, so that the latter region especially had become since the beginning of the 1920s one of the worst casualties of depression.[17]

TABLE 2. (a) *Regional coal production and exports, 1924* (million tons)

coalfield		*exporting ports*	
Northumberland	13·7	North East	21·0
Durham	36·7	Humber	4·8
Yorks., Notts., Derbs., Leics.	80·8	Bristol Channel	25·1
S. Wales	51·1	Scotland	7·7
Scotland	36·2		
Lancs., Cheshire, N. Wales	23·2		

Source: Jones, pp. 49–50.

TABLE 2 (b). *Average annual profits of collieries* (shillings per ton)

	current prices	*1909–13 prices*
1909–13	1·04	1·04
1914–21	2·14	1·05
1922	0·97	0·60
1923	2·17	1·36
1924	1·17	0·68
1925 (January–June)	−0·19	−0·11

Source: Samuel Report, p. 218.

TABLE 2 (c). *Profits and losses by mining districts, 1920–5* (per disposable ton: 1st quarter of each year)

	1920	*1921*	*1922*	*1923*	*1924*	*1925 (1st qtr.)*	*1925 (2nd qtr.)*
Scotland	–2d	–7s 7d	11d	3s 3d	2s 8d	–1s 1d	–1s 3d
Northumberland	18s 5d	–9s 7d	1s 9d	3s 2d	2s 0d	–9d	–1s 10d
Durham	8s 5d	–4s 2d	1s 1d	3s 0d	2s 5d	–3d	–1s 6d
S. Wales	18s 8d	–19s 9d	5d	2s 3d	2s 2d	–4d	–1s 4d
Yorks.	10d	–6d	1s 8d	2s 7d	3s 9d	1s 8d	–3d
Lancs	–4s 8d	–9s 3d	1s 5d	11d	2s 6d	8d	–1s 3d
G.B.	5s 2d	–7s 0d	1s 2d	2s 5d	2s 10d	6d	–1s 0d

Source: from Neuman, *op. cit.*, pp. 40–1.

Even within the same coalfield, individual pits could record very different levels of profit or loss. Of Lord Londonderry's two collieries in County Durham, for instance, the deficits of Dawdon in this period were always far smaller than those of neighbouring Seaham.[18] And the Miners' Federation never wanted for examples of prosperous concerns even in the worst-hit areas. Such variations were partly attributable to managerial ability, but usually the predominant factors were the relative age of the mine, the nature of its lay-out and barriers, and the particular kind of coal which it produced. The sins from which the industry suffered were those of its forefathers.

Analysis of the economic situation of different districts and pits serves to confirm that the *principal* cause of the coal problem in this period was the state of world demand reflected in the volume and value of exports. There were also significant adverse factors affecting supply, but few of these were remediable by entrepreneurial effort. The German coal industry, often held up as a model of managerial efficiency in these years, still suffered from the burdens of low proceeds, unemployed capacity and labour, and deteriorating working conditions.[19] There was thus a narrow limit to the benefits which could be derived from measures adopted in a national context. Although, certainly, productive performance could be improved with advantage, no conceivable reforms could restore coal to anything approaching its pre-war hegemony. Much of the discussion of possible solutions to its troubles therefore exhibited a certain lack of realism –

or else was reduced involuntarily into an argument not about the means to revival but the distribution of the penalties of failure.

The debate on remedies

The future of the British coal industry had, by the end of the war, become the subject of strenuous controversy. The question of its reorganization had been posed inescapably by the adoption of full state control at the beginning of 1917. None of the parties to the subsequent discussion wished to prolong this form of emergency administration; but the alternative plans of reconstruction which they devised were totally incompatible. The debate upon them lasted until, and beyond, the General Strike. It was conducted before the Royal Commission of March 1919, and over the government proposals which followed it in August; it lay behind the national wage disputes of October 1920 and the spring of 1921; it was reopened by the miners' presentation of a nationalization bill to the Commons in 1924, and by the publication shortly afterwards of the first of the Liberal Party's several major essays in industrial policy-making: *Coal and Power*. These extended exchanges were to provide the prologue to the deliberations of the Samuel Commission in 1925–6, and thereby to the argument and conflict which followed.

Three forms of treatment were offered for the plight of the coal industry in the years 1919–25. The Miners' Federation and the Labour Party (with occasional non-partisan support elsewhere) urged nationalization and 'joint control'. The mine-owners, with minor reservations and divagations, called for a return to that system of competitive private enterprise which had prevailed before the war. A third group, more heterogeneous and ill-organized, supported a limited measure of state intervention in the industry to promote 'rationalization' without displacing the existing management. Each lobby, in associating itself with a particular mode of industrial organization took a distinct view of the causes of the coal crisis and of the policies likely to induce recovery.

I NATIONALIZATION

Nationalization of the mines was advocated within the ranks of the Miners' Federation from the late 1880s, and became a plank of their programme in 1894, though not until 1913 did they sponsor their own bill in the House of Commons.[20] The war years intensified, but also modified, their commitment; from demanding simple public ownership they came instead to seek a form of reconstruction which would allow the unions to play a substantial role in the management of the industry. This was a feature common to the private bill which they proposed in 1924, and to the scheme submitted to the Samuel Commission in 1925, which was prepared in conjunction with the Labour Party and the General Council.[21]

The plan of reform which emerged at the end of this period represented an attempt to find a compromise between a number of different influences. It bore the imprint of syndicalist doctrines of workers' control, popular among the rank and file movements of the MFGB since the pre-war years; of Guild Socialists like G. D. H. Cole, consulted by the Federation through the Labour Research Department; and of the more orthodox, Fabian counsels of the Labour Party leadership, especially Sidney Webb.[22] It was the fairly non-committal attitude of the Labour government towards the miners' draft legislation of 1924 which probably prompted the attempt at closer collaboration the following year, giving rise to a revised and largely agreed blueprint for the nationalization and democratic control of the power industries as a whole.[23] A consensus was achieved, however, only by the devising of an administrative system unduly complex and subdivided, the deficiencies of which were to be easily exposed by the Royal Commission.[24]

These organizational problems were in large part a reflection of the diverse objectives which nationalization was intended to fulfil. Its proponents forecast, with varying degrees of emphasis, an increased productivity through 'scientific reorganization', an enhanced status for the worker as producer within a cooperative enterprise and the improvement of working conditions. For the miners themselves, though the former goals were not unimportant, the last had a particular appeal.[25] To them private enterprise had meant the accumulation and dissipation of windfall profits in times of prosperity, a consequently unstable and inequitable wage structure, the intolerable financial exactions of a privileged class of mineral owners, inadequate housing and welfare provision and a persistent record of injury and mortality resulting from avoidable accidents. Neither the partial measure of state control introduced during the war nor the safety legislation of previous generations had succeeded in silencing these grievances.

The critics of nationalization, on the other hand, attacked it precisely on the grounds that its manifold purposes were incompatible.

Good management, it was held, could not be reconciled with democratic control, nor could the miners' interest in uniformly high wages be wedded to the public interest in low costs and prices. Least of all could these contradictions be overcome in conditions of depression. Moreover the miners always resisted the suggestion that as a *quid pro quo* of nationalization they should accept some restriction on their right to strike, thus removing one of the principal attractions which the measure might have had for outside opinion.[26] Nor did such a change of regime have any obvious and immediate relevance to the economic circumstances of the industry. In *The Economic Condition of the Coal Industry*, published jointly with the Labour Research Department in May 1925, the miners themselves attributed the decline of trade 'primarily to the crisis in world capitalism' and secondly to the competition of new fields and alternative fuels. Though public ownership might bring improvements in production, utilization and distribution, there was no expectation even among its champions that it would restore the fortunes of the industry.[27]

The question of ownership was thus almost incidental to the Federation's views on policy. In this regard, the standpoint which they adopted once the brief recovery of 1923–4 had collapsed was simply that mining output must be drastically cut, until prices had been raised sufficiently to cover existing costs. When representatives of the Mining Association brought forward their evidence on the decline of sales in the spring of 1925 Herbert Smith told them that 'if these figures are correct, it points first to the fact that we have too many men in the industry, and secondly that we have too many pits'.[28] The only alternative solution, as yet unmentioned, was the concession of a government subsidy. As the crisis developed it was more and more between these two courses that the MFGB sought to make its adversaries and its allies choose.

2 RATIONALIZATION

The view that the coal industry could benefit from a measure of state intervention falling short of full nationalization appealed to most of those would-be saviours who were neither socialists nor mine-owners. Rationalization meant for them, essentially, the supersession of the myriad small colliery companies by large, modernized units of production more capable of planning and economies of scale. The first scheme of this kind formulated in any detail was contained in one of the four reports of the Royal Commission of 1919, written by Sir

Arthur Duckham. In a modified form ('Duckham and water') this was adopted by the government in its own proposals for the industry published in August 1919.[29] Many parts of the official plan, opposed equally by mine-owners and miners, were abandoned by the time the Coalition ministry introduced the Mining Industry Act of 1920. A refurbished version was, however, put forward by the Liberal Party report on *Coal and Power* in 1924, commanding much the same body of 'neutral' support;[30] and the nostrums of rationalization were to be reiterated by the Royal Commission two years later. The theme common to all these documents was that of restoring the competitiveness of the British industry by reducing costs. The role of the state in this process was to be largely confined to the nationalization of mineral royalties and the encouragement of desirable company amalgamations. Whilst legislative action was thus held to be a necessary element of reconstruction, the management of the mines was for almost all purposes to remain in private hands. Rationalization was seen as an alternative, not an approximation, to nationalization.

The principal difficulty faced by the advocates of rationalization was simply the hostility of those engaged in the industry. The miners thought it no substitute for public ownership, foresaw resultant pressure to increase productivity and prevent disputes, and were concerned at the likely consolidation of the district-based wage system which they wished to replace.[31] The owners objected to even so modified a replication of public control and to any enforcement of industrial concentration.[32] The political difficulties of *imposing* reorganization in face of such resistance were an obvious deterrent to any government initiative, and its benefits uncertain. The appeal of rationalization as a *media via* was thus almost extinguished.

Did it, in any case, offer a credible economic solution to the coal problem? It has been suggested already that its advocates were over-optimistic, assuming in most cases that the industry's future could be as prosperous as its past, and exaggerating the rewards of the unification of mines. In fact the chief potential benefits of rationalization lay rather in allowing a planned scaling down of the industry in order to ensure the profitability of its surviving units. With the return of a trade crisis in 1925–6, and in face of imminent industrial conflict, some proponents of reorganization began to embrace a policy of retrenchment, accepting, though still somewhat vaguely, the need for immediate pit closures and recommending higher selling prices and the agreed reduction of international competition as means of maintaining wages.[33] But the typical adherent of this policy, even in 1926, continued to deplore such restraints on trade, and to equate the efficiency of mining with the cheapness of its product. The Samuel Commission in particular was to follow this prescription with little apparent awareness of its shortcomings.

3 PRIVATE ENTERPRISE

The mine-owners took the view, uncomplicated and almost unqualified, that there was nothing wrong with the coal industry which could not be put right by the existing system of management, free, individualistic and unaided. They held on the one hand that the record of the industry prior to the war testified to the effectiveness of private enterprise in promoting growth and prosperity. On the other hand they associated state intervention after 1914 with the rapid fall in productivity, the short-sighted policy of subsidizing domestic consumption out of export profits after 1918, and the concession to labour's exorbitant demands for wage increases and shorter hours.[34] Even in 1919, when the call for reorganization and nationalization was most powerful, the Mining Association proposed no more to the Sankey Commission than that royalty owners should be subject to a 'sanctioning authority' in the granting of leases, that the miners should be represented on consultative bodies at local level, and that the payment of wages should be put on a new basis. Their chief witness Lord Gainford, asserted, however, that the owners would prefer outright nationalization to any scheme of joint control with their workers.[35]

Since the owners resumed full managerial responsibility for the coal industry only in April 1921, when the depression had already set in, it was easy for them to deny any blame for its advent. Consistently thereafter they argued the cure to lie, firstly in ending any business uncertainty fostered by talk of nationalization, and secondly in the reduction of costs of production, above all wage costs. Like the advocates of rationalization the mine-owners believed that prosperity could be restored to the coal trade by cutting prices and increasing output. Unlike their critics, however, they regarded technical innovations and administrative improvements as of minor importance in comparison with excessive labour charges – from which European competitors of Britain allegedly derived their main commercial advantage.[36] They saw none of the merits in wholesale unification that were discerned by Liberal politicians and others. And they held themselves, as managers, to be invariably and irreplaceably the best judges of desirable reforms. If there were a few inefficient pits in the coalfields, they could be allowed to die naturally, without administering purgatives to the industry in general.

The mine-owners' hostility to the various proposals for rationalization, though it can be partially justified with economic hindsight, was not a mark of their judiciousness. To them, any kind of legislative interference was an instalment of nationalization. Moreover no other view of the future prospects of the industry was so wholly unrealistic. Lord Gainford's attitude to the pit closures proposed by the Samuel Report of 1926 was representative of an unending faith in imminent recovery:[37]

> If permanently closing existing uneconomic collieries is a policy advocated, *that* must mean the national loss of an enormous quantity of coal, which in times of prosperity such as have occurred in the past would undoubtedly pay to work (sic) and be of considerable value to the country.

Instead of planned contraction, therefore, the mine-owners sought to maintain the industry on its existing scale. Instead of promoting cooperation amongst themselves, they continued to believe in unrestrained competition. Instead of welcoming assistance, financial or legal, from the state, they preferred to impose intolerable sacrifices on their employees. It was not simply because they had managed their industry badly in the past the owners deserve their reputation for unintelligence, but because the policies which they devised for its future were so fatally mistaken.

All the solutions for the plight of the coal industry suggested prior to 1926 rested, it has been seen, on unwarranted expectations. There was a general reluctance to admit the necessity of a lasting curtailment of production. The miners came nearest to adopting this pessimistic viewpoint, but there was nothing in the natoinalization programmes of 1924–5 to indicate that this perspective had influenced their original reconstruction proposals – and rather more reason to suspect that joint control would retard rather than advance pit closures. Not until the socialist remedy had been rejected by the Samuel Commission, in fact, did the MFGB assert consistently and publicly its willingness to see the truncation of the industry – a willingness then clearly dictated by their refusal to submit to the alternative of lower wages. The exponents of rationalization and private enterprise, on the other hand, were even slower to reach the same conclusion.

More and more however the principal debate among those involved centred not on long-term reforms but immediate measures of relief. No radical improvement in the coal industry's fortunes could be looked for without lapse of time. The most drastic interim policy put forward was that adopted by the miners after the publication of the Samuel Report: that men should be allowed to fall out of employment until prices rose sufficiently for the industry to pay its way. This did not necessarily involve any of the organizational and commercial innovations recommended by the champions of rationalization. In effect it placed the burden of insolvency on the state and the taxpayer through increased expenditure on unemployment benefits, and on the consumer through increased prices. Alternatively the government might assist the industry more directly by subsidies, tax reliefs and transport rebates. Finally, mining could be left to seek its salvation, as the employers wished, by reducing its labour costs through longer hours or lower wages. Though not mutually exclusive these policies came to be treated by miners, owners and government as if they were. In the last analysis the General Strike was to be fought to determine the choice to be made among them.

Combination and collective bargaining

The economic history of the coal industry prior to 1925 was not so very different from that of other depressed trades; what gave mining an added prominence and notoriety to the observer was the exceptional turbulence of its industrial relations. That the General Strike stemmed from a dispute in this particular industry is an immediately recognizable consequence firstly of the strength and influence of mining trade unionism in the labour movement, and secondly of the peculiarly persistent and increasingly embittered conflicts which engaged the miners and their employers.

The Miners' Federation was formed in 1889 in the midst of that interlude of prosperity and rising prices which also saw the upsurge of New Unionism. It was based initially mainly on the coalfields of Lancashire, Yorkshire and the Midlands – coming subsequently to be known, therefore, with North Wales, as the 'federated area'. Its suzerainty extended to Scotland by 1897, to South Wales from 1899 and finally to Northumberland and Durham in 1907–8. By 1914 its membership stood at 673,000.[38]

As it acquired national coverage, so the MFGB became more attracted to the organizational principle known as 'industrial unionism'.

In its infancy, however, its constituents had sought to cater only for underground workers, and in consequence a number of other unions entered the coal industry to serve the interests of the surfacemen; the general unions attaching the labourers, craft societies like the engineers and the electricians taking in the skilled men. The deputies and winders also formed their own organizations. The Miners' Federation was therefore never fully comprehensive of the labour force in coal-mining (a limitation which somewhat weakened its case for the introduction of a union-based system of workers' control); and its membership throughout its life continued to accept the hegemony of the hewers.[39]

In structure the MFGB remained decentralized, respecting the local autonomy of the county unions which it comprised. Not until 1919, indeed, did it appoint its own full-time secretary. The principal central governing organ of the Federation was the national delegate meeting, which adopted joint trade policies, and which could, under the 20th and 21st rules, authorize financial support for individual districts or initiate collective strike action. The latter recourse had originally been envisaged only for defensive purposes, but from 1911 national stoppages were permitted to obtain improvements in conditions, although it became a strict convention that such a step be taken only when approved by a ballot of the membership showing a two-thirds majority.[40] Indeed, the executive of the Federation, made up of representatives of the various districts, always found difficulty in initiating or altering policy without the mandate of a special conference or a plebiscite and displayed much reluctance even in recommending particular courses of action. It gained a reputation among other unions with whom the Federation collaborated from time to time for an exaggerated constitutional rectitude, bolstered by a jealous concern of its members, despite their ostensible devotion to a national policy, for the rights of their particular areas to a voice on all matters of policy.

The MFGB was brought into being in order to enforce the principle of 'direct negotiation' – that is, of changing wage rates by collective bargaining rather than by automatic sliding scales related to the price of coal which had been common in the industry hitherto. It quickly became identified, however, with other, more radical policies – with the definition of a minimum or 'living' wage below which miners' earnings should not fall even in times of depression, and the legal enactment of the eight hours day. The second objective was accomplished in 1908, the first precipitated the national stoppage, partially successful, of 1912. Shortening hours and maintaining county minima remained the hallmarks of Federation policy in the pre-war years.[41]

By the outbreak of the first world war the MFGB was already renowned for the unshakeable solidarity of its membership and for the unusual militancy of its tactics (and those of its affiliated county unions). The loyalty it commanded was due in part to its successes in the conduct of collective bargaining, and even more perhaps to the successes of its constituents in affecting conditions of work at the most local level.[42] It was equally due, as contemporaries never tired of observing, to the peculiar, self-absorbed and intensely close-knit character of the mining villages of Britain, in which by the early twentieth century unionism had become not just a necessary adjunct of working life, but a social institution with which the identity of the community was bound up. The militancy was displayed in the long and widespread stoppages of 1893 and 1912, in the regional strikes, sometimes even more protracted, in Scotland (1897), South Wales (1898), Northumberland and Durham (1907 and 1910), and Yorkshire (1913), as well as in a myriad local disputes. It was given an additionally acrid flavour by the propaganda of the 'syndicalists' in South Wales and elsewhere and by the violence which accompanied the famous dispute at the Cambrian Combine in the Rhondda in 1910–11.[43]

Yet the strength of the Miners' Federation was not impregnable, nor felt to be so by its leaders. Conditions in the exporting coalfields of the north-east and the Celtic fringe were especially liable to diverge from those of the domestically-based 'federated area'. This economic heterogeneity was reflected in the absence of any authoritative national body on the employers' side, and thus of any negotiating machinery above regional level. The Federation was therefore never free from the fear that, like previous national combinations in the mining industry, it would eventually disintegrate into the county associations of which it was composed. It was this enduring anxiety which pressed upon it a policy of standardizing conditions between the different coalfields, providing the best *raison d'être* of inter-regional organization. Such a policy was clearly embodied in the claims for the eight-hour day and for a national minimum wage in 1912. And the objections of the employers to such demands pushed the MFGB inexorably towards a deeper commitment to nationalization. The new determination manifest in its advocacy of state ownership on the eve of the first world war was the result not just of the advent of a more socialist leadership but of the recent frustrations experienced in collective bargaining on familiar questions of wages and hours.

Between 1914 and 1921 the MFGB came near to having these deep-lying problems solved for it. The introduction of government control in the coal industry in 1917 brought with it national bargaining and the concession of uniform wage increases across the country, paid from a pool of profits to which all the coalfields contributed. This system of administration allowed the Federation to raise the standards of the poorer districts and the lower grades, and obscured the financial disparities between exporting and home-producing areas. The Seven Hours Act of 1919 furthered its egalitarian purposes.[44]

In the event, however, the Miners' Federation failed completely to consolidate these wartime gains. Its attempt to transform government control into nationalization foundered with the Coalition's rejection of the Sankey Report in 1919. Its insistence on standard wage increases was already being opposed by the end of 1920, when the government ended a brief national stoppage by making an agreement tying its wage award to productivity. Finally, state control itself was abruptly terminated in 1921, and with it both the officially administered pool of profits and the centralization of negotiations on terms of employment which this had permitted.[45]

The dispute of 1921, the occasion of the Triple Alliance's collapse, brought the miners for the first time into direct confrontation with a national organ of the employers, the Mining Association of Great Britain. The Association had been established as early as 1854, but its functions prior to 1914 had been restricted largely to the collection of information regarding industrial and labour conditions. Collective bargaining was left to the county associations (of owners and men), although a conciliation board did exist for the whole of the federated area from 1899, and national conferences with the employers took place during the 1912 movement.[46] It was as a result of the war, however, that the Mining Association eventually obtained the authority to represent the owners on wage questions, and the wage proposals which provided the framework of the 1921 agreement derived from this source.

The rise of the Association was marked by the emergence of a settled leadership. Throughout the period from 1919 to 1926 the same small group of officials and ex-officials represented it in all negotiations. The chief spokesman on such occasions was the President, Evan Williams; the Secretary, W. A. Lee, played little part in formal exchanges, though was apparently more active behind the scenes. At least as influential in the affairs of the Association, however, were the foremost members of its Central Council: Sir Adam Nimmo and Lord

Gainford – the chairmen of the Scottish and Durham owners. These men were to acquire an unenviable reputation, even with some of their fellow-employers, for inflexibility, lack of political skill, and a fundamental lack of humanity. Gainford's much-quoted remark to the Sankey Commission dogged him thereafter and Nimmo impressed both Sir Alfred Mond and Tom Jones as one who adhered to reactionary principles with evangelical fervour.[47] It was perhaps significant that both of them, like the Welshman Evan Williams, came from the more depressed, exporting coalfields – although the employers of these areas were not without enlightened and liberal elements. In any case it would be wrong to suggest that the errors of the Mining Association were mainly due to individual leaders, for it was increasingly to become evident that the mine-owners as a whole (including the supposedly 'progressive' elements) were hostile to the very idea of national bargaining institutions. Their main object, certainly after 1925, was to restore the primacy of district negotiations. The Central Council of the Association, in presenting harsh and unacceptable demands at national level, were seeking to commend such devolution to the miners as a preferable alternative. Nimmo and Gainford themselves had appeared reasonable enough when talking to their 'own' men in Scotland and Durham before 1914[48] – and would probably have seemed somewhat more conciliatory there than in London in 1925 and 1926. The officials of the Mining Association, Lee and Williams, appeared inhibited in negotiations precisely because they represented a membership which was anxious to deprive them of this responsibility.

Even after it had gained a new negotiating authority in 1921, therefore, the Mining Association was unlikely to impose itself on its constituent districts, jealous of their own autonomy. The wage proposals it put forward in 1921 departed from the pre-war pattern of county and regional agreements in two ways only. Firstly they provided that the procedure for determining wage rates (but not the rates themselves) should be the same in all areas; and secondly they stipulated that wages should be fixed by ascertaining the proceeds of the industry, not by the selling-price of coal. This scheme was still intended to allow wages to vary substantially between rich and poor districts, the more so since each area would continue to fix its own minimum rate. Only under pressure from the government and after seven weeks of a national stoppage did the Association accept, reluctantly, that districts should be subject to a nationally agreed minimum percentage.

The continued industrial conflict from which the coal industry suffered, especially between 1910 and 1926, can thus be attributed to the rapid fluctuation of its economic condition and to the fundamental incompatability of the objects of employers and employees. On the former count, it can be seen that the miners suffered two periods of relative adversity. Before the war they were affected by inflation in a period of falling output; after 1921, by the impact of depression. Although real wages rose in 1910–14, it was only as the result of sustained struggle by the Federation and its constituents. After 1921 prolonged resistance could not prevent a reduction in the miners' standard of living. In the interval, however, especially between 1917 and 1920, rates of pay improved rapidly, catching and then surpassing the concurrent increase in prices. The difficulty of adjusting to the reverses of the 1920s was considerably greater, therefore, because of the rising expectations and rich gains of the immediately preceding years. At the same time, because the slump affected the coalfields unequally, it called into question the very existence of national bargaining. Owners in the exporting districts took the lead in demanding its dissolution, and also the repeal of the Seven Hours Act, in order to allow the possibility of larger regional variations in wages and conditions.

Ill-feeling was accentuated by the motives which each side attributed to the other. Both saw the conflicts of the 1920s as matters of life and death. The Mining Association regarded the trade policies of the Federation as a covert campaign for nationalization, and its leaders as men prepared to damage the industry in order to undermine private enterprise. In support of their opinion they could cite the miners' hostility to the Whitley reports of 1917 and their initial rejection of the Mining Industry Act of 1920, both of which proposed bargaining institutions adapted to a sytem of private ownership.[49] They were aware, too, that the industrial demands which the miners made prior to the stoppages of October 1920 and April 1921 were designed in part to prolong the necessity for government control.[50] For the miners, their employers' insistence on district agreements represented an attempt to divide and ultimately destroy the Federation, whilst the government's avoidance of nationalization and its decision to end control was evidence of the state's capitalist partiality. From the time of the 1921 dispute until the General Strike mine-owners and union leaders in the industry both viewed the world in terms of stark class conflict, of forces permanently at war, of conspiring and uncompromising enemies arrayed against them. In acting so consistently in accordance with these preconceptions, they widened the already massive gulf which separated them.

The 1921 settlement was thus no more than an uneasy truce. Neither organization was content with its terms for long. The owners had been forced to accept a national minimum percentage which limited the freedom of individual district boards to fix wages having regard to their own financial capacity. The miners, who had at first shown some inclination to be reconciled to the agreement, resumed their hostile stance when they found further encroachments being made at local level and pit closures continuing. In 1924, during the temporary period of prosperity brought about by the occupation of the Ruhr, the MFGB (with the Labour government acting as mediator) raised the minimum percentage on standard from twenty to thirty-three (about three shillings a week on average). They were still not satisfied, however, that this restored their real wages to pre-war level. At the beginning of the following year, with depression returning to the industry, the owners prepared not simply to revise the terms of the 1924 settlement but to eliminate if possible the national minimum itself and with it the legal seven-hour day. To the Federation these were the last cherished remnants of a dispersed fortune for which they might still find force and will to fight.

III The Industrial Alliance and Red Friday

Militancy in the Miners' Federation, 1921–5

Although the owners were critical, the miners bitterly resentful, of the terms of the 1921 wage agreement, its introduction was followed by the longest period of general industrial peace that coal-mining had known since 1910. Because firstly the defeat of the Federation in 1921 and the depression of the next two years had so reduced its strength, and secondly because the recovery of 1923–4 allowed it to obtain a significant wage increase by negotiation, the necessity for large-scale strike action was removed. But it has been suggested already how brittle was this truce. The miners were still engaged in numerous battles to protect their conditions at local level – often, perhaps, with a more direct bearing on the security of particular working communities than national disputes. Relations in this sphere were exacerbated by the employers' constant refusal to institute pit committees for consultative purposes. The owners, for their part, though no doubt grateful for the suspension of warfare, could not indefinitely tolerate a situation in which profits and productivity remained so low. Even in the transitory boom of 1923–4 an average of ten to fifteen per cent of the industry's output was raised at a loss.[1] Their sense of the Federation's implacable enmity remained undiminished, and they asserted with increasing frequency the conviction that its leadership was becoming more, not less, subject to extremist influences.

This view, widely held, that the miners' unions were undergoing a process of radicalization, needs further examination. The miners had ever since the pre-war period sustained a variety of unofficial left-wing movements, strongly supported especially in the exporting coalfields, whose activities had been much publicized. Particularly after the formation of the Miners' Minority Movement, under Communist auspices, in January 1924, such rank and file militancy was conspicuous and widespread. By August 1925 the MMM had established more than two hundred groups among mine-workers and could claim in some instances to have exercised a decisive influence on the policies of at least two districts, South Wales and central Scotland. Both the growing unpopularity of the 1921 agreement and especially the revival of the coal trade in 1923–4, assisted its foundation and progress.[2]

At no time, however, did the unofficial movement control the leadership of the Miners' Federation, or even exert more than a marginal influence upon its conduct. Of the acknowledged left-wing representatives on the MFGB executive probably only S. O. Davies from Wales and John Williams of the Forest of Dean consistently followed the line of the Minority Movement. In all the major industrial conflicts of 1924–6 the Federation sooner or later took a course diverging from that recommended by the Communists and their sympathizers – and after Red Friday the latter moved towards the 'official' position rather than vice versa. If the Federation's conduct in this period appeared intransigent in comparison with that of other unions this was the outcome of industrial traditions, inherited grievances and the behaviour of the owners, not of pressure from the left.

The MMM absorbed much of the support of those multifarious radical elements which had flourished within the mining unions since 1910: former syndicalists and industrial unionists, socialists of various denominations, as well as Communist Party members. Its attention was directed from the outset, however, almost entirely to short-term industrial ends – that is, to pressing an ambitious programme of wage demands and to urging strike action as a means of accomplishing it. Though the Communist progenitors of the Movement hoped that such militancy would have politically educative effects, they placed far less emphasis than had previous left-wing groups, the syndicalists in particular, on organizational or overtly political issues. In consequence, paradoxically, the dichotomy between 'left' and 'right' within the MFGB was probabably less evident than it had been before the Party's foundation.

The Minority Movement was, by design, largely confined to the grass roots membership; it made little attempt to progress by way of the infiltration of union bureaucracies. Even where the causes which it embraced were taken up by the leadership, therefore – as in the case of the Industrial Alliance – there is often room for doubt about whether the connection was causal or coincidental. The Movement did conduct one campaign, exceptional in this respect, in the expectation of gaining a voice at the highest level of the MFGB hierarchy, when it successfully obtained the election of A. J. Cook as

Secretary in succession to Frank Hodges in the spring of 1924.[3] But though Cook was thereafter regarded as a considerable political asset to the left, his importance in this respect can easily be exaggerated. Cook's outstanding talents as a public speaker before mining audiences, developed partly by that missionizing work through which so many other South Wales radicals had entered politics, were coupled with an attachment to democratic principles of union government which tended to abnegate leadership. His oratory itself derived its power by reflecting and recapturing the moods and feelings of his listeners, not by influencing or persuading. When this rapport was absent, he appeared merely incoherent or overwrought. In committee-room and negotiating chamber Cook, though not lacking in intelligence, sometimes appeared unsure and vacillating. Thus both the Cabinet secretary, Tom Jones, and the President of the Mining Association, W. A. Lee, found him in the crises of 1925 and 1926 superficially less uncompromising than Herbert Smith. Even left-wingers within the Federation suspected him from time to time, in his acceptance of the 1921 settlement and later in his attitude to the 'living wage' policy, of temporising and inconsistency.[4]

In the formation and even in the expression of the miners' industrial policy Cook was of far less significance than the MFGB President, Herbert Smith. Widely admired in the labour movement for his veteran qualities, dogged loyalty to his class and blunt honesty of expression, Smith was nonetheless ultimately a miners' man. With little imagination and no subtlety, obstinate and sometimes truculent in temper, he better than anyone embodied that immobile and defensive outlook which governed the conduct of the Federation between 1921 and 1926. To Smith, then still only acting-President in succession to Smillie, the proposals put forward by the miners in the 1921 dispute for the equalization of profits and wages had seemed over-elaborate and prone to misinterpretation.[5] The entrenched position adopted by the Federation in 1925–6, aimed entirely at preserving the status quo, was the tactical product of that preference for marmoreal simplicity. Departing even verbally from such fundamentals led him, habitually, into painful obfuscation.

Smith's preoccupation with holding ground conflicted with and prevailed over the desires of the left, and of the Minority Movement in particular, to convert defence into attack. During the trade recovery of 1923–4 the MMM urged upon the Federation's leadership the objective of the 'living wage' – taken to mean, roughly speaking, the equivalent in purchasing terms of the wage rates secured by the 'Sankey' agreement of 1919. In April 1924 the membership of the MFGB rejected by ballot the owners' offer to increase the minimum by 12½ per cent, and their officials subsequently presented a case for the programme of the Minority Movement to the Buckmaster Court of Inquiry. This probably marked the peak of left-wing influence upon the miners during the post-war period. But the settlement afterwards accepted through the good offices of the Labour government conceded a minimum of only 33⅓ per cent over 'standard'.[6] During 1925, though certain districts urged that a further wage claim be presented, the leadership of the Federation did not seriously contemplate such a demand. Both on this question, and in their acceptance of the owners' invitation to take part in a joint inquiry into the condition of the industry at the beginning of 1925, they ignored the counsels of the MMM.

There was little reason to conclude, accordingly, that the disposition of the MFGB after 1924 was more militant than before. The employers' allegations of extremism rested chiefly on its attachment to public ownership, which even if again a topical subject was nothing new. Moreover despite their recurrent attacks on the miners' leadership when the industry began once more to slide towards depression they still took an apparently optimistic view of their powers of persuasion.

Conditions in the coal trade had again begun to deteriorate towards the end of 1924, with the recovery of the German industry and the depreciation of the French franc. Coal exports reached their maximum monthly figure of 5,488,000 tons in July 1924, falling back to 4,366,000 tons by January 1925, when prices were about 2s per ton below the average for the previous year. The proportion of coal raised at a loss had increased from about ten per cent in January 1924 to about forty per cent twelve months later.[7] Towards the end of that month the Association wrote to the executive of the Federation to propose the establishment of a joint subcommittee to investigate 'the present situation of the industry'.[8]

The miners agreed to hold a meeting of the two full executives, and after prolonged exchanges a joint committee was set up at the beginning of March. Cook advised against participation but was overridden by his colleagues, who were reluctant to have it said that they 'were afraid to face the facts'. But Smith told the employers at their first encounter, 'some of us . . . have strong suspicions about you, and I share these suspicions'.[9]

His mistrust was well-founded. Though the owners insisted that they had no wish to offer proposals until the investigation was complete, the evidence which they themselves submitted was calculated to lead to one conclusion: that costs of production in Britain must be reduced nearer to the levels prevailing in European exporting countries. Sir Adam Nimmo, the leading Scottish representative on the Council of the Association, told the National Liberal Club on 22 January:[10]

> The wages of those engaged in the industry cannot permanently rest upon considerations of cost of living, or what the men may call a living wage. So long as British coal has to compete with the coal produced in other countries it must meet competition by providing similar conditions in respect of the production of coal as obtained in competing countries. It is of no avail to suggest that the wages received do not permit of the miners having a proper standard of living.

What the owners hoped for, as the outcome of the talks was to make clear, was a submission on the miners' part if not to wage reductions then to the alternative of longer working hours.

As far as the Federation was concerned the investigation was agreed to in the hope of postponing such demands. Some districts – South Wales, Scotland and Lancashire – still wanted to persist with the campaign for a 'living wage' but the Special Delegate Conference of 26 February, in approving the joint inquiry, recognized the unreality of this claim and the desirability of prolonging the 1924 agreement. While its sessions still continued, however, the MFGB began the quest for prospective allies in the likely event of renewed conflict.

The Industrial Alliance

The negotiations begun in 1925 to establish an Industrial Alliance between the miners and other unions in transport and heavy industry are poorly documented, and the significance of this project has been interpreted in contrasting ways. Some historians have seen the planning of the Alliance as heralding the General Strike itself, indicating the readiness of the organizations involved to engage in concerted action and strengthening the impetus towards militancy throughout the movement.[11] Others have suggested that its eventual miscarriage exposed the underlying opposition to such a strategy, and foreshadowed the end of the General Strike rather than its beginning.[12]

Both accounts have a measure of plausibility, but neither is complete in itself. The union leaders who undertook to form an alliance were impelled by various and inconsistent motives. The proposal was given serious attention because of the immediate tactical needs of the miners. When the engineers had previously suggested 'an offensive alliance against the employers' to the MFGB and the Transport and General Workers' Union in June 1924 the Federation had shown no interest; and a resolution calling for a coalition had been remitted to the executive and apparently forgotten. It was not until early 1925 that A. J. Cook wrote on the miners' behalf to a number of organizations, including the T&GWU, the engineers, the railwaymen and the iron and steel workers, with the intention of reviving the enterprise. It was now to be given a defensive character, however, to '[render] mutual support to our respective memberships in times of necessity'.[13] Clearly this awakening of interest is to be attributed primarily to the miners' growing apprehension of conflict in their own industry; and their hopes of obtaining assistance were based on the familiar assumption that such a capitalist offensive would be bound sooner or later to extend to other unions.

Not all union leaders, however, saw the Alliance in this light. Ernest Bevin, who more than anyone was to be responsible for the drafting of its constitution, wanted a lasting, not simply an *ad hoc* association, carefully constructed to secure effective collaboration, but intended to give moral rather than physical support in most disputes. 'I am sorry, really, that this Alliance comes just at the time of the miners' difficulty,' he told his delegate conference in July. 'I would rather it be discussed apart from that.' And he went on, significantly.[14]

> We do not think we ought, simply because we have an instrument like this, to be striking every minute. With the Alliance we would have bargaining power that we do not at present possess. If there was an Alliance of this character in being it would not be permitted to side-step it. It could act with tremendous bargaining power and probably lift the whole thing out of the rut it might be in.

For both the T&GWU and the railwaymen, too – and perhaps for some other large unions involved – the Alliance was welcomed in the hope that it would prompt smaller organizations in their industries (the footplatemen and the constituents of the Transport Workers' Federation, for example) to agree to amalgamation.[15]

The Alliance was not conceived, therefore, to fulfil any single purpose. The enthusiasm for joint action which it revealed was neither novel nor unqualified. Organizations involved themselves for reasons which were typically opportunistic, in part if not in whole. But given this ambivalence, it is also mistaken to see the failure of the scheme as reflecting a common objection to joint action. Like the TUC debate on the powers of the General Council, what the discussion of an Industrial Alliance indicated was simply the difficulty, in the face of opposing sectional interests, of obtaining agreement about the method of its accomplishment. There were, it is true, some unions belonging to the Federation of Engineering and Shipbuilding Trades which eventually withdrew from the project because the Alliance seemed likely to disrupt the conduct of peaceful collective bargaining with their employers.[16] But the more fundamental issue, over which – in different guises – other would-be partners always seemed liable to fall out, was that of centralization *versus* particularism. Bevin and the constitutional committee put forward draft rules which were designed both to subordinate individual member unions to the collective organs of the Alliance and to compel each constituent executive to vest in itself, if necessary at the expense of more democratic procedures, authority to act as the Alliance required. This *modus operandi* could not have been accepted in practice by any of the federations considering membership – including the miners'.[17] Similarly, the NUR's demand that the Alliance should assert in principle the need for unity of organization within each of its various trade groups was intolerable to the locomotive engineers and to most other small societies. The existence of these radical disagreements became partly visible by November 1925, when the railwaymen withdrew from the discussions – though other organizations, anxious not to question the ideal of cooperation, concealed their misgivings.[18] But once the General Council had shown, on Red Friday, a hitherto unexpected capacity to coordinate industrial resistance to wage cuts, the need to attempt to resolve such differences disappeared. Most of the participants who, like the miners, had conceived of the Alliance as a convenient, loosely-knit association to be called on when industrial emergencies arose now transferred their allegiance readily and conclusively to its official TUC counterpart.

Despite this disappointing outcome, it is still possible to argue that the attempt to establish an Industrial Alliance was a significant step in the direction of the General Strike. Whatever the reality, it gave the appearance at least of militant intentions, confirming for outside witnesses the willingness of union leaders of different shades of opinion to contemplate mutual industrial support. 'Through the Alliance', claimed Herbert Smith afterwards, 'we got such an atmosphere created in the Trade Union world we have not had before.' Certainly in so far as rank and file opinion accepted these professions of solidarity at face value, the pressure on union leaders to keep their promises increased. Secondly, it might also be suggested that the General Council regarded the Alliance as a potential rival and that the determination with which it supported the miners in July 1925 was the product of a wish to avoid eclipse. This, probably, was the innuendo in A. J. Cook's observation that the Alliance 'was the means which focussed attention upon the growing unity and power that gave courage to the Trades Union General Council to take and use it in the interests of the people that called upon it'.[19]

Though in prospect the Alliance may have had a certain indirect influence, however, this should not be given too much weight. Whatever its popularity, it was allowed to lapse without much protest. What is more, the most energetic radical propagandists active among the union rank and file – the Minority Movement – had become lukewarm in their attitude to it, both because it had a distinctly bureaucratic aspect and because it threatened to dispute the hegemony of the General Council which the MM had committed itself to support.[20] In raising the temper of the rank and file the Alliance was probably less important than the Hull TUC and certainly less so than Red Friday itself. The effect it had upon the General Council cannot be assessed with any confidence. But the progenitors of the scheme, the miners in particular, denied that it was a competitor at all, suggesting rather that it might eventually be integrated into the Council's trade group system.[21] Such assurances were obviously a diplomatic necessity, but were not necessarily disingenuous. Since several prominent members of the Council were also connected with the proposed Alliance, they may well have been believed. In any case it is unlikely that fear of the emergence of this rival was a critical factor in the conduct of the TUC leadership during the mining crisis. Its behaviour then can be explained adequately enough, as will be seen, by reference to its own previous undertakings, its view of the current industrial situation, and its hopes of an easy victory.

The mining crisis

Before the Alliance had obtained a draft constitution the truce in the coal industry broke down. After the usual seasonal improvement in the early months of 1925, commercial conditions worsened considerably from April onwards. Between March and May the proportion of coal produced at a loss rose from about forty to sixty per cent; and between January and June the average price of exports fell by 1s 4d a ton.[22] At the meeting of the joint inquiry on 17–18 June the Mining Association announced that they would give notice to terminate the 1924 agreement at the end of the month, adding that they considered an extension of hours of work to be essential for economic recovery. The last session of the investigation was held on 23 June; when the owners suggested a further discussion early in July they were told by Herbert Smith that 'the duties of our subcommittee are at an end'.[23]

The Association's proposals for a new wage agreement were forwarded to the miners on 1 July. They involved, first and foremost, the abolition of national minimum percentage and subsistence rate, leaving wages to be settled primarily by the revenue-sharing procedure and the conduct of negotiations primarily to the districts. The existing provision that a minimum wage should be the first charge on the industry automatically lapsed. These alarming demands were clearly framed with the intention of compelling the miners to reconsider their attitude on the question of hours of work. The previous day the Association's Secretary, W. A. Lee, had written to Cook to point out that

> The difficulty of drawing up wage proposals . . . has been greatly increased by the unwillingness of the Miners' Federation to consider an extension of the seven-hour day, for the terms which can be offered under a seven-hour day are necessarily much less favourable than those which could be offered under an eight-hour day.

He implied that, on the latter basis, a national minimum might be accepted by the owners, since 'the great differences between district and district have been aggravated by the operation of the Seven Hours Act.[24]

The miners rejected the employers' terms outright at a Special Conference on 3 July, however, and thereafter declined steadfastly to meet the Association until their demands had been withdrawn. In the event no negotiations were to take place directly on the owners' demands at any time during the crisis. The proposals of 1 July, the Federation's executive said in their reply, asked them 'to allow our wages to be entirely at [the owners'] mercy', and meant that 'the burden of bad management, and inefficient methods of production, administration and distribution could all be automatically transferred to our shoulders without any let or hindrance whatsoever'.[25] Calculating the average wage rates which would ensue (on the assumption, which the owners denied, that no higher minima would be established at district level) the Federation claimed that reductions would amount to about 2s per shift in all coalfields except that of Yorkshire, Nottingham and Derby.

TABLE 3. *MFGB estimates of wage reductions under mine-owners' proposals of 1 July 1925*[26]

	Average earnings per shift for month of July	
	under 1924 agreement	*under new conditions*
Scotland	10s 3½d	8s 2½d
Northumberland	9s 5d	7s 3d
Durham	9s 11½d	7s 11d
S. Wales	10s 9d	8s 10½d
Eastern	10s 10d	10s 2½d
Lancs., Chesh., S. Staffs.	10s 0½d	8s 4½d

Recognizing now that the Industrial Alliance could not be mobilized in time to offer support in this crisis, the miners' executive had already by 3 July arranged to meet the General Council. When the interview took place a week later, Smith emphasized the danger of the dissolution of national bargaining arrangements and the withdrawal of protection for the lower paid, and referred vaguely to the need for 'some sort of unification' in the industry. The Council resolved to 'give [the miners] their complete support, and . . . to cooperate wholeheartedly with them in their resistance to the mine-owner's proposals'.[27] A Special Industrial Committee was appointed, with Swales as chairman, to maintain contact with the Federation and recommend action if required.[28]

The wording of its motion was too loose to indicate how far the General Council would be prepared to commit itself to sympathetic strike measures; not for another two weeks did it discuss what form of assistance should be given to the miners. In the meantime the hope that negotiations would get under way was continually frustrated. On 9 and 10 July W. C. Bridgeman, the first Lord of the Admiralty, saw the executive bodies of the Mining Association and the Miners' Federation in an attempt to find a basis for discussions, but failed to persuade the owners to withdraw their conditions. On 11 July, therefore, the government announced the appointment of an independent Court of Inquiry into the dispute, under the chairmanship of H. P. Macmillan, formerly Scottish Advocate during the first Labour administration.[29] But the MFGB maintained their posture of total immobility by refusing to attend any further tribunal 'that has for its object the ascertainment of whether mine workers' wages can be reduced or their hours of work extended'.[30] The Court tried without effect to bring about a direct exchange between the two sides by prevailing on the owners to hold their proposals 'in abeyance'. On 20 July its hearings began in the miners' absence.

At the Federation's conference a number of delegates had been apprehensive of the reaction of the General Council to this boycott, and Herbert Smith admitted that it might have an unfortunate effect on public opinion. Partly for this reason the miners' former President, Bob Smillie, suggested apparently without forethought that the appointment of a Royal Commission similar to the Sankey Commission of 1919 would be an acceptable alternative. The executive incorporated the same suggestion into their statement on the dispute addressed to the TUC on 22 July.[31] Through this cranny an escape from the impasse was eventually contrived.

In the event, the miners suffered no loss of sympathy as a result of their refusal to negotiate and to argue their case. On 21 July the South Wales Coal Owners' Association officially published notices in their own district embodying the original terms presented nationally on 1 July. It was the employers, still, who appeared more unreasonably inflexible, and the Federation took this provocation as grounds for rejecting once again an offer of the Mining Association to begin discussions.[32] On the 28 July, moreover, the Macmillan Inquiry published a report which to the owners' chagrin was markedly receptive to the Federation's unheard arguments. The employers' case for the restoration of the eight-hour day was said to be unconvincing, since their ability to dispose of the increased output, even at lower prices, was doubtful. Without making any positive recommendation on the subject, the Court held that 'wages at some agreed minimum rate must in practice be a charge before profits are taken'.[33] They added their opinion 'that there is considerable room for improving the efficiency of the industry as a whole, and in this way affording some aid to its economic position'. It was questionable whether the industry could be left to 'the unmitigated operation of purely economic forces'.[34] The most urgent need was for the two sides to consult more closely on the means by which problems originating externally could be overcome. The Report seemed to endorse, as did much of the press, the miners' contention that they could not be made the sole sacrificial victim of trade depression.[35]

The intervention of the General Council

On 23 July, while the Macmillan Court was still sitting, the miners' executive held their first consultation with the Special Industrial Committee to discuss the practical aspects of assistance. The Federation urged a boycott on the movement of coal. The T&GWU had already facilitated such a measure by passing a resolution at their delegate conference on 21 July empowering their executive 'to co-operate with the Trades Union Congress General Council for the purpose of assisting the miners to resist to the utmost the imposition of the proposed conditions' of their employers. Marchbank suggested that the NUR would be willing to join forces.[36] The Committee therefore arranged to see the executives of all the transport unions on the 25 July. The following day a special meeting of Congress took place to discuss the unemployment problem, at which, at the suggestion of the General Council, a Coal Embargo Committee was appointed (George Hicks later being made its chairman) to help the transport workers draw up detailed instructions once a decision had been taken.

The General Council and the SIC had thus pledged themselves to take sympathetic action, at least on a limited scale, on the miners' behalf. Their reasons for doing so were twofold. Firstly, they were convinced that the demands upon the MFGB were evidence of the intentions of other employers to reduce wages throughout industry. Secondly, they hoped that the threat of a boycott would be effective in bringing about a settlement on the miners' terms. None questioned these assumptions, though neither, it will appear, could be said to be particularly firmly based.

Some signs of a coming 'capitalist offensive' were visible in the summer of 1925. In June the AEU informed the General Council that it had received demands for longer working hours and a reduction in wages in the engineering industry. Shortly afterwards the woollen textile unions were confronted by a call for a ten per cent wage cut, obtaining the help of two Council members in negotiating with their employers. Almost simultaneously craftsmen in the railway workshops were asked for a reduction of five per cent.[37] These threats stimulated real, though as it proved unjustified, fears.[38] It is possible that labour's disquiet was the more intense because of the government's decision to return to the gold standard in April 1925 – denounced by J. M. Keynes in a series of *Evening Standard* articles as damaging to employment and living standards[39] – though more likely the connection between this measure and the prospect of wage cuts was clarified in the minds of most union leaders only after the decision to support the miners had been taken.[40] It should be noted, too, that the mine-owners themselves expressed the view that the revival of their industry required wage reductions not just among miners but throughout the sheltered trades – an opinion of which at least some other union leaders were doubtless aware.[41]

Such scattered and meagre evidence was hardly sufficient in itself, however, to make of the coal dispute so awful a portent, and it is apparent that the alarm of the General Council was partly irrational – born of the memories of Black Friday and its aftermath, and of the exaggerated conception on the labour side of the powers and conspiratorial character of the employers' confederations. It is clear, nonetheless, that their fears were of considerable significance in bringing the Special Industrial Committee on 23 July to agree to sympathetic action on the miners' behalf. 'Their duty was clear' said A. G. Walkden.

> The General Council was brought into being to deal with that sort of situation. . . . They did not want to see the miners let down. They realised that after 1921 when the miners were defeated, everyone else was attacked. There had been four years of disaster since. The railway magnates were waiting their chance to get his Union down. That would happen in every industry.

And Citrine made the same point: 'If the industries fought singly they would be broken singly. Only if they could get Trade Unions to rally to the support of the miners now had they any chance of settlement in other industries threatened by attacks.'

There was, however, another aspect to the Committee's calculations: that the threat of a boycott would in itself be sufficient to compel the government to intervene and force the owners to withdraw their notices. The NUR President, Marchbank, claimed that 'on Black Friday they nearly had the Government on their knees. If they could bring the Government into a similar position on this occasion, it might not only prevent a stoppage, but save the miners' position. But for this, they wanted more support than was merely necessary.'

And Citrine predicted that the Prime Minister would be anxious to take up the miners' offer of a general inquiry into the industry.

> The coal owners should be told that it was their duty to come to terms with the miners. It should be intimated to them that the miners had the solid backing of the whole Trade Union Movement. The Prime Minister should

be approached with this end in view. If they met the Prime Minister he would ask on what basis the dispute should be settled, and would go tooth and nail for an inquiry.

The SIC thus agreed on 23 July, with the miners' permission, to make an approach to Baldwin, and a meeting was arranged four days later. Though there was no indication that they expected a public subsidy to be conceded at this stage, they manifestly hoped for a peace without bloodshed.[42]

During the next week, besides, it was to become steadily more transparent that the enforcement of an embargo on coal presented major unsolved problems of organization. Though the transport unions were ready enough to undertake action, they were increasingly concerned about the degree of support that would be given them by the rest of the movement. On the twenty-third anxiety was expressed unexpectedly, about certain weaknesses among the miners themselves. Some districts, especially Nottinghamshire, were reported to be unenthusiastic about fighting wage cuts which in their case were to be minimal; and the Federation's failure to ally the unions of enginemen and deputies was also criticized. In addition, the opposition of the leadership of the Seamen's Union to an embargo on coal was already forecast. Two days later, when the Committee met the executive of the railway unions, other difficulties were aired. The imposition of a boycott would almost certainly lead to the dismissal of railway workers for disobeying orders, presenting their organizations with the necessity of ordering a general stoppage. J. H. Thomas even suggested that it would be tactically advisable to authorize an immediate strike rather than risk the confusion which a selective withdrawal of labour would create. The railwaymen also stipulated that financial assistance be afforded them by other unions. This, however, had already struck Citrine as difficult to bring about: 'really sustained financial support is practically an impossibility in consequence of the depression of the last few years'.[43] Though in its public statements the SIC betrayed no lack of confidence in the impending embargo, it had more and more obvious reasons for wishing to avert it.[44]

The Committee again discussed the question of financial support for the transport workers on 28 July, but no decisions on this subject had been taken prior to the meeting of affiliated union executives on the thirtieth. In the Conference notes which Citrine prepared for the General Council chairman, Swales, it was suggested that whatever the legitimacy of the demands of the unions involved in the boycott, 'the very extent of the lock-out makes the problem appear almost insurmountable'.[45] By that time, too, a further hazard had been more clearly appreciated. Bevin told the T&GWU executive on the morning of 30 July that those responsible for planning the embargo had felt that their preparations 'might not in themselves be found to render adequate assistance to the miners by reason of the fact that, according to information received, many industrial concerns had accumulated large stocks of coal sufficient to meet their requirements for a period, of several months, in anticipation of a Dispute'.[46] Though the SIC, when considering the draft report of the Coal Embargo Committee the previous day, had been unwilling to contemplate any extension of the stoppage, the attitude of the transport unions was bound to open up this prospect in the event of any prolongation of the struggle.

At the general conference of executives held that afternoon, enthusiasm for the idea of a boycott was such that these difficulties went almost unnoticed. The transport unions were successful in committing the rest of the TUC, verbally at least, to giving whatever form of additional support their sectional action proved to require. The General Council was instructed, on Bevin's motion, to 'put a definite scheme before the Executives' for the provision of financial help. And though no decision was taken on the immobilization of industrial coal reserves, there was said to be 'general agreement' that the Council should have discretionary power to issue further orders with this object in view.[47]

In no respect, therefore, could it be said that the coal embargo due to begin at midnight on 31 July was carefully planned. Its implementation was thought liable by some of those concerned to lead haphazardly and unpredictably towards a large-scale stoppage possibly implicating numbers of unions which had expected to take no part in the dispute. It may be doubted whether the union movement was prepared, psychologically or organizationally, to engage in a full-scale general strike in July 1925. Though Citrine had raised for consideration, at the meeting of the SIC on the 23 July, the policy of 'collective cessation of work' he had expressed himself 'dubious how far [it] would be translated into practice'.[48] Brownlie, the AEU President, for example, told the executives' conference on 30 July that 'the declaration of a general strike would not help the miners. . . . The Amalgamated Engineering Union could be brought out the next day, and it would not help one iota in favour of the miners.'[49] Only belatedly, and partly involuntarily, was a more ambitious form of collective action to be undertaken the following year. But to whatever extent the General Council were criticized for failure to lay the groundwork for the stoppage of 1926, they had at least drawn some practical lessons from the experiences of the previous summer.

The intervention of the government

The TUC was saved from the exposure of its makeshift plans on Red Friday, as the Industrial Committee had hoped, by the decision of the government to avert a conflict. Their intervention occurred, besides, in such a way as to suggest that the prospective embargo had exercised a critical influence on the Cabinet. Whether this is true in fact is not easily determined. It depends upon an ordination of the considerations which affected government policy during the crisis, which must remain partly conjectural.

The government, and Baldwin in particular, had avoided being drawn into the coal dispute for as long as seemed politically feasible. Evan Williams claimed to have warned them of an impending collision as early as March 1925; the Labour Party asked parliamentary questions on the coal situation the following month; and by the end of May the Minister of Labour had himself told the Cabinet that an August strike was a palpable threat.[50] But in a speech at Welbeck Abbey on 1 June Baldwin had told the two sides in the dispute to 'put the State out of their minds and get down to it'.[51]

Baldwin's administration avoided implicating itself in the settlement on industrial disputes as far as possible, on the general assumption that the state's attempts to act as mediator were usually vitiated by ministerial ignorance and by the undue expectations of public assistance aroused in the adversaries. The Premier's own reputation for fair-mindedness and lack of class prejudice rested on this abstention, for more frequent involvement in such conflicts must have increased the likelihood of being charged with partiality. In the case of the mining industry the government had additional reasons for maintaining its aloofness: the complexity of the wage system to be administered, the past history of government control and subvention which the Conservatives of the post-Coalition period wished to be free of, and the miners' advocacy of nationalization, which was contrary to settled policy. It was for these reasons – and not as a result of any careful assessment of the current disagreement – that Baldwin remained outside the arena until the clamour compelled his appearance.

The first official contact established by the government with miners and owners – by Bridgeman on 10 July – was intended only to try and promote direct negotiations. Both the First Lord and the Macmillan committee failed to bring the two sides together, until on 24 July the former at last managed to arrange a joint meeting, primarily to discuss the possibility of deferring a lock-out.[52] No progress was made, and no further conference took place until the 29 July. Baldwin himself did not make a move until 27 July, when he received (at their request) the Special Industrial Committee of the General Council. There is no evidence that even at this late stage either the Cabinet or the Prime Minister had any solution to the dispute in mind.

The SIC sought to 'impress on the Prime Minister the gravity of the situation and urge him to make an early pronouncement to the effect that the notices and the terms of the Mine Owners should be withdrawn'.[53] The following morning the Cabinet held their first discussion on the crisis and agreed that the owners should indeed be asked to offer unconditional negotiations, but that

> ... there was to be no question of giving any general Government subsidy to the coal industry; that the question of a subsidy would in no event be considered except in the remote contingency of it becoming clear that both parties to the coal dispute had made the largest possible concessions but that there was still a gap which might provide the only means of securing a durable settlement on an economic basis.[54]

At the same time they arranged for the issue of an emergency proclamation in the event of an embargo being declared, though agreeing also to advise the railway managers not to take disciplinary measures so long as it remained 'on a small scale'. Finally, a committee was set up under Churchill to investigate the practicability of the state purchase of coal royalties.

When Baldwin subsequently interviewed the Mining Association he tried to persuade them to concede a national minimum wage, even if it entailed the closure of a number of pits.[55] This, with obvious reluctance, they agreed to do. On the afternoon of 29 July the Prime Minister submitted to the miners' executive the owners' 'first memorandum', announcing that they accepted 'the principle of a minimum', though warning that it 'must be very low, and must be much less favourable to the men than minimum percentages fixed district by district'. The miners, after consulting the SIC, rejected the offer, repeating their standard formula that they were 'unable to accept any conditions that impose a reduction in wages'.[56] In a further exchange of documents during the early evening the owners declared themselves ready to allot all profits made during August to increase wages, and again hopefully held out the inducement that 'considerably better terms could be offered if it were possible to arrange even temporarily some relaxation of the Seven Hours Act'. The miners replied that large profits had been made and dissipated by the employers prior to 1924, and that investigation of managerial inefficiency had been refused; they added that, though national and district minima were now supposedly on offer, no figures were specified, and substantial reductions in pay were still apparently contemplated.[57]

At 9 pm the Special Industrial Committee saw the Prime Minister for a second time. Its members had already discussed whether a subsidy might be forthcoming as a means of averting a crisis, and though opinions had differed as to the government's tractability, it seems clear that such a solution was urged on this occasion. According to the General Council's later report to Congress, 'great pressure was brought to bear upon the Prime Minister to take into consideration the special and abnormal conditions in the industry'. Baldwin gave no immediate sign of having accepted this argument; but the following morning he and Churchill drafted proposals for a grant of ten million pounds to be extended to the coal industry for a period of nine months.[58]

This prospect remained concealed, however, for most of the day. On the morning of 30 August Baldwin reiterated to the miners his earlier assertion that 'the Government are not prepared to give a subsidy to the industry', and pressed them to accept an interim 'readjustment of conditions'. It was during this exchange that he uttered his remarks, their nature afterwards disputed, on the necessity of general wage reductions. But he did not officially propose 'an authoritative inquiry to try to get to the bottom of the economic difficulties of the industry and to see how far the allegations that are made as to the room for improvement in the industry are well-founded with a view to putting the industry as quickly as possible into a more healthy condition. . . .'[59]

The miners reported this suggestion first to the SIC and then to the full General Council, which decided that an answer should be delayed until the conference of executives had approved the projected embargo. They then gave their imprimatur to the Federation's reply:[60] 'we offer no opposition to a further inquiry, provided there are satisfactory terms of reference, and that in the meantime the mineworkers are not asked to submit to either a reduction of wages or an extension of hours of labour'.

This message was received during the evening session of the

Cabinet which began at 6.30. The ministers decided, on a vote, 'that as between a national strike and the payment of assistance to the mining industry, the latter course was the less disadvantageous'. Bridgeman, Joynson-Hicks and Salisbury appear to have constituted the opposition.[61] In the official statement issued in the early hours of 31 July, the subvention was said to have been provided because the miners 'felt that it was not fair to require a reduction of wages with the present cost of living before an attempt had been made by means of an inquiry to secure a contribution towards meeting the difficult situation with which the industry was confronted'.[62] Already there was evident an implication, fatally ambiguous, that the inquiry would produce conditions in which such cuts would be considered fair.

Between 28 and 30 July the majority of the Cabinet apparently performed a political *volte-face* on the critical issue of the granting of a subsidy. It is arguable, however, that this reversal of attitude was at least partly simply a change of public posture, dictated by the state of negotiations between the disputants. On the twenty-eighth the government still hoped to force both miners and owners to make concessions; to offer a subsidy at that stage would preclude any such development. On the other hand the Cabinet did not then consider, except superficially, the effects of a possible lock-out and embargo – whilst on the thirtieth these were the pre-eminent topics of discussion. There is no reason to suppose, in other words, that the factors which influenced the government's decision of 30 July had in all cases come into existence during the two preceding days.

The problems of defining these factors is therefore considerably more difficult. Most historical explanations of the government's conduct on Red Friday comprise three elements: the state of public opinion, the degree of readiness of the emergency services administered by the Supply and Transport Committee, and the expected economic and financial repercussions of a large-scale dispute.[63] This aetiological framework has, however, various shortcomings. Firstly, it makes no distinction between the consequences that might have been attributed to a lock-out of miners and those expected to flow from an embargo involving other unions. Yet in so far as the latter threat was unnecessary, so clearly the lessons which the labour movement drew from the crisis were mistaken. An additional and complicating possibility, however – likewise rarely stressed – is that different groups of ministers were swayed by different influences and calculations. There is no need, on this assumption, to give primacy to any particular factor: rather, we are confronted with the task of tracing alternative mental paths which led to a single point but were thereafter liable to diverge again.

In one respect, however, the conventional explanatory scheme can be simplified. It is difficult to see how the factor of 'public opinion' affected the outcome of events except in its bearing on the state of emergency preparations. Though both the treatment of the mining dispute by the press and the report of the Macmillan inquiry published on 28 July might have been expected to ensure public sympathy for the miners against the owners, this was hardly an influence sufficient to warrant the provision of a subsidy or to secure its popularity. The Cabinet exposed itself to criticism on so many counts by its decision of 30 July that it cannot be thought primarily concerned with its public image. On the other hand the willingness of British citizens probably ignorant of the issues at stake to suffer inconvenience arising from a widespread stoppage, and especially to cooperate with measures designed to counteract it, was no doubt a matter of greater concern.

There was, at the same time, an additional factor which may have influenced the government's conduct on Red Friday to which few historical accounts give much attention. The Conservative administration may well have recognized, by now, the case for a measure of reorganization in the coal industry. In face of the rapid decline in the fortunes of coal, the strictures of Macmillan and the blinkered prejudices exhibited by the owners in the course of the negotiations, it was evident that the question of legislative intervention had again to be seriously considered. The Cabinet admitted as much by appointing the committee on nationalization of royalties, even before the subvention had been conceded. At the very least they accepted the desirability of producing a policy for the industry where they had had none before; and it is clear that the Royal Commission was appointed with the intention of securing an agreed and, it was hoped, a palatable report – not simply of imposing delay. This is not to conclude that all, or even most, members of the government thought an inquiry likely to avert a major dispute, or that a radical policy of state interference was now favourably regarded. But some modest encouragement of reconstruction was almost certainly seen as necessary for the mining industry; and the postponement of a strike was a reflection, in this respect, of the Cabinet's uncertainty as to the form which it should take.

The appointment of the Royal Commission was not, however, the most substantial benefit purchased by the settlement of 30 July; most Cabinet ministers were much more urgently concerned with the damaging repercussions of a mining lock-out on the rest of the economy and on the national finances. They concluded, on the experience of past disputes, that 'the effect on the trade and industry of the country . . . [would] be of the gravest character'. The hopes for a commercial recovery founded on the return to the gold standard would inevitably be dispelled. And the relative expense of a public subsidy was slight in comparison with the expected cost of a stoppage which it was believed must be prolonged.[64]

These considerations might very well have been sufficient in themselves to influence Baldwin and his more conciliatory colleagues like Steel-Maitland in favour of appeasement. But other ministers were almost certainly more concerned by the added threat of an embargo and its implications. Hankey, in his note to the king on the proceedings of the Cabinet, highlighted the distinction between those whose priority was to settle the coal dispute and those whose object was to postpone a fight with the TUC. 'Many members of the Cabinet think that the struggle is inevitable and must come sooner or later – the PM does not share this view. The majority of the Cabinet regard the present moment as badly chosen for the fight though conditions would be more favourable nine months hence.'[65] Even if this statement is exaggerated, it seems clear that the prospective boycott represented a problem larger than the lock-out *per se*. By the thirtieth the Cabinet had become convinced (as they were not two days earlier) that such action would quickly lead to a general stoppage among railwaymen and probably among all transport workers.[66] The question is thus raised: how far did the government feel capable of meeting this challenge?

Emergency organization

It was Baldwin himself who many years later explained the government's retreat on Red Friday to his biographer in the celebrated phrase, 'We were not ready'.[67] The value of his statement as evidence of the inadequacy of the supply and transport organization has rightly been regarded with scepticism by later historians. Yet it is clear that, even at the time, members of the Cabinet actively encouraged this impression. One junior minister, J. C. C. Davidson, was sure that it 'was a major factor in the settlement'. Another, Lane-Fox, was told that the two principal reasons for the granting of the subsidy had been the lack of public warning and the need to make better preparations for carrying on essential services.[68] Baldwin himself informed the Mining Association on the night of 30 August that the unreadiness of this machinery had been the paramount justification for the subvention.[69] And speaking of the decision in the House of Commons in December Churchill said of the Cabinet,[70]

> We considered. . . . that should such a struggle [as a general strike] be found to be inevitable at the very last moment, it was of supreme importance that it should only be undertaken under conditions which would not expose the nation needlessly or wantonly to perils the gravity of which cannot possibly be overestimated. We therefore decided to postpone the crisis in the hope of averting it, or if not of averting it, of coping with it effectually when the time came.

Moreover when the preparations actually made under the aegis of the Supply and Transport Committee are examined more closely, it is evident that until the eve of Red Friday they progressed only slowly. Prior to the 1923 election Davidson and Anderson had managed to appoint prospective civil commissioners in the eleven regional divisions and to find the chairmen of eighty-six volunteer recruiting committees. But neither cadre had any subordinates and neither was yet doing any work. Not until December 1924 was the Supply and Transport Committee itself set up in Whitehall under the chairmanship of the Home Secretary. By the beginning of May 1925 it had designated food officers and road officers for most of the divisional headquarters and made some plans to maintain the supply of power in the event of a strike extending to electricity workers. The regional staff had still taken no steps, however, either to create food stocks or to secure access to means of transport where required.[71]

On 1 April, indeed, the Minister of Transport, Wilfred Ashley, had written to Joynson-Hicks to say that he was 'not at all satisfied' with the measures thus far taken and felt afraid that 'members of the Government, and even members of the Supply and Transport Committee, [were] apt to believe that the schemes which have been prepared on paper mean very much more than they do in practice'.[72] In subsequent weeks Ashley continued to press for the extension and consolidation of the organization, especially in the field of transport. Before the end of July, however, he had apparently achieved little beyond establishing haulage committees, representing road transport firms, to co-operate with the officials of the divisional centres. A fortnight before Red Friday he was finally given permission to recruit chairmen for similar committees in about seventy additional sub-areas, 'every effort being made to complete the arrangements before the end of July'.[73] A week later the chairman of the Supply and Transport Committee told the Cabinet that plans were still in process of being drawn up setting out the detailed responsibilities of central departments and providing for the maintenance of postal services.[74]

It thus seems fair to conclude that the government's counter-strike measures in 1925 had been somewhat hastily assembled, and were still less than complete. As far as can be judged, departmental responsibilities at the centre had been clearly, if recently, laid down, and in the regions the divisional headquarters had acquired a permanent supervisory staff ready for action, though small in numbers (including coal, food and road officers, but none for electrical power or port transport). At local level, however, the machinery so far established appeared more rudimentary. Unpaid chairmen of volunteer service and road haulage committees were expected to ensure the maintenance of services over relatively large areas, though they had been given no opportunity to consult, had made no contact with employers outside their own acquaintance, and had no guarantee of the cooperation of local authorities as yet officially ignorant of the existence of an emergency apparatus. Though the Shipping Subcommittee in Whitehall had made a preliminary and optimistic estimate of national coal stocks, their sufficiency in many urban areas such as London and Birmingham was dependent on the availability of uninterrupted transport facilities; and still, apparently, no similar inquiry had been conducted in connection with food supplies.[75]

The Cabinet was perhaps more concerned, however, about the anticipated problems of activating the machinery which had been created. The discussion on the thirtieth indicated that:

> While the organization was complete it was only a skeleton and could not be put into operation until volunteers had come forward. Volunteers, however, could not be called for until an emergency was proclaimed. . . . Until volunteers had been enrolled and sorted out, the organization could not function, and this would require a few days. . . . There was general agreement that in the event of a strike on the scale now threatened, the maintenance of the essential public services could be effected, but only by a great and costly effort.[76]

The Minister of Transport had grown more confident on this count, forecasting that volunteers could be mobilized in only two days, 'because the goodwill evoked by an Emergency enables things to be done rapidly'.[77] But there were a number of instances like the power and railway industries where skilled and experienced men would almost certainly be more difficult to obtain, and Joynson-Hicks again noted the absence of specialized military service units which had previously been available to support civilian activities.[78] Ashley himself felt some doubts, too, about the provision of additional protection required by emergency operations – 'the essence of the problem' in his eyes.

In short, though Conservative ministers expected the supply and transport system to work adequately if put to the test, they were still troubled in varying degrees by the shortcomings likely to be exposed during the crisis, and in some cases perhaps uncertain about the public response to so sudden an emergency. At the very least, they were aware that considerable improvements in the system could be achieved if greater publicity and expenditure were allowed. Looking back a week after Red Friday Ashley judged that the plans for preserving transport had been 'brought as far forward as was possible under the instructions existing at that time', but added that the threat of a general stoppage justified 'far more complete preparation'. Writing in November, Steel-Maitland acknowledged 'it may well be true that in July last we had not sufficiently developed the system and the staffs of an emergency organization'. The Cabinet had instructed the Home Secretary on 5 August to draft proposals 'with the object of enabling a more effective scheme to be drawn up than at present exists for maintaining vital national services in the event of a strike'.[79] The improvements made in the supply and transport arrangements over the next nine months accurately reflect the awareness of its deficiencies on Red Friday.

Whether the prospect of a TUC embargo was required to induce the Cabinet to buy peace in 1925 is still hard to say. Those ministers chiefly concerned with the economic costs of an industrial dispute may well have regarded a coal stoppage as an evil sufficient in itself to justify the price of a truce; but they were a minority, if an influential one. Those who were more anxious about the disruption and disorder attendant on an embargo were also inclined to regard a mining strike as likely to prove unavoidable. Their agreement to the concession of a subsidy was the result firstly of Baldwin's personal authority and the desire for government unity and secondly of the calculations that, even if an emergency could have been safely weathered in 1925, further time for preparation would afford additional confidence. It is not necessary to see the government's response to this crisis as a merely tactical exercise in order to stress the change of mood with which men like Churchill and Amery faced the same industrial problems and unsettled issues the following year.

'An affair of outposts'

The announcement of the terms of peace aroused anger and disapproval in many quarters. Evan Williams told Baldwin on the morning of 31 July that the Mining Association had received the news the previous night with 'profound disappointment and very serious alarm', and felt that even a strike on a wide front was a 'lesser evil' than the government's proposals.[80] It was not until mid-afternoon, indeed, that Churchill and the government officials finally secured the Association's agreement to the financial conditions of payment. When settled, however, they proved so favourable to the owners that much of the initial criticism on this score was eventually silenced. Collieries claimed a share of the assistance, calculated on a district basis, so long as their profits did not exceed 1s 3d a ton. There was no restriction on the reopening of pits, nor any other measure to restrain price-cutting.[81] The outstanding grievance of the owners, therefore, was not the subvention but the mounting of an inquiry, reviving spectres of the Sankey inquisition. This time, Williams insisted, it should be conducted by 'competent persons within closed doors' and should examine conditions, including wage levels, in all industries and not just in coal.

In the House of Commons Lloyd George in particular ridiculed and excoriated the government's conduct. The ministers were 'afraid of cold steel'. Their supporters were being 'herded into the Red Lobby. The hand that directs them will be the hand of the Patronage Secretary to the Treasury but the voice that compels them is the voice of Mr Cook.' The subsidy was 'a guarantee of wages and profits, without any control, without any limit, without any restrictions'. The Royal Commission would produce predictable recommendations on reorganization whose enforcement would be delayed by its proceedings and which would provide no solution to the immediate issues of the dispute.[82]

The Conservative backbenchers were obviously uneasy, though only a handful openly attacked their government. On 5 August Tom Jones had found Baldwin 'concerned about the attitude of many of his followers in the House', expressed in the party meeting of the evening before.[83] In his speech on the sixth the Prime Minister endeavoured to reassure them with a peroration directed against unconstitutional and undemocratic forms of industrial action and a promise that 'if the time should come when the community has to protect itself, with the full force of the Government behind it, the community will do so. . . .'[84]

But the Cabinet continued to feel vulnerable to rank and file disapproval. The initial revenue grant for the payment of the subsidy was less than half the amount eventually required, and Churchill was forced to return to the Commons in December to seek a further instalment of £9 million.[85] The reluctance of the government to consider any generous terms of renewal in April 1926 was no doubt strengthened by the embarrassment which past debates had occasioned.

The leadership of the Labour Party felt scarcely happier about the political implications of Red Friday. The miners, with the General Council's acquiescence, had deliberately denied the parliamentary party the responsibility for presenting their case. MacDonald saw this aloofness partly as a product of personal vendettas and partly as evidence of a resurgence of 'direct action'. He wrote, immediately after the crisis,

> The sections which believe that governments only yield to force, and that direct action against society offers great prospects for improvement in working class conditions naturally feel that they have scored a fine triumph . . . the mishandling of the Government . . . handed over the honours of war to those who may be inclined to toy with revolution.[86]

J. H. Thomas expressed similar reservations;[87] and though his return to the General Council in September 1925 did not result in any other change of strategy, it was perhaps largely responsible for the fact that, in 1926, liaison with the parliamentary wing was to be considerably closer.

Among the General Council members, however, only Citrine expressed some anxiety on the constitutional question. 'If the challenge of the movement,' he suggested, 'could have been given the appearance of a denial of the Government's right to govern, and as the beginning of open war between society as at present constituted and the whole organized working-class movement, a very serious situation might have arisen.'[88] But the majority of TUC leaders ignored or overlooked this danger. The Industrial Committee, for instance, apparently saw Red Friday largely as a triumph of bargaining powers – evidence of the extent to which the threat of joint action could yield results by means of negotiation. They declined to regard this procedure as a challenge to the state. For them and their colleagues the distinction between a revolutionary general strike and a limited sympathetic strike remained quite sharply defined – though MacDonald was perhaps right to argue that initiation of the latter tended to encourage contemplation of the former. 'When they got down to it,' Swales told the SIC on 23 July, 'their people were not ready for the last struggle and to attempt it would put them back too far.' Ernest Bevin assured his union conference, rather unconvincingly, that since the government had remained inactive during the development of the coal dispute, 'the constitutional issues are out of the way'; but he, too, had added a vague rhetorical flourish:

> We shall not win material gains out of the struggle immediately. Not for one moment do I want you to believe that you will pull down the citadel of capitalism about your ears. I do not for one moment think you will jump a century, but the demonstration of power will usher in an era of constructional effort to follow which will lay a sound basis for generations to come.[89]

The motion of a final victory was thus conjured with but relegated to the indefinite future. And the main consequence of Red Friday was expected to be a further battle in the current war. The telegram which Swales and Citrine sent out on 31 July, cancelling the order for a boycott, warned that the movement 'must be alert and vigilant in case the necessity should again arise for it to act in defence of its standards'. And Herbert Smith wrote in a TUC pamphlet some weeks later: 'The recent crisis was an affair of outposts. It was a mere skirmish. The main battle has still to be fought and won.' On 6 August the first deliberate measure was taken in anticipation of a renewal of the emergency, when the SIC recommended that it should remain in existence 'to apply itself to the task of devising ways and means of consolidating the resistance of the Trade Union Movement should the attack be renewed'.[90]

Thus far there had been no visible sign of disagreement within the General Council about its present conduct or its future responsibilities; to see the events of 1925 as a triumph of the 'left' over the 'right' seems unwarranted.[91] Differences of temper and outlook no doubt existed, but the action taken before Red Friday seemed necessary and justified to all concerned, commanding overwhelming support at every level of the movement. Too much attention has probably been given in this regard to the presence of Alonso Swales and A. A. Purcell as chairman and vice-chairman of the Council, and the temporary absence of J. H. Thomas from its ranks. The radical influence of the TUC officers was at best limited: Purcell belonged to a small union (the Furnishing Trades Association), Swales to an unusually particularist one (the AEU), and neither was a general secretary. It is absurd to suggest that they could determine the decisions of the Council as a whole. As for Thomas, his dislike of militancy was real enough, and as head of a large union and a leading Labour politician he exerted an influence upon other leaders greater than that of Purcell or Swales. But Thomas was also a man who swam with the tide, who had to react to the currents of militancy within his own organization, and who did in fact assent in 1925 to the proposed embargo on coal by the transport unions. To think that as a member of the Council he might have attempted to deflect its policy – and, more, succeeded in doing so – is to credit him, as he complained of later detractors, with the attributes of 'a sort of machiavellian superman of the entire labour movement'.[92]

There was, it is true, more evidence of disagreement in the General Council *after* Red Friday over the tactical lessons to be drawn from it. But this represented a continuation of that earlier debate on the constitutional question, alignments in which were scarcely ever to be understood simply by reading conventional political labels. For Citrine in particular the problems which had obtruded in the planning of the coal embargo pointed to the need for a more thorough preparation of any similar enterprise, and above all the reinforcement of the General Council's authority. He wrote in the August edition of the *Labour Magazine*:[93]

> In my opinion it would be mistaken to overrate the apparent success which attended the General Council's efforts in support of the miners, and later the textile workers, in their struggle to maintain essential Trade Union principles. ... I am convinced that in limiting the scope of the action which it was proposed to take in the mining dispute and in basing our strategy upon the transport and railway unions – which incidentally cannot always be expected to act as the storm troops of the movement – the General Council acted wisely. Had it been necessary to call a general stoppage we should have realized where our weakness lay.
>
> Responsibility for calling a strike and for organizing the necessary financial and other measures is not concentrated in the General Council to such an extent that many – perhaps the majority – even of trade union executives could not constitutionally act without the sanction of a ballot vote of their members.

For unions to review their own rules was thus a first step towards more effective industrial cooperation.

The opponents of organization, as in the past, upheld spontaneity of action and argued Red Friday to have vindicated it. 'It was a magnificent response which was obtained in the miners' case,' proclaimed J. H. Thomas. 'It was the better sense of the movement that said: "We as Trade Unionists will not allow these conditions to be imposed on another section." That spirit, that action, will always be forthcoming at the right time.' J. R. Clynes echoed him: the authority of the General Council in the emergency had lain 'not in . . . resolutions, but in the unanimous feeling of the Labour world that the miners were in the right, and the miners had the support not only of their own class but of the public at large'.[94] Though expressed most eloquently by those unsympathetic to 'direct action', this viewpoint still had the support of many radicals too; and to those outside the corridors of Eccleston Square was a plausible version of the experience of 1925. Even Citrine's belief in careful preparation was modified by an appreciation of the limited degree of centralization which the movement would think justified.

The events of July 1925 had thus bound the General Council to the miners by virtue of a shared victory, whilst doing little or nothing to provide the conditions for a repetition of this success. Not only did the course of events encourage an undue faith in improvised action; it also established precedents for the formulation of policy, advantageous to the miners and prejudicial to their allies. The General Council had accepted without question on this occasion the largely negative and inflexible standpoint adopted by the MFGB in face of demands for a worsening of conditions. At the same time the Federation had successfully insisted on keeping control of the conduct of all negotiations, confining the SIC and the General Council to a role of approval and affirmation. Their officials told the Industrial Committee on 27 July 'that the fullest possible facilities would be given to the General Council to deal with the dispute, but that the actual detailed negotiations should be carried on by the Miners' Federation themselves'.[95] On the renewal of the conflict in the spring of 1926 the TUC representatives were to attempt, slowly and painfully, to extricate themselves from this position of subordination – but achieved, in the end, only a very limited success.

IV Prospects of War and Peace, 1925–6

The Royal Commission

To justify its appointment from the government's point of view the Royal Commission on the Coal Industry had to offer recommendations which displayed independence from undue influence by owners and miners, but secured the approval of at least one side. The Cabinet had no wish to impose a purportedly bipartisan settlement upon unwilling disputants, and like the Coalition ministry in 1920 probably regarded such an attempt as impractical. If, however, the Commission could find the means to reconcile the miners to wage cuts, a stoppage could clearly be avoided. Alternatively, if it could induce the owners to moderate the demands they had made in 1925 and to accept a limited measure of reorganization, then at least the government could take a stand against the unions on secure and apparently reasonable grounds. In fact the Samuel Commission achieved neither purpose. It presented a report objectionable to both parties and to the government itself (and attractive only to the TUC General Council). Thus it brought about a political situation in which Baldwin and his colleagues, while choosing to confront and resist the threat of a general strike, were unable to assert the virtuousness of the owners as an argument for doing so and were left to rely for a defence, not perhaps unwillingly, on the unconstitutionality of the strike itself.

In August 1925, however, the government had conscientiously set out to appoint a Commission acceptable to the Mining Association and the MFGB. This had not proved easy. The miners wanted an inquiry in public, conducted by men qualified through past association with the coal industry, modelled on the Sankey Commission of 1919. The owners wanted commissioners drawn from outside, meeting in private. The Cabinet inclined to the latter's view in the choice of members, as making unanimity of conclusions more likely.[1] But they compromised with the Federation by allowing the two sides of the industry to appoint assessors with the right to take part in the examination of witnesses; and left the Commission itself to decide whether to admit the press.

As a matter of policy, too, the Cabinet evidently decided to find for the post of chairman 'a Statesman of the first rank'.[2] The desire for formal neutrality suggested that he should be a Liberal. The first nominee, Lord Grey of Falloden, declined on grounds of ill-health and ignorance; the second, the wartime Home Secretary and ex-governor of Palestine, Sir Herbert Samuel, accepted after some hesitation.[3] Of the other members – Sir Herbert Lawrence, previously Haig's chief of staff; Kenneth Lee, of the textile firm of Tootal; and W. H. Beveridge, Director of the London School of Economics – the latter two also had affiliations with the Liberal party.[4] Some predilection for progressive but non-socialist schemes of rationalization might therefore have been anticipated, though there is no evidence that the Cabinet sought to predict the outcome of the inquiry. Nor were the predispositions of its members ever conspicuous, for the chief characteristic of the Commission was to be its reluctance to come to definite conclusions except by means of painstaking research. Beveridge's faith in the 'unbiased collection of facts' and Samuel's 'deliberate, precise, exact and unemotional' approach to work were calculated to produce a report which paid more attention to scientific and academic criteria than it did to *realpolitik*.[5]

The difficulties of the Commission's task were of course immense. As its public hearings quickly indicated, any accommodation between owners and miners was almost inconceivable. The Federation sought to repeat the inquisitorial methods used at the Sankey Inquiry, but Herbert Smith had none of the forensic skill of Smillie, nor was the atmosphere of the Commission so highly charged.[6] While these heated exchanges took place within the confines of the Commission's hearings, moreover, owners and men in the coal industry continued to conduct guerrilla warfare in the country. Towards the end of September the Federation's executive were asked by the Durham miners for financial assistance to sustain their opposition to attacks on basis rates and customary hours of work (which in the north-east were below the permitted legal maximum). At a special conference on 8 October, cases of disputes over price lists and piece rate agreements were reported from Scotland, Yorkshire, Northumberland and North Wales as well as Durham. They affected in all some ten thousand men, three-quarters of them in the north-east. Two weeks earlier the miners' leaders had already made complaints on this subject to the Prime

Minister: the owners, claimed Cook, were 'trying to enforce the proposals they put forward [in July 1925] pit by pit, district by district'.[7] Baldwin insisted that the government were unable to intervene, and the special conference decided to refer the dispute, if necessary, to the General Council, only narrowly defeating a proposal to boycott the Royal Commission until a satisfactory settlement had been obtained.

The issue receded in the autumn of 1925, though in Durham it remained sufficiently intractable for an official strike ballot to be held in January, recording a majority insufficiently large to authorize a stoppage.[8] In November, the miners' executive had approached the Mines Department of the Board of Trade in order to seek a written agreement with government and owners proscribing any further wage reductions.[9] This, however, the Mining Association still refused. Lane-Fox, the Secretary for Mines, commented that the owners, 'having, as they think, now secured the tactical advantage of a situation in which wages are regulated without any formal national agreement . . . are not likely to be persuaded to forgo it'. The MFGB had to be satisfied with a memorandum jointly signed with the Department itself, restating the terms on which the subsidy had been granted, though indicating at the same time that the 1924 agreement was no longer in force.[10]

Tension within the mining industry thus remained high throughout the months occupied by the Samuel inquiry. It was maintained with the help on the one hand of the intensive propaganda of the Minority Movement, and by 'what Mr Cook has been saying Sunday after Sunday with regard to a revolution';[11] on the other hand by the activities of the Organization for the Maintenance of Supplies. To those members of the government who had seen Red Friday largely as a delaying tactic, the prevention of a stoppage seemed more and more chimerical. 'If the men's leaders were convinced last August that nothing could be yielded until the men had been got into a proper frame of mind by a stoppage,' wrote Lane-Fox in November, 'they will certainly not be less determined in April, with the recollection of their earlier success to give them confidence.'[12]

The hostile attitude of the principal disputants to the Samuel Commission and its report can therefore easily be put down to the indestructability of old antipathies. In consequence the Commission itself has been largely exculpated by historians from any major part in bringing about the crisis of May 1926.[13] In reality, however, its responsibility was of greater extent. The Samuel Report, though initially well-received by much of the press, had obvious and fateful shortcomings.[14] Some of its arguments were inconsistent or unproven, and dissent from them could be adequately justified on these grounds. Other recommendations were ambiguous or incompletely explained, and their obscurity allowed the contending parties to profess agreement with the report whilst placing opposing interpretations on its meaning. Finally, those proposals which were most clearly and definitely stated were unfortunately least calculated to help avert a further conflict in the industry.

The deficiencies of the report were attributable in part to that detachment of its authors from the affairs of the coal industry which the government had originally valued. It is obvious that the Commissioners had no new ideas of importance to offer on the subject of reconstruction and reform; the only significant proposal which had any claim to novelty was the suggestion, no more than tentative, of a system of miners' family allowances.[15] In other respects their proposals on the long-term reorganization of the industry were the commonplaces of earlier discussions on rationalization. Ramsay MacDonald commented, with a measure of truth, that the Commission's membership was one 'which the Liberal party might have appointed to recommend its scheme of coal and power, and that, roughly, is what happened'.[16]

At the same time Samuel and his colleagues managed to ignore to a surprising degree the fact that they had been appointed to find an escape from a dispute *en train*. They gave little attention to the events of the summer of 1925, and although they saw themselves as working with commendable dispatch, they seemed to the officials of the Mines Department to be unduly slow to come to firm and useful conclusions on the real gravamena.[17]

The bulk of the Samuel Report was in fact concerned with the analysis of the economic condition of the coal industry and recommendations for its rehabilitation. Its view was that the depression in mining was a problem common to the whole of Europe, and that the peculiar difficulties created in Britain by the return to gold and the payment of reparations by Germany were temporary or marginal in their impact. As a long-term remedy it envisaged the creation of large undertakings by amalgamation, the nationalization of the mineral by the state, the more active development of by-products and expenditure on research into other uses for coal, and the formation of cooperative selling agencies to reduce competition between different collieries, especially in the overseas market.[18]

The premise underlying these proposals was a familiar one: that increased productivity and lower costs in the coal industry would restore prosperity. The basis for this supposition was, however, astonishingly vague. The Royal Commission did not expect more than a slight increase in coal prices, nor did they attempt to calculate the optimum price in current circumstances.[19] They demonstrated no reason for believing that the international demand for coal would recover. Thus they seemed to be recommending higher output *per capita* but not higher aggregate output; indeed, they objected to the owners' proposal to lengthen hours of work on the grounds that it would produce additional unsaleable coal. The logical conclusion was that any improvement in productivity must result in a diminution in the number of mining concerns. But though the Report foresaw the elimination of some uneconomic pits, it deplored any drastic contraction of capacity such as would exacerbate unemployment.[20]

Moreover the Commission's principal proposals for improving the efficiency of the industry were highly unpalatable to both owners and government. The former were to object, predictably, to recommendations which envisaged state interference, especially in bringing about colliery amalgamation – though even to some Conservative ministers these appeared timid.[21] The initiative in devising unification schemes was left to the companies themselves, the government being called on only where it proved necessary to coerce a refractory minority in a particular district; or, after a lapse of three years, where a standing commission felt it desirable to transfer leases of unprofitable concerns in one locality to more enterprising firms elsewhere.[22] This half-hearted advocacy of compulsion perhaps reflected doubts about thus linking efficiency with size of company: the Mining Association claimed that the findings of the Samuel Report gave undue weight to the returns of the large and recently developed collieries of Yorkshire, not confirmed by the data from exporting coalfields; and to the Commission itself Beveridge observed privately that 'it is rather the small undertakings which are unsuccessful than the large ones that are successful. There are quite a few large undertakings which do only moderately well.'[22a]

The government's main objection was to the conclusion that mineral royalties should be purchased by the state. Again, the Commission had been hesitant on this point. Between late-December and February they discussed at least three methods of dealing with royalties other than outright nationalization: the creation of a stronger 'sanctioning authority' to regulate the terms of private leases – of the kind already established by the Mines (Working Facilities and Support)

Act of 1923; the acquisition of undeveloped coal only; and the piecemeal purchase of existing leases as they expired.[23] They finally opted 'very reluctantly' for the most radical solution, influenced by the advice of the Mines Department on the practical difficulties of adopting any partial measure, and on the likely objections of the Treasury to financial outlay which did not yield an immediate return in revenue from current leases (though in the event what they proposed met Treasury objections equally strong). It is possible, too, that the Commission expected comprehensive nationalization to appeal to the miners and the labour movement, whose scheme of joint control for the industry had been decisively rejected as administratively unsound.[24] But the *economic* justification for purchasing royalties *en bloc* was even more suspect than the case for amalgamation. It might have been more easily provided had the Commission proposed a programme of mergers enforced by the state, for which the control of leases would have been essential. But they had in fact no intention of significantly changing the terms and distribution of existing leases, nor was it possible greatly to alter the lay-out of mines already worked. Nationalization of royalties promised to facilitate the more efficient development of new fields, but this of course was a very long-run prospect.

The most controversial sections of the Samuel Report, however, were those dealing with conditions of employment – and offensive primarily to the miners. 'We see no escape,' the Commission stated, 'from the giving up of [the] minimum of 1924.' Yet whilst the verdict that rates of pay should be reduced was clear enough, the recommendations affecting the nature and conditions of the reduction were shrouded in obscurity. At least three crucial questions were left inadequately answered. Firstly, how large were the cuts proposed? In an annex to the report the Commission suggested that a ten per cent decrease in the total national wage bill would 'nearly, though not quite, bring about a balance of costs and proceeds'. But because of the varying fortunes of the coalfields they concluded that 'greater reductions are almost certainly needed to give any chance of equilibrium in the exporting districts, and smaller ones would still leave a profit elsewhere'.[25] This phraseology unintentionally provided the owners with justification for demanding draconian cuts in the poorer districts. There was nothing in the report, besides, apart from a caveat to the effect that the lower-paid workers should be excluded from the reductions, to indicate how the economies should be distributed between the many grades of worker. The presumption seemed to be, without regard to equity, that all should suffer alike.

Secondly, how was a wage settlement to be negotiated? Samuel and his colleagues referred to the bargaining procedure they envisaged in four different passages, without ever achieving precision. In one instance they stated: 'it appears to us a reasonable course for the national conference [of owners and men] to refer the question of minimum percentage and such other matters as they think appropriate to district associations to frame proposals. These proposals would be submitted to the national conference for approval.'[26] The retention of a national wages board was obviously intended, but its powers *vis-à-vis* the district boards were left hopelessly indefinite. In subsequent negotiations on this point miners and employers quoted selected passages to each other with emphatic monotony.

Whilst the authors of the report clearly did not intend that wage reductions should be so large as to cover all the industry's current deficits, it was difficult to vary them district by district without conferring the largest benefits on the most inefficient collieries.[27] And it was impossible to reconcile the MFGB to any such revision. Before the publication of the report, Beveridge, Lawrence and Lee had invited Herbert Smith and Arthur Cook to a dinner party, in which unlikely setting they had hoped to 'understand . . . what was in the minds of the miners' leaders'. But since their inquiries were directed chiefly to discovering whether the Federation would prefer wage cuts to longer hours, little enlightenment was obtained.[28] Eventually the Commission came down heavily against an extension of the working day, though with the rider that it should be open to the industry to agree upon this measure if it desired. The report also favoured a family allowance scheme (financed from the wages fund), profit sharing, the creation of statutory pit committees with advisory functions, and the establishment of a welfare fund to provide pit-head baths.[29] The first three proposals were of little or no interest to the miners, however, and the last they regarded as their belated due. They were not distracted for a moment from what was, for them, the vital issue.

On one final matter of policy the Samuel Commission was unusually decisive. They regarded the government subsidy of July 1925 as objectionable in principle and deleterious to industrial performance. And though its members had considered recommending a tapering subvention 'conditional on acceptance of our proposals in principle' and of arbitration on disputed issues, this idea was not referred to in the report. Yet this was one count, ironically, on which miners and owners might have reached a measure of agreement; the former were clearly anxious to see a continuance of financial assistance, and the latter were almost certainly less averse to it than they had appeared the previous year. And though the government were reluctant to consider further outlays of this kind, they had acknowledged the disadvantages of an abrupt cessation of aid. The Commission's recommendation, coupled with official scepticism, were, however, to prevent this element of a compromise agreement from ever assuming prominence in negotiations.[30]

The Samuel Report was thus, in one or more aspects, inimical to all the parties it addressed. Yet it assumed, characteristically, that the implementation of its recommendations could largely be left to the mutual goodwill of owners and miners. Although it suggested that 'impartial' representatives might be attached to the National Wages Board, even this step was made dependent on the assent of employers and men.[31] Moreover subsequent criticism of the government for seeking to evade its responsibilities for assisting negotiations in the industry ignored the fact that the Commission had itself encouraged this abstention. 'Progress must come mainly from within the industry' if prosperity were to be restored, the authors concluded; 'the future depends primarily upon the leadership, and the general level of opinion, among the mine owners of Great Britain'.[32] Events were to force the Cabinet to relinquish the position of bystander, but to do so too slowly and reluctantly for the slender prospects of peace to survive.

Reactions to the Samuel Report

The government clearly could not disclaim all interest in the findings of the Royal Commission. Whilst it might interpret the final paragraphs as an invitation to remain aloof from negotiations on the wage question, the recommendations on reorganization required a more direct response. The course it adopted reflected its embarrassment: whilst giving nominal approval to Samuel's proposals, it avoided any immediate steps to enact them. The effect of this policy was simply to remove reorganization from the agenda of negotiations in the coal dispute, and to leave miners and owners to come to blows on the question of wages.

The standpoint adopted by the government was the product of differing moods and expectations among its members. As in the 1925 crisis there were some conciliators, including Baldwin, who desired peace to be maintained, and who unrealistically regarded the official promise of eventual action on reconstruction as an inducement to the two disputants in the coal industry to reach a voluntary settlement. There were, on the other hand, pessimists who thought such compromise unlikely, and who welcomed the postponement of legislation as promising the final evasion of any commitment on the Cabinet's part. But even the latter element did not as yet openly predict, still less welcome, the prospect of an industrial stoppage. The conduct of the administration gave little evidence of careful calculation of any outcome, and displayed a desire for unity more than support for any considered strategy.

Following the publication of the Commission's report the Cabinet appointed a committee under Baldwin's chairmanship to examine its proposals. Doubts were expressed about the advisability of local authority retailing of coal and the possible expense of transferring unemployed miners to new jobs;[33] but the chief object of disapproval was the recommendation on nationalizing royalties. When the Cabinet had first considered this question in August 1925, though there had been some support for a policy of gradual acquisition of mineral rights, their 'immediate and simultaneous' purchase had been generally deprecated.[34] Opposition was now voiced again, though the issue of political principle appeared to carry less weight than the financial imperatives of the Treasury's current policy of debt conversion.[35] The Cabinet committee suggested, nevertheless, that the recommendation on nationalization 'should not, at any rate at this stage, be resisted' (while still hoping that any eventual implementation of it would be delayed and protracted). And the majority of ministers concurred in this view. One of the dissentients, Lord Salisbury, acknowledged to Baldwin that though on the royalties question 'a large number of our colleagues agreed with me on the merits, like yourself most of them are prepared to accept nationalization as part of an eirenicon'. In the Cabinet meeting of 22 March, when the wording of the official announcement on the Samuel Report was discussed at length, those who wanted a stronger expression of misgivings about the purchase of minerals were overborne by the argument that 'the Government must from the first strike a note of agreement, and that the only chance was to give the other parties a lead'.[36] But provisional acceptance of this proposal was offered 'on the understanding that if either of the other parties to a settlement of the coal dispute made reservations in regard to the Report of the Royal Commission, the subject of purchase of royalties would again be brought before the Cabinet and be discussed in the light of the new circumstances'.[37]

On 24 March Baldwin announced the government's conditional approval of the Samuel Report to the miners and owners.[38]

The Government have considered with great care the Report and conclusions of the Royal Commission. The conclusions reached by the Commission do not in all respects accord with the views held by the Government and some of the recommendations contain proposals to which, taken by themselves, the Government are known to be opposed. Nevertheless, in face of the unanimous report of the Commission and for the sake of a general settlement the Government for their part will be prepared to undertake such measures as may be required of the State to give the recommendations effect, provided that those engaged in the industry – with whom the decision primarily rests – agree to accept the Report and to carry on the industry on the basis of its recommendations.

On the renewal of the subsidy, he took a similar line: a tapering grant, unspecified in amount, would be available only if a settlement were reached by the two sides. Even this offer was made, it appears, solely 'to set the Government right with public opinion'.[39]

Partly with its connivance, therefore, the government had managed to defer action on the proposals of the Royal Commission. No legislative measure was published on any item of the report prior to the General Strike.[40] Baldwin himself, while constantly professing a belief in negotiations, did not seriously begin to devise a possible settlement for another month. Anxious to appear impartial, his disinterestedness was to be reflected chiefly in a reluctance to state, still more to insist upon, any private judgement which he knew to be unpopular: the need for a generous national offer in the presence of the employers; for wage reductions in face of the miners; possibly too for effectual measures of reorganization before the Cabinet. Well-intentioned and indecisive, sincere and unimaginative, reassuring and vague, he was to emerge from the impending crisis which saw the largest and most costly industrial conflict in British history with his reputation as a man of peace almost untarnished.

At least for the moment the government was approaching the coal problem affirming the leading premise of the mine-owners that reconstruction could afford no solution to the current difficulties of the coal industry. The Cabinet was indeed fully aware of the view of the Samuel Report held by the Mining Association, having received a confidential memorandum on the subject on 17 March.[41] Its suggestions on reorganization could have 'no appreciable effect upon the economic condition of the industry', their benefits being 'largely illusory'. To aim at higher prices was self-defeating. It was also still the Association's opinion – and soon to appear as the government's– that 'no practicable solution of the coal problem can be reached' without lengthening hours of work.

The tacit accord between ministers and employers was already perceptible when Baldwin met the Mining Association and the Miners' Federation on 24 March. Throughout the interview the miners' leaders urged the Prime Minister to be more explicit about the measures which the government proposed to take on reorganization. 'You say that you will accept the report and introduce legislative measures necessary to carry out the findings', said Cook, 'but what sort of legislative measures?' The owners showed no interest in the inquiries, however; as Tom Richards afterwards complained, 'they sat silent and allowed us to do our feeble best to probe the Government as to what they meant'.[42]

What was the miners' own opinion of the Samuel Report? Disappointed by the rejection of their plans for nationalization, the Federation's leadership were still prepared, at this stage, to admit that the document contained something of value. 'If the owners, bad as this report is, are prepared to accept it all,' Herbert Smith told his delegate conference on 12 March, 'if there is anything in nationalization this is one of the steps towards it.'[43] Others, including Vernon Hartshorn, as well as the spokesman of the Miners' Minority Movement, Arthur Horner, were much more hostile.[44] But the delegates agreed to accept the standpoint favoured by the executive: to await the proposals of the government and the owners with a seemingly open mind.

This attitude was obviously taken up partly with an eye to the possibility of further monetary assistance. The miners preserved the hope that the Cabinet would eventually renew the subsidy of July 1925 on generous terms even after Baldwin's indefinite but discouraging references to the subject on 24 March. Public opposition to the Report was clearly inconceivable if the chance of financial aid were not to be destroyed. It was even more important, however, to assure the General Council of their reasonableness. When the MFGB executive met the Special Industrial Committee on 11 March, Smith and Cook went out of their way to speak kindly of the Commission's work. Though they objected to its findings on the wage question in particular, Smith averred that 'there were some things in the Report that they had been fighting for years to get a recognition of', and Cook referred to 'revolutionary changes . . . which were to the greatest advantage of the mining community'.[45] It was as a means of preserving a united front with the TUC that the latter urged the policy of 'wait and see' on the delegate meeting the following day: 'All we are doing is to put ourselves right with our membership, with the Trade Union membership, and with the Labour Party membership. . . . Let us keep to the tactics of last year. I think we started right last year. Let us start right again, and I think we shall win again.'[46]

From the miners' point of view, however, as Cook's statement made clear, the original conflict in the mining industry remained unresolved. Whatever momentary and staged applause they gave to the Samuel Report it was never in doubt that they would reject its terms entirely rather than submit to its wage proposals. 'It gives three-quarters and we can't accept it,' Cook told Thomas.[47] And as differences of interpretations arose in the course of negotiations, what the Commission had conceded shrank rapidly in importance.

Herein lay the beginnings of a divorce from the TUC. Already on 11 March, at the miners' meeting with the Special Industrial Committee, John Bromley had seemed to hint, to their alarm, that wage reductions might be the ultimate price of reorganization.[48] None of his colleagues yet echoed this opinion, but there was little doubt that the majority of the SIC believed, as the miners did not, that the measures of reconstruction advocated by Samuel afforded the key to a settlement of the coal dispute. Since a basis for negotiation now existed, for them the situation was essentially different from that of 1925. Whereas to the Federation a strike seemed as nearly unavoidable as ever, to their associates it was to become more and more a hazard to be averted.

With this exception, however, the Samuel Commission had done nothing to alter the stage of affairs which had existed prior to Red Friday. It had failed to dislodge the owners and miners, and had caused the government to accept a degree of responsibility for reorganization in terms so vague as to be nugatory. If the Cabinet subsequently partly detached itself from the employers, this had little or nothing to do with their attitude to the Samuel Report. And although the seeds of dissension between the miners and the General Council had been planted, at no time before the outbreak of the General Strike did this disagreement widen into an irreparable breach. The official attitude to reform remained too non-committal to allow government ministers to exploit, or even fully recognize, this incipient schism – which offered, as it proved, the only possible opportunity of averting the General Strike.

Preparations for the General Strike: the TUC

The hopes pinned on the report of the Royal Commission represent one factor which might account for the omission of the General Council, following Red Friday, to take precautionary measures in anticipation of a renewal of the conflict. Certainly the left wing of the labour movement, then and later vociferous in their criticisms of the lack of 'preparedness', also saw the report as a deliberate attempt to create disunity among the workers' ranks. Yet it has been seen that both the miners and the TUC leadership were aware at the time the coal subsidy was granted of the danger of a further crisis when it expired. Their inertia in the subsequent months was not merely the result of obtuseness; specific proposals for strengthening the unions' defences were made and considered at length, and it is in the light of these discussions that the attitude of the participants must be discussed.

From the point of view of the labour left prior to May 1926 readiness for a general strike required both national and local initiatives. They had supported the cause of a more powerful General Council at the TUC of 1924, and this campaign was continued in the Congress of 1925 through a resolution of the National Union of Vehicle Builders, authorizing the Council to levy financial assistance from affiliated unions, to order them to take sympathetic strike action 'to assist a Union defending a vital trade union principle', and to make arrangements with the Cooperative movement for the supply of food and other essentials to strikers during large stoppages.[49] On the other hand the Minority Movement, with some support from other quarters, advocated a policy of rank and file mobilization involving the reinforcement of Trades Councils, together with the creation of local Councils of Action and workers' defence corps and became increasingly critical of the official union leadership for its evident reluctance to encourage such democratic enterprise.[50]

The General Council and its Special Industrial Committee were, however, unsympathetic to radical proposals for centralization or for devolution. In the 1925 Congress the vehicle builders' resolution did receive the support of the miners, in a relatively moderate speech by Arthur Cook – who pointed out that if it were given power to order strike action, 'the fact of the General Council having that power would save a general strike'. Against him, however, J. H. Thomas and J. R. Clynes maintained that the very success of the Council in affording support to the miners on Red Friday demonstrated the adequacy of the existing standing orders.[51] Although the vehicle builders' motion was not rejected out of hand, but referred to the Council itself with authority to summon a further special conference, there was probably little expectation that this would take place. In February 1926 the Council circulated affiliated unions with a statement drafted by the Industrial Committee, setting out its views on the various aspects of the 1925 resolution. The main conclusion was that members of Congress 'were not likely to surrender such a measure of autonomy until they had had greater experience of the manner in which the Council were able to use the recent powers already entrusted to them'. And against the most radical proposal, to allow them to initiate industrial stoppages, their circular repeated the old maxim 'that any effort in the way of active support to a Union in dispute would be more likely to be successful if coming spontaneously from the Union or Unions whose assistance is required.'[52]

The demand for strike preparations at local level received still shorter shrift. The General Councils had made some attempt since 1924 to reinvigorate the Trades Council and to establish closer links with them. A national conference held in February 1925 had appointed representatives to a joint consultative committee with the TUC, which promoted further regional conferences and drew up model rules for the guidance of individual councils.[53] But the role conceived for them involved little but publicity and propaganda; and these were the only functions expected of them during the crisis of July 1925.[54] The idea that union branches should concede significant power to bodies often unrepresentative in composition was never countenanced; and the proposal to readmit Trades Council delegates to Congress itself was heavily defeated in 1924. The support of the Minority Movement for greater local autonomy, and their adoption of the slogan 'Don't trust your leaders', also produced the first signs of an open rift between the unofficial left and the TUC leadership. In a press statement issued jointly with the miners on 19 February the SIC urged the movement 'not to allow itself to be influenced by unauthorized and unofficial suggestions which are being made in many quarters regarding the mining problem'. And the following month, in the *Labour Magazine*, Citrine asserted the incompatibility of 'rank and file control' with a coordinated industrial policy conducted by a 'trade union general staff'.[55] In neither context was the Minority Movement mentioned by name, however, and in both instances the main object of publication was probably to reassure the union audience that the General Council, in face of threats to their vital interests, would be as vigilant as on Red Friday.

The evident agreement of the TUC leadership that the *statutory* powers of the General Council were sufficient for its present needs did not by any means signify unanimity on the question of 'preparedness'. Within the Special Industrial Committee a prolonged discussion took place at the beginning of 1926 on precisely this issue. It was begun by a memorandum composed by Citrine as Acting Secretary and first presented on 19 January. After a preliminary consideration, the Committee invited him to produce an expanded and revised version, which was again discussed on 28 January.[56] In this form, the document was sent to the executive of the Miners' Federation, who attended a joint meeting with the SIC on 12 February, and then appointed a subcommittee which continued the examination of its contents a week later.[57]

Citrine's efforts to facilitate the General Council's conduct of industrial disputes had been rebuffed after Red Friday, when the other members omitted from the official congressional report on the dispute his proposal that each affiliated union should 'vest in its own Executive Council the power to declare a strike of its members in collaboration and consultation with the General Council'. In his January memorandum he had implicitly criticized the seemingly *fainéant* attitude of his colleagues in face of government anti-strike measures, and urged that 'preparation should be made of a kind which will ensure spontaneity of action and not leave preparations until the eleventh hour'. In his autobiography he attributes to the SIC and the miners a culpable lack of response: 'they did not want to face the issues raised by my memorandum and would do anything to put off a decision'.[58]

This evidence suggests at first sight that the TUC Acting Secretary was in favour of taking practical measures against the event of a general strike which, though perhaps more restricted in scope, were similar in character to those demanded by left-wing spokesmen – and that his foresight was unavailing because of the myopia of those he sought to persuade. But this picture is misleading. In fact there is no evidence to suggest that Citrine was more actively sympathetic to the Vehicle Builders' resolution than the General Council at large: probably he thought it equally unacceptable. More important, though he raised a number of organizational questions bearing upon the prosecution of a general strike both in his memorandum and in subsequent discussions upon it, in neither context did he make positive proposals which were rejected. Indeed, he appeared to be almost entirely in accord with the other members of the SIC on the impossibility of such detailed preparations. Where he *did* come into conflict with the majority of the Committee and with the miners was over the advisability of determining certain objectives of policy prior to the appearance of the report of the Royal Commission. This was a difference of major importance, but on a matter quite distinct from that of strike organization, requiring no enlargement of the powers of the General Council but only a greater determination to make its existing authority tell. 'The mining situation has ceased to be exclusively a miners' question,' he asserted; 'the imperative need is to get a recognition generally that whatever policy is laid down by the General Council shall be the policy of all concerned.'[59] But he did not say immediately what programme he envisaged – making this known only at the joint meetings between the SIC and the miners during February. And this delay, whether due to uncertainty or diffidence, seems to have been fatal to his purpose.

The Committee had no difficulty in assenting to the proposition that it should share in the responsibility for framing policy, but neither did it reveal any clear idea of what that policy should be. On the first two occasions when Citrine's memoranda were debated, much time was given to relatively peripheral questions such as the help which might be expected of the Labour Party, and to complaints about A. J. Cook's unbridled public prophecies of a general strike. As to the settlement of the mining dispute itself, most members of the SIC appeared ready to rely on the Samuel Commission's Report – in which, Pugh hoped, there would be 'some constructive proposals'. As a result, the SIC confronted the miners without any agreed view on a programme for the industry.[60]

At the Industrial Committee's first meeting with the miners Herbert Smith left no doubt that the latter stood by the three 'cardinal principles' adopted in 1925: national negotiations and opposition to wage reductions or longer hours. Citrine was willing enough to support this standpoint; but he now urged, what he had not clearly stated earlier, that existing conditions could be maintained only with the aid of a continued state subsidy for the industry. As he told the miners on 12 February, 'there were still exactly the same reasons for the granting of financial assistance as in July last. . . . Unless they said they must have financial assistance until the Commission's report could be applied, the Government would jettison its responsibilities and the Miners would be in trouble.'[61] He thus proposed that the Federation and the SIC mount a public campaign to bring pressure on the Royal Commission itself to recommend a renewal of the subvention.

This proposal was less than welcome to the leaders of the MFGB. Cook told the joint meeting on 19 February:[62]

> They were not going to make it a subsidy issue. It was a Trade Union issue, a wages agreement question. . . . The main point which affected them was the psychological effect of discussing the subsidy or wages. At this juncture, they could not decide definitely in regard to the subsidy, that would have to be determined in the light of the recommendations for reorganisation contained in the Commission's Report.

What was more, the representatives of the General Council seemed to agree: 'If they talked too much about the continuance of the subsidy,' said Pugh, 'that might be used against them.' Whether in political or economic terms, apparently, the case for relief was felt to be too weak. The meeting of 19 February thus took the firm decision 'that no declaration on this issue be made until after the Commission's report was received'.[63]

The course of this discussion set the pattern which relations between the miners and the SIC were to exhibit throughout the next two-and-a-half months. Among themselves the members of the Committee expressed constant misgivings about the leadership and policies of the Federation. In joint session these anxieties were expressed, if at all, in muted and oblique fashion; no open disagreement was allowed to manifest itself. Dogged always by fear of the demoralizing and divisive effects upon the movement of any breach with the miners, the SIC allowed this apprehension to influence them against any frank expression of judgement. As a result the miners, who knew their own mind, rarely had difficulty in determining the outcome of 'consultation'. Citrine's hope that the TUC representatives would achieve at the outset an equal voice in the making of decisions was never within sight of being realized.

The dominion enjoyed by the miners was confirmed by the outcome of the February meetings. During the exchanges the members of the SIC (with the exception of Citrine himself) had omitted to express either support for or dissent from the MFGB's 'cardinal principles'. Two public pronouncements were then issued, however – their phraseology frequently recited afterwards by the miners and their sympathizers – in which the TUC seemed to have renewed its unconditional backing to the Federation in the terms of the previous July. Yet these declarations were made almost as an afterthought. On the nineteenth both organizations agreed to issue a press statement, but left the two chairmen and secretaries to devise it. In the absence of any new understanding the officials returned, probably willingly enough, to the prolegomena of Red Friday. The bulletin thus accurately reflected what the miners had said in their conversations with the SIC.[64]

> The attitude of the trade union movement was made perfectly clear last July, namely, that it would stand firmly and unitedly against any attempt further to degrade the standard of life of the coalfields. There was to be no reduction of wages, no increase in working hours, and no interference with the principle of national agreements. This is the position of the trade union movement today.

A week later the joint meeting approved a circular to affiliated unions and Trades Councils which naturally employed the same terms.[65] But it is manifestly unlikely that the members of the Industrial Committee expected to be bound by such uncompromising pronouncements once the report of the Royal Commission was published. J. H. Thomas already thought the promises offered to the miners 'too definite'; and John Bromley gave a decidedly equivocal interpretation of their import: the Committee were only 'agreeing to defend those principles so far as they could, and it would not debar the miners from making concessions in the course of negotiations'.[66] By repeating the Federation's lapidary texts, however, the Committee left themselves little room to influence their subsequent conduct.

In retrospect it seems fair to conclude that Citrine was right to urge the Industrial Committee and the miners to press actively for a subsidy before the publication of the Commission's report. The difference with his colleagues was narrow, but it was strategically significant. Citrine was not indeed alone in predicting that the difficulties which would arise from Samuel's recommendations would hinge upon the provisions for the period of their implementation. Having failed to advance the arguments for a further subsidy before Samuel's findings were made known, however, the SIC were to be inhibited from doing so afterwards by the emphatic disapproval which the Commission expressed of its renewal. Dependent upon the report as a means to a settlement, the TUC representatives were loath to contradict it on this count. Whether more energetic advocacy of an extended subsidy would have influenced the Samuel inquiry may well be doubtful; but it would at least have focussed attention on the need for a clear policy during the interim period of reorganization, upon which score Samuel was so sadly deficient. Having once itself postponed the task of formulating such a policy when circumstances were favourable, moreover, the SIC were to delay doing so continually until the crisis had reached its height.

The other aspect of 'preparedness', the planning of strike organizations and tactics, was one which concerned Citrine much less closely at this early stage of 1926. His memorandum of 29 January discussed the problem in general terms. It drew attention to influences upon government policy which 'may create the determination to wage a decisive struggle with Labour' – the attempts of Conservatives to reintroduce legislation on the political levy and trade disputes (on which the view of the Cabinet was not yet clear); and attacks in the press and elsewhere on the settlement of Red Friday. It also pointed to the government's desire for financial retrenchment, and especially its preparations for the maintenance of essential services in industrial disputes, as additional grounds for anxiety.[66a] But how were the unions to respond to these alarums? Four aspects of the general problem of strike organization were touched on in the memorandum or the discussion which followed upon it: cooperation with the Labour Party; the provision of mutual financial assistance within the TUC; the scope and character of sympathetic action which might be taken on the miners' behalf; and the means of maintaining vital services during such a dispute. On none of these, however, did the secretary make any positive recommendations; and on none of them, predictably, did the Industrial Committee deem prior measures practicable.

Citrine had raised the first two topics, indeed, in order to enter caveats. He objected to any close cooperation with the Labour Party until the miners and the SIC had settled their objectives and policy.[67] Thomas and Bromley pressed the Committee to take the opposite line, but the only subject on which consultations with the political wing as yet took place was the question of essential services – and that was at the behest of the party. Similarly, the possibility of organizing financial support in large-scale concerted stoppages was one which Citrine was anxious to discount. When Bromley brought up this issue at the SIC on 12 February the secretary recalled the lesson of the projected coal embargo of 1925: 'They went into this carefully last year and came to the conclusion that it was an utter impossibility for the Trade Union Movement adequately to finance the people affected by the dispute.'[68] And this view was shared by the majority of the SIC and the General Council. The circular sent out to members of Congress on 4 February, in response to the proposals of the Vehicle

Builders, had said simply, 'the Council feel that with regard to the suggested powers to levy affiliated societies, the present time is inopportune to seek any addition to the financial powers already conferred on them'.[69] The small amount of money that it might be possible to procure in the event of a general strike could, it was assumed, be raised after it began.

Without this backing, however, as Citrine appreciated, it was doubtful whether the railway and other transport unions would be willing to act as the forlorn hope of the movement. Yet, curiously, the question of what kind of supportive action might be undertaken if the miners were again embroiled in conflict was considered neither in Citrine's memorandum nor in the discussions upon it. The notes of the private staff meeting of 18 February record that some conversation took place on the relative advantages of different courses of sympathetic action – financial assistance, a transport strike or a general strike – but the only clear view to emerge was of opposition to the first.[70] The General Council's circular on the question of its constitutional powers issued the same month seemed to imply that it still envisaged the kind of limited, sectional support mobilized on Red Friday as most probable. By the beginning of April, however, Pugh appeared to take it for granted that 'in the event of the circumstances being such as to justify anything in the nature of a stoppage, it would not be one or two organizations that would be concerned, but the whole movement'.[71] But this statement was still ambiguous and did not represent any sort of firm official decision. Those members of the General Council, like Bevin, who were not on the SIC remained in ignorance of its opinions until the eve of the critical conference of trade union executives on 29 April.

That the extent of sympathetic action had not been properly considered is confirmed by the discussions held, in the early weeks of 1926, on the final aspect of 'preparedness', the maintenance of essential services. This was a problem which confronted the TUC leadership before the Citrine memorandum was drafted, and which continued to engage them until the General Strike had begun and ended. It was one, however, to which they never found a solution, in theory or practice. The assumption of the militant left, reflected for instance in the vehicle builders' resolution of 1925 and in Cook's speeches in the country, was that an arrangement should be made with the Cooperative movement to supply the needs of union members called out on strike under the auspices of the General Council. The SIC was not opposed to this, but it had become evident by the beginning of 1926 that such an agreement could not be reached. In December 1925 the Cooperative Union itself sought a meeting with the Committee on this subject. At three interviews, before the end of February, their representatives told the SIC and the miners that they would give no undertaking to feed strikers unless their reimbursement could be guaranteed from union funds, pointing out that local cooperatives were already owed over £17,000 in loans and £183,000 for goods obtained during the mining lock-out of 1921. The Miners' Federation, for their part, were unwilling to accept national responsibility for the defalcations of their constituents; and the Industrial Committee were unable to commit their affiliates to repay future losses.[72] Citrine, in any case, seemed to attach little importance to an arrangement with the Union in his memorandum of 28 January, and in a further report, a month or so later, pointed out disparagingly:

> It would require an immense expansion [of Cooperative society membership] before it could become adequate to conduct even a skeleton set of services. Some services such as those undertaken by the municipalities, i.e. water, lighting, and possibly heating, would be entirely outside the ambit of the Cooperative resources. It is even doubtful as to what extent it would be possible for the Cooperative movement to devote its attention to the feeding of the working class.[73]

Negotiations made no further progress. On 15 March the Cooperative Union Board wrote to the SIC, officially to ask that the funds of the whole trade-union movement should be offered as security for credit afforded to strikers. They repeated this request twice more before May. First the Committee and then the General Council turned it down.[74] When the General Strike began, local union organizations were left to seek from their own society whatever terms they could get.

The jettisoning of the Cooperative movement left open only one possibility. 'If the Trade Union Movement assents to the necessity for the carrying on of essential services,' wrote Citrine in March, 'it is to the Government, rather than any other agency, that attention must be turned.'[75] The political aspects of this problem had already occurred to the Labour Party, the issue having been raised at their Annual Conference in October 1925. Following this, Arthur Henderson had brought the matter before the National Joint Council (representing the party executive and MPs, and the TUC) in January. A subcommittee was appointed with the General Council, to which body Citrine addressed his memorandum of 3 March.[76]

In this document, examining the question of relations between unions and the state in the event of a general strike, Citrine confronted explicitly the intractable practical implications of that strategy. On the one hand no stoppage could be envisaged which would have the effect of depriving the community (including the strikers) of *all* services: 'A general strike . . . is a literal impossibility, and behind the reasoning of those who support it is always present the feeling that in some imperfect way services essential to life must be carried on.' Yet on the other hand, an offer by the TUC to cooperate with the government in this sphere, if not rejected outright, was unlikely to be accepted 'in a proper spirit'. And the unions, by reducing the extent of their action, were obviously surrendering 'a very powerful weapon'.

This predicament was never solved. In what appears to be the report of the subcommittee to the National Joint Council, dated 12 April, the only definite recommendation put forward was that Labour councillors and local authorities should refuse any help to the Organization for the Maintenance of Supplies. But on the attitude that they should adopt to *official* counter-strike preparations, no advice was offered. And on the main question of the policy to be followed by either section of the movement in future large-scale disputes, the subcommittee had nothing to propose except delay.[77]

> We would suggest that in accordance with previous practice, the National Bodies in conjunction with the Trade Unions should be left to improvise machinery to safeguard the public against unnecessary inconvenience according to the exigencies of the disputes. . . . We would . . . recommend that no cut and dried scheme be formulated at the present juncture, as . . . any such scheme as evidence of good-will on Labour's part would be ruthlessly exploited by our opponents.

The General Council's offer to the government on 1 May to assist in the maintenance of vital services, was apparently unpremeditated. The conduct of the unions during the General Strike itself was to be the product of that improvization which had, beforehand, seemed the only option.

The Industrial Committee had thus been as backward in planning a general strike as they had in settling a negotiating policy. But their failure on the former count seems the more excusable of the two. To begin with, there was a natural reluctance to talk about preparing for a major stoppage before any negotiations on the mining dispute had taken place or any issues highlighted. Those who urged mobilization were not trying to rectify a particular industrial grievance but proclaiming assumptions about the malevolence of capitalism and the inevitability of class war. The TUC leadership had no wish to act upon these premises, whatever their anxiety about the official and unofficial measures being taken in readiness for a general strike by the other side. It was, after all, difficult to portray preparations for such an undertaking as other than wilfully aggressive, whilst preparations to resist it, however provocative, were still only precautionary and contingent. Secondly, prior arrangements for a general strike were almost wholly precluded by the narrow constitutional powers of the General Council, unable directly to instruct union executives on even the smallest matter of organization. It is true that they had declined to seek additional authority after the 1925 Congress; but they had done so in the belief, almost certainly valid, that any such recommendations would be as objectionable to affiliated organizations as they had been earlier.

Finally there is no reason to doubt that the union leaders primarily concerned were confident of their ability to take action at the eleventh hour. The railway leaders in particular believed that to give advance warning of a stoppage would actually lessen its impact. And Bevin, though personally somewhat resentful of the uncommunicativeness of the SIC beforehand, pointed out in his union report after the strike,

> There is a good deal of talk about the Movement not being prepared for strike action, but it should be borne in mind that with a Transport Union of this character, it is so built that its machinery can be put into operation almost immediately when it is attacked, and no special plans have to be thought out or devised in advance.[78]

While other organizations might have been less complacent, their role in the conflict was very obviously a secondary one.

Criticism of the Council's failure to prepare for the General Strike can be justified, in the last analysis, only if its omission significantly reduced the chance of victory. In fact scarcely anyone argued this; and it would have been implausible to do so. The TUC leadership could claim with some justification that in the event most of the problems and difficulties of organization confronted during the nine days were overcome, in however makeshift a fashion, with reasonable success. On the other hand almost none of the specific proposals made in advance by the Minority Movement – arrangements with the Cooperative Society, greater financial power for the General Council, the prior creation of local Councils of Action – could have affected the issue to any marked extent. The most fundamental weakness of the stoppage, once it began, was the result of the maintenance of large-scale commercial road transport services, the bloodstream of the government emergency scheme. This resource could have been denied to the opposition, however, only by a vast improvement in the organization of haulage workers or by mass picketing and obstruction. The former objective was evidently unattainable, the latter would have implied an unrestricted use of physical force against the authorities and an attempt systematically to deprive the community of food and other necessities, which not even the union left had envisaged. As the more perceptive TUC representatives appreciated, no general strike could be *wholly* effective which did not threaten civil war or inflict hardship upon the working class itself. A partial stoppage which avoided these dangers, however lengthily planned, could not exercise the same powers of coercion. The controversy over 'preparedness' merely served to obscure this insoluble dilemma.

Preparations for the General Strike: the government

The decision of the Cabinet after Red Friday to strengthen the counter-strike organization administered by the Supply and Transport Committee was quickly effected. On 7 August 1925 the Home Secretary, Joynson-Hicks, submitted a report which led to a number of important developments. The specialized staff at the divisional headquarters of the supply and transport system was considerably expanded to a normal strength of six or seven. Employer representatives were recruited in port and railway centres, to collaborate with the official apparatus there. The national committee was given permission to establish contact with local authorities and police forces to secure their cooperation in its plans. And the Home Secretary was allotted £10,000 to spend on the stockpiling of resources.[79] Joynson-Hicks had also suggested, with the approval of his committee, that the local volunteer service and haulage committees should, if they found it practical, enlist lorry drivers and electrical engineers in advance of any emergency.[80] On this issue, the Cabinet postponed a decision. Within a few weeks, however, they were largely relieved of the necessity to authorize such recruitment by the establishment of an ostensibly independent voluntary body for this purpose, the Organization for the Maintenance of Supplies.

The OMS announced its existence to the press on 25 September.[81] Its founders constituted an impressive list of former public servants and retired military officers, headed by Lord Hardinge of Penshurst.[82] Its purpose was to register and if necessary to train, under private auspices, those classes of volunteer labour which would be most valuable to the government during a general strike. It thus promised to assist the administration in precisely that area where overt official preparations were most difficult. Moreover some government ministers were certainly privy to the plans for its formation. Wilfred Ashley, the Minister of Transport, had appended a note to the Home Secretary's memorandum at the beginning of August, saying, with what looks like more than prescience, 'I feel that an organization outside the Government could do a very great deal in enrolling in advance capable and willing volunteers and giving them instructions where to report and for what duties'.[83] And Joynson-Hicks himself welcomed the formation of the OMS in a letter to the press which indicated that prior consultation had taken place.[84]

> I told the promoters . . . that there was no objection on the part of the Government to their desire to inaugurate [this] body; that, if and when an emergency arose, the Government would discharge the responsibility which is theirs and theirs alone, but that it would be a great assistance to us to receive from the OMS or from any other body of well-disposed citizens, classified lists of men in different parts of the country who would be willing to place their services at the disposal of the Government.

Not all ministers and government officials were so favourably inclined towards the Organization, and some chairmen of Volunteer Service Committees regarded it as an intrusive rival.[85] But by November 1925 the alternative of enlisting volunteers under official auspices had been finally ruled out, and the OMS thus appeared at least a potentially useful auxiliary.[86] On 7 December, accordingly, Mitchell-Thomson, J. C. C. Davidson and other representatives of the Supply and Transport Committee interviewed leading members of the OMS to clarify and regularize its relations with the government.[87] It was agreed that the Organization should not attempt to establish branches where there were local objections, but that where possible the divisional commissioners would encourage unofficial contacts between it and volunteer service chairmen. The OMS was advised, however, to concentrate on the recruitment of lorry drivers rather than those categories of labour which local authorities would be likely to employ. It was also asked to circularize its branches to make clear that its activities would come to an end and its lists of workers be handed over to the government once an emergency was proclaimed. Finally, its officers were told that political contacts with them would be ended, although communications could still be maintained through the civil servants employed in the emergency apparatus.

The practical value of the assistance provided by the OMS was, in the end, relatively small. Its principal difficulty proved to be lack of funds. 'It will surprise many of my readers' wrote one of its officers in March 1926, 'to learn that among the big industrial firms, manufacturers, bankers, and shipping companies, so far the response to an appeal for funds has been almost negligible.' Its activities remained largely confined to the south of England; not until April 1926, for instance, were committees set up, with the help of local Conservative officials and councillors, in Northumberland and Durham, whilst scarcely any footholds were secured in the north-west. Whilst such patriotically inspired and right-wing support as it received in the north-east may have been acceptable to the Organization *faute de mieux*, its pretensions to political neutrality were destroyed and its practical purposes probably little advanced.[88]

The OMS was, however, valuable to the government in another way: it acted, as John Anderson afterwards noted, 'as a useful lightning conductor'.[89] The criticisms and complaints which might otherwise have been levelled at the counter-strike measures of the state were instead diverted here. From early October 1925, when MacDonald wrote to *The Times* protesting that 'private enterprise is being entrusted to maintain order in such a way as to make a breach of order inevitable', to the eve of the General Strike itself when the industrial committee of the General Council and the printing workers condemned the publication of OMS advertisements, the attention of the labour movement was focussed almost entirely upon it.[90] By the time of the strike most trade unionists no doubt regarded the OMS and the official emergency machinery as one and the same – a confusion which was indeed to be encouraged by their leadership. Previously, however, ministers had found it easy to meet inquiries that were mainly concerned with the latter body by pleading ignorance or absence of responsibility.[91] These disclaimers, even if disengenuous, were difficult to disprove.

Under this smokescreen, Whitehall proceeded steadily with its own preparations. After the civil commissioners' staffs had been strengthened the appointment of food officers on a local basis was set in motion. In November the Cabinet was informed that the government could have full access to broadcasting facilities during a general strike. During the same month the Ministry of Health sent out 'Circular 636' to local authorities, instructing them on their responsibilities in relation to the government's emergency provisions. Some steps were eventually taken through the official machinery, besides, to ensure the availability of alternative labour for various specialist tasks. About a thousand civilian volunteers were enrolled from engineering colleges and electrical firms to man the London power stations if required, whilst on the eve of the General Strike road commissioners were ordered to organize training schemes for heavy lorry drivers. By 22 April 1926 Joynson-Hicks was able to report that the Supply and Transport Committee had approved the appointment of 98 volunteer service committees, that 147 haulage committees were in existence (almost double the number available in 1925), each with a road officer attached, that 331 local food officers had been selected, and that arrangements for food convoys, the maintenance of the London milk supply and emergency electricity generation were at or near completion.[92] The rickety structure of July 1925 had been wholly transformed.

V The Coming of the Strike

The government's evasive response to the Samuel Report on 24 March had left the miners and mine-owners face to face. Baldwin was to remain aloof from their negotiations for another month, until the mining lock-out was a mere ten days away. Both sides had during the interval taken up predictably irreconcilable positions and declined to modify them. Not until 21 April, therefore, did serious diplomatic activity begin. Subsequently the Prime Minister made an effort, painstaking but nonetheless unsuccessful, firstly to discover a compromise which would prevent a stoppage in the coal industry; then, on 1 and 2 May, to produce a formula which would postpone and possibly avert a general strike. Even after the Cabinet had delivered its 'ultimatum' on the night of 2nd May, demanding the unconditional withdrawal of strike notices, unofficial communication continued until nearly midnight the following day, when the General Council's instructions to its affiliated organizations began to take effect.

The complex and sometimes ill-recorded dialogue of these six weeks, between miners, employers, government and TUC, warrants attention both because it was through these transactions that the issues of the General Strike were focussed, and because such chances of peace as existed can thereby be assessed. It will be seen, however, that each party perceived the issues differently; and in addition that negotiations were ultimately abortive, not just as a result of the inflexibility of the Miners' Federation and the Mining Association, but also because the government and the General Council proved unable to reach an understanding with each other. Less inclined to submit to a conflict than the principal combatants, they still ended for all practical purposes by identifying one with the miners, the other with the owners. To account for this alignment is sufficient, therefore, to account for the General Strike itself.

Entering the impasse: 31 March–22 April

Some explanation must first be offered of the intransigence of owners and men in the coal industry. In neither case, it has been seen, had the report of the Royal Commission affected the standpoint adopted in 1925. The owners, it is true, purportedly accepted its findings; but having told the Cabinet privately that they placed little or no value on reorganization, they drew up a formal statement on the Samuel recommendations – presented to the miners at their first joint meeting on 31 March – which referred all important items under this heading to the government and to parliament.[1] On the wage question the owners simply reinterpreted the proposals of the official inquiry to suit their own wishes. They proposed a national agreement which would be restricted to 'general principles' such as the rules governing the ascertainment of revenue and its distribution between wages and profits. But the Association held 'strongly and absolutely that the question of the minimum percentages . . . can only be dealt with, and must be dealt with, in the districts themselves'. The central organizations might 'approve' such district bargains, but they were to have no authority to alter them.[2] The very existence of national negotiations was again placed in the balance.

The employers' side did not take up this uncompromising position, however, without some element of tactical calculation. In spite of their continued vocal objection to any suggestion of 'political interference', the owners' representatives doubtless expected the government ultimately to intervene in the dispute. By taking a hard line on wages, therefore, they hoped to direct ministerial attention to the possibility of lengthening hours of work. The central committee of the Association told their constituent districts on 12 March that it was 'essential, despite the adverse report of the Royal Commission on the subject of hours, that the Owners should not give up their view that an extension is necessary'.[3] 'We look upon that as the greatest measure of reorganization that is possible for the industry and the only measure of reorganization that will bear fruit immediately,' Evan Williams told the miners' executive on 31 March. And when the Association finally confronted the Prime Minister in the fourth week of April their secretary at once urged on him the repeal of the Seven Hours Act.[4]

More surprisingly, many owners were by no means unwilling to contemplate a prolongation of some form of state subsidy to the industry. The leadership of the Mining Association gave no *official* recognition to this predilection, declining the invitation of the miners to join in its advocacy. But among their rank and file, Malcolm Dillon, Lord Londonderry's agent, detected a persistent opinion in the north-east that 'notwithstanding the Report of the Commission . . . the Government would continue the subsidy at any rate in a modified form'.[5] The Yorkshire owners, too, alarmed that they might be excluded from a further grant in view of the prosperity of their district, offered an unchanged minimum to their employees on 21 April 'on condition that any continued subvention payment granted by the Government shall be received in full by the Yorkshire collieries on the same basis as all other districts'. By this stage the central committee of the Association was clearly under some pressure to convey to the government that the low wage rates put forward, in the export districts in particular, could be improved only by 'the Government making up the difference'.[6] If they omitted to make this point to Baldwin, it was almost certainly because they thought him more likely to be persuaded to suspend the Seven Hours Act than greatly to prolong financial assistance. From his first encounter with them, the Prime Minister himself indicated that he would be receptive on the former count, but gave no sign of softening on the latter. In consequence the government had no knowledge that the Association's attitude to subsidization had altered since their submission to the Royal Commission. If the topic was never properly discussed prior to the General Strike, it was at least partly because of this misunderstanding.

The leadership of the Mining Association was the more guarded in its conduct of negotiations because it was aware that divisions existed within the ranks of the coal-owners. It was, indeed, subjected to a good deal of open criticism from the more liberal employers for its unyielding and parsimonious policy. The critics generally consisted of industrialists whose interests lay only partly in coal-mining, whose public eminence was reflected in their titles and who included a significant leavening of Conservative and Liberal MPs.[7] Both their political influence and their articulate opposition to draconian wage cuts created a certain vulnerability in the apparently entrenched positions of their fellow-owners.

The dissentient voices of the Association did not, however, win much backing within it. The moderates formed only a small minority of its membership, unable to sway even their own district organizations.[8] And precisely because of their discontent with the national spokesmen of the employers, they were probably more strongly in favour of the decentralization of negotiations even than other mine-owners.[9] More optimistic about the possibilities of reorganization than most colliery proprietors, they were still no more enthusiastic about legislative interference in the industry. On the issues of a continued subsidy and the lengthening of hours they held no agreed view. The common ground they shared with the Miners' Federation was thus severely limited. And though certain individuals among them, especially Sir Alfred Mond and Lord Londonderry, may have exercised a measure of personal influence upon Baldwin, collectively the progressive elements of the employers had a negligible impact on the course of events.

In the Miners' Federation a similarly statuesque posture was adopted by the majority of the national executive and supported by the overwhelming body of rank and file opinion. There was never any doubt, of course, that the owners' proposals of 31 March would be rejected. On 9 April the delegate conference of the MFGB reiterated, and even reinforced, the three 'cardinal principles' which had been its motto since the previous year: 'That no assent be given to any proposal for increasing the length of the working day. . . . That the principles of a National Wage Agreement, with a National minimum percentage be firmly adhered to. . . . That inasmuch as wages are already too low we cannot assent to any proposal for reducing wages.' The only opposition to this resolution came from the militant minority who wished to revive the demand for a 'cost of living' wage and to reject the Samuel Report, root and branch.[10]

On 12 April, when the miners and owners met again, negotiations came to a dead halt. The Federation submitted their own statement on the Samuel recommendations, rejecting not only its wage proposals but even such relatively minor changes in conditions as the redistribution of working hours, and contesting the employers' view of the negotiating procedure which the Commission had favoured. 'We are still prepared to discuss with you the national wage question as we define it,' Smith told the Association representatives. '. . . If you people have any desire to settle wages now we ought to sit down and start to discuss that national minimum.'[11] Instead the owners issued invitations in the districts, and on 15 and 16 April the majority posted their new wage schedules.[12]

Whether the miners yet regarded a stoppage as inevitable may still be doubted. Smith had expressed earlier in April his continued hope of government assistance, and two days before the lock-out advised the delegates, 'we should save a conflict if that can be avoided, and conclude a peace with honour'. In Tom Richards' view, 'every time we have had any serious situation between the employers and ourselves . . . we have always had this period of bluff, manoeuvring for position, propaganda to prejudice the other chap, and all that kind of thing. We have had a long period of that, longer than usual probably this time.'[13] On the other hand, as the crisis dragged on, the utterances of their leadership seemed to become more uncompromising, their token interest in reorganization to dwindle, their overt distrust of the government to increase. The Industrial Committee, at first a restraining influence, was told by Smith on 8 April, 'there was not three per cent [of the Samuel Report] that he would value with a Tory government like the present'; and that he was accordingly prepared to accept that

> . . . if the miners retained their position for no reduction in wages, they were going to put upwards of 200,000 men out of work. They realized all that. . . . It was a big proposition, but as they told the Owners, they had to face it. They were determined that if the country wanted coal, it had to give the men who got it a respectable living.[14]

What chance of peace existed, in the Federation's eyes, depended on its own total intractability.

There was less evident disagreement with official policy in the MFGB than in the Mining Association, but latent tensions were present even in the former. It was already apparent by the beginning of April that on the basis of recent returns the Yorkshire, Nottingham and Derby coalfields would suffer little or no reduction in their minimum wage rates even after the withdrawal of the subsidy. Large-scale pit closures, on the other hand, would probably hit export areas, especially the north-east, with exceptional severity. It was an awareness of these disparities, no doubt, which led Arthur Cook to suggest to Tom Jones on 15 April that 'while a lot of our chaps won't agree with me, we shall have to have a national minimum, not only with pluses above it, but minuses below it'.[15] And the TUC officials were later to comment to Horace Wilson (how knowledgeably it is difficult to say) on the mutual suspicions harboured by the district spokesmen on the miners' executive.[16] The unity of the miners was preserved, however, by powerful countervailing forces: the fear that the owners wished 'to break up the Federation'; the desire to see the government play a fuller and more constructive part in the affairs of the industry; and the threat of longer working hours – affecting all districts alike and increasingly visible as the crisis persisted.[17] These pressures were sufficient to keep them together, not just prior to the outbreak of the

General Strike, but for many bitter months of the dispute which followed.

For the miners' executive, therefore, the question in doubt when they devised their motion for the special conference of 9 April was not whether it would be approved by their own organization, but how far it would be supported by the General Council. On the eighth they met the Industrial Committee to communicate the terms of their resolution and to ask 'how far they could recommend the movement to stand by the Miners on those three things'. The response was profoundly disappointing. Although the SIC were willing to back the demand for a national agreement in the coal industry, they declined to take up so dogmatic a position on the wage question. The request for such a promise was unreasonable, said Jimmy Thomas; 'the Committee could not possibly give any such reply. . . . Speaking plainly, who was there on the Committee who could commit his Union to anything?' 'It was quite obvious that if they made any definite statement on the three points,' added Pugh, 'it would prejudice negotiations.' Only Swales was in favour of issuing the declaration for which the miners asked; the majority view was conveyed in Citrine's carefully phrased letter to Cook, later that day:

> The Committee fully realize the seriousness of the present position, but they are of the opinion that matters have not yet reached a stage when any final declaration of the General Council's policy can be made.
>
> It appears to them that negotiations are as yet at a very early stage, and that efforts should be made to explore to the fullest extent the possibility of reducing the points of difference between your Federation and the Coal-owners, and for that purpose to advise the immediate continuance of negotiations.[18]

Twice more, at joint meetings on 14 and 23 April, the miners' representatives sought to win the SIC to their viewpoint on the wage question, only to be met by similar equivocation. The Committee issued a second public statement on the 17 April, protesting at the owners' attempt to move negotiations to the districts. But they would still neither affirm nor deny the propriety of the miners' attitude on other issues. Predictably, in consequence, the MFGB leaders became more suspicious of their allies' fidelity: 'Was the General Council prepared to say that the miners ought to submit to a reduction in wages?' asked Herbert Smith at the session of 23 April. The SIC 'wanted to proceed on the basis of no reductions', replied Pugh, 'but they must see what that would involve on the Government and everybody else'.[19]

The Committee, even more than the miners, pinned their hopes on obtaining a renewed government subsidy. In their view, however, it was to be justified for the specific purpose of facilitating reorganization in the industry and probably terminated by its completion. At the first interview with the miners on 8 April Pugh suggested a three-year 'stabilization' period, and outlined the scheme for dividing collieries into three categories – profitable, remediable, and uneconomic – which was to form the basis of the General Council's official proposals three weeks later. But he also argued, in the miners' absence, that 'if it is thought that the whole Trade Union Movement could be brought on the field in order to support a subsidy, that was a profound mistake'.[20] And though Pugh himself was prepared to make representations on this subject to the government, here his colleagues proved reluctant. Citrine, for instance, though he had been anxious to give public backing to the renewal of assistance before the Samuel Report was published, regarded its advocacy now as tactically unwise, until the owners had been forced to improve their offer.[21]

The Committee's position in the evolving dispute was thus an ambiguous and ineffective one. Hoping for a peaceful settlement on the lines of the Samuel Report, they were nonetheless aware of its failure to make recommendations of immediate applicability. Disapproving of the miners' premature and rigid stance on the wages issue and increasingly conscious of their lack of interest in measures of reconstruction, they remained unable to influence the Federation's conduct of negotiations. They were, indeed, strongly bound to the miners by the apparent unreasonableness of the Mining Association, and by the ever-present sense of the hopes and expectations of the labour movement. The only development which might have relieved their difficulties was the presentation of a constructive and acceptable solution by the Cabinet. 'The sooner the Government come in the better,' Pugh told his colleagues on 8 April. If the TUC was to remain reluctantly committed to the MFGB until the outbreak of the conflict, it was primarily the result of the timidity and backwardness of the political initiatives of the Conservative administration.

The government intervenes: 23–30 April

Baldwin and his Cabinet had decided, following the report of the Samuel Commission, that any immediate intervention in the negotiations of miners and owners would simply diminish the inclination of the two sides to make an independent agreement. This passivity continued even when the question of the scope of national agreements had brought about a complete deadlock. On 12 April the Minister of Labour, Steel-Maitland, saw Pugh and Citrine, but governmental intervention was evidently not discussed. When, the following evening, he met representatives of the Mining Association, he made no attempt to dissuade them from posting notices in the districts.[22] On the fourteenth the SIC attempted to disturb this seeming complacency, visiting the Prime Minister with the consent of the miners to urge the need for 'a definite guarantee from the government that the Report was going to be fulfilled and a different interpretation put on the national negotiations from that given by the Mining Association'.[23] Clearly Baldwin made little positive response. The Cabinet had agreed earlier in the day that he should emphasize to the Committee the impossibility of further public expenditure beyond the temporary assistance offered on 25 March. And though it was felt 'that the most hopeful prospect of averting a strike was to be found in the action of the Trade Union Council' there was no sign that any particular 'action' was expected. The only conciliatory move undertaken after this meeting was another private conversation between Steel-Maitland and the owners, in which he stressed the damaging effect on public opinion of their 'offering inadequate wages in the various districts'.[24]

When, on 15 April, Baldwin discussed the dispute with the Miners' Federation, he had no intention of taking their part. According to Middlemas and Barnes this meeting came 'closer to true understanding and frankness than any other in the pre-Strike period'. In reality the miners disguised their true priorities to make it appear again that a wage agreement was dependent on the reorganization of the industry. 'We ought not to be called upon to make a single sacrifice,' said Smith, 'until there has been a thorough investigation as to what this reorganization is going to be, and until the men have appreciated the benefit of it from that standpoint.'[25] Baldwin himself had no proposals to make; and though he implied that he could consult with the owners in an attempt to bring about renewed national negotiations, he took no further action for almost a week.

The government involved itself in the diplomacy of the dispute in the end not because of pressure from the labour side, but because of the drastic wage cuts sought, despite Steel-Maitland's plea, by the owners' district organizations. On 21 April the Mining Association presented to Baldwin their token national agreement together with the schedule of proposed district minima, which had already been dispatched to the miners' executive. Their offers were for the most part even lower than the rates of pay suggested in 1925.

TABLE 4. *Mine-owners' wage proposals, 1 April 1926*

District	*Average rate per shift*	
	current	*proposed*
Scotland	10s 4d	8s 3d
Northumberland	9s 3d	6s 11d
Durham	9s 11d	7s 2d
Lancashire and Cheshire	10s 1d	8s 6d
Yorkshire	11s 2d	10s 2d
Notts and Derbys.	11s 1d	10s 0d
S. Wales	10s 9d	7s 11d

Reductions in the case of piecework coal-getters were significantly larger than the averages set out above. In addition, various local agreements and conventions were now to be withdrawn, such as the practice of paying six shifts for five to South Wales hewers and the housing and coal allowances in the north-east.[26]

Neither Baldwin nor the Mining Association had any expectation that the Federation would look twice at such an agreement – which was in fact formally rejected at a joint meeting on 22 April. The same day, the Industrial Committee again saw the Prime Minister to urge him to take part in negotiations.[27] This time, sensitive to the danger of appearing to condone the employers' harsh demands, he consented; and on the twenty-third the two sides in the dispute were summoned to a general conference at Downing Street.

Since his first interview with the SIC the previous week Baldwin had given some thought to, and received much advice on, the composition of a settlement. One possibility considered, though not pressed against the declared opposition of both employers and men, was the concession of a national minimum to which reductions would be permitted in the most hard-hit districts.[28] The Prime Minister placed much more faith, however, in the idea of an agreed extension of the working day. He told Tom Jones on the twenty-first that 'he was building his hopes on some concessions from the men in regard to hours', and at his interview with the Mining Association suggested that this might be 'the crux of the whole situation'.[29] The proposal was not necessarily inconsistent with an elastic minimum wage, but its appeal for Baldwin was clearly that it would permit a uniform national percentage. It was perhaps as a step towards eliciting such an offer from the employers that he asked Birkenhead to give an interpretation of the findings of the Samuel Commission on the disputed question of the powers of the national wages board.[30] In addition Baldwin held the opinion – influenced possibly by the *Daily Mail's* investigations of the state of feelings in the coalfields, possibly by the convictions of the owners themselves – that the rank and file of the Miners' Federation were 'much keener to give in on hours than on wages'.[31] If by holding out the hope of a change in the Seven Hours Act he could prevail upon the Mining Association to alter their position on other points at issue, a settlement seemed conceivable. Without as yet deciding finally to take this course, he set out to explore its promise.

The possibility of seeking a solution to the mining crisis by way of reorganization had comparatively little appeal for the government, for reasons already considered. The principal advocate of rationalization at this juncture was in fact the Conservative backbench *rallié*, Sir Alfred Mond, among whose industrial empire was the Welsh colliery combine, Amalgamated Anthracite. Mond argued, as he had done the previous year, that the central problem of the coal trade lay in overproduction and the ultimate remedy in international price agreements. He presented his own proposals, for the closure of uneconomic pits, cooperative selling and government loans for amalgamation schemes, firstly to Baldwin (in a memorandum of 18 April) and a few days later to a selected group of prominent coal-owners.[32] Despite the author's optimism, his ideas were bound to run foul of the *laissez-faire* principles and competitive instincts of the latter; and whilst the Prime Minister did not wholly ignore the promise of rationalization, especially of cooperative selling agencies, he was clearly disinclined to consider anything which increased the government's anticipated financial commitments to the industry. The views of the miners, which might have been relatively favourable to a plan promising the elimination of surplus production and higher prices, were never canvassed.

The chief object of Baldwin's conciliatory endeavours after 23 April, therefore, was to persuade the owners to offer a reasonably high national minimum on the understanding that a longer working day would be reinstated. He achieved a measure of success in the diplomatic exchanges prior to 30 April, though significantly less than he had hoped. Furthermore, the outcome of his mediation resembled, inevitably, an *entente* with the Mining Association rather then an independently sponsored compromise. Tom Jones commented during the negotiations: 'It is impossible not to feel the contrast between the reception which ministers give to a body of owners and a body of miners. Ministers are at ease at once with the former, they are as friends jointly exploring a situation. There was hardly any indication of opposition or censure.' And Baldwin himself acknowledged the element of discrimination, in his own fashion, when talking to the committee of the Mining Association: 'I have to try to be as perfectly fair as I can to all the parties. It very often happens that we are apt to speak a little more frankly to the ones that belong to you than to the others, though I do say straight things to the miners.'[33] Neither the General Council nor the miners' executive had any reason to suspect, in fact, until two days before the lock-out, that the government were contemplating longer hours as an answer to the crisis.

It was not, of course, Baldwin's wish to appear thus biased, and he made some attempt also to win the goodwill of the Industrial Committee. On Sunday 25 April, at Tom Jones' suggestion, he invited the TUC chairman, Arthur Pugh, to Chequers to discuss the crisis in informal fashion. The latter gave his opinion 'that the negotiations had been too much on the wages issue and too little on reorganization', but admitted the rigidity of the miners, and may have proposed the introduction of members of the SIC into the Downing Street meetings.[34] The following day the Prime Minister saw the Industrial Committee as a whole, retailing these opinions as his own: 'The result of this concentration on wages and wages alone' had been 'the exclusion of all other considerations.' He invited the SIC to depute one or two representatives 'who perhaps are more useful in negotiation' to accompany the miners. Then, on the afternoon of 27 April, Baldwin introduced the subject of reorganization, for the first time, to the Federation and the employers.[35]

This discussion seems, however, to have been a placebo only. The Prime Minister, perhaps influenced by Mond's advocacy, did suggest an inquiry into the possible benefits of cooperative selling agencies; but otherwise the dialogue was unprofitable and without sequel. Baldwin did not deviate significantly from his chosen path of seeking a settlement through the Mining Association: he had continued to press for a modified offer, confined to the gravamena of wages and hours, in private conversations with them on 23 and 26 April.[35] And on the morning of 27 April he conveyed to Tom Jones his own conception of a suitable agreement the essentials of which had been little altered since his original intervention. If asked to arbitrate on the dispute, he would recommend the maintenance of existing wages for two years, the suspension of the Seven Hours Act, the formulation of cooperative marketing schemes and measures to deal with royalties 'without damage to the country's finances and to the debt conversions which the Treasury have in prospect'.[36] Generous by the owners' standards, this formula still envisaged immediate and precise concessions from the miners in return for circumscribed and indefinite promises of governmental action. It was, furthermore, soon to be whittled down.

At midday on Tuesday 27 April (prior to the evening discussion of reorganization) Evan Williams told Baldwin that the owners would be prepared to discuss a uniform national minimum tied to an eight-hour day, since 'it is clear that the disparity between the different districts on an eight hour basis would be bound to be much less than it is on a seven hour basis'.[37] This, in all probability, was enough finally to commit the Prime Minister to devising an offer along these lines. The following afternoon the Association's committee suggested a conditional wage rate of twenty per cent above standard (the 1921 minimum), though admitting that the more prosperous districts could afford a higher figure.[38] The recommendations which Baldwin presented to the owners that night, however, proposed that a twenty per cent minimum should be offered without any extension of hours, provided that individual districts could apply to the national board (or to its independent chairman) to be allowed to vary this rate temporarily, by negotiation or arbitration. On the other hand, if the working day were lengthened to eight hours he suggested that the prevailing national minimum remain unchanged.[39]

This was far too much for the Mining Association to contemplate. Early on Thursday afternoon they returned with a list of objections, declining to improve their original terms on the existing working day, or to raise the offer of a twenty per cent minimum on an eight hour basis. They rejected Baldwin's request that the minimum might be fixed by arbitration. The Prime Minister did not resist, and it was the employers' proposals, accordingly, which were forwarded to the miners on 30 April. Moreover, though not warranted by the government, they were given a measure of apparent approval by Baldwin's accompanying letter announcing his willingness to suspend the Seven Hours Act until December 1929 (when its reinstatement would depend on another investigatory commission), and his intention of setting up 'an authoritative inquiry' on cooperative selling agencies and amalgamation.[40]

Whilst the Mining Association had been prevailed upon to offer a national minimum wage, it was on conditions significantly less generous than Baldwin had wished. Ready to engage in a conflict even with public opinion against them, the owners were still bent on restoring the financial viability of the entire industry. 'I did what I could to press them into making the best offer which they possibly could,' Lord Londonderry wrote after the meeting of his own district association on 30 April, 'but they do not look very far ahead . . . with the result that they only made the offer which assured them a profit'. Nor did Baldwin himself expect these proposals to be accepted by the MFGB; such a settlement, he had commented when it was first outlined, 'would be a remarkably good one if it could be got by agreement. I do not see much chance of it in any circumstances'.[41] Yet the Prime Minister had made no real attempt to impose his will on the Mining Association, whether by threatening compulsory reorganization and pit closures, by offering fuller financial assistance, or even by contradicting their interpretation of the Samuel Report.[42] And though during Friday he tried to gauge the miners' feelings on the question of extending hours, Smith's negative response perhaps helped to discourage him from communicating his own proposals to the Federation.

In giving the owners their way, besides, Baldwin abandoned hope not only of pacifying the miners but also of creating a rift between them and the General Council. On Monday (26 April) he had thought it was 'still in the power of the Trade Union movement to pull the miners from the position they have taken up and make them negotiate'. On Tuesday he suggested, with a certain irony, 'I do not think there is that enthusiastic friendship between the Miners' Federation and the Trades Union Congress that we would like to see'. By Thursday night he was telling the owners: 'I think they [the miners] will very likely bolt. It is impossible to say whether they would draw everybody in, but they all say they are going to be drawn in.' And the following morning, with the Association's final terms before him, he predicted unhesitatingly that 'of course there will be a general strike', though one, he hoped, which 'would not carry much conviction'.[43] The sole remaining purpose of the offer of 30 April, it appears, was to disarm that public hostility invited by the wage reductions which the Mining Association had demanded ten days earlier.

Reluctant allies: the Special Industrial Committee and the miners

Was this resignation justified by the attitude of the TUC? The Industrial Committee, which retained responsibility for negotiations on behalf of the General Council until the lock-out began, was manifestly a reluctant adversary. Its refusal to approve the miners' standpoint on wages, its constant efforts to secure effective negotiations and its unwillingness to take any measures which presupposed their failure, demonstrated its continued desire for peace. On the other hand the engagements made before Red Friday and the potent fears of appearing to betray the miners and declare its own bankruptcy precluded any act of surrender. Crippled by these conflicting desires, and by no means wholly free from internal dissension, the SIC found it difficult to take any initiative at all. It was afflicted, throughout the prologue to the crisis, by an inability to make its mind known.

In private, the members of the Industrial Committee had little difficulty in identifying the elements of a settlement of the mining dispute satisfactory to themselves. The first necessity was a detailed programme of reorganization. As early as 8 April Pugh outlined the scheme which would eventually be recommended to the trade-union executive conference at the end of the month, involving the classification of individual collieries, the closure of the most inefficient and the continued assistance of those capable of rehabilitation but unable to pay standard wages in the meantime.[44] In the next two weeks the staff at Eccleston Square produced a series of memoranda which envisaged the formation of a joint board of miners, employers and government to carry out the investigations required for this purpose. Though its form was left unspecified, it was obvious that the continuance of a subsidy was an essential ingredient of these proposals, both for the maintenance of wages and perhaps for the reconstruction of the industry itself.[45]

It is no less apparent, from their reports and transactions, that the SIC and the TUC staff were already reconciled to the imposition of wage reductions on the miners. The Research Department favoured a national minimum which individual districts were permitted to undercut within a fixed margin. Citrine and Pugh seemed to prefer the revision of differentials between various grades of employees so that cuts would fall chiefly on the higher paid.[46] In the meeting of the Committee on 21 April (the first time since the eighth that its members had discussed the crisis separately from the miners) both Pugh and Thomas gave their opinion that some such sacrifices were unavoidable. 'On wages,' said the chairman, 'as a Committee they could not see the miners getting out of that without some adjustment.' 'The miners' slogans would get them nowhere,' Thomas agreed, adding that he had raised the possibility of returning to the 1921 minimum with Vernon Hartshorn – 'who pooh-poohed the idea.' Of their colleagues only Swales objected vocally to the assumption that such cuts must be faced.[47]

The Committee naturally concealed these opinions from the miners; but thereby its contribution to negotiations was gravely handicapped. Reluctant to make any move which would increase the Federation's suspicions of its infidelity, it baulked at discussing with them how the crisis might be resolved. Not all its members, it is true, were happy at this evasion. On 13 April Citrine urged the SIC to prepare recommendations on a settlement with which the miners could be presented 'in the event of their asking . . . for advice'.[48] The following week he suggested that they should seek to be represented at negotiations with the government. But, as Pugh observed, 'the difficulty was that if they took part they would have to have a policy. At present the Committee had none.'[49] Tillett, Swales and Thomas all objected to Citrine's proposal, the first two because it implied interference in the miners' affairs, the latter presumably because of his unfriendly relations with their leaders. Not until Baldwin himself put forward the idea on 26 April – prompted, perhaps, by Pugh – did the SIC assent to it in principle.

The Committee set the mechanism of a general strike in motion almost casually. On 23 April John Bromley told his colleagues that the locomotive engineers had already begun to discuss the question of strike pay, and added that most other union executives thought 'it was time something was done'. Pugh also mentioned that the remainder of the General Council were expecting a conference to be summoned. The impending lock-out of the miners left little opportunity for further postponement. But the SIC still had no clear strategy in mind at the time they issued invitations to their affiliates; the extent and organization of a sympathetic stoppage was not officially considered until the meeting of the General Council on 27 April. And none of the Committee, with the exception of Swales, spoke of the advantage of threatening a general strike for bargaining purposes. The summoning of the executives was not a calculated *démarche*, but a reflex action.

Once the union conference was arranged, however, there was no doubt in the minds of the SIC that, unless the miners' stoppage were averted, a general strike in some form would ensue. They could not defer any longer, besides, the task of producing a declaration of policy, and on 27 April finally agreed with the miners to set up a joint committee to prepare such a document.[50] Approved by the General Council, this statement, *The Mining Situation*, was laid before the executives two days later.

The Mining Situation emphasized, what had been unforcefully argued by the Industrial Committee and inconsistently by the miners, that reorganization held the key to peace in the coal industry. This was seen to entail the closure of uneconomic pits (so that prices would rise); the compulsory amalgamation and financial assistance of the more viable, and the introduction of cooperative selling and municipal trading. But on the wages question, the statement seemed to reproduce the miners' views, almost intact:[51]

> The wages and working conditions of mine workers are already so depressed as to render it imperative to seek for remedies other than a further degradation in their standards of life, or abrogation of the present standard hours. . . . The figures given in the [Samuel] Commission's Report show quite clearly that to seek any further degradation of this level [of wages] is indefensible.

Though not wholly unambiguous, this phraseology was much more dogmatic than any which the Industrial Committee had used hitherto. Like the General Council as a whole, it felt obliged to present to the movement a bold and resolute face. Whilst both bodies (the SIC in particular) hoped that further negotiations would produce concessions, the expression of their true feelings was out of the question.

The TUC leadership did nonetheless contrive for a time to restrain any open display of belligerence by the conference of executives, when it assembled at Farringdon Street Memorial Hall on the morning of 29 April. The delegates heard Pugh give a lengthy *résumé* of the history of the negotiations and express optimism about the outcome of Baldwin's intervention. They approved a resolution proposed by J. H. Thomas authorizing the SIC to continue its efforts to obtain 'an honourable settlement', unless and until a lock-out was imposed on the miners. They accepted Bevin's view that no threat of a general strike should yet be uttered, as it would 'place a weapon in the hands of our opponents'. For almost two days thereafter the members awaited the outcome of discussions at Downing Street, their boredom relieved by impromptu choruses and occasional progress reports, whilst the General

Council itself (with the exception of the members of the Industrial Committee) sat in similar lethargy upstairs.[52]

Throughout Friday negotiations continued. The owners' offer was rejected by the miners in mid-afternoon, but the Cabinet agreed that Baldwin should make a final attempt to avert a dispute by at last bringing the SIC directly into the discussions. He, Lane-Fox and Steel-Maitland ('conciliatory in manner but ineffective and uncertain') were now joined by Neville Chamberlain and Birkenhead on the government side.[53] Between about 6 and 11 pm four successive sessions of negotiations took place, separated by brief adjournments, the first two between the government team and the Industrial Committee, the latter attended also by the miners' leaders. The presence of the committee seemed at first to offer a real chance of escaping from the impasse. Pugh urged the need for an inclusive agreement covering specific measures of reorganization as well as conditions of work – 'everything everybody has to undertake'. In response the members of the Cabinet offered 'an Advisory Committee (on which the miners as well as the owners will be represented) to advise the Mines Department as to the steps that can be taken to put into operation whatever proposals for reorganization are of benefit to the industry'. Herbert Smith, pressed by the ministers and prompted by the TUC spokesmen, also made what looked like a major concession, agreeing that once the terms of reorganization were clarified he was 'prepared to start on page one and go to the end of the book [Samuel Report], which would have meant examining a reduction in wages'. But this did not imply agreeing to cuts *ab initio*: 'I am not prepared to accept a reduction in wages until I see what horse we are going to mount on'. And on this point the Industrial Committee agreed with him: 'I should feel myself guilty,' J. H. Thomas told Baldwin, 'if I led you to believe that we had discussed possible reductions in wages with the miners.'[54]

This measure of accord did momentarily conjure up the vision of an agreement, or at least led the participants to consider how they might postpone the lock-out to allow conversations to continue. Much time was spent in attempting to determine what interval must be allowed to secure an understanding on reorganization.[55] A rupture could not be prevented, finally, however, since the government's spokesmen were sure that the miners would remain, no matter what the delay, immovable on the wages question. It was Baldwin himself, throughout these exchanges sounding more pessimistic than his colleagues, who concluded the discussions on this note:[56] 'We are not convinced that there is a better chance of progress at the moment in pursuing negotiations. We have no assurance that they will lead to any fruitful result; and we fear that a continuation of negotiations may end again in a second deadlock which would leave us in a worse position than we are in tonight.'

The breakdown of negotiations was reported to the conference of union executives late that night, whereupon the General Council distributed its 'Proposals for Co-ordinated Action'. Affiliated organizations were to be asked to vote next day on the question of whether to hand over to the TUC power to order and conduct a stoppage on these lines. On the morning of 1 May the miners' executive agreed that, on acceptance of this resolution, the General Council should assume primary responsibility for negotiations, provided that there was 'the fullest consultation between the two bodies in respect of any developments which might occur, and no settlement would be reached without the miners' consent'.[57] Shortly after midday it was announced that a stoppage had been authorized by 3,653, 577 votes to 49,911.[58] Both Bevin and Ramsay MacDonald indicated to the delegates, however, that discussions might be expected to continue in an effort to prevent a strike. Smith made two statements, their significance afterwards disputed, on the miners' willingness to consider the Samuel Report *in toto*.[59] The Red Flag was sung; and the officers of the organized labour movement dispersed to pass on the word of battle.

The miners and the TUC leadership had thus, in the end, made a sort of common cause, though not without an increasing mutual unease. 'We felt all along the great danger of asking other people's help,' Cook told the Federation's conference on Thursday evening; 'they want to decide their position and that has meant a terrible struggle with your representatives.'[60] But by treating agreement on reorganization as an absolute priority, the two sides had successfully disguised their basic conflict on the question of whether wage cuts were ultimately necessary – and had, indeed, appeared to conspire to avoid and suppress the issue. The miners, despite their decisive resolution of 9 April, had never repudiated the Samuel Report with its prescription of lower pay, and at the height of the crisis Herbert Smith had obscured their position again and again. The Industrial Committee, for its part, had been most willing to be misled by his statements on the Royal Commission, never seeking even in private to clarify the enigmatic utterances on which they asked the government to rely. Against all the evidence, they chose to act as if the miners would finally accept a compromise settlement; an illusion they could preserve until, but only until, an adequate compromise was assembled.

Negotiations under threat: 1–3 May

During the next two nights members of the General Council and the government sought, strenuously and even desperately, to find a formula which would still prevent a general strike. They never came within measurable distance of success. The principal reason for this failure was not the inflexibility of the union side, but the inability of the politicians to distinguish between the strategic objective of solving the mining dispute and the tactical objective of avoiding its issuance in a general strike. Baldwin and his colleagues assumed that all concessions on the government's part should be assessed in terms of their likely acceptability to the miners. With some element of justification, though also with considerable lack of imagination, they treated the representatives of the General Council as mere auxiliaries of the Federation. Such chances as there were of engineering a breach between them were thus forfeited.

The history of these negotiations was much distorted by subsequent propaganda. The miners, unsympathetic witnesses, afterwards claimed that they had come close to success: that an understanding had been reached, only to be repudiated by the diehards of the Cabinet. Their allegations were lent force by J. H. Thomas's statement in the House of Commons on 5 May, giving a similar account of a Cabinet *volte-face*.[61] Many other labour spokesmen, whether or not close to the events, proceeded to offer their own versions (albeit conflicting) of the supposed rebellion by Baldwin's ministers against his conciliatory policy.[62] In fact these reports had little or no validity, though their currency was in itself revealing of the Prime Minister's imperishable reputation as a peace-lover. Though there is no doubt that, once the representatives of the General Council were able to confront Baldwin in the absence of the miners, both sides were impressed by the change in atmosphere and convinced of the other's *desire* for an accommodation, it is equally evident that no common view of a settlement emerged, and that the Cabinet broke off negotiations because they appeared abortive, not because they were productive. The hopes that had been aroused, however, did have a significant effect in widening the division between the General Council and the MFGB leadership – which by 3 May became overt and explicit for the first time.

On 1 May, following the conclusion of the conference of union executives the General Council sent two letters to the Prime Minister, the first offering to cooperate with the government for the purpose of maintaining essential services in the event of a stoppage, the second indicating that they would 'hold themselves available at any moment' if the government wished to meet them for further talks.[63] Despite the failure of the negotiations on the previous evening the members of the Industrial Committee still evidently hoped that Herbert Smith's 'acceptance' of the Samuel Report on that occasion, reiterated at the trade-union conference, afforded the chance of peace – which their own direct responsibility for negotiations, and perhaps the prospect of a general strike, would enable them to exploit. Why the Prime Minister accepted their invitation is less clear, for the miners' change of heart seemed insincere to the government representatives, and the threat of a stoppage moved them to defiance, not conciliation. When the conversations were renewed on Saturday evening, Birkenhead again emphasized to the SIC (now renamed the Negotiating Committee) that Smith's approval of the Commission's recommendations was insufficient unless accompanied by an explicit recognition of the need for wage reductions. Baldwin's own inclination appears rather to have been to explore the idea of a 'comprehensive' agreement, embodying long-term and short-term provisions, which Arthur Pugh had suggested the day before. With this in mind, perhaps, he proposed the creation of a subcommittee of four members from each side to continue the discussions informally and without record. After some hesitation the Negotiating Committee agreed; Pugh, Thomas, Swales and Citrine were chosen to represent them, Baldwin, Birkenhead, Steel-Maitland and Horace Wilson acted for the government.[64]

The subcommittee found itself immediately barred from entering upon new ground, however, by the obligation of the Negotiating Committee under the resolution of the conference of executives to secure the withdrawal of the lock-out notices in the mining industry prior to further negotiations.[65] As a result, the two sides were immediately diverted from discussing specific terms of agreement to arguing over the conditions upon which a public subsidy might temporarily be renewed to maintain the miners' wages. And the Royal Commission's report presented itself, despite its obscurities and the ambiguity of the miners' response to it, as the only source from which such a provisional truce could be extracted. The extended dialogue of 1–2 May never escaped these frustrating confines.

The object of the ministers on the subcommittee thus became once again that of winning from the TUC representatives, in return for a promised subvention, an admission that the application of the Samuel proposals involved unavoidable wage cuts in the coal industry. But in pursuit of this end they produced a second problem, of uncertainty about how far the Negotiating Committee were speaking for the miners. Ambiguous formulae based upon mutual good faith might have been satisfactory for the government and the TUC, but Baldwin and his associates were ultimately unwilling to allow the same latitude to the miners. So long as the power of the General Council to impose a diplomatic understanding upon the Federation remained in doubt, agreement was obstructed. 'I never lost my belief,' Birkenhead maintained afterwards, 'that the limited authority with which the TUC was negotiating disabled them from agreeing to the only basis which we were authorized to discuss.'[66]

In the amicable climate of the subcommittee, nonetheless, some semblance of agreement appeared at first to be reached. The result of its opening session was a formula, evidently devised by Horace Wilson, submitted to the Negotiating Committee in the early hours of Sunday morning.[67]

> The Prime Minister has satisfied himself as a result of the conversations he has had with the representatives of the Trades Union Congress, that if negotiations are continued (it being understood that the notices cease to be operative) the representatives of the Trade Union Congress are confident that a settlement can be reached on the lines of the [Samuel] Report within a fortnight.

The status of this declaration was, however, ill-defined and its meaning highly disputable. It had been devised while the two sides were in separate rooms and never in fact discussed at all. Wilson, who had acted as intermediary, told the ministers that in conversation with the members of the Negotiating Committee 'it had been made clear to me that the statement was intended to mean that the Miners accepted the Report, recognizing that it meant a reduction in wages'. And it was this interpretation, next day, which Baldwin and Birkenhead reported to the Cabinet.[68] But this rendering was, almost without doubt, in conflict with the understanding of the labour spokesmen. According to Citrine, the exchanges with Wilson were brief and vague, and Thomas in particular resented the attempt to conduct negotiations through 'a permanent official'. During or after the discussion, moreover, Thomas evidently drafted a formula of his own which he later gave to Tom Jones. Though subsequently discarded, this may well reflect fairly accurately the opinion which he and his colleagues had intended to convey to Wilson:[69] 'We are satisfied that a settlement on the lines of the Report could be obtained within a reasonable period (fortnight), it being understood that the notices cease to be operative, the General Council undertake to use their influence to obtain this result (facilitate this object).' Altogether looser in its wording, this signified much more obviously that the TUC representatives were unwilling to commit themselves to dictating anything to the miners, least of all wage cuts.

On the morning of 2 May the full General Council met and asked the Negotiating Committee for a written report on the proceedings of the previous night.[70] The miners' executive, ignorant of what had transpired, had departed for the coalfields and had now to be recalled. But about 1.15 pm the Committee heard Arthur Cook give his personal opinion that the Wilson formula was unlikely to be acceptable, that the Federation had never intended to accept the Samuel Report unconditionally, and that Smith's statements on the subject should have been taken to promise no more than its thorough examination.[71] Pugh thereupon suggested that the General Council could not agree to the document 'until they were perfectly clear as to precisely where the miners stood with regard to what is meant by "negotiations on the lines of the Report".' Moreover, the Negotiating Committee's own view was that the formula was too indefinite about the government's responsibility for the implementation of reorganization, and that therefore 'a concrete document would have to be secured from the Government to the items on which they would take measures'. A fortnight was felt to be inadequate for this purpose.[72] At 4.30 the General Council reconvened to hear Cook repeat his earlier objections. The members of the Negotiating Committee were evidently evasive about whether the formula would eventually result in wage reductions, which aroused the suspicion of some of their colleagues that they had said more to the government than they admitted. Nonetheless the consensus of the meeting was 'that the formula . . . could be accepted in substance', but that the Negotiating Committee should 'find out more specifically what were the Government's intentions with regard to its interpretation'.[73]

Despite the subsequent assertion of the miners, and of J. H. Thomas, the General Council thus gave no unqualified approval to the first subcommittee formula. Nor was the qualified assent which it did record thought, by either the Council or the Negotiating Committee, to imply the immediate and definite acceptance of wage cuts. Though the members of the latter body had always been willing to contemplate reductions at some time in the future, they continued to be deterred from saying so by fears of the miners' objections. They had in fact offered assurances to the government representatives in the same, indefinite terms as had Herbert Smith himself. Their prevarication at the Council meeting was almost certainly the product of their own ambivalence, not a concealment of any actual misconduct as negotiators. Like the Council as a whole, they still wished to avoid any official discussion of the wage question until undertakings on reorganization had been obtained. The events of Sunday night were amply to confirm the significance of these reservations.

Notwithstanding the reading offered by Birkenhead and Baldwin, the Cabinet gave the Wilson statement a decidedly more hostile reception than the TUC. According to Hankey's report to the king on its midday meeting of 2 May:

> The general view . . . was that the above formula was too vague and indefinite, and gave no assurance that the proposed negotiations were likely to lead to a successful issue; and that taken in conjunction with the menace of a general strike, it would be regarded by public opinion as a yielding by the Government to threats. It was felt that negotiations involving the payment of a subsidy ought not to be resumed without a definite answer from the Miners in regard to their acceptance of the Report of the Royal Commission, which, of course, would commit the Miners to make some sacrifice as indicated in that Report.
>
> It was assumed that in any event the complete withdrawal of the threat of a general strike was *sine qua non* to any resumption of negotiations involving a subsidy.[74]

The understanding, Amery noted in his diary, seemed 'both meaningless in itself and likely to lead to some very feeble and ineffective negotiations while in practice accepting the general strike as a natural thing'.[75]

Although there appears to be some evidence here of a growing intransigence on the part of the ministers not involved in the negotiations, no split in the Cabinet developed. Baldwin himself had already expressed misgivings about the formula to Tom Jones before the meeting, and his doubts were reinforced by the prediction of the Conservative Chief Whip, Eyres Monsell, that it would be badly received by the government's backbenchers. Wilson and Steel-Maitland likewise felt its inadequacy; apparently only Birkenhead made any serious attempt to meet the criticisms in the Cabinet.[76] On the other hand no objection was made as yet to the continuance of negotiations. Members of the government still seemed to hope that the General Council could be propelled into making definite pledges or even cancelling the strike.

During the afternoon, however, these hopes dispersed. The failure of the General Council to appear at Downing Street at 1 pm as expected frayed ministerial tempers.[77] The Cabinet were also told by the Postmaster-General that telegrams were already being dispatched by several unions ordering a stoppage from midnight on the third. When the meeting reconvened at 6.45 pm there was still no definite news from Eccleston Square. About 7.30 pm the draft of an ultimatum was approved, which both required the TUC and the miners to 'say plainly' that they would accept 'interim adjustments of wages and hours of work' prior to negotiations on reorganization; and demanded an unconditional withdrawal of the threat of a general strike.[78] Even now, however, it was agreed that Baldwin should present this missive only *after* he had again seen the representatives of the Negotiating Committee at 9 o'clock, the time finally fixed for their delayed meeting.

When the General Council arrived at Downing Street the miners' executive had still not returned to London. But the joint subcommittee with the Cabinet representatives soon ran into difficulties. Pugh insisted that the undertaking to withdraw the lock-out notices be made more precise; and at the same time emphasized that the General Council could not *guarantee* a settlement, but only a discussion which would consider wage reductions *inter alia*: 'they were not prepared to say, either on their own behalf or on behalf of the miners' that the phrase 'an agreement on the lines of the Report' meant *acceptance* of wage reductions. Baldwin and Birkenhead described the adverse reception of the formula in the Cabinet, and alluded briefly to the animosity aroused by the general strike instructions. The latter now pressed for the inclusion of an explicit reference to wage reductions and produced a new version of the statement with this object. Though the original form does not survive, it evidently required the General Council to 'accept the report' and to 'take the responsibility of advising the Miners that either in the matter of hours or wages there must be a concession whilst the matter of reorganization was under adjustment'.[79]

The fate of this 'Birkenhead formula' is the subject of conflicting testimony. Citrine's autobiography suggests that it was rejected by the labour representatives without even being submitted to them in writing. But both Horace Wilson's minutes and the memorandum later written by Birkenhead indicate that discussion was more prolonged, and that J. H. Thomas put forward at its conclusion an amended and much diluted draft of Birkenhead's proposal, by which the Council were to agree to 'urge the miners to authorize us to enter upon a discussion with the understanding that they and we accept that it may involve some reduction in wages'. The discrepancy between these two accounts is not, however, of much significance. Birkenhead agreed to put the new formula to the Cabinet, but averred that 'there is no chance whatever that an assurance so vague and so limited will be accepted by them'. No record of the meeting indicates that the representatives of the Negotiating Committee undertook to present it to the miners or even to the General Council. Neither in its initial nor its ultimate form, therefore, did the 'Birkenhead' declaration secure any measure of mutual approval. When the miners' executive finally arrived at Downing Street at about 11.15 pm, all witnesses are unanimous that the meeting of the joint subcommittee was at an impasse.[80]

When the Negotiating Committee rejoined the General Council, the Birkenhead/Thomas formula was thus not discussed. Citrine remembers that Pugh made an obscure reference to 'a note which Baldwin had drafted to read to his Cabinet, showing the basis upon which the negotiations could proceed'. He adds, however, that the TUC members of the subcommittee did report how the government ministers had sought a commitment on wage reductions, and were warned by Smillie that the miners 'will never do it'.[81] When the miners' executive attended the Council, it was the formula of the previous night that was made the subject of discussion. The Federation's subsequent account alleges that this was actually turned down by them; but the other evidence does not corroborate this. The minutes of the General Council record only a statement by Herbert Smith that 'they would not be prepared to go into the question of a reduction of wages until everything else recommended in the Report had been tried', and that a month at least would be needed for the purpose of further negotiations.[82] It seems that the General Council, aware of the attitude of the government and themselves already dissatisfied with the terms of the statement, did not press the matter. Instead, Bevin now proposed that they 'should get on rather different lines to discussing these wretched formulas – taking a word out here and putting one in there'. His alternative suggestion was that heads of agreement providing the means by which reorganization could be implemented should be formulated on the spot.[83]

Bevin had been privately considering ways of settling the mining dispute for ten days or so. Like the Industrial Committee he was resigned at any early stage to some wage cuts – and wrote accordingly to Arthur Cook on 22 April. During the next four days he produced two memoranda developing a plan for a national wages board and a graduated minimum wage. Neither proposal was original; but at some point prior to the deadlock of Sunday night he conceived of the more novel idea of making the wages board (with independent representation) responsible for ensuring the execution of reorganization as well as and in advance of adjudicating wage rates. This body would in effect recommend and approve the legislation necessary for reconstruction, and the government as well as employers and mine workers would accept its final decisions.[84]

Bevin's device was seized on by the TUC leaders since it once again delayed the threat of enforced wage cuts. The board's projected role in reorganization was the first, and probably the only, aspect of the proposed settlement which was discussed on Sunday night. Before the thorny question of wage arbitration arose – and of course before the government heard anything of the plan – the delivery of the Cabinet's ultimatum brought the course of negotiations abruptly to an end.[85]

Opinion in the Cabinet, hardening against the General Council since midday on the second, crystallized in its closing hours. When, about 11.30 pm, Birkenhead reported the amended version of his formula as 'the uttermost point to which they [the TUC] would go', the reaction was as unfriendly as he had predicted. Most ministers, according to Amery, 'thought FE had gone much too far in the way of compromise . . . [and] thought that there was no real assurance that it would lead to anything, nor did it take any notice of the general strike'.[86] There was, for a moment, a danger of conflict, with Baldwin and Birkenhead urging (though with little support) that negotiations should continue at least until the miners' position was known. The news of the refusal of the *Daily Mail* printers to set up that paper's editorial on the impending strike terminated the argument, silencing the voices for conciliation. Baldwin too was led to conclude that the orders for the General Strike were already taking effect. The decision to end negotiations until 'an immediate and unconditional withdrawal of the instructions for a general strike' had been secured was taken without dissentients.[87]

At about 1.15 pm Pugh, Thomas, Swales and Citrine were called out of the discussions between the General Council and the miners to be told by Baldwin of the government's resolution and handed a newly revised version of the note which had been approved by the Cabinet earlier in the evening, which now referred to 'overt acts . . . including gross interference with the freedom of the Press' as grounds for the cessation of talks. Its terms were read 'imperturbably' by Thomas to the assembled committees, amid 'laughter and growls'. But the union side did not wish to accept so apparently misapprehended an incident as the pretext for an ultimatum, and Pugh and Citrine were soon sent back to tell the Prime Minister that the General Council 'were entirely without responsibility for the "overt acts" referred to'. They were told by the Office Keeper that Baldwin had already retired and shortly afterwards returned with their colleagues to Eccleston Square. There, during the next hour or so, the Council approved its reply to the Prime Minister, disowning the printers' strike and deploring the 'precipitous and calamitous' curtailment of negotiations.[88] It also appointed a subcommittee with the miners (consisting of Bevin, Pugh, Citrine, Smith, Richardson and Cook) to complete the outline agreement which had been under consideration when the government's missive was delivered.[89]

Attempts at peace-making were not yet over. But the events of 3 May showed the government inflexibly determined on forcing a retreat by the TUC, while the latter remained confused and divided about its course of action. The dissension in the labour ranks became apparent as soon as the joint subcommittee of the General Council and the miners had finished drafting their proposals for a settlement. These now stipulated that once the national wages board had decided upon the requisite measures of industrial reform and provided it was satisfied that 'economic prices' were being charged by the owners, it could consider what conditions of work were appropriate in the interim period of their application, 'subject to the maintenance of a national minimum and the Seven Hours Act'. This manifestly implied the threat of a wage reduction, albeit a uniform one.[90] Although the terms were evidently accepted by the miners' officials, therefore, when the document was put to their full executive that body – encouraged, according to Citrine, by Cook and Richardson – voted by twelve to six to insist that *the* national minimum be retained. The amendment was considered by a joint meeting with the Negotiating Committee, whose members expressed openly, for the first time, the view that the miners must be prepared to compromise for the sake of a settlement, and asserted, through Bevin, the authority of the General Council to 'take its own decision'. The full General Council approved unanimously the original wording of the proposal on the wage question. Even now, however, the extent of the rift was still largely obscured. It appears that the Council's decision was never officially communicated to the miners – according to whom all their own copies of the joint document were destroyed to safeguard security. Though the General Council met the MFGB executive, together with the parliamentary party, early in the afternoon, Bevin then referred to the scheme only indirectly, and without mentioning the element of controversy.[91] Nor were the miners aware of the surreptitious efforts to restart talks on this basis later in the day.

These attempts, ill-prepared and mismanaged, were in fact undertaken without any very clear authority. According to Horace Wilson's account, written the following day, Bevin rang him at 5 pm to inform him that new proposals had been approved and to suggest a meeting, adding that MacDonald would probably refer to the document in his speech to the Commons that evening.[92] Bevin later claimed, with support from Citrine, that a definite arrangement had been made by the Council with the Labour Party leader.[93] An official of the Ministry of Labour collected the memorandum from the TUC offices on Wilson's behalf. The latter concluded, on examining it, that it needed amendment but had 'certain merits'. Shortly afterwards, in the Commons lobby, Arthur Henderson proposed independently to Wilson that the government might be prepared to negotiate on this basis with MacDonald, himself, and (possibly) J. H. Thomas, on the labour side.[94]

Wilson warned Baldwin that a new initiative might be launched by the Leader of the Opposition; but in the event neither MacDonald nor Thomas mentioned the document or its contents during the evening debate. MacDonald may well have been unwilling to do so because of the uncertain attitude of the miners, whose MPs had been enjoined not to speak in the adjournment, but clearly could not be held to this promise if a compromise settlement were publicly aired.[95] Immediately after the main speeches, therefore, Baldwin and some of his colleagues attempted to find out, through Wilson and Tom Jones, 'what was afoot' at Eccleston Square. Wilson again contacted Bevin, urging the necessity for strike notices to be withdrawn before negotiations, to which Bevin replied that this might be possible if the General Council could be privately assured that their scheme would be accepted 'not in detail but in principle'. A meeting between the two civil servants, Bevin and Pugh, was arranged for 9 pm. But Citrine, who was also at Westminster, told Wilson shortly afterwards that the trade unionists had been instructed not to attend unless accompanied by the full Negotiating Committee.[96]

A little later, however, Henderson repeated to Wilson his offer to act, with MacDonald, as intermediary. Citrine, who was still present, did not demur, though it is clear that Henderson had no mandate from the General Council. About 10 pm an interview finally took place between the two Labour Party leaders and Baldwin, Churchill,

Chamberlain and Steel-Maitland. The conversation was unrecorded, but Wilson heard afterwards that the ministers had taken the line that the withdrawal of the strike notices was a prerequisite of any agreement; and Henderson told Citrine that both the ostensibly conciliatory Steel-Maitland and the bellicose Churchill had appeared to regard the experience of a general strike as certain to be salutary and chastening to union pretensions.[97] By the time the outcome of the meeting was made known to the Council, the General Strike was already under way.

Was the General Strike avoidable?

The General Strike occurred, it has been suggested, firstly because the miners and mine-owners were incapable of settling their own dispute, and secondly because the General Council and the government were unsuccessful in coming to terms independently of them. Enough evidence has been put forward to indicate that the latter circumstance was not a simple and direct outcome of the former. The General Council were very unlikely ever to have prevailed upon the miners to accept a compromise peace. But it is still possible that they might have been dissuaded from undertaking sympathetic strike action by government ministers more enterprising or more machiavellian in negotiation. The Council and the Cabinet were subject to other, external constraints, however; and it remains to ask whether these were sufficient to preclude agreement between them. The question, What caused the General Strike? poses inescapably the question, Was it avoidable?

The most important factor governing the conduct of the General Council and its Negotiating Committee was their sense of accountability to the movement they represented. They were bound to the miners less and less by any sense of common interest and objectives, more and more simply by fear of the repercussions of a supposed 'betrayal', reminiscent of 1921. The apprehension, so marked before Red Friday, that a general attack on wages would follow a defeat of the miners, seems to have receded, and even at the conference of union executives it was scarcely mentioned. What was now at stake was the value of earlier pledges and the credibility of the General Council itself as a 'general staff' of labour.

The leaders of the TUC were thus constantly concerned to avert the effects, demoralizing and divisive, of an open rift with the MFGB. This impulse was evident as early as February 1926, in the circular then issued to reassure the movement of their continued support for the miners' case. It was equally evident in the terms of the statement on the dispute put before the trade-union conference at the end of April. Above all, it was evident in the last phase of negotiations after 1 May – the only time when representatives of the Council took the responsibility for finding a peace formula upon themselves. Though no doubt tempted to accept what Baldwin and his colleagues initially offered as a basis for continued negotiations, the Council held back. 'We had visions of Black Friday on our minds,' writes Citrine of the discussion of 2 May. 'On the present occasion the miners had expressly handed their powers to the General Council, but it would not do to attempt to force a decision upon them.'[98] Later that day, according to Bevin, before the Council left for the final round of talks at Downing Street, 'there was a discussion as to whether the risk should not be taken of calling the notices off in view of the desire for a settlement. Personally, however, with the feeling in the country I thought that unless it was a pretty clear statement we should continue or else we should all be accused of creating another Black Friday.'[99]

Looking back on the General Strike afterwards some union leaders claimed that the demands and expectations of the rank and file had deprived them of any freedom of choice.

> It is alleged that . . . knowing inevitably what would happen, I at least ought to have chucked it up [J. H. Thomas told the railwaymen's delegates in July]. Well, I hope I have never been a coward, and if I had chucked it up, it is a foolish person who would assume that that would have stopped the strike. It could not have stopped the strike. It had gone too far for that.

His colleague, C. T. Cramp, made the same point more emphatically to the combined executives in January 1927: 'I do not blame the General Council for calling off the strike, but I do blame our people who for years had made it impossible for the General Council to resist the general strike.'[100]

Such alibis are of dubious validity. For at no stage between the publication of the Samuel Report and the outbreak of the strike did the General Council abandon hope of a negotiated settlement. Nor, it has been seen, did they expect such a settlement to exclude wage cuts. What the fears of another Black Friday did was to lead the Industrial Committee and its successor to obscure, as far as possible, their differences with the Federation, and to rule out any capitulation which made no visible concessions by way of reorganization and financial assistance. Had the latter requirements been taken seriously by the government, however, it seems reasonable to assume that the TUC leadership would have been prepared to face a rupture with the miners and the discomfort of popular criticism rather than undergo a trial of strength in impossible conditions. The fact was that their requirements were never met, and it was the government's unwillingness to tackle the question of reconstruction which was the critical consideration in leading the General Council to threaten and, ineluctably, to implement a general strike. The most convincing statement of their own view of the reasons for the stoppage focussed precisely on the intractability of the Cabinet:[101] 'The Government were less mediators than a directly interested party even before negotiations broke down. [They] were as much concerned to limit their obligation in any settlement to be arrived at, as the Mine Owners and Miners respectively were to make terms advantageous to themselves. . . .'

The General Council could not have maintained a resolve so brittle, however, had they not been hopeful that a general strike would advance – at least not prejudice – their cause. Although its constitutional implications had been foreseen, with more or less alarm, none of the TUC leadership had expected the government to sever all communications with them. To some, Thomas in particular, it probably seemed only a matter of time, on 1 and 2 May, before a form of words could be agreed allowing negotiations to continue. Even after the official ultimatum of Sunday night the secretive exchanges in the Commons on Monday appeared to indicate that contact would be maintained. Not until the strike was some three days old did the impenetrability of the administration come to be appreciated.

If the TUC were to this extent optimistic about the outcome of the General Strike, however, they were, in matters more essential, profoundly defeatist. Eventually the stoppage had only one stated object: to achieve a temporary suspension of the miners' lock-out. On no other point had the General Council formulated a positive policy on which they felt able to fight. The proposals of *The Mining Situation* prepared for the trade-union executive conference at the end of April had no such status; hastily drafted and insincerely advocated, they were ignored from the moment the conference dispersed. The scheme approved on 3 May perhaps aroused more confidence, but partly because of the opposition of the miners was never publicized. Both documents were mainly concerned with procedures for reorganization. Far from defending the major principle asserted by the MFGB – no loss of wages – the General Council had, in a sense, declared a general strike to allow themselves to clarify the conditions on which they would sacrifice it.

Nowhere is this self-doubt more marked than in the Council's attitude to the particular question of the subsidy. Although there was a case to be made for further governmental assistance to the coal industry, on the grounds both of social justice and economic advantage, the TUC (like the Labour Party) consistently failed to present it. This was a crucial symptom of the underlying illogicality of their position, and the essential absurdity of the General Strike itself. The justification for such an action had necessarily to be political, not in the sense that it challenged the existence of the government but in that it protested the inequity and irrationality of specific Conservative policies. Yet no demand for financial aid was ever effectively argued. In part this was because labour representatives were intellectually ill-equipped to formulate controversial economic proposals except in the familiar categories of rigid liberal orthodoxy or crude socialist polemic. In part it was because both wings of the movement were burdened with a mechanical and blinkered concept of parliamentary sovereignty which led them to view their own actions with uncertainty and trepidation.

In labour eyes Baldwin appeared, even at the last – and in contrast with some of his colleagues – well-meaning if weak. But his part in the Cabinet's failure to produce any fruitful suggestions during the course of negotiations seems in retrospect more decisive. Until the end of April he had committed himself entirely to the tactic of persuading the mine-owners to improve their wage offer and even refrained from objecting openly to their wilful misinterpretation of the Samuel Report. Eventually he allowed the Mining Association to overrule his own judgement of what a fair settlement would be. At no stage in the crisis did he or his fellow-ministers consider putting forward specific recommendations on the reconstruction of the coal industry, offering a subsidy proportionate to wage reductions for a fixed period of time; or devising a new authority for the fixing of wages. Positive ideas on these lines came always from the TUC.

It was not simply capitalist economic dogmas which ruled out such solutions. A subsidy, for example, had been granted to the coal industry in 1921 as well as in 1925, and a 'tapering' subsidy was not opposed even in 1926. Selective industrial protection had already been adopted and justified in the shape of safeguarding tariffs. And resort to arbitration, too, was a remedy that the Cabinet itself put forward immediately after the strike, and again during the extended coal dispute which followed, despite the objections of the employers. Later in 1926 the administration was eventually to enact a measure of reconstruction, albeit an unambitious one, in the Mining Industry Act. The arguments against more radical state-sponsored reorganization, on the other hand, tended to be pragmatic and short-term: the financial problems stemming from nationalization of royalties, the lack of *immediate* results likely to avert the dispute in hand, the necessity of coercing private industrialists (currently well-disposed) and perhaps of enforcing against opposition the closure of some collieries. Underlying this half-hearted and inconsistent policy, however, was the conflict, endemic to Conservative politics, between an intellectual recognition of the *need* for change and an emotional aversion to implementing it. Conscious of the ills of the coal industry the government were also afraid that reform initiatives on their part would encourage the expectations of root-and-branchers, compel their own involvement in every subsequent dispute in the industry and lead step by step towards public ownership.

It was these unrealized or half-realized fears which fostered the reluctance to set reorganization on foot. Between the publication of the 'fourteen points' in the Samuel Report requiring administrative and legislative action and the outbreak of the stoppage the Cabinet made scarcely a move in this direction. A draft bill on local authority trading in coal, the offer of an inquiry into cooperative selling, and the last-minute proposal for an advisory committee on the implementation of the Royal Commission's recommendations were the full fruits of ministerial endeavour in this regard.[102] On 3 May the Minister of Education, Eustace Percy, admitted the plausibility of the labour argument 'that they have no certainty as to "re-organization", that the Owners are known to be reluctant to "re-organize", and that the Government have taken no definite action'.[103] And in this crisis such an omission was fatal, even in terms of the government's own pragmatism. For the General Council attached such importance to this subject, were so convinced that here lay the solution to the dispute, that only concessions on this count could afford any prospect of industrial peace. Proposals on industrial reconstruction, even if lacking any obvious economic utility, might still have facilitated negotiations. Denied any foothold of this kind, the TUC was dragged with little effective resistance into an unwanted conflict.

The government's clumsy handling of negotiations indicated, no doubt, that like the General Council they were constantly aware of their constituency. The strictures levelled by Conservative press and

MPs at the settlement of 1925, the public warnings then given to the unions, and the findings of the Royal Commission itself made the offer of any generous subsidy hazardous on this occasion. Furthermore, any indication that hostages had been handed to the General Council in the form of promises to legislate on particular aspects of colliery organization and the like would be liable to be interpreted, especially after the meeting of the union executives' conference, as a further capitulation to unconstitutional militancy. The attitude of the Cabinet on 2 May and of the ministers who confronted MacDonald and Henderson on the third was testimony to their growing consciousness of representing democracy in danger.

There was, on the other hand, little awareness of the possibility of manoeuvring a rift between the miners and the TUC. While Baldwin had been apprised of tensions in the labour camp, the General Council had done nothing to suggest that a rupture was imminent. As late as 30 April it delivered, through the MFGB, proposals for a settlement which deemed wage reductions 'quite indefensible'. Though some hint of an incipient split appeared during the negotiations of that evening, it quickly passed out of view. The General Council's unwillingness to accept, unamended, even the statement drafted by Horace Wilson on 1 May – a reluctance which could not readily be attributed to the influence of the absent miners – was deeply disillusioning. From that point on it became ever more tempting for the Cabinet to conclude that the best method of forcing the two sides apart was to subject them both to the heat of battle.

This they did with manifest confidence. Both the comprehensiveness of their emergency measures and the high level of unemployment led the government to feel that a general strike was unlikely to be completely observed, and they were surprised by the actual response.[104] Thus the Cabinet of 2 May decided to ignore or to decline the Council's offer to cooperate in the distribution of foodstuffs, and to introduce legislation restricting the right to strike, if the TUC's notices were not withdrawn.[105] Throughout the period prior to 12 May the government were far more concerned to contradict any suggestion of willingness to bargain than they were doubtful of their capacity to obtain an unconditional surrender.

The fear of conflict, potent in 1925, was thus largely absent in 1926. Even so, conflict was not entered upon because it was desired. The dominant impression created by the course of negotiations prior to the General Strike is of a lack of determination and direction, not of a rooted inflexibility or (until the end) a spirit of aggression. The problems which gave rise to this industrial war were not immune to treatment, nor assumed to be so by either side. Nor did the treatment required demand of the government a departure from cherished principles. It may have required an intellectual capacity to grapple with complex industrial issues, an imagination to take the long rather than the short view, and the courage to meet ill-informed criticism; it may, perhaps, have called for no more than diplomatic skill sufficient to exploit the weaknesses and inhibitions of the opposition. Baldwin's administration, it is fair to conclude, lacked any of these virtues, even while preserving the aura of virtue. If the TUC fought the General Strike with little semblance of purpose, the government fought it with none at all, save the sterile and pointless satisfaction of punishing an apologetic militancy and the freedom gained to continue to ignore responsibilities it found too laborious to assume.

VI The Conduct of the Strike: Eccleston Square

The General Council first discussed the organization of a national stoppage in support of the miners on 27 April, on the eve of the conference of union executives, and appointed a Ways and Means Committee to prepare detailed proposals which were approved the following day. This first plan 'for co-ordinated action' was distributed to the delegates late on 30 April. On 1 May the Ways and Means Committee was replaced by the Powers and Orders Committee, which produced an amplified version of the original instructions, slightly amended by the Council next day and dispatched to the various union offices.[1] These two documents represented the manual with which the labour movement, not without difficulties, dissensions and misunderstandings, conducted the General Strike.[2]

The strategy approved by the General Council was principally the work of Ernest Bevin. It projected a stoppage initially limited in coverage to selected industries, with other organizations retained as a reserve which could be called out subsequently to reinforce and revitalize the 'first wave'. Unions not involved in the strike effort were later approached for financial assistance, though there is no evidence that this was part of the original intention of the Ways and Means Committee. The withdrawal of labour on 4 May was to be effected by four groups of unions. By far the most important were the transport organizations, upon whom the TUC relied to ensure the immediate impact of the strike on the economy and on the public. They were to be supported, however, by printers, metal and chemical workers (mainly those in iron and steel manufacture), and building workers. Engineers and electricians engaged in construction or maintenance in these industries were likewise brought out.

The implications of this strategy were, it appears, less than fully appreciated by many of the Council members who endorsed them. In making provision for reinforcements, Bevin was assuming that the strike might continue for some time; after the constitution of the Strike Organization Committee on 5 May, indeed, he and Purcell were contemplating the possibility of its lasting for three or four weeks. Other union leaders, particularly the railwaymen (unrepresented on the Ways and Means Committee) had neither experience nor expectation of so prolonged a struggle.[3] If they assented to the idea of a strike initially so circumscribed, it was probably in the hope that this limited conflict would in itself prove sufficient to sway the government, avoiding an engagement whose control would become uncertain and whose manifestations revolutionary.

The strike could thus be labelled 'general', as its architects afterwards insisted, only at the cost of a certain imprecision. It was, on the other hand, much more extensive than the action contemplated before Red Friday. The decision to broaden the union front originated, almost certainly, in the difficulties apprehended in imposing a boycott the year before, but it was finally confirmed by the refusal of the transport workers to fight in isolation this time. 'We should know definitely,' wrote Bevin on 26 April, 'what unions are prepared to support the miners to the UTMOST EXTENT to secure an honorable [*sic*] settlement.' He made it clear to the General Council, on behalf of his own union, 'that what we did in the July previous we were not prepared to repeat. That just meant that we should endeavour to hold up coal – to boycott it – and any one who knew the Government's plans knew very well that would be absolutely ineffective and foolish. I found . . . that as usual there was a lot of talk on the General Council by people who thought they were not going to be involved.'[4]

The choice of auxiliaries was, however, somewhat random. The printing organizations were, it is true, the instrument of a deliberate tactic of silencing the anti-union press – though Bevin himself at first hoped that the threat of a newspaper strike would itself cause 'the tune of the press [to] alter in support of the miners'.[5] The iron and steel workers were enlisted, on the other hand, despite the financial embarrassment of their union and their inexperience of large-scale stoppages. The main justification for their inclusion was evidently that metal manufacturers were large consumers of coal, and had a vested interest in reducing prices and wages in that industry. The decision to call upon the construction industry may have been influenced by the numbers of firms likely to be affected and the wide distribution of the labour force; but it was said afterwards to have come 'much to the surprise of most of the Executives of the Building Trade Unions'.[6]

While the Ways and Means Committee wished to ensure that the effect of a stoppage was felt without delay, they were understandably reluctant to take measures whose most obvious consequence would be to inconvenience the public, including the working class themselves. Thus in the case of the building industry, for example, the memorandum of 1 May proposed to distinguish between 'luxury and commercial building' and ordinary housing, creating an exemption which caused considerable difficulties of interpretation and enforcement. The same hesitancy was displayed in instructing the electrical workers. The Committee was at the outset unwilling to interfere with the supply of electricity, especially for domestic purposes; but the ETU, and especially its militant London district, was equally anxious to join the stoppage.[7] No orders were issued to power workers on 1 May, except for those employed in industries directly affected by the strike; but under pressure from the unions the General Council first set up a Public Services Committee to consult with the organizations concerned on the advisability of a selective withdrawal of labour, and then on 3 May authorized the unions to close stations supplying power exclusively for industrial use, and to seek to negotiate arrangements in other plants enabling lighting alone to be maintained.[8]

These attempts to delineate the permissible range of strike action exhibit once again that preoccupation with the safeguarding of 'essential services' which had exercised the Special Industrial Committee and the General Council for several months past. In its principal aspect, the supply of food, this problem was no nearer to solution. According to the orders of 1 May the transport organizations were to establish local subcommittees, assuming responsibility for the release of foodstuffs and the provision of transport for sanitary and health services. The circular accompanying this memorandum said no more than that they should 'adopt the most suitable method open to them' in carrying out the order.[9] Nothing more fruitful of confusion or conflict could have been devised.

The strike plans were also ambiguous about who should direct operations at local level. The first Ways and Means Committee document of 30 April recommended that 'the actual calling out of the workers should be left to the unions, and instructions should only be issued by accredited representatives of the unions participating in the dispute'. But it also provided that Trades Councils should be 'charged with the responsibility of organizing the Trade Unionists in dispute in the most effective manner for the preservation of peace and order'. The instructions of 2 May further envisaged the creation of larger area organizations, based on groups of Trades Councils and union district committees, with even more indefinite responsibilities for discipline and organization. In addition, local joint transport committees were given control over their own sector.[10] Although the area 'circles' were to materialize in only a few centres, as a result of local efforts, there was still ample room within these terms of reference for rival authorities to emerge. When they did, there was frequent difficulty in settling their differences.

At the centre the General Council allocated responsibilities with equal open-handedness. Its members constituted themselves on 1 May into six committees: for negotiations, food and essential services, powers and orders, public services, publicity and general purposes. 'Everybody on the General Council wanted to be on a Sub-Committee of some kind,' Bevin complained.[11] The result was a multiplicity of overlapping authorities, all of which were answereable directly to the Council. The pressure of work was such that 'it became difficult for the Council to be thoroughly informed as to what decisions were being taken by the Committees'.[12] This was soon evident enough from its own vacillations of policy.

Some of the subcommittees found equal difficulty in obtaining recognition from the unions. The men responsible for public services (Beard, Kean, Thorne and Clynes) were confronted from the outset by a rival body drawn from the unions in the electricity industry, their principal sphere of action. Although the latter was formally converted into an advisory committee to the former on 4 May, it remained in practice autonomous, both in handling negotiations with the various employers in the capital in an attempt to cut off the supply of non-domestic power, and in the gradual extension of the strike among electrical workers which the Council reluctantly authorized during the nine days.[13] The establishment of a system of communications with local strike organs was meanwhile delegated to the otherwise under-employed General Purposes Committee, presided over by H. H. Elvin of the National Union of Clerks. In this case it was the transport unions which failed to cooperate. No more than seventeen courier routes were successfully established before the end of the stoppage, whilst a separate service inside London, organized by Herbert Morrison, did not begin operation until its last day.[14]

Dependence on the goodwill of the transport organizations proved an even greater liability for the Food and Essential Services Committee. For four days its chairman, Margaret Bondfield, was to struggle without effect to formulate an acceptable policy to safeguard the supply of food by means of official union permits. Though both the T&GWU and the railway unions had ostensibly agreed in principle to such measures, when they met privately on 1 May they offered no suggestions for their introduction. Instead, they produced a statement primarily reflecting the views of the railwaymen, which proposed to form a new committee, staffed by themselves, to initiate policy in this field, but to delay any immediate issue of permits in order to give 'an opportunity for the Government to accept [the General Council's] offer of assistance'.[15] The Essential Services Committee itself, with the help of officials of the T&GWU (following inconsistent policies at this juncture) dispatched a standard permit for the guidance of local transport committees, but gave no instructions on its proper use. 'It was thought that as soon as applications for permits began to come in they would be able to issue examples of how demarcation in withholding or supplying permits should be made.'[16] On 2 May the Council again asked the unions concerned to submit plans for their distribution, 'if that stage be reached'. When they reconvened next day, however, the full extent of the disagreement between the T&GWU and the NUR became clear.[17]

> The decision of the railwaymen (Marchbank told Margaret Bondfield) was that there should be no movement of any trains or vehicles, no issue of permits or handling of anything. The Transport Workers' Union . . . were prepared to allow their members to work so far as conveying food is concerned. That would immediately lead to a clash between the Railwaymen and the Transport Workers at docks and goods yards, and cases would arise in which the Transport Workers would be issuing permits where Railwaymen had refused them.

The Council proposed a compromise – that union members carry bread and milk to retailers, by road only – which failed to receive approval. Eventually, at its meeting on 4 May, the Council abandoned any hope of agreeing a policy at the centre and decided to leave the local strike organs, already issuing permits under the original TUC instructions, to their own devices.[18]

During this dialogue the one area of accord visible between the two principal organizations concerned was their insistence that 'everything affecting transport should be left to a committee composed of railway and transport unions'.[19] Margaret Bondfield was relegated to acting as messenger girl between them and the General Council. It was evident, besides, that the Council itself was too unwieldy a body to take decisions of a detailed and complex nature on such issues. Both union offices and local strike committees embarrassed it with direct requests for orders and advice. On 5 May, in face of mounting confusion and frustration, the original committee arrangements at TUC headquarters were dissolved, and a new apparatus for the conduct of the strike was set up.

The Strike Organization Committee

The architect of this reconstruction was, once again, Ernest Bevin. On 4 May he had already suggested to the General Council that he should take supreme command of the organization of the strike. His audience was predictably unflattered.[20] The following day, however, with a greater show of protocol, the Powers and Orders Committee brought forward a scheme for a new administrative arrangement which had much the same effect. The Committee itself, hitherto responsible simply for answering questions of interpretation arising from the initial strike orders, was to be renamed the Strike Organization Committee and to exercise overall responsibility for the conduct of the stoppage. Its chief potential competitors, the committees for food and public services, were abolished, and their roles taken over, in the one case by the advisory committee of unions in the electricity industry, and in the other by a central transport committee of the kind persistently sought by the railway unions – both subordinate to the SOC. The scheme also involved the establishment of a phalanx of new committees, for interviewing, intelligence, propaganda and parliamentary liaison, as well as retaining the existing Publicity and General Purposes Committees. But the object of this apparent proliferation was doubtless to distract the attention of the *petits grands hommes* of the Council from matters of major importance.

The Strike Organization Committee was dominated by Bevin and Alf Purcell (its chairman) who were the only members not to be given any additional duties. Though remaining accountable to the General Council, besides, the SOC in practice arrogated to itself the right to issue instructions on behalf of the superior body. It was helped by the fact that the Council was forced to give up the attempt, after 4 May, to keep track of the activities of its myriad off-shoots; and that on 7 May it decided (at Bevin's suggestion) to cease recording minutes because of the danger of arrest and prosecution. From this point on, moreover, the Council became increasingly less concerned with the running of the strike and more absorbed in the negotiation of prospective terms of settlement with Sir Herbert Samuel.[21]

This development in turn led to a further devolution of authority.

Initially the SOC had wished to include amongst its other duties that of establishing contact with outside bodies with the object of promoting a settlement. But this was too blatant an instance of Bevin's self-aggrandisement to be tolerated. When the talks with Herbert Samuel were undertaken, therefore, it was the Negotiating Committee which conducted them. The revival of the latter body – which included all the most prominent officers and ex-officers of the TUC: Swales, Hicks, Thomas, Pugh and Citrine – served to restore the political equilibrium which the creation of the Strike Organization Committee had tended to upset. The 'strong men' of the General Council pushed the rest on to the sidelines.[22]

The atmosphere of Eccleston Square became, from now on, somewhat less febrile. The anxiety and uncertainty which had prevailed at the outset of the strike was at least temporarily dispelled, as a result both of the obvious loyalty and enthusiasm of the strikers and of the absence of any drastic measures of repression on the part of the government. Though Bevin was still able to conjure up the apparition of mass arrests on 7 May (possibly from ulterior motives), Citrine found that Jimmy Thomas, earlier the most gloomy of oracles, had changed his mind on this subject.[23] John Simon's speech in the House of Commons on 6 May, pronouncing the strike outside the protection of the Trade Disputes Act, seems not to have alarmed the General Council, which almost certainly remained entirely ignorant of the government's projected trade-union legislation. Though their disquiet about the prospects of the strike was soon to revive, it was no longer to be a reflection of self-doubt as to their own capacity to command and organize.

It should not be supposed, however, that the overhauling of the TUC strike machinery on 5 May solved all previous problems. The Strike Organization Committee still found difficulty in reconciling inter-union conflicts and in securing uniformity of policy among local strike executives. Both the obscurity of the original strike memoranda and the discontent caused by the partial character of the stoppage in certain trades remained a source of trouble. The Committee moved only slowly towards clarity and consistency.

In the electricity industry, for example, the stoppage continued to spread in the same uneven fashion as before. In London, by 10 May, the unions claimed to have secured ten working agreements to cut off the supply of industrial power, and to have withdrawn the labour of 18 out of 33 municipal undertakings and 19 of 31 private concerns. But the efforts to keep the stoppage within bounds still aroused intense dissatisfaction, especially among the local ETU members, who complained to the Strike Organization Committee on 8 May that the arrangements negotiated with the borough councils were being infringed. The SOC in turn complained of unofficial stoppages; and at least one power station supposedly exempted was struck by 10 May.[24] Elsewhere in the country the SOC tried in a fairly haphazard manner and with only limited success to apply the same policy of selective stoppages, encountering unpredictable local pressures for militancy and restraint.

Discontent with the circumscribed coverage of the strike was also repeatedly voiced in the building industry, similarly affected by official orders which kept some men at work. After receiving numerous queries and complaints from local bodies the Strike Organization Committee eventually decided, on 10 May, to constitute the National Federation of Building Trade Operatives as an 'advisory committee' analogous to that in the electricity generating industry. This remedy was by no means certain of success, however, because the principal builders' union, the Amalgamated Building Trade Workers, was unaffiliated to the Federation and reluctant to accept its authority. The Amalgamated had indeed already set out on a more militant path. 'As we felt that the fight had to be short and sharp we were concerned more with finding excuses for bringing men out in support of the miners than in finding reasons for keeping them in.' They ordered a stoppage in the construction of private houses worth more than £1,200, and on new building work on hospitals, schools, gasworks and dockyards. On 11 May their President, George Waddell, wrote to Citrine protesting that the Federation 'has already by its interpretation of the Trades Union Congress instructions in the matter of housing and hospitals created well-founded fears that it appeared to be chiefly concerned with finding excuses for keeping men at work. . . .'[25] No solution to this conflict was in sight before the strike ended.

As the strike continued, increasingly and from all sides pressure was exerted on the SOC and the General Council to widen it. Workers withdrawing their labour unofficially demanded retrospective endorsement for their action, and those employed in firms dependent on government transport services objected to any requirement to cooperate with blacklegs. In centres where a resumption of work was threatened or took place in some sections the local strike committees usually wished to offset the defection by calling more men out. And on the General Council itself, where the diachronic strategy adopted at the outset was debated at some length on 5 May, the demand for a more complete withdrawal received support both from Citrine and, in some degree, from J. H. Thomas.[26]

On 7 May, therefore, the Strike Organization Committee raised the question of extending the strike with a deputation from the Amalgamated Engineering Union, who agreed to take part 'on condition that all other Engineering Workers affiliated to the Trades Union Congress are called out simultaneously' and that adequate notice were given.[27] Official instructions were issued by the General Council on the ninth, that all workers in shipbuilding and engineering, chemicals and cement, were to withdraw their labour from the first shift on 12 May. This decision might have been expected to increase the breadth and solidarity of the strike in many northern and midlands towns, and especially on Clydeside, and to place the unofficial stoppages that had already occurred in the ship repairing and motor car industries on a legal footing. But even the enlistment of the 'second wave' was far from rendering the strike comprehensive, and might in certain areas have created further problems of the kind that builders and electricians had encountered. Since neither the gas nor the cotton industry were affected, for instance, engineers in these were excluded from the order.[28] Nor, in the event, did the General Council place much faith on the buttressing effect which these new recruits would have on the forces already in the field.

The plans to bring out the engineers did, nevertheless, represent an obvious attempt to tighten the hold of the strike. A similar tendency is observable in the handling of the permits question. As soon as the Central Transport Committee had been constituted on 5 May (with Marchbank, the NUR President, as its Secretary), an effort was made to restrict the issue of permits at a local level. The NUR circular which announced the formation of the Committee repeated the instruction 'that nothing whatever be released or handled'. By the seventh the Transport Committee, with the SOC's assent, was ordering strike committees to rescind all permits, on the grounds that the operation of the government's emergency supply system made it impossible to afford such facilities without conniving at strike breaking. Though this general prohibition was subsequently relaxed to allow cooperative societies to supply bread and milk to their customers, no other exceptions were made prior to 12 May.[29]

The difficulty which still confronted the TUC committee (as in all cases of policy revision) was that of securing adhesion to its orders by the congeries of strike organizations throughout the country. Although the bodies which had been given official responsibility for the granting of permits were the joint transport committees, in many centres this power had been assumed by others: the Trade Councils (under various titles) and their subcommittees, regional federations constituted by them, or even individual road transport unions. As the Food and Essential Services Committee later reported,

> There is evidence that – as at Headquarters – there were conflicting opinions in the localities in regard to the issuing of permits. Trade Councils were not in receipt of instructions sent out as to the policy adopted by the Central Transport Committee until the strike had been in progress for some days. This resulted in a lack of uniformity, which continued in many places throughout the strike.[30]

On the whole, however, despite manifest errors and omissions, the General Strike was not maladministered. It might, certainly, have been more officially conducted had more time been given to planning it beforehand, but this point should not be exaggerated. The primary sources of confusion and dissension – the lack of communications between local and central authorities and the restriction of the stoppage to specified groups of unionists – would have been hard to eliminate in any case. Even had they been solved, the impact of the strike upon the government may not have been much increased.

It is, of course, true that the TUC pulled its punches. The wish of the General Council to avoid a widespread stoppage in the food and retailing industries, their initial willingness to create some kind of permit system, their reluctance to bring about a total stoppage in the power industries, indicate a tentativeness, even an anxiety, about the use of the weapon of the general strike. But to say that the TUC did not wish to cause severe food shortages or to bring about a cessation of all normal processes of life, is merely to repeat the obvious. The general strike had never been regarded as a revolutionary weapon. Its lineaments were moulded by its confined and modest purposes.

Intelligence and forecasts

Most TUC leaders afterwards averred that the response to the strike call on 4 May had exceeded their expectations, though there had been little to indicate what those expectations were. There is no doubt, however, that as news from the districts came in the mood at Eccleston Square grew more confident. Optimism about the strike's effectiveness was at its peak by the Thursday and Friday of the first week. Thomas told Citrine on Thursday 6 May that 'the railway situation, from the standpoint of the completeness of the strike, is the best that they have ever known in their history'. 'The report of the Strike Committee today,' the Secretary wrote on the seventh, 'showed the position throughout the country to be as solid as a rock.'[31]

The prevailing view of the state of public opinion was apparently equally sanguine. Great store was set by the statement of the churches on the crisis, issued by the Archbishop of Canterbury on 7 May, proposing a negotiated settlement and renewed subsidy. Though receiving no publicity from the BBC or the *British Gazette*, it was widely advertised by the TUC itself, through pamphlet literature as well as in the *British Worker*. The Intelligence Committee had also recommended labour speakers, the previous day, to give attention to similar resolutions, passed by the Caernarvon and Newcastle Councils.[32] Inside the General Council Thomas and Bevin adduced evidence, allegedly representative, that business opinion favoured an initiative to end the strike as quickly as possible.[33]

At this stage, too, the General Council probably still hoped that the government's emergency services would fail. On 6 May the Intelligence Committee informed Marchbank that although supplies to retailers had been successfully maintained, there had been no movement of stocks to wholesalers since the strike began and that this was 'giving rise to anxiety', particularly in the capital. The next day the Strike Organization Committee was told that the official system of distribution had 'broken down' in Plymouth, Salford and Newcastle, and that in all three places the authorities had sought union help in maintaining supplies.[34] The withdrawal of permits elsewhere, ordered by the Central Transport Committee, was clearly expected to increase the pressure on the machinery of supply and transport.

Over the weekend, however, this sense of security began to suffer erosion. Uncertainty revived, not as a result of any marked diminution in support for the stoppage, but because of the growing realization that, despite its acknowledged solidarity, the success of the government's counter-measures might necessitate an indefinite prolongation. Two particular events emphasized this danger. On 9 May the miners rejected the first Samuel memorandum as a basis of negotiation, thus substantially weakening the immediate chance of an agreed resumption. At the same time the government made a sustained attempt, beginning on the night of 7 May, to lift the siege of the London docks. The show of force here laid on, coupled with incidents of aggressive police activity against strikers elsewhere in the country, appeared to indicate the readiness of the state to break the hold of the stoppage on vital services, if necessary by *force majeure*.

By the following week, expectations that the government's emergency apparatus would collapse in due course had largely disappeared. Ben Turner, recounting a weekend visit to his native Yorkshire, was one who expressed a change of mood and judgement:[35] 'On our way home on the Friday the roads were nearly empty of transport. On our way back on the Monday, the nearer we got to London the more one became convinced that it would be well if we could find a means to end the dispute.'

Though Citrine was less anxious on this particular count, he too thought a speedy resolution more and more unlikely, and was writing by Sunday of holding out 'for three or four weeks at the longest' – a forecast the more uncertain since 'even the most ardent advocates of the General Strike have usually reasoned in terms of a few hours' or days' stoppage at the most'.[36]

The possibility of a long-drawn-out strike raised fears, as will be seen, of growing disorder, gradual defections, and widespread victimization. The most immediate and tangible problem actually to be confronted, however, was that of finance. As it had anticipated, the TUC soon found itself faced by claims for monetary assistance from embattled unions which were hard to satisfy. On 4 May the Council requested accounts of their resources from those organizations not directly affected by the stoppage. But the Finance and General Purpose Committee subsequently reported that 'in the majority of cases the replies pointed out that the position of the unions was changing every day as the membership participating in the strike or being thrown out of work increased daily. Trade Unions could therefore not guarantee what funds would be available. . . .'[37] On the eighth the SOC issued a direct appeal to employed union members to forward five per cent of their earnings to their head offices. But there was little prospect of this request, even if observed, yielding substantial sums in the short term. While the strike lasted the Council had perforce to rely on such *ex gratia* contributions as its affiliates were willing to make.[38]

It was quickly evident that these would be insufficient. Prior to 13 May the Finance and General Purpose Committee had been given £13,000 by various donors and promised another £14,000.[39] During the strike demands for help came mainly from small unions heavily committed by it – though also from the more important National Union of Printing and Paper Workers. But in the week following its termination similar applications were made by the T&GWU, the

Locomotive Engineers and the Electricians – followed later by the Iron and Steel Federation, the Boilermakers and the Typographical Association.[40] And had the General Strike continued it is clear that almost every union would quickly have faced a simple choice between bankruptcy and the cancellation of dispute benefits. Some had already done so; the iron and steel workers had been unable to afford national strike payments from the outset, whilst both the paper workers and the engineers could pay only a reduced rate of assistance.[41] Even wealthy unions like the NUR could not have expected to survive insolvency for any length of time; commanding £2 million in assets on 1 May, the railwaymen had spent almost £1 million on strike benefits by 12 May. At least one organization, the Workers' Union, was irreparably ruined by the events of 1926, being left with debts of £35,000 which it could never repay.[42]

The General Council had no chance of offsetting losses on such a scale. In all, eventually, it disbursed some £17,000 to member unions other than the miners – much of it to compensate workers victimized or prosecuted after the stoppage was over. A rather larger sum was made available in the form of loans, from credit obtained mainly through IFTU; but whilst the strike continued this recourse was legally hazardous.[43] Nor, at this juncture, was the Russian support upon which the miners chiefly relied during the subsequent lock-out either desired by or permitted to the TUC.

The Council in fact deliberately refused help from this source. On 6 May it received a telegram from the Russian Central Council of Trade Unions to say that a donation of 250,000 roubles had been made to the strike, and a cheque for £26,247 arrived next day. On Saturday morning the TUC leaders discussed what to do with this unsolicited aid and, concluding that its acceptance would be 'wilfully misinterpreted and misunderstood', returned the money to the Soviet Union.[44] If this decision had not been taken voluntarily it would certainly have been constrained, for three days later Lloyds Bank told Citrine that a further grant of £100,000 was being withheld under the emergency regulations, and a cheque from IFTU was unpaid for the same reason. The government's decision to cut off external aid of this kind was the one significant legal restriction imposed on the unions during the stoppage.[45] It was, however, manifestly their own sense of vulnerability to allegations of revolutionary sympathies that prompted the Council's decision of 8 May – and caused it thereby to compound one difficulty whilst admitting another.

The government's attitude to financial assistance from abroad might well have suggested the possibility of more crippling measures to follow; but there is, in fact, surprisingly little indication that the General Council took this threat seriously. The decision on 7 May to suspend recording minutes was ostensibly taken for security reasons, but it was also readily explicable as a consequence of the reduction of the Council's responsibilities; the SOC adopted no equivalent precautions. There was evidently no subsequent talk of likely police action.[46] Moreover, it seems that neither of the two supposedly authoritative pronouncements on the illegality of the General Strike during the nine days caused disquiet. Sir John Simon's speech in the House of Commons on 6 May was answered relatively briefly in the *British Worker* two days later by the blunt assertion that the unions were acting within their rights. On the tenth it was dealt with more lengthily by Sir Henry Slesser, the most eminent expert on trade-union law among the Labour MPs. According to his account, however, this reply was made against the specific instructions of Ramsay MacDonald; and whether or not the Labour leader had been asked by Eccleston Square to let sleeping dogs lie, it is obviously unlikely that he would have recommended silence if the TUC leadership had desired a public rebuttal.[47] The stoppage was also declared illegal by Mr Justice Astbury on 10 May in response to an application by the seamen's union for an injunction restraining dissident branches from paying out strike funds; but this again attracted only passing attention from the TUC. An unsigned note of a phone conversation on the morning of 12 May records that a legal opinion was sought on the judge's *obiter dicta*. This was, of course, after the termination of the strike had been decided; and in any case the advice received was that Astbury 'had not decided anything about a general strike'.[48] In the aftermath Citrine was to dismiss this episode, too, as without significance.[49]

Their complacency over the legal issue raised by the stoppage strengthens the impression that the General Council knew nothing of the government's deliberations on the possibility of legislation.[50] The official decision to allow the *British Worker* to continue publication, the gradual cessation of governmental philippics on the unconstitutionality of the strike and the very prolongation of the conflict, tended to quieten any fears on this score. What did create alarm, as will be seen, were the divinations of an increasingly rigorous enforcement of the existing law, and the emergency regulations which had supplemented it. Preoccupied with outbreaks of violence in the localities, the union leadership could not conceive that the Cabinet was looking elsewhere.

As the strike entered its second week, therefore, the General Council displayed an increasing ambivalence, conscious both of present achievements and of future dangers. Their perception of both can be judged from two reports submitted to them by the Intelligence Committee on the mornings of 11 and 12 May (each based on information gathered, and perhaps partly communicated, the previous day). On nearly all counts the two documents offered similar, though not identical, appraisals. The strike was being loyally observed almost everywhere: 'The reports show no weakening on the part of the workers' (11 May), and 'indicate no real breach in the solidarity of the strike' (12 May). Its economic effects were increasingly deleterious: 'the grip of the strike is now exerting pressure through transport difficulties, coal shortage and shortage of raw materials. Even the Government admit . . . that factories and workshops are closing down . . . relatively little production is going on' (11 May); 'many factories are stopping work owing to shortage of fuel, shortage of raw material, lack of power, or inability to get their output transported' (12 May).

In other respects, however, these surveys were less comforting. They noted some initial defections among the strikers, the earlier survey mentioning printing workers, the later adding tramwaymen at Portsmouth, Southampton and, imminently, Reading. And though on 11 May the Intelligence Committee had appeared undisturbed by these symptoms, on the twelfth they were distinctly more pessimistic: 'There is evidence that a slight leakage is beginning to take place, which may or may not tend to spread . . . the position on the fringes is not so firm as it was. . . . As a whole, the strike is perfectly solid but these elements of uncertainty cannot be altogether disregarded.' Both reports admitted, too, if they did not emphasize, the government's success in maintaining food supplies in most areas. Almost no goods trains were running, according to the bulletin of the eleventh, but 'food and other supplies are being carried by water or by road (under strong military protection)'. 'The position with regard to food is somewhat obscure,' it concluded. 'The Government are in serious difficulties in some areas, e.g. the North East coast, but it is now forcing greater supplies through the docks.' Next day, again, the verdict was more pessimistic. Though local shortages were still alleged to exist, 'the Government organization is improving'. Both documents referred, besides, to the arrest of pickets and strikers, and the latter suggested that 'it is clear from yesterday's events' – in Birmingham, Chesterfield and London – 'that the Government is becoming more aggressive.'

It would be difficult to regard these assessments as alarmist. They indicated a marked inadequacy in the General Council's information, the effect of which was indeed to foster a somewhat sanguine view of the success of the strike. The claims about economic disruption were vague and undocumented, those about local dearths probably outdated. The instances of resumptions of work, on the other hand, were certainly understated. The Intelligence Committee's retrospective report to the General Council in June 1926 was on all these counts more reserved.[51]

The surveys did provide grounds for the belief, however, that the indefinite continuance of the General Strike could not be borne. Despite the discernment of a prevalent public desire for peace, there was no sign that the government would be required or inclined to come to terms. Nor were the Intelligence Committee disposed to think that the withdrawal of the 'second wave' would reduce its resistance.[52] The only prospect which the reports offered was a war of attrition. From this perspective even small-scale breakaways and scattered confrontations with the police appeared as premonitions of what was to come.

The leading members of the Strike Organization Committee were, it is true, still relatively phlegmatic. Although Bevin had evidently little confidence in the advantages of widening the stoppage, he did not anticipate any rapid decline.

> You could not sit in that Strike Organization room with the deputations and committees coming in all the time from all over the country without sensing pretty clearly about how long we could carry it, having regard to all the positions of the different industries, and I felt and said [on Friday and Saturday] that we would reach the maximum of strength about the following Tuesday, – then it would be a case of 'holding out', and I thought approximately three weeks would be necessary after that to clear up. . . .

From Citrine's account, and Bevin's later comments, it seems unlikely that his estimate altered much until the strike was over.[53]

In contrast, the railwaymen especially thought that the stoppage could not be maintained for so long. J. H. Thomas expressed growing anxiety about the threat of dismissals; his fellow-secretary, C. T. Cramp, agreed with Ben Turner on Monday night that the strike 'must not go on much longer' than that week; the footplatemen's leader, John Bromley, was already predicting 'a débacle'.[54] Both were influenced by the fact that previous disputes in the industry had been of short duration.[55] And even if the membership of the NUR and the ASLEF remained firm, both the uncertainty among the railway clerks and the increasing success of the companies in restarting services made their continued loyalty dubious. The majority of the General Council almost certainly shared this opinion. Citrine, consistently unemotional and detached, wrote an assessment of the situation on 9 May full of foreboding. 'I have never heard anyone previous to this event who had contemplated a general strike lasting even a fortnight. . . . Can we afford to risk . . . the disintegration that may follow rapidly from a return to work in certain sections. The logical thing is to make the best conditions while our members are solid.' And he reports discussion among his colleagues on Monday night which led to the same conclusions: 'while the position of our forces was strong, we could not count upon a continuance of the dispute without serious danger of breakaways'.[56]

The expectation of growing disorder constituted a further, pressing anxiety for the General Council. The occurrence of blacklegging, the intensification of emergency services, the imminent stoppage of the engineers, the exposure of many strikers to increasing financial hardship and the supposed aggressiveness of the police alike accentuated this fear. 'The principal danger' of the well-publicized military convoys to the docks, Citrine considered, was 'the effect . . . on the morale of our men. When some of them see their jobs being filled by scallywag volunteers they may get desperate and resort to forcible means. That means disorder; and that in turn means an excuse for police and military intervention.'[57] Harold Laski reflected Pugh's susceptibility to the same alarm in a letter to Felix Frankfurter: 'They [the unions] had reached the peak with group one. To call out group two, postal workers, electricians and so on, would have meant violence and from that anything.'[58] And it may well have been this concern, primarily, which was recalled in J. H. Thomas's vague and melodramatic statement to the Commons the day after the stoppage ended: 'What I dreaded about the strike more than anything else was this: If by any chance it would have got out of the hands of those who would be able to exercise some control, every sane man knows what would have happened.'[59] What most union leaders feared, it may be assumed, was not a Communist conspiracy, but the spread of local and individual acts of indiscipline, and the consequence of systematic repression.

The General Council's doubts about the future course of the strike was not based upon much tangible evidence, but they were not for that reason chimerical. Whatever losses the stoppage inflicted on the economy and whatever hardships on the community, these were insufficient to force the government to come to the negotiating table.

The reinforcement of the stoppage was possible, but there was no indication that this would produce the desired effect, and considerable worry that it would provoke strict counter-measures by the public authorities. The tactical consideration, that victimization could only be prevented if the stoppage were called off while still at its most effective, was plausible and at least partly justified by events. Doubtless many employers would have preferred to see a more disorderly retreat.[60] At the same time, the reluctance to prolong the stoppage did distort the Council's view of the Samuel memorandum, the so-called settlement which was exploited to call it off. It will be argued that the TUC leadership, deeply anxious to bring the conflict to a close, wilfully deceived themselves about the status of Samuel as a negotiator and the authority of the terms which they agreed with him. Whatever the merits of those terms in themselves, their acceptance in the circumstances was a *de facto* surrender signifying that, limited though its objectives had been, the General Strike had no power to achieve them.

VII The Conduct of the General Strike: Whitehall

As the threatened General Strike drew nearer, the government's battery of emergency measures was primed. The names of civil commissioners and their divisional staffs were communicated to local authorities on 30 April. The first emergency proclamation came into force at midnight on that date, and the provisions for rationing and distributing coal were introduced as the lock-out began. On 1 May, prompted by the decision of the conference of union executives, the Supply and Transport Committee moved the commissioners to their posts, authorized volunteer service committees to start enlisting labour from the second, alerted naval ratings and civilian recruits to be ready for a stoppage of power workers and arranged to take over Hyde Park as a transport and milk depot. On the third, advertisements for special constables were published precipitating the first, unofficial, strike action in Fleet Street.[1]

Once the national stoppage had commenced the emergency machinery had to prove its effectiveness in four principal spheres: providing volunteer labour; affording means of transport, especially by road; ensuring adequate food supplies; and preserving order. The difficulties encountered varied considerably from region to region, depending on the extent and proximity of food sources, the distribution and density of population, the number and temper of the strikers, and the competence and energy of local and divisional officials. A definitive judgement on the success of the counter-strike measures would thus require an examination of each of the fifteen divisions of the country. But in only a handful of cases was there any suggestion, even from the labour side, that a breakdown of services had occurred; and most such reports were ill-informed and probably exaggerated. The performance of the emergency organization in general was one factor which created among ministers in Whitehall a growing sense of confidence and even complacency.

The problem which before the strike had appeared most incalculable and raised most official doubts was the recruitment of volunteers. In the event, however, this difficulty proved to have been largely imaginary. Those who attested a willingness to work during the strike numbered over 300,000 and perhaps as many as half a million. The manpower was not distributed evenly throughout the country; the one source which offers a regional breakdown (unofficial, but plausibly conservative in its estimates) indicates that nearly half the enrolments in England and Wales were in London and the home counties.[2] But in only two divisions did the stated numbers available fall below 20,000: the Northern, with 18,000, and South Wales with 12,186. In neither case would an efficient supply of such dimensions have been inadequate. In the London region, for instance, of 114,000 men coming forward by 11 May only 9,500 had been given work, and in the South Midlands only about 10,000 jobs could be found for double the number of volunteers.[3]

Broadly speaking, the supply and transport organization seems to have commanded a superfluity of unskilled labour and an adequate supply of those key workers whose absence might have seriously affected vital services. The latter had because of their importance sometimes been specially enlisted independently of the Volunteer Service Committees. The preparations made for running the London power stations had involved the selection of about three thousand trained or expert staff capable of assisting the engineers in charge of the generating plant. The recruitment of locomotive drivers was left to the railway companies, but they were supplied with official information about suitable colonial servants and military personnel on leave. Car drivers were obtained, outside the capital, through the good offices of the motoring organizations, and some temporary lorry drivers were provided by special training schools established during the stoppage both in London and on a small scale in South Wales, Liverpool, Cambridge and Bristol.[4]

The volunteers recruited by the OMS, in contrast, were evidently more impressive for their quantity than their quality. Though it claimed before the stoppage to be performing an essential function in registering potential replacements for strikers, the importance of the Organization was afterwards dismissed in a casual note by Sir John Anderson: 'apart from the fact that it trained a few drivers its practical utility was almost nil'. 'Only a very small proportion of the names on the OMS lists were used,' said the official Home Office report. 'Our experience during the General Strike,' Joynson-Hicks told Lord Hardinge afterwards, 'goes to show that so far as general labourers and special constables are concerned, there is no need for any recruiting machinery in normal times.'[5]

In fact, the OMS boasted of having handed over 100,000 names to the Volunteers Service Committees in England and Wales in 159 centres (a figure excluding some of the special police constables offered to the police authorities). Of these just over 5,000 were certainly employed, mainly in a variety of transport services.

TABLE 5. *Employment of OMS volunteers*[6]

lorry drivers	1,312
bus drivers	144
car drivers	1,345
motor mechanics	351
Post Office drivers	250
tramway men	91
power station workers	1,194
inland waterway workers	116
railway workers	640

Although other OMS recruits may have been engaged in more menial tasks, this was the full extent of its assistance in what might be regarded as essential occupations. And even on the quoted list it seems probable that most of the men supplied to power stations and to the railway services were unskilled.

The placement of the OMS volunteers can be instructively compared with the distribution of jobs undertaken – outside their own district, and mainly in the capital – by the more indiscriminately enlisted Cambridge students.

TABLE 6. *Employment of Cambridge undergraduates*[7]

London underground staff	137
London special constables	710
London bus operators	100
London tramway drivers	36
Air Ministry employment	64
car and lorry drivers	99
dock workers	460
railway workers	63
power station workers	64
general labour	308

On this evidence, it seems that the bulk of the voluntary labour was divided into five significant categories. Those who could drive were almost always employed doing so, acting usually either as supplementary lorry drivers, or providing courier, passenger and newspaper services by car. The only other class of strategical importance were the small number of hand-picked students drafted into the London power stations – accompanied by a much larger body doing unskilled jobs, primarily stoking. The third, and probably the largest group overall, were the special constables, mobilized in most large towns but particularly numerous in the capital. The other major occupations of volunteers were those of docker and general labourer. In the ports they were employed mainly in clearing goods which were already unloaded, for which neither manual skill nor mechanical equipment was needed. Some of the London volunteers (and probably others too) were later used on board ship, but their numbers were somewhat restricted by the lack of lightermen to remove cargoes by river. The residual body of general labour performed a variety of auxiliary functions: loading and discharging cars and lorries, delivering newspapers and messages, operating catering units and so forth.

How this amorphous mass of temporary labour was composed it is not yet possible to determine. Strike propaganda, and much subsequent historiography, asserted it to be largely or wholly middle- and upper-class in character. Peers working in Printing House Square, ex-army officers driving trains, students and club-men patrolling city streets, were certainly part of the picture. Car-owners were obviously unlikely to be working-class, and the motor pool administered by Lord Curzon in Horse Guards Parade was a particularly popular rendezvous for London Society. It is also plausible to suggest that the OMS had attested volunteers mainly from the higher social strata.[8] But it is probable, too, that a large proportion of the emergency manpower was drawn from clerical and manual labour. The most natural and effective substitutes for strikers in 1926, as in the past, were those industrially and socially homologous to them: the non-unionists, the unemployed, retired or white-collar staff from the same establishment or trade. In the industrial north it seems likely that middle-class volunteers were more scarce than in London, and that reliance upon those of wage-earning status who stood outside the ranks of the strikers, was correspondingly greater. It may be suggestive that, in Newcastle for instance, the Civil Commissioner reported difficulty in recruiting special constables, but none in finding alternative dock labour.[9]

The extent to which voluntary labour was obtained from such sources as these can be illustrated, but not quantified. The workers sent to the London docks were partly, perhaps mainly, unorganized Covent Garden porters. On the Liverpool waterside they were ships' clerks. Elderly and retired engine drivers were to be found working in southern England, and perhaps elsewhere, outside their own home districts. Railway clerks remaining at work, according to the unions, were liable to be shifted to manual jobs. Non-unionists (and blacklegs pure and simple) helped to maintain provincial bus services and road transport of goods. In Swindon, Great Western Railway employees on strike enlisted with the local volunteer committee, and some Plymouth tramwaymen were retrained as lorry drivers.[10] But what, perhaps, affords the most positive evidence for the presence of manual workers among the ranks of volunteers and substitutes is the incidence of victimization once the strike was over. The dismissal of former employees was clearly facilitated in many cases by the willingness of those who had replaced them to accept permanent jobs. Many casualties of the strike could only have been, in one form or another, victims of the action of fellow-workers.

The supply of voluntary labour was one factor, though only a marginal one, in securing the successful operation of road transport during the strike. Many of the haulage committees responsible for organizing and allocating motor lorries were able to rely on regular drivers. In London the special convoys to the docks and the Hyde Park milk scheme were largely dependent on temporary recruits. But such highly centralized operations were uncommon; elsewhere in the country individual hauliers were normally left to carry out the instructions of the committees and food officers on their own initiative, applying for additional labour if they required it, but retaining and paying it thereafter as part of their own workforce.

The efficiency with which commercial road transport functioned during the crisis appeared afterwards to be the most vital if not the most spectacular aspect of the success of emergency administration. The Ministry of Transport concluded the day after the strike terminated, 'it is apparent that the local road organization has worked satisfactorily in all Divisions, and has been quite equal to meeting the demands made upon it'.[11] The road commissioners had no need to resort to requisitioning vehicles in any area, and only in two divisions, the North West and the South Midlands, was it even necessary to introduce a compulsory system of priorities, requiring lorry owners to carry food and other necessities in preference to alternative loads.[12]

In general, the system of distribution worked without any marked sense of strain.

This success is traceable to several factors. Undoubtedly the road transport organization was a tribute to the voluntaryist principle. The haulage committees, composed of transport proprietors and firmly rooted in their own localities, found no difficulty in adapting themselves to the needs of the occasion, prompted by a satisfying admixture of public spiritedness to private interest – anxious to avoid any enlargement of public control, and happy no doubt to appropriate new business from the railways. They were helped by the fact that the full weight of the task of distribution fell on them only two or three days after the stoppage had begun, when retailers' stocks grew low, and when the strikers' own readiness to distribute permits for the purposes of food supply was diminishing. By that time the haulage committees had already improved their own service, by process of trial and error. Throughout the stoppage, besides, the amount of normal carrying to be done was constantly being reduced, whilst by its end the renewal of a skeleton rail service had partly relieved the burden on road transport.[13]

There were a few, not very serious, criticisms of the working of the scheme. In some places the members of the committees used their influential positions to raise charges for their services, and the Minister of Transport afterwards echoed his officials' opinion that haulage users were inadequately represented in the organization. Relations between the chairmen of haulage committees and the road officers subordinate to the divisional commissioners were not always good – the former being inclined to regard the latter as superfluous. The co-ordination of local agents for transport, food and volunteer recruitment was more difficult because they frequently worked within different territorial boundaries, and had differing notions of their mutual responsibilities.[14]

It was road transport, nonetheless, which provided the effective key to continued food supply during the General Strike. Once consumables could be moved easily from wholesalers and millers to retailers and where necessary to customers by this means, the danger of shortages became slight. The London and Glasgow milk schemes – the former covering a radius of a hundred miles or more – worked so well that both Scotland and the capital enjoyed a surplus of milk before the end of the strike. The *production* of food presented little difficulty in the case of the most basic manufactured perishable, bread, since workers in the flour and baking industry at first remained at work and never struck more than partially and spasmodically. To ensure continued output, naval vessels were used to distribute yeast from Scottish and Irish distillers to the major English ports.[15] Thus although the President of the Board of Trade had acquired powers to impose rationing under the emergency regulations, these were exercised only in the case of coal.[16] Price controls over foodstuffs were administered by voluntary arrangements between civil commissioners and local retailers. Here again, as in the case of road haulage, the system of modified *laissez-faire* worked well, preventing increases in the case of fruit, vegetables and dairy products, and restricting them to no more than ½d to 1d per pound for meat, bread and sugar.[17] The public, for its part, reassured probably by the appearance of normality and the obvious evidence of continuing supply and distribution, showed no inclination, except in the few days prior to the strike, to resort to hoarding.

One revealing index of the effectiveness of the voluntary system of food control was the willingness of the Co-operative Society at national level, and sometimes of its local branches, to rely upon the state emergency machinery in the manner of other shopkeepers. The co-operatives were liable to suffer more than most retailers from the stoppage in view of the relatively high unionization of their employees, and many of their officers were resentful at the common reluctance of the unions and the General Council to afford them immunity. Some of their representatives pressed the government to publish a promise to afford statutory protection to union members remaining at work. On 8 May, moreover, a deputation of their directors saw Cunliffe-Lister to ask for the assistance of government agencies where necessary to maintain their services.[18] This step may have been taken in order to put pressure on the TUC to be more indulgent to its supposed ally and associate. But the divisional food officers were instructed to provide volunteers, transport and police protection where requested; and in the northern region, at least, the co-operative management had officially applied for such help before the end of the strike.[19]

The efficiency of distribution would not of course have safeguarded the food situation unless stocks had been sufficient and capable of being released. It was this consideration which focussed attention on the ports, where large reserves of foodstuffs were available but pickets were in some cases concentrated. Volunteer labour was moved into the docks at Liverpool, Bristol, Cardiff, Glasgow and Leith during the first five days of the stoppage. Before the end of the strike the majority of provincial English ports had been mobilized, sometimes under police protection, but with only occasional obstruction.[20] A more acute problem of access was, however, encountered in the port of London, the main artery of food supply for southern and central England, whose scattered conduits were heavily guarded by strikers. By 6 May stocks of flour and sugar in the capital and elsewhere had fallen alarmingly low, and apprehension about the effects of the blockade was expressed also in the south west and the south midlands.[21] The ministers concerned, however, were not unduly disquieted. The Supply and Transport Committee minuted on 6 May that they 'were satisfied that as soon as the dock area had been opened up so as to enable movement of food from the docks, the problem of food distribution would be solved'.[22] The previous evening Moore-Brabazon had been given the post of special commissioner for the post of London, with a staff of eight. Some 550 volunteers were introduced into the Victoria docks by river on the night of 7 May and increased to 1,000 by 10 May. 111 lorries travelled through the East End under military escort during 8 May, principally to bring away loads of flour and sugar. On Monday, the London and St Katherine docks and the south side wharves were also being worked – and Cunliffe-Lister was able to tell the Supply and Transport Committee that the reports of the food officers to the Board of Trade were the best since the strike had begun.[23]

Was the relief of the food situation likely to be permanent? The Road Commissioner in the North West believed that 'if the strike had not been called off . . . we could have gone on working foodstuffs without any serious difficulty indefinitely, and in fact improvements might have been made so as to facilitate the movement of many other commodities'. This view was evidently shared by most other divisional officials.[24] Only one significant note of dissent was sounded, by the food officer of the south-west division, E. F. Strange, who contended after the strike was over that 'the huge problem of replacing rail by road-borne transport was never thoroughly tested. Had the General Strike lasted another fortnight or even another week, a very different story would have had to be recorded.'[25] Strange's pessimism was based on the prediction, not unrealistic, that as reserves of food in local shops and warehouses fell, the necessity of moving supplies over longer distances, particularly from the ports, would rise proportionately. But even he did not expect the emergency machinery to collapse, anticipating only the prospect of gradually tightening controls. The pressure in any case might well have increased less than he expected. Road transport was never the sole means of distribution: the slowly reviving railway service (already carrying food again by the end of the stoppage), coastal shipping and inland waterways, were all useful auxiliaries, capable of further exploitation.[26] The chief threat to the emergency operations probably lay not in dwindling supplies but in increasing interference on the part of the strikers. But there is no indication that such action would have been authorized by the unions at any stage; and so long as it remained sporadic and unofficial, police counter-measures were almost everywhere effective.

Law and order

The actual and potential level of violence had been the principal source of anxiety for the Supply and Transport Committee during the first week of May. The movement of troops after 1 May, though inconspicuous, was some indication of this; and throughout the strike messages from the provinces were gathered and collated by Sir John Anderson at Whitehall, to assess the extent of obstruction and disorder. Against both, the Committee's precautionary measures were increasingly elaborate.

Symons and Farman, repeating allegations made at the time by the TUC, suggest that the authorities became more aggressive and determined in their enforcement of law and order as the strike proceeded.[27] Whatever the justification for this view it is apparent that, at the centre, the chief measures of security were taken in the first few days of the stoppage. On 5 May the Home Secretary prompted the Supply and Transport Committee 'greatly to augment' the force of London special constables, fixing a target of 50,000. The following day the Committee decided to recommend a new force of full-time police auxiliaries to the Cabinet. The Civil Constabulary Reserve was accordingly set up, recruited from Territorial Army units and other former soldiers, controlled by the War Office (though deployed by the chief constables) and designed, though never in the event used, specifically for crowd control. The police authorities were also instructed by the Home Office, again at the beginning of the stoppage, to apply the most stringent interpretation of the laws concerning peaceful picketing.[28] After this initial burst of zealous activity, however, the government were evidently satisfied with the course of events. Between 10 and 12 May Anderson's reports to his colleagues suggested that the danger of serious disturbances had lessened; and although the Committee continued to discuss the possibility of further restricting peaceful picketing, this seemed to represent a major hindrance to traffic only in the northern division. Where there were more arrests of strikers during the second week than the first, this could reasonably be attributed, in the absence of contrary evidence, to local initiative, as individual police forces, strengthened by newly enlisted special constables, reversed their initially lenient or passive attitude towards picketing.[29] The pattern of arrests remained much too variable, however, to suggest that increased severity was the result of influence exerted from above.

By the latter stages of the strike, the forces at the disposal of the authorities, central and local, were sufficient to quieten almost all apprehensions. The number of special constables recruited in the capital rose from 3,035 on 4 May to 51,807 by 11 May. The Civil Constabulary Reserve, which remained inactive, reached a total of 9,000. About 200,000 'second reserve' policemen were mobilized elsewhere in England and Wales. Under the control of local police forces, these part-time volunteers were probably used in differing degrees. In London some of the local stations were grateful for the private cars which they provided for police transport; but in the opinion of one of the metropolitan chief constables, 'on the one hand much valuable assistance was lost through want of proper organization and control, whilst on the other many desirable and enthusiastic volunteers were disheartened through the use, or want of use, made of their services.[30] Elsewhere, if the numbers retained on the 'second reserve' in September 1926 are an indication, they were enlisted mainly in the counties rather than the boroughs, and were more numerous in the South and West than in the North and Midlands.[31] They were, however, occasionally transported from one area to another during the strike. If they were unpopular with trade unionists, they did prevent extensive use of the military, something for which both sides were grateful.

Apart from giving protection to the London docks and the Hyde Park convoys, the army appears to have taken little or no active part in the General Strike. Despite the sabre-rattling of the *British Gazette*, soldiers were given no special powers under the Emergency Regulations; and their attendance on the caravanserai to the East End, though dramatically impressive, was not necessitated by any inadequacy in the police. Otherwise, though troop movements continued to take place between 1 and 12 May the army remained almost invisible, stimulating scattered rumours – whose propagators were heavily punished – of mutiny and confinement to barracks.[32]

The other services played a slightly larger role in events, though not a particularly combative one. The RAF helped to distribute the *British Gazette*, and later *The Times*, to areas distant from London. Naval vessels maintained surveillance at Hull, Liverpool, Clydeside, Newport and other ports, and their crews protected waterside installations. The navy also took over Tilbury ferry, running it with a certain lack of proficiency. Four submarines provided electricity for some of the reopened London docks and sailors acted as dock gatemen and tugboatmen there. Ratings helped to move petrol by barge from Thamesside depots into the city. But their most important role was to man the capital's generating stations where affected by the strike, and by 9 May thirty-three of sixty-one establishments were at least partly dependent on their assistance.[33]

Local and private enterprise

In the establishment of public services during the strike responsibility did not always, of course, lie with the central government. Local authorities supervised the rationing and distribution of coal and maintained public utilities, including the electricity supply outside London. The restoration of municipal tramway services depended on their initiative, though in the capital, and probably in most other centres, private bus services were relatively more successful in continuing operations.[34] Even among Labour councils, only a small minority tried systematically to reinforce the stoppage by refusing facilities for the recruitment of volunteers or by restricting power for industrial uses.[35] Those who threatened such obstruction were liable to penalties under the Emergency Powers Act. But the majority of Labour councillors (like the mayor of Birmingham, who chaired the city's Emergency Committee) probably thought their first duty to be owed to their local electorate as a whole, and displayed in more pronounced form the strikers' own inclination to preserve the essentials of communal life.[36]

The railways were also largely outside the state's purview, counter-strike measures being left to the companies. Though their representatives were present at some divisional offices, and though official advice had been given them concerning military staff and other public servants with useful experience, the predominant part of their labour needs were provided by the volunteer service committees or by their own efforts. These needs were to remain severely limited. Though the LM&S claimed after the strike that it 'would very soon have been in a position to deal effectively with all railway business offering', this statement itself testified that both passenger and, even more, goods traffic was greatly curtailed by the stoppage. In fact the company enrolled nearly 22,000 volunteers, but could find jobs for only 7,662. Clearly the crucial factor in restoring services was the availability of enginemen and these remained in short supply. The Great Western Railway – with the Southern the most successful in restoring services – had according to Dr Bagwell enlisted only 760 volunteer enginemen by the end of the stoppage; and the figure for trains run on 12 May suggests that this constituted about half their current strength in the department, the remainder presumably being drawn from their own employees. With the aid of this miscellaneous manpower, the railway combines had still made significant improvements in their schedules by the end of the stoppage. It seems almost certain, however, that further restoration of services would have depended on the return of strikers, both footplatemen and engineers, of which there was little sign.[37]

TABLE 7. *Number of trains run, and percentage of normal service, 5–12 May*[38]

		5 May	%	*8 May*	%	*12 May*	%
LMS	passenger	423	3·8	861	7·6	1,494	13·4
	goods	23	0·5	55	1·2	169	3·4
LNER	passenger	281	3·4	757	8·0	1,107	13·4
	goods	6	0·1	23	0·5	171	3·6
GWR	passenger	194	3·7	612	11·6	1,170	22·2
	goods	8	0·5	47	2·9	128	8·0
SR	passenger	335	5·1	794	12·3	1,462	22·7
	goods	9	0·8	27	2·5	48	4·5
Total		1,279		3,176		5,479	

The Trade Disputes bill and its postponement

The government's confidence in the adequacy of the emergency provisions made before the General Strike proved, in general, to be fully justified. Though there were occasional signs of nervousness in the early stages, both ministers and officials at Whitehall acquired a growing sense of security. Not only the efficiency of the machinery they had set up and the response of volunteers, but also the normal good temper and discipline of the strikers themselves buttressed their optimism. No-one displayed assurance more overtly, according to J. C. C. Davidson, than the Home Secretary Joynson-Hicks, who

> . . . up to the beginning of the strike had been known as Mussolini Minor and about whose possible conduct of affairs many despondent Civil Servants had grave doubts [but who] not only handled the [Supply and Transport] Committee with supreme skill, but showed that he really understood his own countrymen. Jix was never rattled, was most businesslike and adopted a policy with regard to the police which it is not too strong to say was superb.[39]

Though Churchill and Birkenhead continued, at their irregular appearances on the Committee, to commend drastic policies, they were outweighed by their more moderate and phlegmatic juniors: Mitchell-Thomson, Cunliffe-Lister, Ashley and Davidson – supported by the departmental officials; and the diehards themselves were probably belligerent from native temperament rather than from fear of a débacle.

The dwindling appeal of extremist measures for the Cabinet was visible also in its changing point of view on the question of anti-union legislation. At the outset of the stoppage penal measures against the organizations involved had been considered a matter of some urgency. But by its second week they were felt to be both superfluous and inadvisable. Though the government remained committed to enacting restrictive measures of industrial law in the future, the defeat of the General Strike was regarded as certain without them.

Baldwin had apparently warned J. H. Thomas after his first encounter with the Industrial Committee that 'if there was a general strike the pressure . . . to restrict the powers of the Trade Unions would become irresistible; he would be driven to deal with a Political Levy, the Ballot, and the Trade Disputes Act'. On the first day of the strike itself he talked in similar vein to Tom Jones: the government must respond to the 'tremendous centralizing' of union government by enforcing fuller consultation of the rank and file.[40] These intimations of eventual action, however, did not bear upon the problem of defeating the strike itself, which seemed primarily to require restrictions on the use of union funds. In this matter it was probably not the Prime Minister who took the initiative.

The first target of governmental proscription was in fact financial help, or prospective help, for the TUC from overseas. On 3 May the emergency regulations were supplemented so as to permit Secretaries of State to hold up such payments 'for any purpose prejudicial to the public safety of the community'.[41] The amendment was clearly prompted by the abiding preoccupation with Russian gold; indeed, the Home Secretary remained convinced even after the strike, and despite the General Council's public refusal of Soviet aid, that some £200,000 had been made available indirectly through the Co-operative Society.[42] In fact use was made of the regulation to hold up payments from the anti-Communist IFTU as well as the USSR. A few days later, besides, the government bent its eyes upon the resources of the unions at home.

On 7 May, when the apprehension of strike disturbances was at its height, the Cabinet instructed its lawyers, Birkenhead, Cave and Hogg, to consider 'what legislation, if any, to strengthen the powers of the Government is necessary and possible, either at the present juncture or in the near future'. This relatively 'diehard' committee, probably influenced by Simon's parliamentary disquisition of the previous evening on the state of the law pertaining to general strikes, recommended the immediate introduction of a simple three-clause bill 'declaring' as illegal any strike of a sympathetic character 'calculated to intimidate or coerce the Government or the community', authorizing the restraint of funds assigned to it by the unions and prohibiting the expulsion of members refusing to participate.[43] On 8 May the Cabinet agreed that the bill should be introduced the following Tuesday, but should be made effective as from 10 May. To prevent the withdrawal of bank deposits in anticipation of this measure, it was intended to issue a further regulation under the Emergency Powers Act through the Privy Council on 9 May, the day before publication.[44]

Though having the appearance of an act of overt repression, however, this proposed legislation seems on closer examination to have been largely symbolic in form and psychological in intent. Trade-union funds were to be immobilized but not confiscated. There was no likelihood that this, in itself, would bring the General Strike to a rapid conclusion: indeed the Cabinet had already authorized increased rates of poor relief to the dependants of workmen on strike. Further, though the bill was to make it a misdemeanour to instigate or join an illegal strike there is no indication, despite superficial symptoms of alarm at Eccleston Square, that the arrest of any of the General Council was contemplated. Even if the government had an exaggerated notion of the scale on which union finances were being deployed to maintain the General Strike, therefore, it is likely that the chief object of the measure *en train* was to reinforce the impact of previous propaganda on the legal and constitutional status of the stoppage, and thereby to hasten a voluntary capitulation.

Most of those ministerial confidantes who after the weekend sought to reverse the policy undertaken, certainly appear to have inferred that this was its purpose; they argued, that is to say, that legislation would intensify union resistance instead of undermining it. Tom Jones, who rallied the support of Baldwin's other private secretaries and of senior civil servants like Niemeyer and Warren Fisher, told the Prime Minister that 'Eccleston Square was already beaten' but that the bill 'would profoundly change the quite peaceful temper of the men now on strike'. The representatives of the LMS and Great Western Railways who saw Baldwin on Monday afternoon likewise forecast that legislation would delay a resumption of work; whilst the Conservative chief whip reported to the Cabinet that backbench opinion was in favour of delay. Within the Cabinet Salisbury, Balfour and even Churchill were by this time inclined to a deferment, the first two on the grounds that a bill passed by so drastic a procedure would be inconsistent with the constitutional principles which the government claimed to uphold.[45] Finally, the king's reluctance to sanction the emergency regulation on union funds was expressed privately to Baldwin and officially by a letter to the Cabinet which in all probability deprecated the bill it was to precede.[46]

On the afternoon of 10 May the Cabinet took stock of the opposition to their proposals and of the 'indications of a tendency towards uncertainty' among some of the strikers, and though agreeing that there was no immediate likelihood of a widespread desertion among the unionists decided to postpone a decision on legislation for another two days. In the meantime they agreed to announce in the Commons their intention of introducing a measure to clarify the state of the law in respect of the strike. The next day Baldwin cancelled this announcement, in expectation of the General Council's termination of the stoppage.[47] The Trade Disputes Act, never a markedly heroic venture, was thus condemned to be no more than a tedious and irrelevant postscript to the General Strike.

VIII News and Propaganda

Whilst the government was clearly the victor in the war of supply and transport in 1926, the struggle for dominance in the field of communications was less decisive in its outcome. Both the Conservative administration and the TUC were inexperienced in this sphere, and both displayed, though in contrasting ways, their lack of expertise. The General Council's failures were partly due to a want of ambition; it produced a newspaper whose primary function was to maintain contact with the men on strike and which only incidentally sought to influence a wider range of opinion. It measured its achievement, therefore, in the discipline and obedience of the trade-union rank and file and their insulation from the propaganda of the opposition – even when it was clear that the attribute of durability alone would not be enough to make the strike prevail. The government, on the other hand, possessed more means of publicity, and was anxious to secure 'public' approval of its own conduct. If it too was less than successful, this was largely because of the shoddiness of its main organ of propaganda, highlighted by the superiority of rival media of news and opinion. In many respects, indeed, these 'neutral' agencies played the most important role in determining the way in which the strike was perceived – by non-participants and even by participants. The lack of panic and even of marked controversy or ill-feeling, so remarkable to foreign observers, was nowhere more assiduously cultivated than at Savoy Hill or Printing House Square.

The *British Worker*

When the General Council decided to include the printing workers among those withdrawn at the outset of the strike, they had evidently intended a complete closure of the national press. A Publicity Committee was appointed on 1 May, consisting of E. L. Poulton of the

Boot and Shoe Workers, J. W. Bowen of the Post Office Union, and Willie Henderson and Herbert Tracey from the TUC staff; but its original purpose was simply to arrange for the passage of information to the ordinary press while it remained active. The committee continued to perform this function after 4 May for the international news services and the foreign press, for which it held twice-daily conferences. Its members had thus no initial orders to establish an organ of their own, and their decision to do so, like most of those taken at Eccleston Square, was the product of hasty improvization.[1]

As soon as the stoppage began, however, the Publicity Committee obviously felt that some means of communication with the strikers should be created. Its first solution was the brief and inadequate *General Council Bulletin*, comprising two or three cyclostyled foolscap pages of miscellaneous strike news and instructions. The opening number of this series was compiled on the morning of 4 May when the Committee discovered that two large vehicles were about to depart for Liverpool to return stranded railwaymen to their homes.[2] The *Bulletin* remained in existence subsequently, as a kind of condensed substitute for the *British Worker*, but its publication and distribution was left largely to the London headquarters of the ILP. Although 25–40,000 copies a day were produced there between 9 and 13 May, it is likely that distribution remained unsystematic and probably restricted largely to the London area.[3]

The suggestion that the General Council should publish its own newspaper was first made to the Publicity Committee by the national officers of the Printing and Kindred Trades Federation on the evening of 3 May. Their request that the *Daily Herald* be allowed to continue production for this purpose was evidently put aside.[4] But the following day Hamilton Fyfe, the *Herald*'s editor, accompanied by representatives of his managerial staff, visited the Committee to urge the same course, on the grounds that the government was about to issue its own paper and that some counterweight was therefore required. The Committee now acceded to this view, and during the evening interviewed officials of the four London-based printing and paper unions, securing their approval for a TUC publication. They decided to produce an evening paper, eight pages long and costing a penny, to begin on 5 May.[5]

Once Poulton and his colleagues had been convinced of the possibility of running their own paper, they saw increasing advantages in doing so. The *British Worker* afforded the General Council a powerful instrument of control over the conduct of the strike. It justified the attempted prohibition of any local publishing ventures and the silencing of the labour press, on the argument that competitors might promulgate conflicting and confusing orders or advice to the rank and file. 'The real reason for [the] close shut-down of all printing,' Tracey told the London Society of Compositors on 6 May, 'was to enable [the] General Council through its Publicity Committee to maintain absolute control of all news or propaganda connected with the strike.'[6]

The appearance of the *British Worker* did, however, create considerable problems which the Publicity Committee had only partly foreseen. Just as the granting of food permits prompted accusations of blacklegging among transport workers, so the publication of a newspaper, albeit a labour one, caused considerable disquiet among the printers. Those required to work felt some doubt to be cast on their loyalty; those not involved saw less reason for the continuance of an incomplete stoppage. The former reaction was encountered by Hamilton Fyfe when he first tried to get the *Herald*'s employees to begin work on the night of 4 May: their objections were overcome only with the help of a written authorization from the General Council.[7] Two days later a deputation from the London Society of Compositors approached the Publicity Committee to propose that since the strike in their industry had failed to prevent a government publication, and since some at least of the papers affected by it were not unfavourable to the TUC's position, the embargo on the national dailies should be lifted.[8] This point of view was not supported by NATSOPA, the principal metropolitan union. But the force of the compositors' argument was strengthened the larger the *British Worker*'s scale of output became.

The necessity of enlarging the production of the TUC paper, and thereby the labour force required for it, was the result simply of difficulties of distribution. The number of copies printed was gradually increased; but although wholesalers and newsagents were usually willing to handle them, the movement of this output from London to the rest of the country continued to present insuperable difficulties. The compositors had maintained that 'the *British Worker* was being published, but was not getting into the hands of the general public', and as late as 9 May William Mellor, its assistant editor, told the Publicity Committee that 'there were whole districts in the southern counties to which they were not going, and to which it was impractical to go'. The committee later admitted that it had turned a blind eye on the production of unauthorized strike bulletins at Gloucester and

Southampton for this reason.[9] Elsewhere the problem of circulation was tackled by the launching of provincial editions; but this, as will be seen, only heightened the disaffection of the printing workers.

The problems of the *British Worker* were further exacerbated by official harassment. A police raid on the offices of the *Herald* on 5 May was undertaken by the city police commissioner. It perhaps had some ministerial approval, but no formal Cabinet authority and threatened the existence of the new paper only momentarily.[10] There followed, however, a more indirect but effective attack on the *Worker*'s vitality. On 7 May Churchill, in his capacity as production manager of the government's *British Gazette*, requisitioned the bulk of the *Herald*'s supply of newsprint. The immediate result was to compel Fyfe and the Publicity Committee to cut the size of the paper to four pages, and it probably also caused them to refrain from further increases in output. The Victoria House press tried, without success, to obtain the release of its reserves.[11] The *British Worker* kept going thanks to some swift adaptation of its machines and the acquisition of further paper from *Racing and Football Outlook* as well as the *New Leader* and *Lansbury's Labour Weekly*, which Churchill had overlooked.[12] Mellor nonetheless described the situation as having again become 'critical' by 11 May and the continuance of publication remained uncertain until the government lifted their embargo two days later. Meanwhile, Churchill's depredations had provided a further, though perhaps superfluous, reason for decentralizing production.

Before recounting the story of the provincial editions, however, it will be convenient to look at the editorial policy of the *Worker*, which remained unchanged throughout the strike. The content of the paper was from the outset rigidly controlled by the Publicity Committee, at least one representative of which was constantly at Fyfe's office to act as censor.[13] The Committee quickly made its weight felt. On 6 May Fyfe wrote to Tracey proposing (while the paper was still in its eight-page format) that some general news should be included in addition to strike news: 'cricket we certainly ought to give'. The Publicity Committee refused; and its secretary replied to Fyfe that in their opinion

> The only news that need be included in the *British Worker* is such as to show the spirit of our own people, the unity of our own action, and the enthusiasm and loyalty with which the General Council's instructions are being carried out. We do not want to publish anything that will frighten or demoralize the public. It is the view of my Committee that the whole contents of the journal should be such as to convince the public that the General Council is in strong

control of the strike situation and that everything which occurs is according to plan, and no apprehension need be entertained by the public regarding the course of events.[14]

The *British Worker* in fact had three main objects. To maintain the morale of the strikers required the constant rebuttal of government claims of defections among them, and repeated instructions not to believe the news retailed by the *British Gazette* or the BBC. The paper naturally suppressed references to such resumptions of work as did take place. It did not deny coverage to Simon's speech on the illegality of the strike, but attempted to answer his arguments on the front page of the edition of 8 May – and it made no mention of Astbury's subsequent judgement on the same issue. It reported the military convoy from the London docks on the ninth (as well as the Plymouth football match), but presented it as an unnecessary show of force calculated to create an undue sense of alarm. The maintenance of strike discipline was urged in daily calls for exemplary conduct by all workers, and orders to pickets 'to avoid obstruction and confine themselves to their legitimate duties'. Occasional warnings were issued of particular troublespots like the London docks. The occurrence of disturbances was given little or no attention. 'Dangerous rumours' printed by other, less responsible, organs were contradicted. The other purpose of the Publicity Committee, though less consistently and deliberately pursued, was to help create a body of public opinion favourable to a negotiated settlement. Besides reiterating its assertion that the strike was constitutional, the *British Worker* gave large coverage to proposals for peace made by the churches, sundry local authorities, Oxford dons and others. The thesis was again advanced, subsequently to remain a part of General Strike mythology, that the stoppage had been precipitated by a *diktat* to Baldwin from the diehards of his Cabinet. A somewhat irregular attempt was made to keep the Samuel Report in the minds of the paper's readers.

The *British Worker* was no less propagandist in character than the *British Gazette*, but in the circumstances of the strike it was less tempted to falsification. In some respects it might be said to have had the better of the polemical arguments. It successfully communicated the message that the General Strike was not revolutionary in its aims, thanks particularly to the orderly behaviour of the strikers for which it also claimed some credit. By the end of the stoppage the *Gazette* had itself ceased proclaiming that democracy was in danger, its original *leitmotif*.

On the other hand, paradoxically, the General Council's newspaper afforded little reassurance to its authors. Though the Publicity Committee worked hard to extend its distribution they could not but be aware that the *Worker* did not reach all strikers, still less the general public. On the other hand, the General Council were probably more conscious of the volume of the government's propaganda and of its breadth of readership than of its lack of credibility. And during the initial absence of an independent press they had no litmus with which to test the effectiveness of their own publicity. The hyperbole of the *British Gazette* displayed an aggressive confidence in its editors of which the prosaic moderation of the *British Worker* gave no hint.

The General Council's doubts about their own publication increased rather than diminished when efforts were made to start its provincial editions. The *Worker* was eventually established in various centres outside London, but only after considerable delays and only at the cost of seeming to weaken the strike, at least in the printing industry. The operation in fact demonstrated a confusion over tactics and a conflict of sectional interests which was typical of many other aspects of the strike at a local level.

The Publicity Committee's decision to launch its provincial editions recognized the needs, and was perhaps encouraged by the demands, of strike committees in the country. From the outset of the strike a number of local organizations urged the importance of improved publicity in their own areas. The north-east regional council put out one issue of its own newspaper on 4 May, but were immediately forced by the Typographical Association to suspend it. They promptly sought the support of the General Council to renew publication and their officials informed the Newcastle committee on 7 May that 'every telephone conversation had emphasised . . . up till then [the necessity] of having in the Newcastle district a paper which would give accurate information, up-to-date information, and local information, to meet the extremely virulent poison that was being poured out from the the blackleg sheets'.[15] Ellen Wilkinson and J. F. Horrabin reported from Manchester on the same day that not even a strike bulletin was being produced, and that news and information was seriously lacking. The Glasgow strike committee, among others, constantly pressed the Scottish TUC to print a paper of its own.[16]

Poulton and his associates did not need much prompting, however, clearly appreciating the likely difficulties of communication with unionists in distant strike centres. As early as 6 May they successfully recommended the General Council to establish editions of the *British Worker* outside London. Their urgency may also have been increased by the unofficial printing of labour papers, not only in Gloucester and Southampton, but also in Bradford, Leeds and Preston.[17] They perhaps feared, too, the effects of active Communist propaganda in certain localities.[18] By Thursday night they had already selected Manchester and Newcastle as the first two sites for the purposes of reproducing the *Worker*, and obtained the permission of the Printing Trades Federation for the operation, whilst the Co-operative Printing Society had been asked to provide its presses. The following day Poulton contacted the main provincial union concerned, the Typographical Association, and the Committee appointed and dispatched Fenner Brockway and Arnold Dawson as its plenipotentiaries and editors.[19]

Both immediately encountered hazards. At Manchester Brockway had to find a replacement for the local union official, Skinner, who had been deputed to assist him but had fallen ill – his wife standing guard awaiting the arrival of the police following news of Simon's speech pronouncing the strike unlawful. By the evening of 8 May a more serious difficulty was created when the board of the Co-operative Printing Society refused to put out the *British Worker* on the grounds that they had been prevented by the strike from undertaking any other work. Not until Brockway managed to find a second Co-operative printing establishment, based on Southport, which was prepared to produce the *British Worker*, though having only a limited supply of paper, could production begin.[20] A first Manchester edition of 50,000 copies was produced on 10 May. The following day Brockway obtained additional newsprint and he was able to double his output by the twelfth. The paper was distributed from this centre, partly through newsagents, in the Midlands and Yorkshire as well as the North West – though because of the insistence of volunteer drivers in charging mileage expenses the costs were relatively high. Publication continued until 15 May, though the editor reported a decline in sales once the strike had been called off.[21]

At Newcastle, Dawson was less successful in grappling with similar problems. He managed to persuade the regional strike committee to accept the *British Worker*, albeit reluctantly, as substitute for their own projected newspaper. He was also able to obtain volunteers for his needs from NATSOPA and, with more difficulty, from the Typographical Association. But he, like Brockway, discovered that the Co-operative Society were unwilling to provide their printing services; his attempts to persuade the local directors to ignore the Manchester board's decision were rebuffed, because of local resentment at the refusal of permits by the Newcastle strike committee for deliveries of food. Eventually Dawson obtained the use of a small Sunderland printing shop (which had also produced the first and only edition of the regional strike bulletin on 4 May). 20,000 copies of the *British Worker* were printed here on the night of the eleventh, but only 16,000 could be distributed by next morning. The Sunderland edition also continued after the stoppage had been ended, however, and about 60,000 copies were put out by 15 May.[22]

On 8 May the Publicity Committee at Eccleston Square were informed that the Scottish TUC intended launching their own paper, the *Scottish Worker*, in Glasgow.[23] This news occasioned the decision (already discussed) to increase the number of provincial editions of the *British Worker*. The Committee wired the Scottish TUC to propose that they relinquish their plans in return for the publication of the official paper on Clydeside. Later that day they agreed to send dispatch riders to Leicester, Swansea and Cardiff, as well as to Glasgow, to inquire about possible local printing facilities. On 10 May Tracey also wrote to Councillor W. J. Armstrong in Leeds, asking him to take charge of a similar duplicate from the offices of the already active *Leeds Weekly Citizen*.[24]

Only in South Wales were these plans effectively carried out. The *British Worker* was printed in Cardiff and Newport, under the supervision of W. H. Stevenson, from 10 May. His intention to produce it in Swansea had to be abandoned, however, in face of the objections of the local organization of the Typographical Association.[25] The Glasgow edition could not be undertaken so promptly, and the General Council agreed on 9 May that the Scottish TUC should go ahead with the first number of their own paper. In the event, the local *Scottish Worker* appeared throughout the period up to 15 May – after one unsuccessful attempt to deliver a dummy copy of the *British Worker* from Manchester. It remained independent of London, although the editor appointed by the Publicity Committee, Thomas Johnston, took up his position on the twelfth. 25,000 copies of the first of six issues were produced on Monday, 10 May, but this figure was little increased before the strike had ended, owing to shortage of paper in Glasgow.[26] In Leicester and Leeds the printing of the *British Worker* came up against further, formidable opposition from the Typographical Association. At Leicester the Publicity Committee had arranged for printing by the Blackfriars Press and had put W. J. Chamberlain in charge; but after one number had been published on

10 May, the local typographers refused to continue work. In this they were apparently acting on the instructions of their executive: the Association's secretary, French, told Willie Henderson by phone that his members 'were clamouring to go back and in some cases had returned on capitalist papers as permission had been given in our [Publicity Committee's] case'. He was unwilling now to see the *British Worker* published outside Manchester and Newcastle.[27] The Leicester edition had to be abandoned. The Publicity Committee decided to proceed with the Leeds project despite the Association's objections, but for reasons which are unclear the original printing arrangements broke down, and the strike had ended before any publication took place.[28]

By 12 May, about 700,000 copies of the *British Worker* were being produced. Given more time, it is quite possible that the paper could have been successfully launched in several major provincial strike centres. It seems, too, that the Publicity Committee were contemplating further decentralization during the last phase of the strike, to facilitiate circulation in areas which had still not been penetrated. Tracey wrote to the secretary of the Preston strike committee on 10 May, deprecating the continued publication of the local printed strike bulletin, but adding that 'my committee is now considering the possibility of these local centres [i.e. Manchester, Newcastle and Cardiff] arranging with organisations like yours to reproduce, under their directions, a still more localised edition of the *British Worker*. . . .'[29] But it is thus also clear that, prior to 12 May, the Publicity Committee had by no means satisfied the demand for local news outlets. The provincial editions of the *British Worker* were apt to be out of date by the time they had reached the North or South Wales from London. Their treatment of *local* events was in any case haphazard and incomplete. Any strike committee which, like Preston, had managed to put out its own paper was unlikely to be content with the official alternative. The Scottish TUC were of the same opinion, for the abortive attempt to produce the *British Worker* in Glasgow was made only on condition that a page of it was reserved for Scottish news.[30] And the Secretary of the Northumberland and Durham strike committee, Charles Flynn, wrote a long complaining letter to the Publicity Committee on 10 May recording his failures to get the General Council's permission to continue publication of the regional strike bulletin, and arguing that the *British Worker*, even if printed in Newcastle, was no substitute for such a vehicle.[31] The further extension of the provincial network of the *Worker* was not likely to silence this sort of criticism.

The *British Worker* was thus at best a qualified success, serving the purposes of Eccleston Square better than those of local strike organizations. Furthermore, the measures taken by the Publicity Committee to widen its circulation led to an incipient weakening of the strike – and a stronger apprehension of it – within the main provincial printing union. The Typographical Association were tentative about the Newcastle publication, adamantly opposed to those of Leeds, Leicester and Swansea. The *Scottish Worker* was produced with the co-operation of the Scottish Typographical Association, but this too may have contributed to a wavering loyalty among the rank and file.[32] With the papers of the TUC, the government and the 'independent' press expanding their activities *pari passu*, the stoppage in the industry was bound to seem more and more futile.

The history of the *British Worker* thus reflects, on many counts, the error of the General Council's original decision to call out the printing workers on 4 May. The justification offered for this measure was the need to prevent the strikers' being misled or demoralized by either left- or right-wing propaganda. In fact it obviated neither. Unauthorized strike bulletins flourished, many under Communist influence, and if their output was limited, the scarcity of 'official' news probably increased their readership. Thus whilst the Northumberland and Durham strike committee continued to appeal unavailingly for official sanction to print their own newspaper, the militant issues of the *Northern Light* and *Workers' Chronicle* were circulating on Tyneside.[33] Ironically, the extent to which the TUC was relieved of such embarrassment was largely the result of police vigilance in suppressing subversive literature under different auspices. Furthermore, the strike prompted the establishment of a government paper whose bias and factual inaccuracy went largely uncorrected. However unsympathetic Fleet Street might have been towards the General Strike, the pressure of competition and the conventions of professionalism would have afforded a measure of security against undue distortion of events. In addition, the Conservative press were somewhat more successful in bringing out emergency editions during the General Strike than were organs of Liberal views.

Newspaper workers themselves, especially in London, may well have been more inclined to endorse the kind of action taken unofficially by the *Daily Mail* staff on the Sunday before the strike than to support the General Council's policy. The Printing Trades Federation had recommended on 3 May that their employers be allowed to continue publication on giving an undertaking that 'nothing of an extreme or controversial character should appear in the papers'.[34] In retrospect the Publicity Committee themselves concluded that 'it is unquestionable that as a measure of policy the closing down of the press intensified feeling against the General Council'; in a future crisis, they suggested, it might be preferable for the unions 'to claim for proprietors a pledge that full publicity should be accorded to the Trade Union case'.[35] Given fair play, it seemed best to leave journalism to the specialists.

TABLE 8. *Circulation of the 'British Worker' from different centres, 5–15 May*

	London	*Manchester*	*Cardiff*	*Glasgow**	*Sunderland*	*Leicester*
5 May	320,000					
10 May	n.a.	50,000	n.a.	25,000		20,000§
11 May	n.a.	70,000	n.a.	n.a.		
12 May	514,000	100,000	n.a.	30,000	20,000	
13 May	n.a.	60,000	37,000†	n.a.	n.a.	
14 May	n.a.	100,000	n.a.	n.a.	n.a.	
15 May	n.a.	50,000	n.a.	70,000	n.a.	

* Figures for *Scottish Worker*.
§ The only edition published.
† Excluding Newport. Together Cardiff and Newport produced a total of 205,910 copies between 10 and 15 May.

The *British Gazette*

The government decided to create its own news organ only on the brink of the General Strike, and with as little forethought as the General Council had given to the *Worker*. Although it began this project fractionally ahead of the TUC, the *British Gazette* encountered even more problems in its early stages than did its rival. That the difficulties were overcome relatively successfully was the result of the contrasting but complementary abilities of the two ministers primarily responsible for the paper: Winston Churchill and J. C. C. Davidson.

The Cabinet were warned of the probable closure of the national press on 1 May. When Davidson saw Lord Burnham, the president of the Newspaper Proprietors' Association, on that day, the latter probably suggested that the Association itself should be allowed to propose counter-measures. On the second the NPA meeting asserted the impossibility of publishing any joint private paper, but stated its willingness to cooperate in producing, under government auspices, 'daily bulletins giving essential news'.[36] Burnham offered to arrange an interview between the owners and government representatives to discuss the Association's offer. At this point, Baldwin and Davidson agreed to involve Churchill in the negotiations, partly with the object of withdrawing him from other battlefields.[37] When the NPA met the Chancellor and the deputy chief civil commissioner on 3 May, however, they proved unable to fulfil even the modest promise of assistance held out the previous day. 'So many different shades of opinion were represented at the meeting of the Association that it was felt impossible to organize by agreement a committee of management.'[38] The proprietors suggested that the Stationery Office should take charge of the official bulletin with such help as it could obtain from individuals among them. Davidson, disappointed by the 'mugwumpishness' of the Association, wrote immediately afterwards to H. A. Gwynne, editor of the *Morning Post*, asking whether it were possible for him to provide the offices and machinery of his paper to produce 'a four-page sheet' for the government. Gwynne agreed 'without any condition'[39]

With some hesitation, and after considering various alternative establishments, the ministers ordered the occupation of the *Morning Post* building at 11 pm on 3 May. But production of the *Gazette* was interrupted by the withdrawal of the *Post*'s printing workers the following afternoon, and the simultaneous destruction by other typographers of the duplicate type set up by outside contractors. The first issue of the *British Gazette*, appearing on the morning of 5 May, was reduced to two pages in consequence, and various stock items of the *Post* included to make weight.[40] Thereafter, though the finished article retained a somewhat amateurish look, the efficiency and scale of production of the government paper improved rapidly. The small body of supervisory technicians remaining at work were supplemented by a volunteer staff of employees from independent printing firms, engineering students and naval reservists. The government also requisitioned the Argus Press (next door to the *Daily Herald*), Bowater's paper works at Northfleet, a London wharf to receive imported paper supplies, and one of W. H. Smith's warehouses for distribution purposes. By 13 May the *British Gazette* was said to enjoy the largest newspaper circulation in the world.[41]

TABLE 9. *Circulation of 'British Gazette', 5–12 May*

5 May	232,000	10 May	1,127,000
6 May	507,000	11 May	1,801,000
7 May	655,000	12 May	2,209,000
8 May	836,000		

The principal difficulty which confronted the *Gazette* – as it did the *British Worker* – was that of distribution. Unlike the TUC paper, moreover, the *Gazette* was produced only in London, although Davidson mentions that preparations were being made for facsimile editions in Aylesford, Grimsby and Aberdeen had the strike continued. During the nine days from 5 to 13 May supplies were moved as far as practicable by road, through the machinery of the supply and transport organization and with the help of a large number of volunteer drivers. To the more distant centres, Plymouth, Liverpool and Catterick, some supplies were flown from Biggin Hill by the RAF. But the *British Gazette* was never seen in Scotland, and there were almost certainly other outlying areas where it failed to reach.[42] It is likely, too, that provision in some places exceeded demand. *The Times*, antagonized by the requisitioning of its newsprint, claimed that the *Gazette* was circulated to non-subscribers and surplus copies left unsold.[43] And certainly in the north of England some were distributed with optimistic extravagance by the local airforce unit, which dropped them in bundles, street by street, on selected Durham mining villages.[44] Even the Catterick squadron leader told the Air Minister that he had no need for further supplies.

The concern of the authors of the *Gazette* to increase output and extend distribution, even wastefully, indicated both their pleasure in their own enterprise and a strong tendency to exaggerate its importance. Churchill, full of the 'Gallipoli spirit', portrayed it to the editor of *The Times* as the sole guardian of patriotism: 'This is the one means that at present exists of holding together, in direct contact with the Executive Government and Parliament, the whole loyal mass of citizens throughout the nation, on which success depends. It is the only vehicle left for concerting action simultaneously in all parts of the country. . . .'[45] And in the columns of the *Gazette* itself, in unmistakable Churchillian style, it was characterized as a safeguard against a *grande-peur*:[46]

Nearly all the newspapers have been silenced by violent concerted action. And this great nation . . . is for the moment reduced in this respect to the level of African natives dependent on the rumours which are carried from place to place. In a few days, if this were allowed to continue, rumours would poison the air, raise panic and disorders, inflame fears and passions together, and carry us all to depths which no sane man of any party or class would care even to contemplate.

The editorial policy of the *Gazette*, though described by Davidson as a 'fair compromise' between his own circumspection and Churchill's bellicosity, was at first consistently and naïvely partisan.[47] The early issues printed repeated denunciations of the unconstitutionality of the General Strike; gave substantial coverage to Simon's speech on its illegality but none to Slesser's reply (and little to parliamentary debates on any subject); attacked the Trade Union Act of 1913 for turning the unions into 'a vast political body, spending money to the end that the capitalist state may be overthrown'; and assured the armed forces that 'any action which they may take in an honest endeavour to aid the Civil Power will receive both now and afterwards the full support of his Majesty's Government'.[48] News of returns to work, of increasing transport services and of numberless active volunteers paid little attention to credibility.

From about 10 May the tone of the *Gazette* did become rather more moderate.[49] This perhaps partly reflected the more frequent use of Davidson's 'blue pencil': as early as 6 May Gwynne, the *Morning Post* editor, had criticized the confusion created by a divided command and Davidson himself acknowledged in a note to Baldwin the disruptive effect which Churchill's undue interference was having on the staff of the paper. But the change was probably mainly due to other factors. The strident propaganda on the danger to the polity could not be sustained in face of the TUC's determined denials and the strikers' general restraint. The appearance of other papers, especially *The Times*, and the news service of the BBC, exposed the *Gazette* to unfavourable comparison. Criticism in the House of Commons, especially on the omission of any report of the churches' appeal for peace, proved more than a little embarrassing.[50] Finally, the growing indications that the General Council were contemplating the abandonment of the strike – though the *Gazette*, unlike the BBC, made no mention of them – might have helped to discourage continued philippics.

The importance of the *Gazette*, however, lay in its existence rather than its content. No matter how ineffectual its propaganda, its appearance testified to the determination and capability of the government in face of the emergency. Indeed, the very centralization of the printing and distribution, though a handicap in practical terms, reinforced the impression of executive control. The other aspect of the usefulness of the *Gazette* was in providing the excuse to restrict the output of the *British Worker* by confiscating its newsprint – a measure which promised increasing government domination in the field of publicity, the longer the strike continued.

The 'capitalist' press

It should be remembered, too, in considering the balance of forces in the propaganda war, that the independent press which appeared during the General Strike largely sided with the government, at least to the extent of condemning the strike itself. Davidson estimated afterwards that ninety per cent of the provincial dailies had managed to produce some sort of edition before 12 May and about sixty per cent of the weeklies.[51] After the stoppage, the LSE library conducted its own survey of newspapers publishing during the strike, which though incomplete tended to support this assessment of widespread if improvised output. Only one letter (from Llanelli) reported an inability to continue any form of production. Whilst many of these organs were of small importance and parochial outlook others were valuable allies of the administration. This was particularly true in Scotland, which the *British Gazette* had not reached. In Glasgow all the local dailies cooperated (as they had declined to do in London) to produce a joint paper, the *Emergency Press*. The *Scotsman* managed to publish independently in Edinburgh, whilst the Dumfries *Courier and Herald* was kept going with union labour. At the end of the country the *Exeter and Devon Daily Gazette* claimed to have put out the most voluminous strike edition in Britain.[52]

The bias of party loyalties in the national press, which normally favoured the Conservatives, was even more inclined to the right during the General Strike. The *Manchester Guardian* was the only one of the great national newspapers to make a moderate and liberal voice heard; and even its four-page emergency edition was largely restricted to straightforward reporting. During the first week of the stoppage the remainder of the radical press was silenced. On 5 May a proposal was made on Lloyd George's behalf to the directors of three Liberal papers, the *Daily News*, the *Star* and the *Westminster Gazette*, to pool their resources in a single publication. Talks between the party leader and the editors of the *News* and *Gazette* subsequently took place at Churt, and a leading article for the first issue was actually composed.[53] But on 9 May the board of the *Daily News* rejected the scheme, perhaps because of hostility to Lloyd George personally, or because of the difficulties and dangers created by the Liberal Party's internal divisions. The first Liberal paper to print during the stoppage was the *Daily Chronicle*, which started publication by its own efforts on 10 May. The *News* and the *Star* eventually brought out separate emergency editions on the last day of the strike.

Of the right-wing Fleet Street papers the *Daily Mail*, importing its Paris edition as well as producing an emergency version in London, was the most intemperate and productively the most successful. According to the *British Gazette* it had achieved a circulation of 750,000 by the end of the strike, as against 250,000 by the *Express*, 200,000 by the *Mirror* and 150,000 by the *Telegraph*.[54] It was *The Times*, however, which attracted most publicity during the stoppage. Though adopting a line hostile to a negotiated settlement it maintained the distinction between an impermissible general strike and a partially justifiable mining strike; and it upheld its reputation, even with labour sympathizers, for impartial reporting. Its independence of the government was also usefully confirmed by the dispute which arose over the requisitioning of its newsprint for the benefit of the *British Gazette*. Geoffrey Dawson, the editor, having received notice of the impending losses the previous day, told Baldwin on 7 May that 'publicity . . . in my view (and he agreed) was being mishandled by Winston'. His subsequent formal protest was supported in the House of Commons by the redoubtable Lady Astor. The complaints were unavailing, and the appropriation was carried out on 11 May.[55] The government was less sympathetic because *The Times* had by then increased its circulation from the normal figure of about 80,000 to some 250,000 – and was to reach a peak of 342,000 copies on 12 May. Indeed Davidson heard criticism from Lord Burnham, representing other proprietors, that Printing House Square was taking advantage of the General Strike to poach new readers 'at the expense of more patriotic papers'. But the chief motive for the government's insistence on carrying out the requisition against all papers was the necessity to disarm the protests of the main intended victim, the *British Worker*. *The Times*' vociferous objections served official purposes admirably by making this camouflage more effective.[56]

The relative success of the press in maintaining some form of existence during the strike once again leads to the conclusion that in trying to stop newspaper publication the General Council had overreached itself. The journals printed were truncated in form and unevenly distributed. But the expansion of sales of *The Times* suggests that these handicaps were largely offset by the increased popular demand for news. Moreover, the effect of the General Council's tactics meant that the press (and the BBC) were for the most part boycotted by the labour side. The fact that the government thereby became the main supplier of news served to accentuate, even to necessitate, that political bias which had supposedly justified the withdrawal of the printers in the first place. Whether, without such a stoppage, a movement for conciliation would have received much backing from this source may well be doubtful; but it would certainly have received more publicity. And the TUC would have been spared the anxiety of witnessing the gradual restoration to life of a press whose hostility it had done much to incite.

The BBC

Some provisional arrangements for the use of broadcasting facilities by the government in an emergency had been made in November 1925. These were completed by J. C. C. Davidson and the Director-General of the BBC, John Reith, on 1 and 2 May. The Company agreed to deliver additional news bulletins throughout the day and to relay all government announcements forwarded to it by Whitehall. The content of the news broadcasts was to be approved by Davidson's officials in the Admiralty; the announcements were to be given verbatim.[57]

The Deputy Commissioner found that 'relations with Reith were very favourable' – partly, perhaps, because by a stroke of fortune (more significant though less ironic than the General Council's occupation of Churchill's former dining-room) they lived next door to each other. Both agreed that the BBC should retain its nominal independence from the government. Following the midday news bulletin of 4 May, the Company announced what its own policy was ideally to be:[58] 'The BBC fully realises the gravity of its responsibility . . . and will do its best to discharge it in the most impartial spirit that circumstances permit. Nothing is more likely to create panic than the complete interruption of authentic news. . . . We will do our best to maintain our tradition of fairness and we ask for fair play in return.' This was the posture which, with diminishing credibility, Reith was to try to preserve throughout the stoppage.

The reasons for his insistence on presenting a facade of independence are not difficult to understand. The Company's long-term reputation could only suffer if the government assumed control, for annexation to the civil power during a crisis could not but raise suspicions of official influence in normal times. In addition, however, Reith wanted the BBC to be, if not the mother, at least the midwife of peace. In a policy memorandum written during the emergency he stated: 'in the end conciliation of some kind must supervene and . . . the BBC could act as a link to draw together the contending parties by creating an atmosphere of good will towards the service on both sides'. And in his letter to Baldwin on 6 May urging the case for continued autonomy he made the same point, if more obliquely: 'Speaking with the authority of its own reputation for sincerity and impartiality it [the BBC] would emphasize and initiate statements likely to counteract a spirit of selfishness and hostility.'[59]

For Davidson this relationship was felicitous. It secured a broadcasting service efficiently run and free from the threat of disruption, which was nonetheless subject in all vital respects to his supervision. Both he and Baldwin, moreover, desired to foster that atmosphere of calm and security which Reith promised to evoke. Not all government ministers, it was true, took the same view; first in the Supply and Transport Committee and then in the Cabinet Churchill and Birkenhead pressed the case for governmental requisition. Reith's understanding with the Prime Minister and the deputy commissioner made the adoption of such a measure unlikely, but a decision against it was not taken until 11 May.[60] In the interim the threat of appropriation, perhaps by design, acted as a further constraint on his conduct and enhanced the effectiveness of informal control. At two critical moments he proved willing to sacrifice his supposed independence for the sake of preserving the government's benevolence. On 7 May the BBC agreed that the Archbishop of Canterbury should broadcast the proposals of the churches for a negotiated settlement; but Reith felt it necessary to show the appeal first to Baldwin, who deprecated its contents without explicitly forbidding its transmission; then to Davidson, who took the stronger line that if the appeal were put out the likelihood of government control would be increased. The archbishop's broadcast was not made. The Director's subsequent attempts to exonerate himself with Randall Davidson could not disguise the fact that the principal moral ground on which he had founded the Company's claim to autonomy was being eroded. This was, in the view of its historian, 'the low water mark of the power and influence of the BBC'.[61]

The other outright refusal of broadcasting time was suffered jointly by MacDonald and Lloyd George, though in this instance Reith was less at fault. The first request for such a facility was made on the Labour Party's behalf on 7 May by William Graham, a former junior minister in the first Labour government and a member of the Crawford Committee on Broadcasting. Reith passed the request to Davidson, who said that it should be refused. Following Baldwin's wireless speech on 8 May, however, Graham renewed his request and was now seconded by MacDonald himself. On 10 May Reith saw the Labour Party leader and obtained a manuscript of what he proposed to say. Lloyd George also approached the BBC with the same object, and the Cabinet discussed both requests at its meeting on 11 May. Contrary to what Professor Briggs suggests, the decision to deny permission was taken here, though Reith was told to convey the refusal on his own authority and to give as the reason the illegality of the General Strike, now purportedly established by the Astbury judgement. The Director concealed the manner in which this decision was taken even after the strike, however, and his apology to the Labour Party implied his personal acceptance of responsibility.[62]

Incapable of acting as a *vis mediatrix* during the General Strike, the BBC also fell short of what was perhaps a more attainable objective: the provision of a reliable and objective news service. Here again, aware of Churchill's susceptibilities, Reith did not assert any unfettered freedom to report the facts. To Davidson on 6 May he wrote that 'this is not a time for dope', but added that a reliable news service 'might inspire appreciation of the fact that a prolongation of the stoppage is a sure means of reducing wages and the standard of living, which it is the avowed intention of the Trade Unionists to improve. . . .'[63] Directed to a prejudiced ear, this was perhaps a disingenuous promise; but to his senior officials, after the strike, Raith acknowledged that the Company 'were unable to permit anything . . . which might have prolonged or sought to justify the strike'. He claimed to have achieved no more than 'an appreciable degree of impartiality in the broadcasting of general news'. And in his autobiography his verdict is equally cautious: 'Though complete impartiality during the emergency was, in the circumstances, not to be expected, the BBC had endeavoured to preserve its tradition of accuracy and fair play.'[64]

In so far as it did achieve this much, the Company had to thank the conduct of the strikers and their leaders rather than the tolerance of the government or its own fearlessness. Reith instructed his regional station directors 'not . . . to exclude items from TUC sources provided that they were objective and you are convinced of their truth', but at the same time to broadcast 'nothing calculated to extend the area of the strike'.[65] Since few statements by trade union spokesmen could be regarded as in any way inflammatory, the BBC was free to mention their speeches and to cite the *British Worker* – though it could not, for instance, announce the impending stoppage of engineering and other workers in the last two days of the stoppage. Since there was relatively little violence the news bulletins did not suppress information on what there was; but they did, like the *British Worker* and *British Gazette*, contradict rumours of bloodshed and mutiny. While Reith felt obliged to ignore archbishop Davidson's appeal, he gave little attention to the more extreme utterances of the strike's opponents – though the Cardinal of Bourne's partisan sermon was summarized in the news on Sunday evening.

The picture conveyed by the BBC was of a strike that was solid and disciplined, though showing no signs of militancy or enthusiasm. The evening news bulletin of 4 May announced that 'reports from every part of the country to-day reveal that the General Strike which began at midnight last night has caused an almost complete industrial paralysis'.[66] Thereafter the reports did feature occasional misinformed but uncorrected statements about strikers resuming work – often in rather vague and impressionistic terms: 'A steady stream of railwaymen who have been on strike, presented themselves to the Great Western Railway Company's officials at Slough tonight for re-engagement, and the excellent service of trains now running will be increased as soon as possible', claimed a bulletin of 10 May. But the number of these misstatements was not so great as seriously to distort the true position.[67] Reith did attempt also to keep the prospect of peace before his listeners as far as possible. Whilst the churches' declaration was banned on 8 May, an odd item was allowed to slip through concerning an offer by the Bishop of London to allow Fulham Palace to be used as a negotiating centre. Reference had been made on 5 May to the resolution passed by Newcastle council in favour of a negotiated compromise. On 11 May the clerical manifesto was at length reported – after the government's change of heart – and so also were Simon's proposals for a settlement based on mutual concessions. The outward signs of the General Council's activities that day were constantly observed, and expectations of a peace settlement strongly encouraged.[68]

Among non-participants the reporting of the BBC during the strike was certainly calculated to offer comfort. Its account of the stoppage was probably felt to be authentic, partly because of the normal reliability of its news service and partly because its bulletins situated the truth somewhere in the middle ground between the claims of the *British Gazette* and the *British Worker* – though, it must be admitted, closer to the former than the latter. It was, in other words, the tone rather than the informativeness of the BBC's output which commended it, for its news sources were no different from, and certainly no better than, those of the General Council and the government. Indeed, the factual content of the news and the anodyne commentary of the 'editorials' provided less material for an independent public opinion than the partisan press. The cartoonist Low's rendition of the wireless news bulletins captures exactly its mixture of rapportage, uplift and triviality: 'Mr Baldwin has eaten a good lunch and is hopeful . . . it is denied that the Albert Memorial has been wrecked. There will be several trains and the other six millions of you can walk.'[69]

To the government, therefore, on balance the BBC appeared a distinctly friendly neutral.[70] To the strikers, however, it could scarcely avoid appearing biassed. The *British Worker* published regular instructions to them not to rely upon its information, and occasional corrections of its untruths. The fact that the BBC broadcast official announcements along with its own news strengthened the impression of partiality.[71] A failure to report the appeal of the Archbishop of Canterbury, to which the TUC attached such importance, was confirmation for labour of the company's involvement with the government.

Nevertheless the General Council did not show any unanimous wish to boycott the BBC. The Publicity Committee, it is true, adopted a policy of total aloofness on 1 May and adhered to it thereafter. But they did so, not because of the Company's inherent untrustworthiness, but in view of the Council's previous warnings to the rank and file to disregard its transmissions, after which 'to authorize the BBC to broadcast statements in the name of the General Council would be unsettling and confusing to the movement'. On 4 May, however, representatives of the *Daily Herald* suggested that the Committee should at least supply press statements to Reuters and the Press Association which would be available for broadcasting; and the General Council decided to allow this step as a way of 'testing' the Company's reliability. Subsequently, on 9 and 10 May, a number of Council members including Bevin, Hicks and Walkden urged the Committee to obtain permission for a representative of the TUC to make a broadcast. Presumably they felt it advisable to try to counteract the effects of Baldwin's wireless address of Saturday evening, and perhaps preferable that this should not be done by MacDonald. The Committee again referred this question to the General Council, though again recorded its own dissent.[72] No decision was taken before the stoppage ended – albeit the fact that J. H. Thomas was eventually authorized to go on the air on 14 May perhaps indicates the trend of opinion at Eccleston Square. Given the shortcomings of the *British Worker* and the importance it attached to 'neutral' public opinion, the General Council found it increasingly difficult to disregard the BBC's influence. But its doubt and indecision in this connection reflected once more its dwindling confidence in the potency of the weapon it had deployed.

IX On the Field

The lack of prior attention given to the provision of a local organization for the General Strike, the complicated nature of the strike orders and the difficulty of communications between the General Council and the myriad union bodies acting in its name, make the impact of the nine days upon the country at large difficult to portray. The surviving local records convey a confusing series of blurred and transient images of a stoppage constantly changing in character and extent. The overall picture which forms is, nonetheless, one of a wholehearted and surprisingly efficient response on the part of the movement's rank and file to the problems and demands of the crisis. The General Council had set up no single authoritative local agency for the conduct of the strike; it had, indeed, multiplied delegates by leaving union officers to transmit instructions to their members, setting up joint transport committees to administer permits, and giving Trades Councils a vaguely defined responsibility for 'organising the trade unionists in dispute'.[1] In face of the uncertainty thus created, the success of the arrangements made at the great majority of strike centres was markedly impressive.

The effectiveness of these local initiatives was owed primarily to the work of the Trades Councils. They emerged, manifestly contrary to the intentions of the TUC, as the principal executors of its orders. It was they who, at the outset, formed joint strike committees or Councils of Action – probably between 400 and 500 in number all told; and these latter bodies, through their many subcommittees, acquired and performed a collection of vital functions.[2] Their responsibilities came to include, in almost every area, the management of publicity, the maintenance of communications with other strike organs and with Eccleston Square, the conduct of relations with the police, the entertainment of the strikers themselves and the important task of settling inter-union disputes arising from the interpretation of the General Council's strike orders. Frequently, too, they assumed control over the issue of permits for essential supplies, treating the transport unions as a more or less subordinate authority. Local union branches normally retained an independent power only for the purpose of transmitting the order to stop work to their own members at the outset, and sometimes in the conduct of picketing.

The hegemony gained by the Trades Councils, though unforeseen, is not difficult to understand. At least in towns where several unions were simultaneously involved in the stoppage, they were the only established representative bodies capable of acting as vehicles of joint action or even as media for regular communication. The very suddenness with which the General Strike had happened largely precluded any attempt to create alternative machinery for co-ordinating local activities. In addition, many union activists in 1926 were guided by the precedents of 1920, when Councils of Action had been formed, often under Trades Council auspices, to prepare for a collective stoppage of work in opposition to the threatened war against Russia. If the necessity for *some* administrative centre were acknowledged, therefore, there was usually little doubt about the Trades Councils' suitability for this role. And the recognition of the necessity may be explained, to a considerable extent, by the fact that the General Council had increasingly conferred on Trades Councils since 1924 the functions of propaganda agencies on its own behalf – a responsibility which now clearly assumed a critical significance. The publication of local news and information was a task of obvious importance for all local union leaders, and one which Trades Councils were usually readily equipped to undertake. This, indeed, apart from the distribution of food permits, was the principal *ongoing* duty which local organizations were required by the TUC to perform in the course of the strike. The day-to-day responsibilities of individual union branches, once the stoppage was under way, were almost wholly unspecified in the official instructions. There was an obvious likelihood, therefore, that the bodies chiefly responsible for handling publicity would tend to acquire the authority to take those decisions which they found needed to be communicated. And it was, significantly, on this count more than any other that local strike committees sought for the specific elucidation and extension of their powers by Eccleston Square.

Local strike committees; composition and structure

The energy and enterprise shown by the Trades Councils at the outbreak of the strike may have owed something to left-wing influences. They had tended, in previous years, to accept the leadership of Communists and other militants, perhaps partly because of the indifference of most union members and local officials to the affairs of organs lacking any industrial power. This aloofness had probably diminished only slightly with the increased recognition afforded the Council movement by the TUC since 1924. The representation of fifty-two trades councils at the Minority Movement's national conference in March 1926 was a measure of their political sympathies; and especially in central Scotland, South Wales and east London, Communists were often a major force on their executives.[3] From the beginning of 1926 the MM had urged the formation of Councils of Action under their auspices as part of its 'programme of action'; and at least in a few localities such bodies appeared some time in advance of the General Strike, though rarely in a form suitable to undertake its administration.[4]

Whatever the extent of committed left-wing strength in the Trades Councils prior to the strike, however, it was lessened rather than increased during the first few days of May. Though the Councils might be able to seize the initiative in creating a local strike organization, they could not expect to run that organization by themselves. Most joint strike committees and Councils of Action were made representative of all the unions in their vicinity, or at least of all those directly involved in the stoppage. Nor did the Communists themselves seek to prevent this process of co-optation. On the contrary, the instructions which the Minority Movement sent out to its branches on the evening of 2 May stipulated that 'the Councils of Action were in no circumstances to take over the work of the unions', and that where possible 'no political, industrial, Co-operative and unemployed organisation . . . should be left outside'.[5] There were, in fact, a number of committees to which spokesmen of the Labour Party and the Co-operative Society were appointed; but the official presence of the Communist Party was extremely rare.[6]

Whilst members of the CP and the Minority Movement were often conspicuous in the local strike agencies, therefore, they were scarcely ever dominant. The details of participation of party members given in the *Workers' Weekly* of 21 May suggest that they held a higher proportion of seats on strike executives than on full committees; but only in one instance – that of Battersea – did they form a majority even there.[7] On the other hand, though there were obviously some centres where left-wing pretensions or the suspicions of the moderates produced conflict, this too was unusual.[8] At least within the ranks of the activists, differences of political opinion assumed little significance amid the continuous and arduous effort to fuel and service the stoppage.

The general absence of partisan rivalries at local level probably reflected, in part, the relative ineffectiveness of the Communist Party's central control over its constituent and auxiliary bodies. Before the stoppage, the leadership had positively discouraged a revolutionary posture: 'To entertain exaggerated views as to the revolutionary possibilities of this crisis and visions of new leadership "arising spontaneously in the struggle", etc. is fantastic.'[9] Once the stoppage had begun, moreover, the central committee of the CP and the executive of the Minority Movement alike found the task of co-ordinating their forces impossible. To the inherent difficulties stemming from the nature of the strike itself were added the further problems of police harassment and arrests. The national organizers of the MM were forced to move their offices to escape pursuit and the special party newspaper, the *Workers' Daily*, was suppressed after the first edition on 3 May. Thereafter, as the party itself admitted, contact with the districts outside London was 'rudimentary'.[10] Thus although the Communist leadership adopted a new and more militant line of official policy on 5 May, calling now not just for the defence of the miners' standards but for nationalization of the industry and the formation of a Labour government, this shift had apparently little impact upon the provincial movement.[11]

To attempt to gauge the Communist contribution to the policies adopted by local strike organizations is therefore hazardous, and not particularly rewarding. Not all measures supported by their adherents in particular districts had official approval. Though, for instance, both in the north-east and London, party members were associated with proposals for federating strike committees over a wide area, this had never been an article of the 'programme of action' in previous months, nor was it found appropriate in all cases now. On the other hand the organization of mass picketing, though it had an appeal to almost all Communist members on local bodies, was not their peculiar property. Even the formation of Workers' Defence Corps, which had certainly been propagated by the Minority Movement since the beginning of

1926, probably owed as much to local circumstances and the state of relations with the police across the country, as it did to Communist support *per se*.

It would seem wise, accordingly, to eschew the task of attributing responsibility for variations in local strike tactics to any particular political influences, and to regard them instead as for the most part an index of the varying capacities and priorities of strike organizations in different settings, and facing unequal difficulties. Strike committees can be seen as more or less militant, and more or less efficient in their conduct of the stoppage, partly according to the *organizational* talents of their chosen leaders, but even more according to the extent and character of the support for, and opposition to, the General Strike in their own districts. And though, in broad terms, the accepted account of a strike commanding widespread allegiance and eliciting unsuspected administrative abilities from its rank and file may be allowed to stand, the degree of contrast and diversity of local level should not be overlooked.

Strike committees and Councils of Action varied enormously in size. Even within the boundaries of London, for instance, the Stepney organization had fifteen members, the one at Battersea a hundred and twenty-four. But in most all cases the larger bodies set up executive committees, under various titles, to handle routine daily business. They in turn were normally supported by a greater or lesser number of subcommittees performing special jobs.[12] Most of these agencies operated within narrow geographical confines, and often in comparative isolation. In the less urbanised areas they sometimes represented no more than one or two unions. In many mining districts, especially, the lodges of the MFGB exercised an almost autarchic authority which sometimes obstructed what opportunities there were for cooperation with other sections – and which may well, eventually, have made it easier for the TUC to terminate the strike without effective opposition.[13]

In the larger cities, the common pattern of organization which emerged during the stoppage was one of a congeries of area committees formally subordinate to, though not always effectively controlled by, a central organization. In London some seventy borough organs had come into existence by the end of the strike, and they maintained an almost total independence of the London Trades Council. The latter body, together with the local NUR leadership, called a meeting of union district officials on 4 May to attempt to set up a co-ordinating authority, but though a Central Strike Committee was formed 'nothing in the way of organisation was agreed upon'. Such uniformity of policy as was achieved within the capital was almost wholly due to the General Council's own advisory committees for transport and power. On 6 May the London Trades Council called a meeting of the representatives of the various local committees, but it is unclear whether this conference took place before the strike ended.[14] The Communist secretary of the central strike committee reported afterwards that 'the organization was of a most unsatisfactory character. . . . No effective contact was maintained either with the local councils of action or Strike Committees.'[15] A not dissimilar situation prevailed in Glasgow, where the central strike committee, handicapped by ill-feeling between left- and right-wing factions and encroached on by the Scottish TUC (which assumed direct control of permits and later of the publication of the *Scottish Worker*), lost much of its remaining authority to the fifteen area committees established after the strike had begun.[16]

In other large cities and conurbations, the sovereignty of the central strike organization appears to have been somewhat more willingly accepted. Such nuclear bodies were established, under the auspices of the Trades Council, in Birmingham, Bristol, Nottingham, Sheffield and Edinburgh, and all seem to have worked efficiently, though only the first is adequately documented.[17] On Merseyside a single Council of Action was established to cover the towns of Birkenhead, Bootle and Wallasey, though its principal orbit of operation was almost certainly Liverpool itself.[18]

Apart from the questionable examples of London and Merseyside, there were apparently only four areas in which efforts were made to link together strike committees on a large scale. In Lanarkshire the establishment of a county federation of Councils of Action apparently owed much to the enterprise of the Minority Movement in that coal-field. An organization of the same kind existed in the similar industrial context of east Glamorgan.[19] In south Lancashire another fairly shadowy body, the North West Area Strike Council, evidently connected various strike committees around Manchester, and obtained a degree of recognition from Eccleston Square – though both its territorial coverage and its constitutional authority remain uncertain.[20] Undoubtedly the most ambitious attempt to set up a regionally based administration for the strike, however, was that undertaken by Robin Page Arnot and various local union officials on Tyneside. Intended originally to oversee the whole area of the northern division of the

Supply and Transport Organization, the Northumberland and Durham joint strike committee and Council of Action were constituted, mainly from the district organizers of the unions involved in the stoppage, on 4 May. But this caucus, too, though it had some irregular contacts with centres as far away as Teesside, could probably make its writ effective only in the districts immediately adjacent to the Tyne.[21] In particular, its efforts to attach representatives of the Durham Miners' Association, patently the most influential union in that county, were resisted prior to 12 May.

The proliferation of strike organizations typically parochial in character was not wholly a disadvantage to the labour cause. Unpaid and subordinate union officials were more likely to concede power to agencies with which they could be in constant touch than to more distant and less familiar overlords. Strikers themselves could be more effectively exhorted and encouraged by a united command that was close at hand. Relations with the police, and occasionally with other public authorities, were eased by the influence of local loyalties and connections. If, therefore, the General Council seemed ready to approve the advent in Manchester and Newcastle of bodies with a wider field of action than the purely local strike organs, this reflected a certain difference of local and central perspectives.[22] In the first place, from the point of view of Eccleston Square there appeared an obvious danger that the isolation of individual strike centres would in the long run undermine their confidence and morale. This problem of maintaining communications naturally became more acute in the less industrialized regions and the smaller towns;[23] but many more important cities, including even the capital, furnished complaints of lack of contact with TUC headquarters. The Secretary of the National Union of Corporation Workers, for instance, wrote to Citrine on 8 May from South East London:[24]

> We have a very large number of workers affected by the dispute and we are not getting the information through your Council to allow us to act promptly and in harmony with your decisions . . . the information regarding men in ordinary maintenance and repair to roads reached me 2½ days after the decision had been reached, in the meantime other union officials who had received the necessary information were calling my members out and although we repeatedly, by phone, by letter and also by personal application to your office, asked for up to date information, it did not reach us until nearly all our members had been withdrawn by other union officials.

The Council's first response to this pressure was to attempt to decentralize the publication of the *British Worker*, and to establish certain other nodal points for the distribution of strike news.[25] But it was obvious that these measures would not solve the difficulties of strike committees which themselves wanted better access to TUC headquarters. Eventually, probably the most useful function which could have been performed by regional strike organizations was to provide a means, not just of transmitting information, but of settling disputes over the interpretation of strike instructions, the issue of food permits and so forth, thereby relieving the burdens of the central machinery in these matters. The existence of such chains of command was only occasionally and dimly perceptible even at the close of the strike, however, and their further reproduction would have taken much time and tact to achieve.

Local strike committees: power and policy

Whatever their diversity of character and scope, it is evident that a comprehensive network of local strike organizations had come into existence by 4 May. Moreover, while the General Council had certainly not planned the process, and was perhaps at first inclined to deprecate the transference of responsibility from the individual union organizations to bodies of an unknown complexion, it generally acknowledged them readily enough once they were established, and used them to make known and effective many of its own policy decisions. At the same time the authority and unity of the strike organization in the country was by no means universal and unquestioned; and where a division of command persisted the General Council was, on the face of things, largely to blame. Two important decisions taken at the centre continued to militate against successful union cooperation in a local context, and sometimes wholly precluded it. One was the designation of union head offices as the medium through which to issue strike instructions in the first instance – which was to provoke many complaints during and after the stoppage from representative local bodies faced with the task of reconciling contradictory orders to workers in the same trade. The second was the instruction that a separate and independent authority be formed for the administration of permits for essential services: the joint transport committees projected by the memorandum of 1 May and mandated once again by the new central transport committee on 5 May.

Whilst the Council might be criticized for failing to foresee the difficulties which such a proliferation of executive agencies would bring about, it must also be pointed out that politically it had very little alternative. The union councils which had approved the General Strike were not likely to accept the transference of their control over their own members, least of all to local bodies lacking settled authority or previous experience in the conduct of industrial stoppages. And the leadership of the transport organizations had likewise made clear at the outset their reluctance to delegate the issue of permits either centrally or locally to representatives of unions without any knowledge of the consequences of such a policy. To expect the Council to have set up, by fiat, a nuclear local strike organization on the lines which many strike committees subsequently recommended was to expect nothing less than a complete reconstruction of the movement from top to bottom in a couple of days. In addition, it must be recognized that not all the mutual suspicions and jealousies within the unions were confined to their principal officers. The very fact that in some strike centres an integrated local administration was established and in others was obstructed suggests a variety of response in the rank and file itself. It was as an almost inevitable by-product of the chosen strike strategy that such differences manifested themselves at the grass roots: so that even if the Council were to be held responsible for incidents of local maladministration, it was by virtue of an inability to predict the implications of decisions taken for quite other reasons.

Discord at a local level seems to have originated in three main ways. In a few centres the Trades Council was evidently too unrepresentative or politically suspect to provide an acceptable medium of union co-ordination. This, almost certainly, was the source of the problems encountered at Leeds, 'the worst organized town in England' according to the account of the Plebs League, where at least two rival strike committees were in existence after 3 May.[26] It was rather more usual for representatives of the transport unions (or the railway unions alone) to form joint executives independently of the central strike committees as, for example at Birmingham, Gloucester and Stoke, either to ensure the effectiveness of their own stoppage or to assume responsibility for whatever permits were given out.[27] Finally, and most typically, quarrels were sparked off in particular localities by the ambiguity of the strike instructions on the question of who should work and who should not, and by the contradictory information received on this subject from different union offices.[28] Although such confusion did not always produce open ruptures, at its worst it did prompt individual unions simply to ignore the authority of the joint strike body in their own area. In Sheffield, where the strike committee found at least some local unions unwilling to allow it to adjudicate disputes over the TUC orders, its secretary commented that 'this to a certain extent militated against close cooperation, and if the strike had proceeded for long, would have had a considerably weakening effect on the general position, owing to the creation of internal jealousies'. At St Albans and Middlesbrough a similarly rampant desire for sectional autonomy handicapped the strike committees; and many others complained that their own powers of decision had proved too slight.[29]

In the end, however, despite these manifold problems it seems evident that local queries and disputes about strike instructions were usually resolved and that the General Council's intention of limiting the scope of the stoppage to specified industries and groups was respected, in large if not in detail, across the country. Where clashes between different unions could not be averted on the spot, local strike committees which were unable to enlist the help of the Council's Strike Organization Committee were apt to appeal to visiting labour speakers to arbitrate.[30] But on whatever authority, whilst the official strike orders were sometimes liberally interpreted, they were almost never wilfully transgressed. Unwarranted extensions of the strike were accepted of necessity where they had occurred, but they were rarely initiated by local bodies.

The same uniform obedience was not, it is true, given to national instructions with regard to the issue of union permits, but the movement of essential supplies was a subject on which the General Council had difficulty in making up its own mind and changed it several times. Both the initial decision to set up joint transport committees for the purpose of distributing permits, and the subsequent proposal to leave it mainly to their discretion to determine policy in this connection, seemed to give local organizations *carte blanche* to follow their own inclinations. As a result, in the early stage of the stoppage, the movement of foodstuffs (and sometimes other commodities) by road from wholesalers to retailers and thence to customers was approved almost everywhere – whether by transport unions acting on their own behalf or by joint strike committees and their satellites. This was the practice of militant Councils of Action at Sheffield, Coventry, Preston, Cowdenbeath and the 'red village' of Chopwell in County Durham, as well as of organizations of more moderate complexion at Liverpool, Birmingham, Edinburgh and Cardiff.[31] It seems probable that, at this juncture, local strike leaders in many centres hoped to demonstrate the impotence of the government's emergency provisions; and in Salford, Plymouth, Nottingham and central Scotland as well as at Newcastle there were assertions that the supply and transport system had broken down.[32] But the real objective of 'the struggle for food control' was not simply to secure a symbolic victory; if the unions could indeed establish the supremacy of their own permit system they would thereby be in a position to prohibit the movement of all 'inessential' commodities, and ensure that the General Strike established a stranglehold upon the whole economy.[33]

Where permits began to be withdrawn, usually about the weekend of 8–9 May, it was because this policy had proved so difficult to apply and so doubtful of success at local level. The new line adopted by the Strike Organization Committee at TUC headquarters was in several instances a retrospective endorsement of action already taken. In a few cities, such as Manchester and Edinburgh, food and other passes had been found open to abuse by the unions themselves, having been issued indiscriminately and without authority from the strike committees by the local road transport organizations.[34] Elsewhere – in Glasgow, Cardiff and St Helens for example – their distribution had led to disputes between the T&GWU and the railway unions similar to those which had embarrassed the General Council.[35] In Oldham, Doncaster and probably a number of other places where the strike committees had not successfully subordinated the transport unions, a conflict of authority developed with the joint transport committees.[36] Most importantly, however, the efforts of the government's officers in almost all urban areas to operate their own services independently of the unions, with the aid of volunteers, made it all but imperative to withdraw the offer of assistance and tighten up the strike.

The most publicized change of local policy was carried out at Newcastle. The regional strike committee there cancelled all permits on 7 May, after negotiations with the Civil Commissioner, Kingsley Wood, to exclude non-union labour from the vicinity of the docks had broken down. The committee, and the Newcastle MP, Martin Connolly, subsequently claimed that the labour side had been offered a form of 'dual control' of the waterside in an effort to keep them at work and it seems that some bargain of this kind was indeed contemplated by Wood; though the assumption that, in its absence, the supply and transport agencies in Tyneside were rendered ineffective is much more disputable.[37] The report of the joint strike committee itself firmly stated, after the stoppage, that in the region as a whole 'it should be clearly understood that there was not, so far as can be ascertained at any time during the strike, any shortage of essential foods in any village. . . .'[38]

In other cities, too, the strike was intensified as alternative local transport services were built up. The Liverpool, Birmingham, Bradford and Glasgow strike organizations had placed at least a partial ban on permits for private traders by the end of the first week of the stoppage.[39] Birmingham and Glasgow were both in touch with TUC headquarters on this matter, and took their decisions directly as a result of the orders of the Central Transport and Strike Organization Committees; but in the other towns (probably in this respect more typical) the provision of transport for essential purposes was apparently ended without reference to external authority.[40]

The abandonment of the permit was, however, at no stage universal or absolute. The Unity House Committee itself allowed strike organs to continue supplying the Co-operative Societies and their customers with bread and milk; and this decision was, like the previous policy of *laissez-faire*, both a reflection of and an encouragement to the practice of discrimination at local level. Strike committees were usually susceptible to the pressure exerted by local co-operatives, on the grounds that their clientele was mainly working-class, that their employees were more highly unionized than those of local traders and hence more affected by the stoppage, and that it was undesirable to force a section of the labour movement into the arms of the official emergency system. Thus at Newcastle the decision to withdraw permits, originally providing for no exceptions, was relaxed in the case of bread and milk at the behest of the local co-operative union on 7 May – before the Central Transport Committee had issued its edict to the same effect. Even then the problem was scarcely less acute, and the committee acknowledged two days later that 'the Co-operative Wholesale Society and possibly the retail Societies had before them the very difficult choice of closing down many of their activities or of openly becoming suppliants for the aid of a strike-breaking organization..[41] In Birmingham and Preston, special treatment was afforded to the co-operatives from the outset, though on a similarly restricted basis. Elsewhere, it is clear that the assistance allowed to the societies went well beyond anything approved by the transport union executives. Burns records that at least twenty-nine strike organizations had made specific agreements with their local stores for the provision of necessities or credit vouchers to the men standing down and that others were being negotiated at the time the stoppage ended.[42] Where such arrangements existed, permits on a large scale could hardly have been denied. Moreover, it seems that when the Central Transport Executive sought to impose its policy of limiting aid it encountered a certain amount of resistance, not only from local co-operatives themselves but also from the unions. The Sheffield strike committee, for instance, wrote to Citrine on 10 May seeking permission to grant permits more freely, and meanwhile continued to supply coal as well as food to its co-operative society's customers. Even where the TUC's strict instructions were observed, it was probably often with reluctance.[43]

In addition, a number of strike organizations continued to give permits even to private tradesmen, though how widespread this practice was by 12 May it is difficult to estimate. As late as 10 May, however, the National Transport Committee reported, without giving details, 'that permits were being issued in large numbers in certain parts of the country', and decided to send telegrams to all local bodies reiterating their instructions to withdraw them.[44] The Food and Essential Services Committee attributed this seeming indiscipline to the lack of effective communications between London and the provinces, but a further factor was the desire of smaller road transport unions to ensure that necessities did not run short in their own areas. The Strike Organization Committee were told on 10 May that the Liverpool Carters and Motormen's Union intended to continue supplying at least bread and milk to local residents on behalf of private retailers, since the co-operative societies could cater for only a small proportion of the population. Other union members in Liverpool were said to have consented quite willingly to load and unload vehicles bearing 'official' permits provided by the north-west road commissioner.[45] And elsewhere in the country, civil servants attached to the Supply and Transport Organization who had noted the prevalence of labour permits early in the stoppage remained manifestly unaware that union policy in this connection had undergone any change.[46]

Local strike committees: pickets and police

If the TUC representatives at Unity House sought to obtain the cancellation of all but a minimum of permits, they were nonetheless aware of the dangers liable to arise from this policy – in particular, the occurrence of more aggressive and large-scale picketing. Once the unions were committed to refusing cooperation in the maintenance of essential services, it was only a short step to active and systematic interference with 'blackleg' transport. Even if the national leadership would never have considered endorsing so drastic a measure, local strike organizations were likely to be impelled in this direction the more the tempo of the governmental emergency machinery quickened.

Prior to the end of the General Strike, there was little overt sign, it is true, of such increased belligerence. Most strike committees abided loyally by the instructions, constantly reiterated in the *British Worker*, to preserve law and order and avoid trouble with the police. They spent much ingenuity on arranging entertainment for the strikers, in the form of concerts, sports and cinema concessions.[47] In a few areas, however, more intensive methods of picketing were intentionally adopted. Their occurrence may be partly attributable to left-wing influences, since Communists especially were apt to disapprove of 'the "go to bed till the strike is over" theory of the leaders'.[48] But more particularly it reflected the character and attitudes of the working-class communities themselves, for it was in the coalfields and around the London docks that the most serious incidents of obstruction of traffic took place. In the capital the first, small-scale, attempts to unload food cargoes on the South Side were almost on the point of being abandoned in face of popular harassment on 7 May, and continued only under heavy police protection, while the general blockade of the roads leading to the port was not finally lifted until the introduction of the convoy system.[49] In north Durham miners from Chopwell and neighbouring districts clashed with police whilst attempting to hold up vehicles on the main Newcastle–Durham road on 10 May. Local strike organizations at Airdrie and Coatbridge in Lanarkshire claimed to have mobilized four thousand men for picket duties, and similar large-scale surveillance was mounted, especially by miners, at Fauldhouse and Falkirk in Scotland, and around Doncaster.[50]

It was often – though not always – where such activity caused conflict with the police that 'Workers' Defence Corps' were organized, partly for the purpose of protecting strikers. Probably the largest of these bodies, about seven hundred strong, was formed in Methil, Fife; but other such units were set up at Coatbridge, in the London boroughs of Willesden, Croydon and St Pancras, at Selby and Sowerby Bridge in Yorkshire, and, more surprisingly, at Cheltenham, Gloucester, Chatham, Aldershot and Colchester.[51] Once formed, however, they appear to have created little trouble and may actually have prevented it; the object of the Sowerby Bridge contingent, for example, was said to be 'maintaining peace in the streets and highways'.[52] In most areas, on the other hand, measures of this kind were felt unnecessary or positively undesirable. Even in towns where the police were more than usually hostile to the strike, including Edinburgh and Brighton, the creation of such formations could be seen as unduly provocative by the local leadership.[53]

The pattern of arrests made under the Emergency Powers Act during the General Strike traces quite accurately the frontiers between a relatively small number of districts subject to considerable disturbance and a broad expanse where orderliness prevailed throughout. Of three major troublespots the worst was almost certainly Glasgow, where there were a hundred and twenty arrests between 5 and 7 May, and a further eighty or so during the weekend which followed. Clashes with the police began when Cambuslang miners marched into the city on Wednesday to picket a private bus depot, and further arrests were made as a result of attempts by strikers to stop trams driven by student volunteers. But the confrontations arising from the strike were accompanied by outbreaks of night-time rioting and looting in the city centre.[54] The same conjunction of purposeful obstruction and apparently anarchic violence was present at the other major flashpoints, in the north-east and London. In the former region police were simultaneously engaged in counteracting the intensive picketing of roads through the Durham coalfield, and in restraining destructive weekend rampages within Newcastle itself.[55] In London, too, by no means all those arrested were trade-union members, and in the principal theatres of Paddington, Bethnal Green and St Pancras it seems probable that only a minority were.[56]

Elsewhere in the country there was a significant though somewhat smaller amount of conflict between police and strikers in Yorkshire, South Wales, various other Scottish towns including Edinburgh, Dunfermline and Stirling, and isolated English centres such as Brighton. But only one or two Yorkshire towns, notably Hull and Doncaster, appear to have furnished incidents of physical combat on a scale approaching that experienced in Glasgow or on Tyneside.[57] On Merseyside, in south Lancashire and throughout the industrial midlands, as well as in the less urbanized areas of the country, the number of arrests were few, and even in many London boroughs the peace seems to have been relatively undisturbed.

Statistical evidence on the number of arrests and prosecutions resulting from the General Strike is far from complete. In the House of Commons on 2 June the Home Secretary reported that, in England and Wales, 1,760 arrests had been made under the emergency regulations between 1 and 12 May and that, of the prosecutions that followed, 1,389 had been for acts of violence and disorder and 150 for incitement by speech or writing. He gave no regional breakdown of these cases beyond indicating that of those charges brought by county police forces, 396 out of 583 were in Northumberland, Durham and the West Riding of Yorkshire.[58] A somewhat more detailed picture of the incidence of police activity is provided by the T&GWU's record of prosecutions among its own membership, though the sample thus constituted was obviously unevenly distributed. Of 174 charges listed, however, 79 were in the London district, 36 in Glasgow, 24 in Birmingham and 14 in Leeds.[59]

One further estimate of police proceedings which has some interest is that of the Communist party. The *Sunday Worker* of 6 June suggested that approximately 2,500 people throughout Britain had been charged under the emergency power regulations prior to 12 May – and at the Congress of October it was claimed that about half of these were CP members.[60] This represents an extraordinarily high proportion of total prosecutions and amounts to one-fifth of the party's strength – figures for which there is no means of providing satisfactory corroboration. It is however almost certain, from the local evidence on the stoppage, that *outside* the areas of exceptional disturbance the Communists bore the brunt of police action. Other sources – admittedly mostly sympathetic – suggest that in many places they were its sole victims.[61] And it is clear that, wherever the Party or the Minority Movement undertook the publication of its own local strike bulletins, their adherents were liable to be indicted almost as a matter of course. From the raid on the party's head office on 5 May, which permanently stopped the printing of the *Workers' Daily* to the arrest of the distributors of 'The Great Betrayal' in Manchester on the last day of the strike, Communist attempts at propaganda were subject to constant and ubiquitous harassment, confiscation and suppression.[62]

Other strike publications were not entirely free from such interference, and where they allegedly published false news they were equally likely to be severely dealt with. In London arrests were made at Lambeth and St Pancras on this count; and in Birmingham the whole strike emergency committee was summoned on 10 May, as a result of a report in its *Bulletin* that the government had been defeated in the Commons on an amendment to the emergency regulations.[63] But most strike publications under non-Communist auspices managed to stay out of trouble and it seems, moreover, that those charged for incitement and the like were usually penalized for repeating rumours circulated by Communist sources or printed in the Communist press.

Two conclusions may tentatively be drawn from this evidence on the relations between the strikers and the police authorities. Firstly, it is probable that in most districts the latter set out to hinder or to silence the most readily identifiable vehicles of militant propaganda – and that this frequently involved a considerable degree of discrimination between different elements of the local strike leadership. The differentiation between the *British Worker* and the *Workers' Daily* was widely paralleled. Secondly, and consistent with this observation, in the general maintenance of law and order during the nine days the police did not display any marked hostility towards either those who led the strike locally or those who supported it. In particular, there is little reason to uphold the assumption made by the Intelligence Committee of the General Council of 11 and 12 May, that a police aggressiveness towards the strikers was significantly increasing. Where arrests had been made in large numbers, they had taken place, in London and Glasgow at least, in the early stages of the stoppage and in its second week showed signs of falling off. In both capitals the police themselves, and in Newcastle the civil commissioner, attributed the scale of disorder to elements outside the strikers' ranks. 'It is now perfectly clear,' asserted the London Police bulletin on 9 May, 'that the hooligans, incited and helped by paid Communist agitators, are responsible for disturbances. Trade Unionist leaders are now frightened by the storm they have created, and are urging strikers to wear war medals and refrain from violence.'[64] In a number of other places, including Edinburgh, Hull, Brighton and Tredegar for instance, hostility towards organized labour was more evident; but it was primarily the result of local officiousness or prejudices, or perhaps to the use of unpopular special constables – and not of any widespread concern about the preservation of law and order, still less of central policy directives.[65] The fears of the General Council seem to have been aroused by the arrest of the Birmingham strike committee, another case of excessive zeal in a local police force, and by an exaggerated impression of recent and minor incidents in the capital. Of the significant offensive measures against workers at the close of the General Strike – in Doncaster and Gloucester in England, Coatbridge and Bellshill north of the border – the Intelligence Committee made no mention in its reports.[66] Alarming episodes of this kind were, in any case, still more than counterbalanced by examples of relations of singular cordiality between trade unionists and police.[67]

Taken as a whole, this mass of local evidence suggests that the majority of Trades Councils and strike organs were no more aggressive in temper or lawless in their behaviour than the General Council itself. They displayed on the contrary a strong determination to preserve discipline and demonstrate obedience. The avowal of the Northumberland and Durham strike committee was, in this respect, representative: '[We] were resolved even when it was against the most obvious requirements of the emergency not to go a single step beyond the Trades Union Executives' instructions or prohibitions. . . . The disciplined attitude of the Joint Strike Committee towards Eccleston Square and the Trade Union Executives was assumed from the beginning and never questioned at any moment.'[68] There were, as this statement implies, many complaints from below about the confusion resulting from the official strike orders, and the partial character of the stoppage gave rise to frequent demands for its extension. But for the most part these demands concerned workers in those trades where the strike had been deliberately left more or less incomplete: building, electric power supply and engineering. There was no common insistence, at the grass roots, on an immediate and comprehensive withdrawal of all forms of union labour. Furthermore, in the handling of permits, strike bodies in the country were often less strict than the leadership in London desired. Neither in this regard nor in their anxiety to maintain the peace and inhibit large-scale picketing did the local organizations show themselves particularly conscious of the conditions requisite for the victory of the stoppage. They, just as much as the TUC, were governed by a conception of the General Strike as a form of passive resistance – a conception which, whatever its shortcomings in practice, they showed little sign of abandoning.

The extent of the stoppage

The legend of the General Strike, fostered during its course and established in its immediate aftermath, treated of a heroic, working-class solidarity. 'To the last hour the workers' ranks were unbroken and triumphant,' proclaimed *Lansbury's Labour Weekly*. 'When the strike was off, is there a man here that was not surprised and shocked?' Arthur Cook asked the Trade Union Executive Conference in January 1927. 'Was there not consternation from John O'Groats to Land's End? I had hundreds of telegrams and telephone messages asking: "What is the matter?" They could not understand it.' 'There has been more diarrhoeia in the headquarters than what there has been outside,' his President laconically told the miner's delegates two days after the termination.[69]

There is much reason to regard this picture as accurate. It is not in dispute that the initial rank and file response to the strike call of 4 May was enthusiastic; that even at this stage many left work unofficially, ignoring the letter of the strike instructions; and that the boundaries of the stoppage constantly and irresistibly widened in the next few days. The numbers involved grew steadily throughout its course – some groups of workers received their strike orders only after a delay;[70] some union executives and district officials interpreted the instructions in a deliberately latitudinarian fashion, calling out all men who could possibly be regarded as within their compass;[71] workers not at first called out were authorized or incited to join it where their continued employment brought them into contact with volunteers or otherwise exposed them to charges of blacklegging;[72] more were persuaded to leave work by union pickets;[73] and the General Council eventually brought out its 'second wave' of engineering workers on the last day of the strike. All these factors seemed to give the stoppage a momentum far from exhausted at its conclusion. Indeed, when it was officially terminated there occurred a remarkable and spontaneous resistance in many sections to the imposition of humiliating and penal conditions of resumption of work by the employers, which clearly belied the existence of any widespread sense of demoralization and defeat.

Nonetheless, it has already been seen that by the second week of the strike the General Council were convinced that it had reached its peak and, what was more, had already begun to reveal certain symptoms of weakening. This feeling prevailed despite the fact that the central organization of the stoppage had improved substantially and that there were grounds for expecting it to continue to do so. Nor was it diminished by the expectation of the withdrawal of the engineering workers on 12 May. How far, then, were the Council's fears exaggerated or imaginary? Or how far, on the other hand, were they justified by the condition of the strike in the country?

One of the difficulties confronting the General Council, and also the historian of these events, is that most of the evidence bearing on the progress of the conflict at a local level derives from sources exceptionally prone to brevity and optimism. The activists of the front line – union branch officials, Trades Council secretaries, shop stewards and the other functionaries of the *ad hoc* strike organization – were precisely the elements most committed to the success of the stoppage, most convinced by the dogmas of its invincibility and most conscious of their responsibility for maintaining morale among the rank and file in general. Engrossed in and buoyed up by the struggle, preoccupied with the tasks presenting themselves from day to day in their own vicinity, pressed for time and lacking assured means of communication with London, they despatched reports which typically confined themselves to claiming a unanimous response to the strike orders and an unquestioning enthusiasm among the strikers. The comments they offered after the stoppage were sometimes more informative, but also influenced, in their criticisms of the General Council, by a wish to acquit themselves of any share in the manner of its ending. To have drawn attention to what were certainly no more than minor exceptions to the general truth of working-class unity would have seemed an absurdly academic and self-derogating exercise.

This is not to suggest that the portrait of the strike obtained from these witnesses is seriously distorted. Their disagreements with the assessment made by the General Council, it should be remembered, was one of diagnosis rather than factual description. It was, therefore, their contrasting perspectives which first need to be appreciated. The local strike leadership was predominantly aware of the present state of the conflict; Eccleston Square was constantly considering future prospects. The former attached little, the latter great, significance to minor defections. There was also a natural divergence between the views of those who saw the stoppage from the principal industrial centres, where support was certainly massive and morale usually high, and of those who were conscious of the difficulties experienced in the isolated outposts and smaller battlefields where sometimes – though by no means always – the front was weaker. Given these dissimilar vantage points, it is not necessary to accuse the correspondents of the strike committees of unduly misrepresenting the coverage of the stoppage in order to discharge the General Council of entertaining unwarranted anxieties.

The fact remains, however, that even in the larger cities the General Strike was not uniformly solid. Exceptions are mentioned, though obviously not stressed, in the local progress reports themselves. The General Council's own couriers, and the full-time officials of affiliated unions provide an additional body of qualifying information. And the provincial press, though often hostile to the strike, was probably less inaccurate in describing its successes and failures than was the *British Gazette*. From this varied testimony the impression which emerges is of a stoppage nearly complete and apparently resilient in well-organized trades and in most heavily industrialized regions – but nonetheless ragged at the edges, where lack of financial support and the threat of dismissal or other forms of retribution from employers were most pronounced.

In considering the scale and durability of the General Strike, it is evident that the chief potential dangers faced by the participants came from members of their own class. The largely uncontrollable reaction of non-unionists on the one hand and the out-of-work on the other could exercise a powerful effect, potentially, on the outcome of the stoppage. Unfortunately it is difficult to make any informed generalization about the behaviour of either group. A few unions certainly made special provision for the admission and support of non-members after 4 May and others occasionally refer to the willingness of non-unionists to come out.[74] It seems almost certain, however, that their response depended on the relative strength of union organization in particular areas and industries, coupled with the intensity of picketing. In weak sections, like that of the road-goods workers, non-unionists were probably immune to pressure. The unemployed represent an even more imponderable category. Though the National Unemployed Workers' Movement instructed its members to stand by the strikers, it had recruited only a small minority of the jobless. The attitude of the rest remains obscure. Liverpool was one city in which unemployed men formed a substantial proportion of the official volunteers, and here their presence led to a severe problem of reinstatement after the stoppage for tramwaymen and flour mill workers.[75] In the absence of more reliable information from other centres, it is perhaps reasonable to accept the extent of deliberate victimization after the strike as a fair index of the number of jobless workers in the emergency labour force.

Among the employed and unionized wage-earners of the 'first wave', the success of the General Strike depended critically upon two industrial groups: the railwaymen and the transport workers. They were represented in nearly all industrial centres; in many smaller towns the railwaymen were – like the miners on the coalfields – almost the only workers affected.[76] They gave the stoppage its immediate impact on other industries not themselves stopped, and on essential services. It is with respect to these two elements, therefore, that the effectiveness of the strike is primarily to be measured.

As far as the railwaymen were concerned, the attendance figures provided by the companies to the government showed an almost unanimous obedience to the strike call among the engineering and traffic grades, but a substantially less complete one among the clerical and supervisory staff.

TABLE 10. *Railwaymen available for duty on the four national networks, England and Wales, 5–12 May*

	normal staff	*5 May**	*12 May*
clerical/supervisory	91,213	51,525	55,704
drivers, firemen, guards	81,674	881	1,381
signalmen	24,522	1,443	2,278
shopmen	136,092	8,913	9,540
other grades	217,983	25,683	26,865

* In the case of the LNER the first available figures are those for 6 May.
Source: MT 45/248/5; Bagwell, *op. cit.*, p. 476.

Of the former classes, members principally of the NUR, the ASLEF and the AEU, only the lower-paid manual workers showed signs of weakness – rather more than twelve per cent of them declining to stop work. Even so, there was no sign of the situation worsening appreciably during the course of the strike. Among white-collar workers non-compliance was more substantial. The Railway Clerks' Association organized chiefly booking clerks and ticket inspectors, and few of the supervisory grades were union members. Even the subordinate sections of the non-manual workforce had never been involved in large-scale industrial action and both the character of their jobs and the promotion system of the industry tended to exercise a restraining influence on

TABLE 11. *Railwaymen available for duty by company, Great Britain, 5 and 12 May*

	total	*5 May*	*12 May*	*(clerical etc.) 12 May*
GWR	111,418	20,270	21,554	12,058
LNER	191,070	24,942*	27,949	18,295
LMS	267,799	41,213	46,770	26,319
SR	70,848	14,171	13,448	6,054

* Figure for 7 May.

them. Thus from the outset of the stoppage nearly three-quarters of the Great Western Railway's clerks and supervisors and nearly two-thirds of the Southern Railway's were at work. How many of these were RCA men it is more difficult to say. The union claimed on 4 May that about 50,000 of its 67,000 members were on strike, but this was certainly an exaggeration.[77] By 12 May in Britain as a whole just over 40,000 clerical and supervisory workers were idle; even if all were members of the Association, therefore, this would represent no more than sixty per cent of its total strength. Allowing for non-unionists who had stopped work and for a minority belonging to other organizations, a figure of between fifty and fifty-five per cent seems likely.[78]

The partial nature of the response among white-collar grades was not in itself too serious a matter. The rate of *resumption* of work on their part during the nine days was, in the circumstances, surprisingly slow, and does not suggest any probability of an imminent and complete collapse of the stoppage. Moreover, although there was some reallocation of duties among non-manual employees remaining at work, the value of clerks in the absence of traffic sections was obviously limited so far as the companies were concerned. Nonetheless, the more services could be restored by other assorted means, the more the weakness of the non-manual staff (and to a lesser extent of the 'other grades') caused disquiet, to the leaders of the NUR and the footplatemen as well as the RCA. Nor on balance was this an unreasonable anxiety.

The remaining elements of the labour force in transport cannot be discussed with the help of such precise strike statistics. But in other cases, too, there were obvious contrasts of strength and weakness. The Transport and General Workers' Union, by far the most important organization among road and port workers, clearly gave full and effective support, but many of its smaller neighbours were much less secure or enthusiastic. The most conspicuous example of waywardness among the union leadership in the transport services, however, was set by the officials of the Seamen's Union, and especially by its autocratic President, Havelock Wilson. Due to his overriding authority within the organization and his devotion to the principles of industrial pacifism, this was the only important constituent of the TUC which refused to take part in the General Strike – instead conducting a ballot of its membership on the question, which was eventually said to have yielded an adverse majority.[79] Wilson buttressed his position by suspending dissident local officials in Liverpool, the north-east and

London for attempting to initiate local action and by arranging the collusive court appeal which gave rise to the Astbury judgement.[80]

The seamen's ballot was of little significance as a democratic device and Wilson was quite willing privately to discount rank and file opinion in his determination of policy.[81] But the NSFU operated one of the most effective systems of union job control obtaining in any trade, and most of his members, if they were on shore at all during the stoppage, were doubtless conscious of the dangers which indiscipline might hold. Thus only in Newcastle and on Merseyside did seamen actually cease work unofficially, and this limited revolt did little to obstruct shipping even in the ports affected. The rival Marine Workers' Union, with some footholds in London, Glasgow and Southampton, did support the stoppage, but its contribution had little significance to any large shipping companies.[82] The government never had reason to doubt, during the strike, that both coastal and overseas vessels would continue to bring in essential supplies.

The seaman's non-compliance created a serious breach in the stoppage on the waterside, but it did not apparently affect the solidarity of the other major industrial group there, the dock labourers. Their strike, according to both local and national sources, was as complete as that of the membership of the NUR and ASLEF. On Merseyside, there is some evidence that dockers on strike may have volunteered to work on official emergency services and in Bristol Ben Turner mentions a report that they were weakening by 12 May.[83] But the T&GWU showed no sense of alarm: according to Bevin, 'the dockers could not be persuaded back to work for weeks'.[84] It was the arresting of the ports, indeed, which caused such signs of anxiety as the authorities revealed about supply and transport, notably in London and the north-east.

In contrast, in the sector of road transport, both of passengers and goods, the number of defections from the strike was considerably larger. The reason differed in each case. Tramway and bus workers were in normally secure jobs in a sheltered industry, but they were relatively easily replaced when the need arose, and both local government authorities and private bus companies were particularly likely to adopt strong counter-measures to defeat the strike. The councils often regarded the re-establishment of tramway services as an objective second in importance only to the maintenance of law and order (their responsibilities did not, of course, extend to the supply of food). Bus companies were exposed to possible competition from pirates and non-union operators, as well as from trams; and union organization in this industry was in any case weak outside the capital. In face of such threats passenger transport workers sometimes responded half-heartedly to the strike call or returned to work well before 12 May. This was true not only in towns that were little-industrialized, like Yarmouth, Lowestoft, Maidstone, Brighton, Portsmouth and Perth, but even in the larger cities and trade-union strongholds.[85] Eighty per cent of Liverpool tramwaymen were back at work by 8 May; the Southampton men, members of the T&GWU, came out only partially at the beginning of the strike, as did those of Bristol – and the latter, at least, resumed work completely within a few days.[86] Further instances of desertion occurred in Birmingham and Edinburgh, and there were reports of weakening among this section at other places too.[87] Among bus workers, evidence of 'leakages' was less common, but this was almost certainly because they were in any case less well-organized. Their strike was relatively solid in London, where nonetheless it was unable to prevent the restoration of a substantial bus service by 12 May. In the provinces the unions were probably more widely disobeyed and the extent of victimization here following the strike was some indication of the problems they had faced.[88]

The condition of the strike in road-goods transport was affected both by the heavy unemployment found in this industry and by the relative weakness of union organization. There were 392,000 workers (employed and self-employed) in this occupation in Britain in 1921; at most 60,000 were organized in trade unions in 1925–6.[89] After the stoppage the Intelligence Committee commented:

> One of the weak links in the chain was the inadequate organization amongst the commercial transport workers. The difficulties of organizing commercial transport where only two or three men are employed by a business firm are obvious, and even where commercial transport workers were members of trade unions there were cases where they did not respond to the call.[90]

The hesitancy of the organized men can probably be attributed to the lack of enthusiasm of certain local unions for the strike. Both the United Road Transport Workers in south Lancashire and the Scottish Horse and Motormen gave little more than token assent to the stoppage and both proceeded to distribute work permits wholesale to their members. Examples of men returning to work after coming out on strike seem to be found mainly in the sphere of operations of the Lancashire union: in Burnley, Radcliffe, Ashton and Stalybridge.[91]

No other group of workers had the strategical importance of those in transport. Nonetheless, the symptoms of weakness noted in other industries had a measure of influence on the General Council's view of the security of the strike. This was especially true of the printing trades, where the need to ensure the success of the stoppage was held to be vital to the outcome of the propaganda war; but where, again, implications of infirmity were widespread. Among the unions in this industry both the London compositors and the Scottish typographers had been somewhat reluctant to order a strike in the first place, whilst the principal English provincial union, the Typographical Association, had shown itself to be increasingly anxious about the loyalty of its members. In some cases this apprehension clearly proved justified: in Edmonton, Wolverhampton, Newark, Bristol and Edinburgh breakaways occurred in this section.[92] By 12 May the TUC Intelligence Committee was seriously alarmed about the scale on which private newspapers were reappearing, as both reflecting and contributing to 'the uncertainty of the printers'.[93] No other labour organizations were to encounter, in the aftermath, such major problems in securing reinstatement for their members.

Among electrical power workers the strike was even more varied in its coverage. The responsibility for its patchiness in this case lay primarily with the General Council itself, which had proposed not to shut down generating stations except where this was held to be necessary to reinforce the stoppage. The result was an ill-fated attempt to get electricity authorities to differentiate between the supply of power for domestic and for industrial uses, leading to a confusing succession of local withdrawals of labour, authorized and unauthorized, never by any means comprehensive and not always effective where undertaken. The Council's policy was, however, partly influenced by recognition of the incomplete organization of power workers, and by the fact that one of the main supervisory unions in this industry, the Electrical Power Engineers' Association, was unaffiliated to the TUC and refused to accept its orders. The rank-and-file workers may also have been affected by the elaborate government precautions taken to maintain an emergency service by means of naval ratings and volunteers. Thus even in London, where the strike of electricity workers was most actively prosecuted, twelve out of forty municipal power stations and ten out of thirty-one private ones appear to have escaped it, and in another five cases its coverage was partial.[94] In the provinces, stoppages had taken place in the generating plants of Bristol, Coventry, Bedford and much of the north-east in the first few days of the General Strike; and on 10 May the Strike Organization Committee authorized its extension to Nottingham, Warwick, Leicester, Birmingham and

Leeds.[95] But attempts to withdraw these workers elsewhere, probably largely on local initiative, were less successful. In Glasgow power workers supplying the tram service went back to work on 10 May, and efforts to arrest tramway services at Yarmouth and Lowestoft by stopping this section proved abortive.[96] In Southampton, Portsmouth and Cambridge proposals to strike local power stations of all kinds likewise could not be implemented, and in Liverpool the workers at the largest undertaking were brought out only very briefly.[97] Even in Birmingham, where the decision to enforce a stoppage had been centrally approved, it was evidently applied with some hesitation and with far from complete success.[98] It was small wonder that the ETU Executive claimed after the event that the method of carrying out the strike in the electricity industry had produced 'a state of chaos'.[99]

There were no recorded breaches of solidarity among iron and steel workers during the nine days. Among the engineering workers, on the other hand, the impact of the stoppage is exceptionally difficult to assess. They were not called out at the beginning of the conflict except where employed in the maintenance of transport services and in railway shops. These latter sections appear to have responded promptly, with only one or two cases of disobedience, like that of the Southampton ship repairers, explained chiefly by the ambiguity of the strike orders.[100] Moreover some local branches of the AEU and the Vehicle Builders, particularly in the midland car industry, took action unofficially. It is perhaps significant, however, that this kind of unauthorized stoppage did not occur in the major engineering centres of Clydeside, Tyneside, Sheffield and south Lancashire. Even where local militancy was conspicuous it did not necessarily produce a general solidarity: in Coventry, the strike of car workers involved about a quarter of the local AEU membership, but the remainder, less well-organized and more scattered, apparently often failed to obey the *official* strike instructions which became operative on 12 May.[101] How complete the engineering stoppage then was across the country it is almost impossible to say. Rumours of an impending settlement of the dispute may well have curtailed its extent, and the news of the termination began a rapid move back to work. Afterwards the AEU executive estimated that no more than fifty per cent of its membership had actually downed tools – a figure which is probably little more than a guess, though sufficient to indicate that the strike was far from unanimous.[102] Most of the retrospective reports of the Organizing District Delegates of the AEU were concerned with problems of reinstatement rather than the impact of the strike itself – though it is perhaps again significant that the official employers' federation took an unusually tolerant attitude on this question.[103] The response of ship-building workers is even more difficult to assess.

The analysis of the effectiveness of the General Strike industry by industry can be complemented by a consideration of its variable regional impact. This perspective, as might be expected, suggests a tendency for 'leakages' to occur particularly in the isolated towns of less-industrialized areas: the east and south coast resorts of Lowestoft, Yarmouth, Brighton and Portsmouth, and small inland towns like Stafford and Newark. But the biggest cities of the south, the west, and the midlands, Southampton, Bristol and Birmingham, were also relatively insecure, at least in some sections.[104] It is thus possible, starting with these examples and making some qualifications, to maintain the view that the solidarity of the General Strike became more assured as one moved from south to north, reaching its fullest extent, probably, in the great coalfields. South Wales and the north-east certainly seem to have been immune even to peripheral weaknesses – though evidence on the former region is scarcer than on the latter. Lancashire and Yorkshire appear a little less uniform in their allegiance. In Lancashire a few of the smaller urban centres gave grounds for anxiety; but the only large city of the north which showed signs of frailty was Leeds, whose divided strike organization not unnaturally demoralized the local leadership. From here the acting chairman of one of the local committees led a deputation to Eccleston Square to recommend that 'the great body of trade unionists' should 'retire gracefully from the dispute with the feeling that the whole Trade Unionists of Britain have made a great gesture in support of the Miners' case'.[105] This was, indeed, to be the only recorded instance of an appeal to terminate the stoppage originating at local level.

The contrast between south and north is, in some measure, heightened by consideration of the case of London. The capital did not, it was true, offer many examples of outright defection from the ranks of those on strike; such instances were minor and confined to outlying or partly middle-class boroughs like Edmonton and Marylebone.[106] But London did display an imbalance, increasingly marked, between the relatively inefficient strike organization and the government system of supply and transport ever more impressive and invincible. Nowhere were the signs of official activity, and the forces of order, so visible. Moreover the most overt exhibition of this superiority, in the military convoys dispatched to the London docks from 8 May, represented a direct defeat of local efforts at mass picketing; thereafter obstruction of traffic and street disturbances seem steadily to have declined. On 11 May, from the heart of the working-class East End, the acting secretary of the Poplar trades council wrote to the General Council that the growing number of vehicles on the road and the mobilization of the port 'are tending to make the rank and file affected by the strike question the correctness of the TUC publications'.[107] It would be surprising if this experience were not widespread. Even three days earlier Fenner Brockway had noted, on arrival in Manchester to edit the local edition of the *British Worker*, 'realization of the strike is much completer here than in London. At Westminster one was conscious of the power of the Government. Here the men are absolutely on top.'[108]. In part at least, as has been suggested, the General Council's view of the strike can be understood only by appreciating the nature of its situation 'in the heart of the enemy's camp'.[109]

These numerous though still, on the whole, isolated cases of defection and loss of confidence did not represent a serious attenuation of the General Strike in the national perspective. The scale of such sectional and local breakaways was small, reflecting the failings of particular unions or the vulnerability of particular minorities of wage-earners; and their occurrence was in any case not always known to the General Council itself, still less to the mass of strikers. Nonetheless, Eccleston Square had gained the impression, however blurred, of an accumulation of slight casualties which created an understandable fear of larger losses. From this viewpoint, moreover, it seems artificial to differentiate between the deliquescence of the strike on the one hand and the expansion of government services on the other; their psychological effects were complementary and mutually reinforcing. Official anti-strike measures would have been less alarming had there been no evidence of their ability to bring about a resumption of work; such desertions as had occurred would have appeared less significant in the absence of volunteers and the barrage of government propaganda. If the strike committees in the country remained largely oblivious to the danger of collapse, manifesting rather that self-absorbed confidence which prevails in almost all industrial stoppages, the General Council was naturally more sensitive to it and more fearful of it. And it was their reaction to the symptoms of waning support, incipient and obscure as they were, which was decisive of the fate of the General Strike.

The number of workers involved in the General Strike

The Ministry of Labour estimated that, excluding the miners, 1,580,000 workpeople were affected by the stoppage of May 1926. They did not however offer any breakdown of this figure by industry or union. The Strike Organization Committee, on the other hand, claimed that two million men had stopped work by 8 May.[110] The main difficulty in assessing these figures arises from the partial character of the strike in some industries, and the constant shifting of its boundaries. An attempt to do so may begin, however, with the returns which individual unions made, during or after the stoppage, of the numbers of their own members withdrawn – though some of these statements are, clearly, fairly impressionistic.

TABLE 12. *Union estimates of workers on strike, 4–12 May**

Workers' Union	58,000
General and Municipal Workers	74, 398 (8 May)
Distributive and Allied Workers	10,000
Transport and General Workers	353,000
Vehicle Builders	22,450 (10 May)
Federation of Building Trade Operatives	200,000 (4 May)

* Where the statement relates to a particular date, this is given; otherwise, it can be taken as the maximum involved at any one time. The Building Trades Operatives' estimate applied to all building workers on strike.

In addition, the four national railway companies calculated that just over 540,000 staff had failed to report for duty on 5–6 May. This number excludes the employees of the Metropolitan and London Underground railways, and may be raised by, perhaps, 20,000 on that count. Estimates in other cases have to be based, unreliably, on the membership affiliated to the Trades Union Congress in 1925. The following figures are thus very approximate, especially in the two latter instances.

TABLE 13. *Supplementary estimates for other trade groups involved in the General Strike*

Printing and paper workers	165,000
Metal workers	140,000
Electrical workers	15,000
Transport and general workers (in unions other than those listed in Table 12)	50,000

This yields a grand total of just over 1,650,000, excluding engineering and shipbuilding workers, the bulk of whom were brought out only on the last day of the strike. The addition to be made on this count is very difficult to assess (see p. 215). 516,901 members in these two groups were affiliated to the TUC in 1925, including electricians and vehicle builders. Those in the railway, power and motor industries having already been partly or wholly computed, it seems possible that another 150,000 were brought out on 12 May. It is thus reasonable to conclude that the Ministry of Labour underestimated the scale of the strike by at least 200,000 and that the Strike Organization Committee perhaps exaggerated it by about the same margin.

X The Search for a Settlement

The government's *non-possumus* to further negotiations while the General Strike lasted and the General Council's insistence that the lock-out of the miners end before any concessions be expected of them, appeared to close all avenues to peace save that of unilateral surrender. In fact, however, not even the Cabinet was wholeheartedly intent on a fight to the death. Though ruling out agreement on independent mediation, Baldwin and some at least of his colleagues were still willing to entertain the hope that the TUC might be prompted by other means to end the stoppage voluntarily. The General Council, on the other hand, were anxious to find a suitable intermediary to operate behind the scenes. When the chairman of the Coal Commission, Sir Herbert Samuel, proposed to intervene in the dispute, therefore, each side saw some use for him, though of a very different kind. The government sought to dissociate itself from his peace-making activities, but not actually to obstruct them – and Baldwin in particular was probably optimistic that Samuel might persuade the union leaders that withdrawal from the battlefield was a price worth paying for the resumption of official talks. The General Council convinced themselves that Samuel had sufficient political influence or authority to enter into a surrogate agreement with him which was, in reality, an act of surrender.

The Liberal Party and the strike

In assuming the role of peacemaker Samuel was largely, though not wholly, without competitors. Of the public men and organizations which might have been attracted to the role, the one enjoying the most obvious opportunities and perhaps offered the highest prospective reward was the Liberal Party. Through lack of political unity and effective leadership, however, the chance was lost. On the eve of the

General Strike the Liberal shadow cabinet had agreed to take up a middle position in the crisis, supporting the necessary emergency measures to maintain essential services and protect the authority of the government, but declining to endorse its handling of the dispute or its veto on negotiations.[1] Asquith's speech in the House of Lords debate on 4 May was accordingly moderate in tone.[2] Thereafter, however, the majority of the party leaders moved, apparently without forethought or collusion, into a strongly anti-union position. The articles which Asquith and Grey wrote for the *British Gazette* and Sir John Simon's disquisition in the Commons on the illegality of the stoppage removed any claim which the party might have asserted to neutrality. Simon did something to try and restore the balance on 11 May, when he and other Liberal MPs put down a Commons motion calling for a simultaneous withdrawal of strike and lock-out, unconditional acceptance of the Samuel Report by the government, miners and owners, and the renewal of the subsidy 'for a brief period'. But this came too late, and from a source now too distrusted, to make any impact.[3]

Lloyd George, alone of the Liberal hierarchy, had taken a line more critical of the government. In the Commons on the first day of the strike he had pronounced it 'an ordinary trade dispute', and criticized the owners' delay in making a national wage offer and the administration's failure to put forward detailed schemes of legislation.[4] Thereafter, however, he was unable to play any significant part in the emergency, inhibited possibly by his colleagues' pro-government posture and frustrated certainly in his attempts to launch a Liberal paper. His disapproval of the conduct of the other Liberal leaders caused him to refuse to attend the meeting of the shadow cabinet on 10 May; and in the belief that the stoppage would continue for some time he may have been envisaging a further personal initiative, probably in support of the churches' appeal. Its rapid closure left his plans obscure. But in view of this the Asquithian attempt to make his self-imposed isolation during the strike a *casus belli* in the aftermath, partly by alleging a desire on his part to defect to the Labour Party, was primarily the outcome of longstanding rivalries in the party rather than of the disagreement, slight in real import, over this crisis.[5]

The Archbishop of Canterbury calls for peace

The one significant attempt to launch a public movement for a negotiated peace was that undertaken by the churches. Even in this case it is questionable how far the clergy concerned hoped or intended to do more than make a well-intentioned gesture. Certainly Randall Davidson, the Archbishop of Canterbury, associated himself with the appeal only as a result of pressure exercised by others, both anglicans and non-conformists. The sentiments he had expressed in the House of Lords on 5 May had revealed little sympathy for the strike; and though he suggested very tentatively the reopening of negotiations, he had seemed disposed to leave this to the discretion of the government.[6] The instigators of the call for peace among the clergy were the bishops of London, Southwark and Ripon, and various prominent dissenters such as Scott Lidgett.[7] As a result, on 7 May, Davidson issued a statement – 'the mildest version he could secure after several hours effort', Tom Jones reported to Baldwin – which asked for the termination of the strike, the renewal of the subsidy 'for a short, definite period' and the withdrawal of the owners' district wage demands, 'simultaneously and concurrently'.[8]

The appeal had plenty of backing from the labour side. It was endorsed beforehand by Ramsay MacDonald, and was subsequently widely distributed by the General Council. But the organization of opinion in its favour, outside the ranks of the strikers, had to be left largely to others. Labour sympathizers at Oxford University circulated petitions; a few local government bodies passed resolutions on the same lines; the headmasters of Eton, Harrow and Charterhouse, and an unorthodox Conservative backbencher, Sir Henry Cavendish-Bentinck, conveyed their support to Baldwin privately so as not to embarrass the government.[9] But the prospects of winning mass approval for such a proposal, never good, were destroyed by the refusal of John Reith to allow Davidson to broadcast his message.

The archbishop, perhaps partly because of divisions within the church itself, made little subsequent attempt to garner support.[10] Informed from the outset of Baldwin's own objections to his recommendations, Davidson probably never expected to change his mind. On 11 May, when he finally interviewed Baldwin, he made no attempt to press the case for the appeal.[11] 'I told him that . . . we had very deliberately come to the conclusion we had formulated as a suggestion for the Government to consider, but that the responsibility must now be his as to whether or not they turn our suggestion down and go forward on what they believe to be a sounder and more excellent line. . . .' Nor did the Prime Minister's continued indifference to the churches' proposals prevent the archbishop writing, a week after the General Strike was over, to praise his 'firmness, persistent conciliatoriness, and solid practical counsel'.[12]

The fate of the ecclesiastical appeal served to highlight the inadequacy of 'public opinion' as an agent of reconciliation during the General Strike. The same quiescence was observable even within the ranks of those most directly affected within industry. Lacking a unitary organization to represent them, unequally disadvantaged by the stoppage, and almost certainly in disagreement about how it should be ended, private employers were unlikely to be able to play any successful mediatory role. Though there is some indication that the General Council looked to them to put pressure on the government, no open intervention was forthcoming. Only one industrialist, Sir Allan Smith (President of the Engineering Employers' Federation), saw Baldwin during the stoppage to discuss the question of a settlement – and his views, though unexpectedly pacific, were also unofficial.[13] Only one other, Sir Alfred Mond, sought to mobilize opinion among fellow-industrialists for a similar purpose. He arranged a further meeting, primarily of mine-owners, on 7 May, to renew the advocacy of his own scheme for reorganization of the coal industry; but there was no suggestion of putting this forward as an immediate solution to the General Strike.[14] Otherwise, the forces of capital appeared concerned only with the smooth running of the emergency machinery and, in a few cases, with the issues likely to arise when work was eventually resumed.

The Wimborne – Thomas talks

There were in the end only two serious attempts to intercede between the government and the TUC away from the public eye. The first, which remained the more closely guarded at the time and afterwards, was the initiative of two former Liberal ministers, Lord Wimborne and Lord Reading.[15] A luncheon at the house of the former on 8 May, which J. H. Thomas and Lord Gainford attended, began a series of conversations between the NUR Secretary and his host, with Reading usually in attendance, which continued until the strike had ended. The Cabinet were aware of them from the outset, Churchill, Birkenhead and Tom Jones all being informed of the first meeting, and the latter channelling information to Baldwin on subsequent transactions.[16]

Thomas's reasons for taking part in the discussions at Wimborne House are unclear. It seems extremely unlikely that he expected to secure a settlement by these exchanges; and the General Council as a whole were evidently not informed about them. The only indication of his intention is given by the 'formula' which he agreed with Wimborne, and which was conveyed to Baldwin on 10 May:[17]

If some assurance could be given that negotiations would be resumed for the purpose of bringing the recommendations of the Report into operation without delay, it is possible that the TUC might call off the General Strike and indicate that miners accept the Report unconditionally with all its implications, including the question of possible adjustment of wages as the basis of a settlement. This assurance might be accepted if it were made by some person of influence, not a member of the Government.

The non-committal phraseology of this statement suggests that what Thomas perhaps hoped to obtain from the liaison was some unofficial reinforcement of the status of the concurrent negotiations with Sir Herbert Samuel. Certainly the Negotiating Committee of the General Council were anxious to establish Samuel's credentials more fully at this point – and entertained the belief that he had a larger measure of government approval than he admitted to them.[18] But whether this speculation has any basis or not, Baldwin's evasive response to the formula was simply that his broadcast of two days before had already given a promise of the government's willingness to renew its efforts for a settlement of the coal dispute if the general strike were called off. Wimborne's attempts to obtain a more explicit indication of 'what it was the intention of the Government to do, if and when coal negotiations were resumed' were ignored. The only information given to him or to Reading concerned the Cabinet's intention to introduce emergency anti-strike legislation – intelligence which, though they did not disclose it to Thomas, prompted them to urge upon him, at their final meeting on 11 May, the advisability of a unilateral withdrawal from the strike. It is possible, though again conjectural, that the railwaymen's leader concluded from their emphaticness that the cancellation of the strike was regarded as a worthwhile risk.[19]

The repercussions of the Wimborne conversations are thus entirely uncertain. It is possible that they prompted the government to select Lord Reading as the prospective chairman of the national wages board which they proposed to the miners on 14 May. It is likely that they encouraged Wimborne himself to continue to play the role of conciliator during the mining lock-out. It is also possible that Selwyn Davies, his private secretary, was the informant who led Baldwin to believe that the General Council would end the stoppage on the night of 11 May. Finally, it is possible, if Thomas made his dealings with Baldwin through this channel known to his colleagues on the Negotiating Committee, that they attached more weight to the indefinite undertakings of Baldwin's broadcast than they might otherwise have done. With a generous allowance of guesswork, it is thus permissible to see events at Wimborne House as making a contribution, small but significant, to the negotiations between the TUC and their own chosen mediator, Sir Herbert Samuel.

The Samuel memorandum

Sir Herbert Samuel was at San Vigilio in the Italian Lakes when the General Strike broke out, working at a book on 'what is wrong with the world'.[20] On 3 May he telegraphed Baldwin, offering to return to England to assist in re-starting negotiations between the disputants; but the Prime Minister, no longer interested in such help, replied the following morning that the stoppage had begun and that he would contact Samuel again 'when opportunity arises'. The latter did not wait for more than a few hours, however, before leaving his retreat unbidden – and by enlisting the aid of the Chief Civil Commissioner he was able to reach London by the evening of 6 May.[21]

Samuel's inclination to intervene in the dispute reflected his natural dissatisfaction with the misinterpretation and neglect of the Royal Commission's report. The wage cuts proposed by the owners, he told Baldwin later, 'went far beyond anything contemplated by the Commission'. The government, too, had failed 'to explain to public opinion the reasons for the proposals in the Report'. And to the TUC Negotiating Committee he criticized the Cabinet's delay in involving themselves in peace-making, adding that he and his colleagues 'always regarded national negotiations as imperative'.[22]

Samuel's own ideas on how to achieve a settlement were at first ill-formed. On the evening of his return he saw his fellow-commissioner and principal confidant, Sir William Beveridge, who provided him with an *aide mémoire* outlining an agreement involving a National Wages Board including members from outside the coal industry, an advisory committee on reorganization and a further fortnight's subsidy.[23] These proposals were sketchy, but did introduce the themes which Samuel was to elaborate. Later that evening, he contacted J. H. Thomas, who offered to arrange a meeting with the Negotiating Committee of the General Council the following day.[24] Samuel also drafted a letter to the miners and owners, which obviously anticipated a direct approach to them; and, probably at some time during 7 May, held conversations with representatives of the Mining Associations. These talks, however, 'made no headway'.[25] The proposals which Samuel described in his unposted letter envisaged the retention of the existing national minimum wage on the understanding that reductions were made in basis wages at district level, and the establishment of a National Wages Board (as well as an advisory committee) sharing responsibility for reconstructing the industry. In neither aspect would they have been acceptable to the owners. The TUC Negotiating Committee, on the other hand, received similar suggestions with much more cordiality; and it was for this reason, no doubt, that Samuel left the employers alone, abandoned any idea of a separate approach to the miners, and concentrated his attention on them.

The Negotiating Committee were favourably disposed, as they always had been, towards an agreement which associated wage adjustments with reorganization. They liked the idea of a National Wages Board with an enlarged competence – indeed, Citrine presents it as their own idea.[26] They were not, in principle, averse to cuts in basis rates – and, according to their interlocutor, 'gave me a definite assurance that the miners' attitude had changed . . . that the principal difficulty was the intense suspicion of the miners that while wage reductions would be a certainty the reconstitution of the industry would prove in fact dilatory and doubtful. That if this suspicion could be removed the wage question would fall into the background.' As a further assurance on this point, therefore, Samuel suggested a wage settlement to last only a year in the first instance. The one proposal which he tentatively advanced and which the Committee found 'disastrous' was for a half-hour extension of the working day.[27]

It was readily agreed that the conversations should continue. Samuel told the Committee that he was about to see the Prime Minister, and it was doubtless hoped that this would give the talks some kind of official standing. But when, next morning, Smith and Cook complained to the General Council, with some heat, at their exclusion from the meeting, they were partially reassured by the statement that nothing more than a preliminary discussion had as yet taken place.

Later on 8 May Samuel told the Negotiating Committee of the disappointing outcome of his interview with the government's representatives; ministers 'were not prepared to negotiate, either privately or openly'.[28] He showed the trade unionists the formula he had put before Baldwin, however – which proposed that the TUC accept wage reductions in principle and that the government temporarily renew the subsidy – and suggested that its publication with their approval 'would place the responsibility on the Government of saying whether they accepted my [Samuel's] letter or not'. From Citrine's account it seems that the Committee were willing to adopt this procedure. On the other hand they were not disposed to accept a settlement unless it had been worked out in some detail, and they now set out to formalize and elaborate the points which Samuel had discussed with them the previous day. But it is clear from subsequent events that they did not reveal either to the miners or to the other members of the General Council how their go-between had been rebuffed by Downing Street.[29]

The first 'Samuel memorandum' was circulated to the General Council on the evening of 8 May, and presented to the miners' subcommittee the following day. It envisaged the establishment of a National Wages Board with a neutral element, empowered 'to keep a constant watch' over the progress of reorganization in the mining industry; reductions in basis wage rates for a provisional twelve-month period, to be agreed initially at district level, or else fixed by independent chairmen of district boards (subject to national approval); and legislation to facilitate the amalgamation of pits on lines recommended by the Royal Commission. Probably at the Committee's insistence, the Prime Minister was to give a categorical promise 'that no Parliamentary methods in either House would be allowed to defeat or impede . . . legislation' on this subject. The TUC were required to end the stoppage, and to accept, thus reinterpreted, 'the general proposals in the [Samuel] Report which deal with wages', whereupon the government were to extend the subsidy until 1 June, or for another twelve days if the state of negotiations warranted it.[30]

These terms remained ambiguous in several respects, especially in regard to the powers of the national board over local pay agreements, on whether the miners themselves were to pronounce their readiness to receive lower wages and on the extent of the cuts thereby approved. They reproduced, in fact, some of the obscurities of the Royal Commission report and of the proposals adopted by the General Council on 3 May. In particular, though compulsory arbitration was envisaged in connection with district wages settlements, the miners were still apparently to have more freedom to bargain at national level: the final clause of the memorandum read, '*If it becomes clear that a settlement is being arrived at*, the subsidy [may] be extended to, say, June 12th, to enable the negotiations to be completed'.[31] These uncertainties were never to be effectively removed. Neither now or later, however, did they concern the miners. On 9 May Samuel's proposals were rejected as a basis for negotiation, first by their subcommittee, then by the full executive, on the grounds that any wage reductions were unacceptable – in basis rates (which Herbert Smith held it impossible to revise so completely) or in the national minimum, by arbitration or by voluntary agreement, with or without an understanding on reorganization.[32]

It seems, from the very imperfect evidence on these exchanges, that the Negotiating Committee made little effort to press the miners to change their minds. But doubt must have been cast on the value of the assurance given to Samuel that a compromise was now feasible. 'It was evident to me,' Citrine wrote in his diary, 'that the General Council were coming to the conclusion that it was simply hopeless to continue the strike if the intention was that in no circumstances and in no conditions would the miners accept any reductions.'[33] Apparently undeterred by this reverse, however, the General Council – or more probably the Negotiating Committee – went on to prepare a list of amendments and additions to the Samuel document, which were to be presented to its author the next day. These were probably influenced largely by the proposals drawn up jointly with the miners on 3 May, though they also took account of the suggestions contained in Ernest Bevin's memoranda, prepared in the latter part of April, which were now transmitted to the Committee (perhaps in a refurbished form) through Milne-Bailey.[34] Bevin, in particular, had for some time favoured a wholesale restructuring of the wage system of the mining industry, creating new and consolidated standards and pruning the myriad local rates. Now that straightforward cuts in the minimum or in basis rates seemed out of the question, it was in this direction that the Negotiating Committee turned.

When they saw Samuel again, on the morning of 10 May, this was the only one of their ideas which the Committee seem immediately to have pressed. Instead of rewriting the letter of 8 May, they discussed with their intermediary a 'formula', more briefly expressed, which sought simply to define the general principles of a possible agreement, with a view to gaining the miners' assent. It showed a number of significant differences with the first document. The negotiation of a new wage agreement was clearly to take place only *after* measures of reorganization had been agreed. A committee, including representatives of the miners, would be appointed to cooperate in the preparation of legislation – the National Wages Board retaining responsibility for overseeing its application. The wage settlement then drawn up was to be 'on simpler lines than those hitherto followed', though stipulating 'reasonable figures below which the wage of no class of labour should be reduced in any circumstances'. The idea of an interim agreement was tacitly dropped. No procedure for ending the dispute was now set out: it was merely asserted that 'negotiations cannot . . . be begun until the lock-out notices at the mines are withdrawn'.[35]

On Monday afternoon the Negotiating Committee brought the national officials of the Miners' Federation to discuss this formula with Sir Herbert Samuel. He recited its clauses to them verbally; but argument focussed thereafter entirely upon the justifiability of wage cuts. The meeting served only to show the miners' hostility to Samuel, therefore; it was not to be repeated.[36] That evening, for the first time during the strike, the full executive of the Federation attended the General Council. The formula was now given them in writing, and the breach between the two bodies at last became explicit. 'Miner after miner got up,' Citrine recorded, 'and, speaking with intensity of feeling, affirmed that the miners could not go back to work on a reduction in wages.' Pugh, with equal intensity, put the view of the Council: the adoption of Samuel as a mediator was necessary since neither the government nor the TUC could engage in direct negotiations; the miners were rejecting his proposals without offering any alternative; to suppose that the prolongation of the strike would obtain a continuation of the subsidy was 'living in a fool's paradise'; the outcome would merely be defeat by 'process of attrition'. 'Our men in the coalfields have given us our instructions and we cannot depart from them,' replied Smith.[37] Following an adjournment, the miners' executive finally delivered their reply at about one o'clock: they would accept the formula only if it contained, in place of the proposal for a new wage agreement, the statement that 'they [the TUC] are of opinion that there should be no revision of the previous wage rates or conditions, because if the measures for reorganisation are actually put into effect such revision would be unnecessary.'[38]

The Council discussed the miners' attitude after their departure, but came to no decision about how to proceed. Samuel was informed at first simply that they had proved intractable, for the following morning (11 May) he prepared a letter to Baldwin which assumed that his attempt to conciliate had been abortive.[39]

> The TUC were deceiving themselves when they informed me that there was no longer an absolute veto upon any kind of reduction in any circumstances. My clear view is that the veto remains exactly the same now as it was throughout the negotiations. This is due not only to the suspicion, which is undoubtedly a real one, that reconstruction will not eventuate to any full extent in the near future, but also to the conviction that the miners' wages are already low and are not susceptible of any further reduction at all.

The only feasible course, he concluded, was 'to continue the contest until an assent is secured, to the wage reductions on the scale suggested in the Report'.

Before this letter could be sent, however, the General Council communicated their fateful decision to send the Negotiating Committee back to Samuel with a view to composing a settlement which they could adopt on their own authority.[40] That afternoon the final version of the memorandum was drawn up, based on the terms of Samuel's letter of 8 May, but incorporating most of the amendments put forward by the Negotiating Committee on the tenth and the main clauses, slightly reworded, of the subsequent formula.[41] The only suggestion which Samuel opposed was the introduction of a paragraph ensuring the unions against victimisation – which the members of the Committee 'did not press'. The document completed, Samuel promised to see his former colleagues on the Commission in the expectation of being able to obtain their signatures.[42]

The General Council held a further meeting at 6 pm, heard the report of the Negotiating Committee and summoned the miners for 8 o'clock. It was agreed that 'the General Council would appeal to their executive to assist us by suggesting the termination of the General Strike'. Despite earlier rebuffs, there was some optimism that an assent could be secured.[43] Immediately afterwards Samuel sent for the Negotiating Committee to inform them that his fellow-commissioners had withheld approval of the memorandum, mainly on the grounds that it proposed a renewal of the subsidy.[44] But the Council were not now inclined to change their course. When the meeting with the miners convened, Pugh urged them feelingly to accept the memorandum as 'a fair basis for negotiating a settlement'. According to the Federation's later account,

> The Chairman . . . said that . . . the general strike movement had now reached the apex, and from now onwards every additional hour it lasted would not

increase but diminish its strength and the power of the movement to obtain an honourable settlement. In the light of the latest information which had come into their possession as to the position of the movement in the country, the Council had decided that the time had now arrived when it must face up to its responsibilities, and it had therefore decided to request the miners to come to a definite decision to-night upon the proposals which had resulted from the conversations of the TUC representatives with Sir Herbert Samuel that day.

Mr Pugh then read out the proposals.[45]

The miners' leaders protested at their own exclusion from the afternoon's discussions. In the argument which followed, moreover, the Council's 'request' was clearly transformed into an ultimatum; Pugh, 'tired, worn, and a little bit sick of things – did tell the miners they had to have it or leave it', Bevin recalled.[46] Tempers were high when the miners adjourned to consider their answer. It took them two hours, however, to prepare a reply rejecting the terms offered as involving 'a reduction of the wages of a large number of mineworkers' and dissociating themselves from the decision to end the stoppage.[47] They left Eccleston Square shortly before midnight.

This outright refusal of the Samuel terms, which even if apprehended had not been prepared for, threw the Council into momentary confusion. Bevin suggested that a deputation be sent to the miners next day to try and persuade them to reconsider their decision. The acceptance of this motion seemed conceivably to threaten a postponement of the resolution to end the strike, whereupon both J. H. Thomas and Frank Beard, President of the Workers' Union, asserted that they would not prolong the stoppage without further authorization from their executives. Immediately afterwards the phone call from Downing Street was announced, and Citrine was asked by Gower, Baldwin's secretary, whether there was any prospect of the Council's wishing to see the Prime Minister that evening. Both he and Bevin saw this in retrospect as a catalyst instantaneous in effect. The Council instructed Citrine to arrange an interview for noon the following day: this assignation 'meant plainly . . . the calling-off of the General Strike'.[48]

The origin of this phone call remains mysterious. According to Osbert Sitwell, J. H. Thomas had two brief conversations with Lord Wimborne's secretary, Selwyn Davies, during the course of the evening – the first at about 10 pm and the second around 2 am. At their earlier encounter he told Davies that 'although he was encountering the most formidable obstacles', he thought a decision to end the General Strike would be taken within the next four hours. This information was passed by Davies to Tom Jones (as was the message, later that night, confirming that the stoppage was indeed to be called off).[49] Ernest Bevin, on the other hand, confided in his union's area officials at the end of May, 'I have been told since that the Prime Minister was told from our own side that we might be wanting him early in the evening' – though this, too, might be read as an inaccurate reference to Thomas's contacts.[50] It is also possible, though not probable, that Samuel himself told Downing Street of the apparent success of his efforts. But whatever the identity of Baldwin's informant, the intervention it prompted was the occasion, not the cause, of the General Council's decision. While the latter might have been spared further argument concerning the status of the Samuel memorandum, it is not plausible to think that it would have awaited a second refusal from the miners before following the only course which now seemed open.

The following morning the members of the Strike Organization Committee visited the miners' offices and spent some time in argument with their executive. Bevin, their chief spokesman, laid stress mainly on the danger of victimization which would be intensified by a division in the unions' ranks and the growing danger of breakaways if the stoppage were to continue.[51] The miners, after again retiring, issued a resolution which avoided actually referring to the Samuel memorandum, acknowledged the help they had been given by the rest of the movement, but announced that there would be no return to work on their part before a special conference were held on Friday. When the press were given this decision, however, during the afternoon, they were not in doubt about its implications.

At Downing Street the General Council were met on the doorstep by Sir Horace Wilson, sent to verify that their purpose was to end the strike and not to attempt to engage in negotiations. Baldwin looked 'rather haggard and drawn', though some of the other ministers appeared to Ben Turner to be 'in great glee'.[52] At the interview which followed, Pugh made the most veiled of references to the talks with Samuel; Thomas and Bevin asked the Prime Minister to make 'a general request as head of the government' that victimization should be avoided; but only the latter mentioned the withdrawal of the lock-out, pointing out that 'thousands of our people cannot go back if the colliers are still out. . . .' Baldwin met these demands with characteristic flaccidity: 'I think you may trust me to consider what has been said with a view to seeing how best we can get the country quickly back into the condition in which we all want to see it.'[53] In the garden afterwards conversation continued for a short time while a press statement was being drafted, and Pugh (as he told Citrine) now pressed the same point upon Baldwin: 'Unless the notices were withdrawn at once, it meant that our people would think there had been a complete breach of faith.'[54] He evidently obtained no more positive a response.

On their return to Eccleston Square, Pugh and Citrine dispatched telegrams to union headquarters instructing national executives to arrange a resumption as soon as possible. Later they drafted a letter enclosing the Samuel memorandum and the accompanying correspondence. These were held to represent 'sufficient assurances . . . as to the lines upon which a settlement could be reached to justify them in terminating the General Strike', a decision taken 'in order that negotiations could be resumed to secure a settlement in the coal mining industry, free and unfettered from either strike or lock-out'. The unions themselves had been given the responsibility for organizing the return to work, 'having regard to the varied circumstances and practices in each industry'.[55] The mood of false optimism thus fostered could hardly be expected to last, however, and was in fact shattered within a day.

The ending of the strike

In reaching the decision to withdraw from the General Strike the General Council leaped a number of separate hurdles. Their acceptance of Samuel as an intermediary following his preliminary interview with the Negotiating Committee on 7 May was the first measurable step, though the *need* for some such diplomatic broker had already been appreciated. Their recommendation of both the first and second set of proposals discussed with Samuel to the miners, and the decision to send the Negotiating Committee back to see him again on the afternoon of 11 May, were all significant milestones. They led naturally to the two critical moments of Tuesday evening: the presentation of the final version of the memorandum as a *de facto* ultimatum, and the decision, made shortly before 1 am, to meet Baldwin at midday on 12 May.

When during this sequence the Council reached the point of no return is difficult to ascertain. As early as the night of 10 May some members were suggesting that they must assert their right to override the miners in concluding a settlement.[56] The adoption of the memorandum on the eleventh obviously arose directly from this conviction. On the other hand the extent to which this endorsement would cause the memorandum to be seen as an ultimatum was probably less than fully perceived. And even after its rejection by the miners there was still a hesitation on the part of some TUC leaders to admit the logical necessity of proceeding independently. Indeed, the consequences of that policy were never clearly faced. To the outside observer it may appear that all the ingredients of the final resolution to end the stoppage were present already before midday on 11 May; but for many members of the Council it took another twelve hours or more to overcome the emotional inhibitions and anxieties which held them in check.

What is scarcely in doubt, however, despite these uncertainties, is that the dominant impulse which propelled the Council towards peace was, from the very outset, the belief that the strike itself was bound to weaken and decline. The terms of the Samuel memorandum appeared acceptable because outright victory was held impossible. This was admitted even at the time of Samuel's original intercession. The first advocates of a diplomatic *démarche* were, indeed, the principals of the Strike Organization Committee; on the morning of 6 May Bevin had proposed that Purcell be sent to Manchester to secure the help of C. P. Scott, who was trying to organize local business support for a negotiated settlement. He also hoped to obtain the backing of other industrialists and financiers in the capital, as well as the churchmen associated with the Archbishop of Canterbury's appeal, 'to try and get such a powerful body of people – commercial, religious and otherwise – to appoint a committee which would have acted as a mediatory committee between us and the Government'.[57] Other members, less immediately apprehensive than Bevin about the prospects of the strike, were unwilling to support an initiative by the SOC – but there was no disagreement with its general objective. According to Citrine, Thomas was also 'undoubtedly anxious to get negotiations on foot as soon as possible'; and the sense of the Council as a whole was 'that it was desirable that even though we are certain of the strength of our strategic situation, we should lose no opportunity of getting on to negotiations'.[58]

This remained the critical consideration. The talks with Samuel went well because the Negotiating Committee were willing to show their flexibility on the wage question from the beginning, as well as because of their regard for their intermediary and his report. Although the fiction was preserved that the talks were of an 'exploratory' nature this had clearly ceased to be so by the meeting of Monday morning. By then disquiet about the prolongation of the stoppage had considerably intensified. An agreement with Samuel now afforded the only possibility of an organized retreat, the prevention of a collapse. On Monday and Tuesday, and again on Wednesday morning, this was the main argument employed to persuade the miners to associate themselves with the General Council. It also made a change of mind, or even a further postponement in face of the Federation's obstinacy, impossible to contemplate.

The miners' executive, for its part, was certainly not wholly united; but it contained fewer advocates of moderation than the General Council had hoped and its members were almost uniformly loyal to collective decisions.[59] The majority attitude was determined primarily by an objection to wage reductions in any guise. The other grounds given for opposing the memorandum – its presentation as an ultimatum, the exclusion of the miners themselves from its negotiation, and especially the lack of any guarantees of its acceptance by the government – were, as Professor Bullock suggests, 'beside the point'.[60] None of these arguments had been mentioned in discussion on the first two drafts of a peace settlement which Samuel had put forward. The only additional consideration which might have weighed with the miners (might, that is, have offset their main concern) was their own estimation of the durability of the General Strike. It seems probable, though not certain, however, that they discounted the TUC's fear of defections. But it is also not impossible that their leadership would have been indifferent to such signs of weakening, even had they acknowledged them; the lock-out in the coal industry was to show, in the months to come, for what extremes of sacrifice they were prepared.

Having identified the principal motives of both parties on the labour side, it is still necessary to examine the attitude of the General Council to the Samuel memorandum itself. However strong their wish to accept its terms, they were still bound to insist that it provide an adequate justification in the eyes of the movement at large for their decision to end the strike, and this adequacy depended not just on the reasonableness of its proposals but their enforceability. It was on this issue, of whether faith should have been placed in Samuel's authority, that controversy raged most fiercely in the aftermath.

There need be no doubt about the position of the government. When Samuel saw Baldwin on the morning of 8 May he submitted the first version of the letter which he proposed to lay before the Negotiating Committee of the TUC. Since his discussions with the latter body were still at an exploratory stage, however, the draft contained only a brief and incomplete précis of the memorandum laid before the General Council the next evening; it stated simply that the General Strike should be ended, that the government should ask parliament to renew the subsidy to the coal industry until at least the end of May and that the Council should give an assurance that no part of the Royal Commission's report be ruled out of consideration provided that any agreement negotiated should effectively guarantee reorganization.[61] In this vaguely worded and embryonic form, Samuel's scheme had obviously little to recommend it to his audience. It was scrutinized by the other members of the Coal Committee – Neville Chamberlain, Birkenhead, Steel-Maitland and Horace Wilson – and condemned on the same grounds that previous peace formulae had been found wanting: the miners were not committed to any specific wage reductions. Even more important was the constraint created by the government's own public insistence that the General Strike was unconstitutional and that its withdrawal must be unconditional. It was in these terms that the letter handed to Samuel by Steel-Maitland that afternoon was cast:[62]

> Until the necessary orders have been given to withdraw the Strike or unless the Strike has come to an end we cannot as a condition or inducement take part in negotiations in relation to the mining issue . . . [the Government] hold that the General Strike is unconstitutional and illegal. They are bound to take steps to make its repetition impossible. . . . In these circumstances I am sure that the Government will take the view that while they are bound most carefully and most sympathetically to consider the terms of any arrangement which a public man of your responsibility and experience may propose, it is imperative to make it plain that any discussion which you think proper to initiate is not clothed in even a vestige of official character.

This letter stated clearly the government's stance while the General Strike lasted but was less clear about its intentions if and when the dispute were ended; no thought was given, in fact, to the manner in which an 'unofficial' compromise would then be regarded. Even on the last day of the strike members of the Cabinet seemed concerned only with avoiding the appearance of bargaining. Prior to the TUC deputation to Downing Street, Joynson-Hicks wrote to Baldwin: 'with the concurrence of Sam Hoare, Gilmour, and Philip [Cunliffe-Lister] the only Ministers present, to say that we are very nervous as to the risk of even appearing to enter into any negotiations with the TUC until there has been an unconditional withdrawal of the General Strike'.[63] Once peace was restored, however, since the government had neither discouraged Samuel's efforts on his own behalf, nor explicitly criticized it on proposals made known to them (on 8 May) they were at least susceptible to the exercise of moral pressure; and it was on this, evidently, that Samuel himself prepared to rely.

Samuel did, nonetheless, tell the Negotiating Committee that he had received no authority from the government and they failed to pass the message on to their colleagues. This provides the strongest grounds for accusing the Committee of bad faith. But did they believe him? His first letter to the General Council chairman, revised after two consultations with the Committee, nonetheless contained the assertion, 'I wrote entirely on my own initiative and not at the request of or on behalf of any of the parties concerned.'[64] It was not inherently unreasonable to suppose that Samuel's relations with the Cabinet were similar to his understanding with the TUC. Moreover, on that same Saturday evening Baldwin made his conciliatory broadcast, appearing to promise that the government would recommend its own settlement (more than it had done before) if the strike were ended:[65]

> I did my utmost to secure agreement upon the basis of the Commission's report, and when the time comes, as I hope it soon may, to discuss the terms upon which the coal industry is to be carried on, I shall continue my efforts to see that in any settlement justice is done both to the miners and the owners. . . . We are prepared, as soon as circumstances permit, to consult the owners and the miners, to see in what way effect can best be given to this policy [reorganization], and the country may rest assured that when the time comes the Government will be ready with proposals.

Whether or not reinforced by the Prime Minister's response to Lord Wimborne's subsequent approach, this undertaking seems to have been given some value. Pugh referred to it explicitly when the General Council went to Downing Street on 12 May as 'something which on our side we could not ignore'.[66] And this alone could explain the phraseology of the letter which he and Citrine published on 12 May in reply to the Samuel memorandum:[67]

> They [the General Council] are taking the necessary measures to terminate the General Strike, relying upon the public assurances of the Prime Minister as to the steps that would follow. They assume that during the resumed negotiations the subsidy will be renewed and that the lock-out notices to the Miners will be immediately withdrawn.

For whatever reason, it seems clear that Pugh and Citrine, at least, assumed Samuel to have more official standing than he claimed.[68] The latter wrote in his diary, after the final conversation with him on

11 May, 'Samuel appeared to be speaking with knowledge of the Government's attitude, and from all information at our disposal it looks as though Baldwin has been having a pretty rough time with his Cabinet'. He claimed to be as 'puzzled' as other members of the Council by Baldwin's failure to mention the lifting of the lock-out at the interview with the government next day.[69] And a week later Pugh wrote personally to Samuel complaining bitterly at having been misled:[70]

It is quite true you made it clear that you had no authority to speak for the Government, but I and my Committee placed implicit faith in yourself. Your standing in the Country, your responsibility and that of your Colleagues – whom we understood you had consulted – for the recent Report, gave us the conviction that if the strike was called off, the Government would at least offer the Miners to take your Memorandum as a basis of negotiation.

If not a plenipotentiary, in other words, Samuel was supposed to have provided an accurate reflection of what the government were prepared to do.[71]

In so far as the Negotiating Committee deluded themselves they necessarily helped to delude other members of the General Council. At each meeting of the Council on 11 May, the Committee were pressed to say how far Samuel could be relied on, in the common phrase, 'to deliver the goods'. Assurances were given which, in the aftermath, appeared in some degree reprehensible. On 22 May Bevin, R. B. Walker and Alan Findlay handed a statement to A. J. Cook, subsequently released to the press, asserting that, in their understanding, the Samuel terms had enjoyed governmental approval.[72]

We desire to say that Mr. Baldwin's statement as to the extent to which the Government was committed [to the Samuel memorandum] is not in accordance with our information. We therefore urge Sir Herbert Samuel to speak, and to speak without any reservation. Will he deny that consultations took place between Mr. Baldwin and himself on the terms of the Memorandum?

After Samuel had indeed denied it, Bevin wrote in a draft circular to his union officers and branches,[73]

With regard to the calling off of the strike you may take it from me that we, who were not on the Negotiating Committee, were assured that the Samuel Document would be accepted, that the lock-out notices would be withdrawn and that methods of resumption would be discussed forthwith; and when these assurances had been given us, we naturally felt we had accomplished the purpose for which the strike was called.

Several other Council members clearly acquired the same conviction, on 11 May, that the goods could indeed be delivered.[74] But none of this provides conclusive evidence that the Negotiating Committee said anything which it believed to be untrue. The miners obviously heard nothing which led them to exaggerate Samuel's authority. Ramsay MacDonald claimed afterwards to have understood that Samuel's *locus standi* was simply his chairmanship of the Royal Commission, and added, 'it was made perfectly plain by the [Negotiating] Committee that the General Council had to exercise its own judgement'. Even Ben Turner recalled the members of the Committee as saying only that 'in their opinion and belief' the lock-out notices were to be withdrawn.[75] No doubt in the tense atmosphere of the Council's meetings words were used which could be understood in different ways, and statements of opinion and fact became confused. Their recollections revealed the mood and predisposition of those present as much as actual events.

What is remarkable about the assessment of the Samuel memorandum by the General Council, however, is that *all* its members, both on and off the Negotiating Committee, evidently failed to take account of the implications for its standing of the miners' rejection of its terms. From the evidence considered, it seems that neither such questions as were put to the Negotiating Committee about Samuel's authority, nor such answers as they gave, ever isolated this problem. Yet it was obvious in retrospect (even to those who claimed to have been deceived) that the miners' repudiation of the document undermined any grounds for expecting that the government would renew the subsidy and suspend the lock-out. For if the Federation were declining even to accept the power of the proposed National Wages Board to make a wage settlement *de novo*, then a renewal of the subsidy would have represented a total capitulation by the government on those very issues whose intractability had caused the strike. Yet the signs are clear, from the various sources examined, that this is exactly what was believed – albeit for longer in some cases than in others. Both those on the Negotiating Committee who blamed Samuel for misleading them and those on the General Council who blamed the committee revealed thereby only their own credulity and confusion.[76]

This was further emphasized by Samuel's public utterances. In answer to Bevin, Walker and Findlay he asserted that the government 'were wholly unaware of the contents of the Memorandum, or even that such a Memorandum was under discussion' until the morning of

12 May.[77] The press statement which he issued on that day also made clear that, so far as he was concerned, his proposals would be rendered nugatory by the dissent of the miners: whether negotiations would be resumed or not 'must . . . necessarily depend upon the Miners' Federation consenting to the basis that has been proposed. If they do not, the position so far as the mines are concerned will remain as it was, and the stoppage of the mines will continue.'[78] And he made the same point to Pugh in a personal letter which sought to put the best face on the government's offer of 14 May.[79] Though the General Council had, unknowingly, some grounds for complaint that Samuel did not press his recommendations on the government in private, they had not approved the settlement he offered on the assumption that its acceptance would depend on such confidential advocacy.[80] The various protests made afterwards related solely to the authority with which Samuel had been credited as an 'official' negotiator; and this, it has been seen, was not to any measurable extent attributable to his bad faith.

The endorsement of the Samuel memorandum by the General Council, it must be concluded, was largely due to their psychological need to believe in it. Throughout the course of the stoppage they had deceived themselves in the same fashion – crediting Baldwin with conciliatory intentions which had been restrained by other ministers; assuming, at least in the case of the Negotiating Committee, that the miners had undergone a change of heart on the question of wage reductions; hoping that the strike could be ended without disturbance or friction. The adoption of this 'settlement' formed part of the same pattern of self-induced optimism. This was the only available pretext for concluding the stoppage. It could not be put into cold storage after the miners had refused it; indecision would simply place the Council entirely in the hands of the MFGB, and entail the indefinite prolongation of the dispute. This was a prospect none could look upon. On the other hand acceptance of the memorandum would allow the TUC to claim, with at least a measure of plausibility, that they had negotiated some form of agreement. And such a protective shield against the vilification which all expected and dreaded it was imperative to acquire.

When later they came to seek firmer ground on which to justify their actions, the General Council chose to argue precisely what, at the time they decided to call off the strike, most of them had ignored or overlooked: that the Samuel memorandum could only have been implemented if the miners had accepted it. As early as the night of 12 May Citrine wrote an appreciation of the situation quite at variance with what he appeared to believe a few hours earlier:[81]

The distressing thing is that the General Council's action has been rendered abortive by the decision of the Miners' Federation to call a conference on Friday next, and not to resume work in the meantime. This means, in fact, that all the assurances Samuel gave to us in our private conversations, about the lockout being cancelled, cannot materialize, and we are left in the position of appearing to have been defeated.

Three weeks later, Bevin admitted the same point to Walker and Findlay, who had previously joined him in indicting Samuel:[82]

I signed the letter *re* the Samuel Document believing it might do good and believing the Government had accepted the document; but whether the Government did or did not officially accept it, it now transpires the miners would not, quite apart from any method in which it was obtained.

The fact however remains, that the General Council came to the conclusion that so far as they were concerned they had fulfilled the purpose for which the General Conference gave them powers; and, although I see no good purpose in arguing whether or not the Government accepted the Samuel Document I feel quite satisfied that treatment could have been obtained equal in value to the document.

And in June the Council's official report on the General Strike asserted:[83]

The General Council have never had any reason to doubt that had the miners' Executive accepted the advice of the Council to adopt the Samuel Memorandum and joined with the Council in calling off the strike and obtaining the withdrawal of the lock-out notices, negotiations would have been set on foot and an acceptable arrangement arrived at.

By the time of this official statement, of course, the need to pretend that an agreement had existed on which the government had reneged was less acute. A general resumption of work had been accomplished, and the immediate outcry against the TUC had subsided. The line on which the Council settled was, moreover, circumstantially more convincing: the memorandum did embody proposals and procedures which the government indeed found it difficult to reject out of hand. But what its members said now made what many of them had said at the time of the termination of the stoppage look all the more foolish and dishonest. They were fortunate that, in the exploitation of these inconsistencies, their critics proved comparatively inept.

XI The Return to Work and the Miners' Lock-out

The General Council, as has been seen, had devised no plans for the resumption of work at the close of the General Strike. They delegated the task of negotiating it to their constituent unions in the hope that the continued solidarity of the stoppage in most sections would obviate difficulties with the employers. They also clearly hoped that the government would give a lead such as to encourage magnanimity among employers. And though Baldwin had refused to make any promises when he met the General Council at Downing Street on 12 May, his speech in the House of Commons that afternoon and his broadcast in the evening did contain calls for restraint: 'At a moment like this the whole British people should not look backwards but forwards . . . we should resume our work in a spirit of cooperation, putting behind us all malice and all vindictiveness.'[1] And his appeals were buttressed by a message published by the king:[2]

> Let us forget whatever element of bitterness the events of the past few days may have created, only remembering how steady and how orderly the country has remained, though severely tested, and forthwith address ourselves to the task of bringing into being a peace which will be lasting because, forgetting the past, it looks only to the future with the hopefulness of a united people.

The following morning, however, it became apparent that the hopes for a willing reconciliation in industry were misplaced. Throughout the country union branches, local strike committees and Councils of Action were required by strikers faced with punitive threats from their employers to prolong the stoppage. Their initiative was approved by almost all union headquarters; and later in the day Citrine dispatched a telegram to the affiliated strike executives – 'imperative that agreements, understandings and conditions existing prior to dispute should be maintained' – together with the clause of the original strike instructions which had required that 'there shall be no general resumption of work until agreements are fully recognized'.[3] Though the Council clearly wished to avoid any suggestion that the General Strike had recommenced, they gave a kind of apologetic approval to sympathetic action already taken.[4] In the Commons MacDonald and Thomas denounced the efforts of employers to exploit the situation at the unions' expense, and called for government intervention.[5]

What was really happening in the local strike centres is difficult to discern. Certainly many returning union members were confronted by announcements, sometimes in the form of statements presented for their signature, which seemed menacing or provocative. On the other hand Baldwin claimed that the persistence of conflict was often due to the prevalence of false rumours of wage reductions and the cancellation of seniority rights.[6] Whether justified or not in this view, he was at least right in claiming that very few employers sought to impose pay cuts.[7] The questions which emerged most frequently as the conflict progressed were almost all to do with reinstatement and the status of bargaining arrangements which had often been violated by the withdrawal of labour on 4 May.

It seems unlikely, in the circumstances, that the men who attended their workplaces on Thursday morning were themselves fully aware of what the employers proposed. Baffled already by the manner in which the General Strike had ended they were likely to respond with anger to any posting of notices or presentation of documents. Probably such incidents had only to occur in a few instances in any locality to arrest the process of resumption. It may well be, too, that an equal confusion prevailed among employers, likewise usually taken by surprise by the conclusion of the stoppage, and pursuing no agreed policy towards their workmen. What, therefore, many sought to do initially was not to reinstate their men on *new* conditions, but to avoid committing themselves to old ones. This was a necessary precaution, in any event, wherever industrialists were in doubt about their ability to return immediately to full production in face of the likely prolongation of the coal dispute. Some firms did no doubt contemplate disciplinary measures; but their intentions created such pronounced apprehension, in all probability, just because they were so indefinite.

Within the next day or so the employers' national organizations took on the responsibility for arranging a return to work by the many groups still standing down. Though they were obviously influenced by the continued militancy of rank-and-file unionists, it seems extremely unlikely that it was this factor which drove them to the negotiating table. While some maverick firms did take this opportunity systematically to weaken or destroy union organizations, the majority of representative bodies of industrialists had never considered rescinding recognition. Even an earlier resumption of work would hardly have led to a *fin de non recevoir* when the General Strike itself had been supported so enthusiastically. And in many cases, of course, the employers themselves valued orderly bargaining procedures and stable labour relations too highly to sacrifice them in this way.

The conditions of peace subsequently imposed upon the unions varied, however, from industry to industry and reflected several influences at work. The employers' assessment of the capacity of their respective labour forces to offer further resistance to any *diktat* was, no doubt, one; and this was partially related to the extent to which particular trades had involved themselves in the General Strike and disrupted production thereby. But even seriously weakened organizations which had participated in the stoppage from its outset *might* escape severe penalties if their relations with their own employers had previously been relatively trouble-free and their leaders sufficiently reputed for their moderation.

Employers, industrial agreements and 'victimization'

The existence of these differences in the conduct of employers following the strike, does suggest, on the other hand, that the moral authority exercised by the government was of limited importance. In fact, though Baldwin received much credit for having poured oil on the waters, the policy adopted by the administration during the return to work was by no means consistently generous. On the evening of 12 May an official statement had been published which ignored the spirit if not the letter of the Prime Minister's own pronouncements:[8] 'His Majesty's Government have no power to compel employers to take back every man who has been on strike, nor have they entered any obligation of any kind on this matter.' Moreover the government's conduct towards its own employees was at least as harsh as that meted out by the majority of private employers. The Treasury recommended, and the Cabinet agreed, that government industrial workers should be reinstated only when work became available; that they should, where eligible, forfeit one year's service in respect of pension or gratuity rights; that those guilty of violence or intimidation during the strike should be dismissed; and that the men's 'accredited representatives' should be compelled to acknowledge that the stoppage was 'a wrongful act'. These measures were stringently enforced in the Admiralty dockyards, where established men were ordered to give personal pledges not to infringe contracts again, and where three leaders held responsible for inciting the stoppage amongst them were dismissed.[9] At the Deptford food depot of the War Office Worthington-Evans reported that, following the stoppage, as many as twenty strikers had been refused employment and eighteen volunteers retained. The staff of official printing establishments, notably HMSO and the Hansard Office, were henceforth required to work alongside non-unionists.[10]

Conservative local authorities, whose hostility to the strikers had been most marked during the nine days, also naturally tended to be unbending afterwards. Municipal tramway committees in particular had sought to replace union members in a number of cities prior to 12 May, and were not disposed to restore them. On Merseyside, for instance, the volunteers employed in Wallasey and Bootle were retained subsequently.[11] In Glasgow, according to Patrick Dollan, 368 of about 5,000 tramwaymen were suspended or dismissed after the strike.[12] In Newport 300 volunteers were kept on by the Corporation in place of members of the General and Municipal Workers, whilst the Brighton Council forced its tramway staff to leave their union, the T&GWU. The National Joint Council of the industry did not meet until October, and only then did the employers abandon their attempt to prevent the organization of inspectors' branches during the year.[13] Their ability to revive district agreements varied greatly, but their earliest success, with the LCC on 14 May, was still secured only by a promise, in return for general reinstatement, to allow substitutes engaged during the emergency to remain at work and accept the transference of their own members where necessary to accommodate them.[14]

The position of road transport workers in private employment was also vulnerable. Here, too, organization had been imperfect, the strike sometimes only partial, and volunteers plentiful. The leading London bus company outside the 'Combine', Thomas Tilling's, announced that it would withdraw recognition from the Transport and General Workers and reinstate men only on a day-to-day basis.[15] Bevin told the TUC Assistant Secretary at the end of May that provincial bus workers had been the principal casualties of victimization among his membership. In all, about 1,900 passenger transport workers (busmen and tramwaymen) belonging to the union had not been reinstated.[16] The situation in the haulage industry is less easy to discern: small firms abounded here, and national bargaining machinery had long since broken down. But the subcommittee of the Transport and General Workers' estimated that 1,000 men in this trade group had not been re-employed following the General Strike; and others had been compelled to work alongside blacklegs.[17]

Probably the most irreconcilable body of employers encountered after the strike were those in the printing industry. The newspaper proprietors in particular were outraged by the interruption of publication, regarding the unions as responsible not just for a financial loss but also for abrogating a civil liberty. The fact that, in London, selective attempts had been made to interfere with the editing of newspapers before the General Strike, and that in the provinces some printers had been fairly lukewarm supporters of union orders, intensified the owners' inclination to seek retribution. Whether this resentment was translated into punitive action depended, of course, on the strength of the unions in particular areas or establishments. The most open and effective attacks were made in Scotland, where a strong alliance of employers responsible for almost all daily papers successfully eliminated union organization among their labour. The Scottish Typographical Association tried to resist, but their members, 'who had been looked on for many years as stalwarts of the Associaton . . . instead of loyalty . . . gave a demonstration of treachery by rushing back to work as non-unionists, thus giving up their birthright as free men'.[18] In England the *Manchester Guardian* took less drastic but equally deliberate measures to prevent further stoppages by forming its own house union, which afforded large friendly benefits but outlawed strikes. The Printing and Kindred Trades Federation prevailed upon the newspaper to hold a ballot before requiring its staff's adhesion, but the result was heavily in favour of the company. No strike was attempted.[19]

The Fleet Street proprietors were equally ready to take the offensive, but found the unions more difficult to dislodge. After a week of manoeuvring they eventually came to terms on 20 May. The unions agreed that there should be no future attempt to interfere with the content of the papers or other spheres of managerial prerogative, and no recruitment of secretarial or managerial staff. The owners promised to restore all strikers to their jobs. The Master Printers' Association, representing much of the English provincial press, concluded a similar bargain on 27 May, omitting the limitation on union membership but including further provisions against 'unconstitutional' strike action. Probably neither employers' organization was satisfied with these largely verbal concessions: later in the year, both were to urge the government to include prohibitions on closed shop arrangements in the

Trade Disputes Act.[20] On the distribution side, several London constituents of the Newsagents' Federation did successfully establish open shops following the General Strike, and the employees of W. H. Smith broke away from the Paperworkers' Union, whilst at least two large stationery firms set up their own house societies.[21]

It was the railway directors and managers, more than any other group of employers, who had been responsible for the provocations which had prolonged the General Strike in many areas after 12 May. Subsequently, however, they behaved with a certain prudence or restraint. Although the railway industry had been one of the major theatres of conflict, it had probably attracted few volunteers likely to want permanent employment. On the other hand coal shortages made it impossible to operate more than a restricted service, so that about a third of the labour force was potentially surplus to requirements.[22] And it was this fact, of course, which made both union leaders and rank and file so alive to the dangers of victimization.

The railway managers were atypical, perhaps even unique, in having discussed before the end of the strike the policy they planned to follow on the resumption of work. On 10 May they agreed on what might be regarded as their official demands: whilst 'they did not want to destroy the unions', they should not be compelled to reinstate men they could not use; they should be free to dismiss at will both strikers found guilty of violence, intimidation and damaging railway property, and those previously holding responsible supervisory posts; and they should retain the right to take disciplinary measures against other employees for striking without due notice.[23]

The action taken by the railway companies and their agents on 12 May seems, however, to have differed from place to place. The LNER confined themselves to reserving their rights to exact future penalties in the manner previously agreed; others, including the Great Western at Cardiff, were accused of cancelling entitlements earned by past service and confiscating wages owed from before the strike. And whilst the majority of local officials did no more than post general notices, some actually presented statements for individual employees to sign.[24] But however phrased and delivered, these threats created the impression among railway workers that a meek return would be received in a vengeful spirit.

On 13 May, with the strike as solid as ever, C. T. Cramp wrote to the general managers of the major companies calling for unconditional reinstatement for all workers: 'very large numbers of Railwaymen have definitely refused to take up duty under the conditions which obtain, and it is only right that I should make it very clear that I cannot hope to influence them to speedily take up their duties under present conditions'. When the employers met the railway unions for the first time later that day, though still not in a forgiving mood, they appeared more anxious for a quick settlement. They confirmed their intention to introduce short-time working but promised to prevent widespread redundancies. At the same time they now produced a general proposal to cancel a week's pay for every striker and tacitly maintained their right to dismiss selected men.[25]

Negotiations during the next twenty-four hours whittled down almost all of these demands. Reinstatement was to be regulated by length of service; only those guilty of violence or intimidation were excluded. Employees were liable to be transferred to other posts, but were not to lose earnings thereby, and kept the right to appeal with union representation. The proposal to deduct a week's pay was dropped. The unions, for their part, admitted a 'wrongful act', acknowledged the companies' undiminished legal claims to damages for breach of contract, promised not to strike in advance of negotiations or to support unofficial strikes, and not to 'encourage' the participation of supervisory employees in any stoppage. The guaranteed week was officially suspended on 21 May.[26]

These terms were humiliating for any union to swallow. Charges were made subsequently, too, that reappointments were being carried out to penalize men in higher grades for their association with the strike. Victimization, however, was clearly uncommon in both traffic and maintenance departments. Moreover, although the companies drew up lists of volunteers who wished to obtain full-time employment, they evidently retained almost none.[27] In South Wales, at least, the main complaint of union members concerned rather the preferential treatment of men who had remained at work (or had been on sick leave) during the General Strike.[28] Whilst those clauses in the agreement concerned with contractual obligations and future stoppages were offensive, they had little practical import. As Bromley wrote to Citrine on 16 May: 'It [the agreement] is much better than it looks on the surface as most of the clauses mean nothing detrimental to our people'.[29] While unemployment continued to make life difficult for the railwaymen for the next six months or so, their leaders were inclined to blame this on the miners rather than their own employers.

In most of the other industries affected by the General Strike the repercussions were less serious than in the cases so far discussed. In engineering the stoppage had generally lasted for so short a period that the Employers' Federation felt able to be liberal about reinstatement. 'Whilst protesting most strongly against this irregular action taken by the Trade Unions,' their executive told the electricians that it was 'of opinion that the members of the industry and those engaged in it will best be served by abiding in the future by agreements and recognised procedure.'[30] Local disputes were reported on this score, but they resulted from the actions of individual – often non-federated – firms.[31] In building, where the strike had been of a partial nature from the outset, the National Federation acknowledged that 'the employers did not try to impose any humiliating terms on our members'.[32] In the iron and steel industry the tradition of good industrial relations which had prevented disputes in the past stood the Confederation in good stead when its own financial weakness and the difficulties created by the continued coal stoppage rendered it particularly vulnerable. Dock workers, who enjoyed none of the same good feeling with their employers, were evidently sufficiently well-organized to deter threats of retaliation in the larger ports; and though additional non-union labour may have come into the industry as a result of the General Strike, it could do little to worsen the endemic casualism of employment. Some permanent men in Bristol were dismissed, and others were threatened with disciplinary action by the Port of London Authority. But the waterside interests in the capital were unsuccessful in their attempts to prohibit future stoppages by foremen and other supervisors.[33] In almost all these industries the employers were satisfied with post-strike agreements which asserted principles but did not impose penalties. The unions were usually required to signify that they had violated agreements or caused breaches of contract, and reinforced negotiating procedures were introduced to try and prevent stoppages without notice in future. Few labour leaders offered serious resistance to such demands.[34]

The immediate cost of the General Strike to the unions is difficult to assess. The prolongation of the coal stoppage caused a substantial increase in unemployment until the close of 1926 – the rate rising by 5·3 per cent, the number on benefit from 1,034,000 to 1,675,000 between 24 April and 31 May.[35] Though mainly concentrated in the railway and metal industries, this deterioration of the labour market was felt in almost every sector of the economy. In terms of financial damage and loss of membership the stoppage itself and its final withdrawal probably had more deleterious effects on the union movement than any action taken by employers on the resumption of work. It is also difficult to estimate the real extent of victimization. This was a label somewhat indiscriminately applied, following the stoppage, not only to the dismissal of militants and the replacement of former employees by volunteers, but also to redundancies resulting from the reduced circumstances of many trades and firms. After the coal lock-out was over, therefore, it seems likely that many of those previously affected (outside the mining industry) managed to find new jobs. The T&GWU suggested, for instance, that about 4,500 of their members had lost work as a result of the General Strike, but only some 500 remained unemployed at the end of the year.[36] The incidence of victimization *pur sang* clearly lies somewhere between these two figures.

Whatever costs were charged, however, the worst were not directly inflicted by the employers. Whether because they hoped for an economic recovery, accepted the marginal relevance of the General Strike to the conduct of industrial relations in their own trades, appreciated the general good behaviour of the strikers and their leaders, or simply wanted a quick return to a quiet life, most industrialists were eventually satisfied with largely token concessions from the unions. Though some were to seek to strengthen the controls over strike action by calling for legal sanctions during the next twelve months, even this demand was far from universal. In the end, accordingly, the aftermath of the General Strike created less resentment, at least at national level, than had at first seemed likely. In this somewhat deceptive atmosphere of reconciliation, before the end of 1926, hopes of a lasting industrial peace were being widely entertained.

The mining lock-out

The return to work of other unions left the Miners' Federation apparently undaunted. The dispute in their industry was to continue for more than six months after the General Strike – the longest, the most costly and perhaps the most bitter in British industrial history. Moreover the nine days had little or no perceptible influence upon its course and outcome: if the General Council had been unable to bring about a solution to the conflict by calling a general stoppage, they were still more powerless after ending it. The withdrawal of sympathetic support seemed simply to make the miners' leaders and rank and file more intractable. The single ascertainable consequence of the intervention of the TUC was to prompt the government to present proposals for a settlement in its own name to the miners and owners on 14 May – and even this initiative would probably have been taken in any case. Furthermore the content of the Cabinet offers embodied the views expressed by its members prior to 3 May, and was not visibly influenced either by the collapse of the General Strike or by the terms of the Samuel memorandum. And whilst the General Council still believed that the recommendations made by Samuel could have been obtained from the government, had the miners endorsed them, the conduct of the Federation during the lock-out serves primarily to confirm how much the Council had misjudged the miners' temper. The possibility of making some sort of agreement which would have saved the MFGB from utter defeat was not destroyed by the abandonment of the General Strike, but such compromises remained for one reason or another unacceptable.

Since the mine-owners remained as unyielding as their workers the lock-out in the industry became a war of attrition, punctuated by occasional and ineffective attempts at official and unofficial mediation. The first of these, the government's peace formula of 14 May, fulfilled the pledge given by the Prime Minister in his broadcast of 8 May to renew his conciliatory efforts once the General Strike were over. The Cabinet had given no serious thought to the making of a settlement since the end of April, however, and at no stage had they been prepared to publish proposals of their own. It is clear, besides, that some ministers were now embarrassed and alarmed by the existence of the Samuel memorandum – approved by the TUC, assumed by many union members to have the status of a negotiated agreement, widely reported in the press, and still not explicitly rejected by the Miners' Federation. On 13 May Steel-Maitland, with the support of Lane-Fox, Wilson and Gowers, advised Baldwin to publicly disown the Samuel proposals in the House of Commons. If the miners' delegate conference 'had any sense', the former predicted, 'they would jump at Herbert Samuel's suggestions. This would place us in an exceedingly difficult position.'[37]

The course which Baldwin took, however, was a good deal more devious. It was his understanding, as he told both the Cabinet and the king on 13 May, that the Miners' Federation had already declined the offer in the memorandum.[38] When he saw the miners' executive on Thursday evening, he invited them to confirm their rejection.

PRIME MINISTER: I understand from what I saw in the press, it may not be true, that proposals on the lines he [Samuel] advocated were of no use.

MR SMITH: I think that would be rather foolish as far as we are concerned of anybody else, not because he advocated it, because I want to say I have finished with Samuel as far as I am concerned. I want to make that perfectly clear, to say because somebody else put something down on paper that they rejected entirely –

PRIME MINISTER: That is what I wanted to ask you.

MR SMITH: You may want to re-model it. I would not sweep any man's ideas aside and say, 'that is no good', because I have to watch his point of view as well as my own.

PRIME MINISTER: I ask you that because I saw some difficulties in it. It did not seem to me to promise a quick finality.

On 14 May Baldwin confessed himself to the owners 'a little anxious . . . lest the miners' delegates should adopt the formula and want to negotiate on it', adding that the government had prepared other proposals 'because we want [negotiations] off that basis'.[39] Subsequently, however, it was the evidence of the cryptic exchange with Smith that he cited to justify his neglect of the memorandum. In the Commons next month, though denying that the government had authorized Samuel's mediation, he suggested that opposition to the latter's proposals had come entirely from the miners, who 'had publicly rejected the Memorandum and . . . adhered to that view when they saw me'.[40] He even claimed, quite baselessly, that the terms which the Cabinet presented to the disputants on 14 May 'were almost exactly those, though expressed differently, which were contained in what was called the Samuel memorandum'.[41] It is obvious that the Prime Minister found it difficult to disown Samuel as the author of the memorandum and to uphold him as principal author of the Royal Commission report, still supposedly accepted by the government. To this extent the assertion which the General Council later made that approval of the Samuel proposals by the MFGB would have obliged the government to negotiate upon them appears not unreasonable.

It has been seen, on the other hand, that the government drew up its own peace terms with the primary intention of avoiding this outcome. These were first discussed by the members of the coal committee on the evening of 12 May, provisionally accepted by the Cabinet the following morning, but further amended in committee before submission to the miners and owners on 14 May.[42] In one important respect they followed – or even strengthened – the proposals adopted by the General Council: the recommendation of compulsory arbitration. Already by Wednesday evening Viscount Reading had agreed to act as independent chairman of the projected National

Wages Board. But the conditions under which arbitration was to take place were very different from those envisaged by the General Council. A final wage settlement was to be drawn up – or if necessary imposed by the chairman – within three weeks of the Board's establishment. In the meantime the miners were to accept an interim, uniform reduction in the national minimum. Legislation on hours would be passed at the request of both parties. A subsidy, of the same amount as was offered in April, would be made available to taper wage cuts and assist labour transference.

In the matter of reorganization the government largely ignored the Samuel memorandum. Instead of allowing the proposed joint committee and the National Wages Board to supervise the drafting of legislation and the implementation of reforms within the industry, they offered simply to consult the existing Coal Advisory Committee of the Mines Department on a specific set of legislative measures.[43] These included bills on colliery amalgamation, statutory pit committees, restriction of labour recruitment and the permanent establishment of the Wages Board. An inquiry into selling agencies was also planned. Both the question of nationalization of royalties and that of municipal trading in coal were referred to departmental committees, but on the former at least the Cabinet admitted no obligation to take action in view of 'the setback caused by the strike to the financial position of the country'.[44]

The government's offer is adjudged by Baldwin's biographers to have been 'reasonable and fair'.[45] It might be so regarded, perhaps, in comparison with the owners' attitude; when the spokesmen of the Mining Association saw Steel-Maitland on 13 May they condemned a further subsidy and compulsory arbitration, and demanded strict negotiations and longer hours – resuming, thereby, the position they had taken up prior to 30 April.[46] The government, on the other hand, did at least envisage the retention of a national wage agreement and the machinery to enforce it. But on two major counts the Cabinet was now more exacting than it had been before the stoppage. It had always been intent on securing a promise to accept wage reductions from the miners, but now it sought to impose an actual cut, substantial in amount, in advance of a final wage settlement. On 13 May the ministers had evidently agreed to propose lowering the minimum by five per cent; but five days later, asked by the miners to stipulate what reduction he thought appropriate, Baldwin suggested ten per cent. This would have entailed an immediate return to the 1921 minimum – and though the Prime Minister did not insist on a cut of this magnitude, he did require that any deficits recorded by the industry during the consultations of the National Wages Board would be repaid by diverting the £3 million subsidy to that purpose, whilst only if the Federation accepted an interim cut would the owners be asked temporarily to forego their ascertained profits.[47] Furthermore, although in April the government had seemed to accept the desirability of a uniform national minimum, the Wages Board was no longer to be bound by this restriction, but allowed to lay down variations – pluses and minuses – for individual districts.

There was of course no chance that the miners would accept such an agreement. At their interview with the government representatives on 18 May they drew attention to its obvious weaknesses. Wage cuts were still not effectively tied to reorganization. The procedures for enforcing reconstruction were inadequate: 'we will get a reform in 1,700 years and not before', said Smith. Above all, as Frank Varley among others pointed out, 'there is no motive force in any one of your suggestions to close a single pit in this country – not one'. An arbitrator, confronted by the evidence for the existing financial plight of mining and assured of the miners' tractability by their submission to a provisional reduction, was bound to impose further draconian wage cuts.[48] At their resumed conference on 20 May, discounting all other considerations, the miners resolved once more to reject any reductions in wages or any departure, by arbitration or otherwise, from the existing national minimum.

The Mining Association was, as expected, equally uncompromising. After referring the government proposals to its constituent bodies on 15 May, the Central Committee delivered on the twenty-first a long and unqualified denunciation. Statutory reorganization was self-defeating: it was 'time to state plainly that a number of the conclusions in the Report of the Samuel Commission . . . would spell ruin to British industry'. All forms of government intervention were objectionable: 'it must be stated emphatically that it will be impossible to continue the conduct of the industry under private enterprise unless it is accorded the same freedom from political interference as is enjoyed by other industries'. Only the restoration of the eight-hour day could secure 'the drastic reduction in the cost of production of coal which the situation demands'.[49]

Faced with these negative responses the government had little inclination to persist. The Prime Minister wrote to the Mining Association, condemning the 'incapacity of the industry, unlike other industries, to settle its disputes for itself' – and warned the miners that the offer of a subsidy would be withdrawn at the end of May.[50] Subsequently the Cabinet embraced a deliberate policy of inaction. Baldwin and some of his colleagues had an unproductive conversation with the miners' officials, accompanied by Ernest Bevin, on 31 May. Thereafter it was assumed that, left to contemplate their hopeless situation, the miners could not long maintain their unyielding stance. According to Tom Jones, Baldwin dismissed as unduly pessimistic J. H. Thomas's forecast, at the beginning of June, that the stoppage would last another eight weeks.[51] Attempts at private mediation, by Lord Wimborne and by Seebohm Rowntree and W. T. Layton, were not discouraged – though the public intervention of the Social Christian Fellowship in July was frowned on as liable to increase the miners' intractability.[52] But the government itself showed no further inclination to take part in negotiations for more than three months.

On 15 June, however, the Cabinet decided on the recommendation of the coal committee to suspend the Seven Hours Act for a five-year period. The considerations which prompted this step were those which had already inclined the government towards it before the General Strike. Most ministers were still convinced, as Amery told Baldwin on 1 June, 'that the men would prefer the 8 hours' day to a lower wage'.[53] The coal committee were able to extract promises from the owners that generous wage offers would be made in the districts. Moreover, Churchill, as Chancellor, had been urging for some time the serious financial and economic repercussions of a continuance of the lock-out.[54]

The suspension of the seven-hour day, enacted in the second week of July, had none of the desired effects. Despite the fact that it was linked with a Mining Industry Act which implemented certain measures of reorganization, it was naturally regarded by the Federation and by the General Council as a capitulation of the government to the views of the owners. Although the employers were in a position to offer better wages, they did so, in all cases, only for provisional periods of six to nine months. In the export areas the minima proposed were still below the 1924 level; and in the inland coalfields the prospective increase in the working day often represented a more serious attack on existing working conditions than had been threatened hitherto. Though the prospect of an eight-hour day was no doubt more disliked in some districts than in others, it was a measure against which all miners could readily unite – more easily, in many respects, than on the wages issue.[55] Furthermore, the reintroduction of longer hours was not now tied, as on 31 April, to the offer of a uniform national minimum. Though the Cabinet considered the institution of a statutory National Wages Board through the Mining Industry Act, they chose not to proceed with it.[56]

The miners kept up their rigid resistance until the beginning of September. In mid-July they asked the General Council to impose an embargo on the movement of coal – particularly coal imports – but when this was refused by the railway unions (as it had been already, immediately following the General Strike) Smith told the TUC leaders 'that the Federation did not want the Council to interfere at all at the present time'.[57] Although signs of friction appeared between Smith and Cook by the end of July, it was not until the midlands miners showed unmistakable signs of returning to work that the Federation executive admitted the need to retreat. On 3 September, through the good offices of Ramsay MacDonald, they offered to renew negotiations for a 'new national agreement with a view to a reduction in labour costs'.[58]

There followed four weeks of complex negotiations, principally between the miners and representatives of the government. The Cabinet's coal committee was prompted by Churchill, in charge during Baldwin's recuperative vacation at Aix and now as bold in the cause of peace as formerly in the heat of conflict, to take up the Federation's suggestion. But the district constituents of the Mining Association had during June formally rescinded the authority of the Central Committee to conclude a national agreement, and this veto was now confirmed. Although Churchill was outraged by the obstinacy of the owners, the Mines Department argued that no satisfactory way could be found to enforce a national agreement, and Baldwin was in any case evidently reluctant to envisage coercion.[59] On 17 September, after the Prime Minister's return, the Cabinet approved instead a plan drafted by Cunliffe-Lister to establish a wages tribunal with power to revise, on appeal, district agreements on an eight-hour basis. This was still unacceptable to the owners, who rallied support among other employers' organizations against the enactment of wage-fixing machinery; and to the miners, who declined to resume work on terms negotiated in the districts, and almost certain to embody longer hours. The MFGB suggested instead an immediate return on the basis of the 1921 minimum and a tribunal empowered to implement all the recommendations of the Samuel Report. The Cabinet, with some disagreement, stuck to their own proposals which were decisively rejected by a majority of almost 700,000 on submission to the Federation's membership.[60]

Forced back into a state of siege the miners drew upon their last reserves of militancy. On 7 October their conference reasserted its original 'cardinal points' and decided to withdraw safety men, to call again for an embargo on imported coal and a general union levy, and to send speakers to rally defectors in the midland regions. As a mark of determination it expelled the former President of the Nottinghamshire Miners, George Spencer, for his part in the negotiation of local agreements on behalf of returning workers.[61] But this defiant policy could scarcely be called realistic, and was opposed by more than a third of the MFGB membership. The independent safety men's unions discountenanced any wilful acts of sabotage. The transport unions considered, but for a third time rejected, a boycott on the movement of coal, on 2 November. The General Council summoned a special conference of its affiliates to consider the possibility of further financial aid, but demurred at the idea of a compulsory contribution.[62] In return for more voluntary support, however, it was able to prevail on the miners to allow it to attempt once more to conjure up a settlement.

The proposals which the General Council and the miners were able to obtain from the Coal Committee on 11 November were almost a replica of those rejected six weeks earlier. The miners were still to agree to district negotiations, covering hours as well as wages. They could appeal to an arbitration authority if such terms failed to provide a reasonable minimum (defined as twenty per cent above standard). Even though the wage tribunal was not obliged to enforce any such standard, the executive now decided to recommend this offer to the districts. The lodges, however, reflecting the power of left-wing influence in some districts and the growing indifference to the residual principle of a national settlement in others, voted against the agreement by 460,806 to 313,200. The national conference of 19 November thereupon ordered its constituents to make their own terms, consistent as far as possible with agreed national standards.[63] By the end of the month, resistance at last broken, those miners with jobs to go to were returning to work.

The conditions to which they submitted varied considerably between the coalfields. In most districts the eight-hour day was restored, though in Yorkshire all workers, and in Northumberland and Durham face workers, were put on seven and a half hours. In South Wales, Scotland and the north-east immediate wage reductions were also imposed; but in other areas, especially the old federated districts, pay settlements were relatively generous, so that the majority of miners actually received more than they did before the lock-out. In Nottinghamshire, for instance, those workers who had returned under

Spencer's auspices were granted an increase of about 4s per week.[64] In 1927, however, wages went down throughout the country, though the export areas continued to lead the way. In Durham, the new minimum lasted only until February 1927, after which the increment to standard was cut by fifty-four per cent in the next seven months.[65] Earnings per man shift in Britain as a whole, despite longer hours, fell from 10s 5d in the first quarter of 1926 to 10s 0¾d in 1927 and 9s 3½d in 1928.[66]

The miners could almost certainly have escaped some of these sacrifices by an earlier readiness to abandon their entrenched bargaining position. In the first place it is apparent that until the middle of June the government was unwilling to commit itself to legislate on hours of work. Secondly, at least in the immediate aftermath of the General Strike, the Cabinet showed no inclination to submit to the owners' insistence on district agreements (even on a seven-hour basis). Thirdly, the shape of reorganization measures was still not completely determined, and on certain items – such as selling agencies or even municipal trading – the government might have been flexible in negotiations. Finally, though least significantly, the offer of a subsidy, definite in May and probable in June, had ceased to be mentioned by September.

It has been suggested earlier that the miners did not owe the opportunity to make a compromise settlement, such as it was, to the General Strike. Whilst any possibility of securing the acceptance of the Samuel memorandum might be credited to the larger stoppage, that is, the mining lock-out in itself sufficed, in its early stages, to bring about a search for other negotiated terms. The miners appear to have suffered a crucial loss of bargaining power, however, with the passage of legislation on hours and organization at the beginning of July. Previously the government had seemed willing, if its own requirements could be met, to tackle the owners with a certain determination. It was the miners alone, according to Steel-Maitland and Lane-Fox, who made the deadlock insoluble: 'Employers can be forced by legislation to grant certain conditions to their employees, but employees cannot be forced by legislation to accept them.'[67] But the existence of the July measures, manifestly strengthening the owners' position, substantially changed this view. When Churchill sought to initiate a policy of coercion directed against the Mining Association in September Baldwin wrote to him from Aix, 'My desire, and I think the desire of us all, is to wean the Coal Industry from the Government, and that any agreement must be between owners and men'.[68] The Cabinet would now contemplate compulsory arbitration only in supplementation of voluntary district agreements – and faced, even so, the organized opposition of industrial opinion outside the coal industry. Nor were they certain any longer that the mine-owners could in practice be subjected to compulsion. Cunliffe-Lister, who devised the government offer of 17 September, observed significantly in his memorandum, 'We have lost that control of the conduct of affairs which we should have retained, if we had insisted on the Owners agreeing to our terms before we passed the Eight Hours Act.' That pessimism about its own power to achieve a reconciliation, spasmodically evident before the General Strike, now again dominated the government's mood.[69]

Nor was the cost of the miners' long-drawn-out struggle to be measured only in the adverse agreements of November 1926. After its final surrender the MFGB was effectively destroyed as a fighting force for almost a decade. Loss of membership and of funds was made more irreparable by the emergence, especially in the Midlands and South Wales, of non-political and company unions, and in Scotland of a split between the established old guard and a rival organization under a mainly Communist leadership.[70] A militant policy would in any case have been almost impracticable in circumstances of deepening economic depression, after 1929, but the repercussions of that depression, social and industrial, were doubtless more difficult to avoid because of the wounds suffered in 1926.

What, on the other hand, can be said in defence of the Federation's leadership? They were, it is clear, always under severe pressure from militant spokesmen of the rank and file – especially adherents of the Minority Movement – not to give in at any cost. They, no less than the General Council in May, were aware of the divisions which would be created in their organization if they chose to compromise and were likewise the victims of an inherited conception of leadership evolved and accepted in a period of union growth and strength. The evidence suggests, besides, that the rank and file of the Federation had itself acquired its own ideal of heroic intransigence. The rejection by the membership of the bishops' proposals in August, and of the government's final offer in November, were recorded despite the advice of the executive and the conference delegates.[71] Even at the end of November the Durham miners voted, by a small majority, against the district agreement negotiated by their officials.[72] It is doubtful whether such diehard resistance can be attributed simply to the influence exerted by the Federation's own leaders in the initial phases of the struggle. It was a collective will, not the foibles of individuals, which made the miners appear to outsiders to be governed by an inexplicable, even suicidal, recalcitrance.

The Coal Industry after 1926

The recasting of wage agreements and the lengthening of hours of work were the only important changes which took place in the coal industry as a result of the 1926 dispute. Its methods of production and organization were minimally affected. The proponents of rationalization were conceded the Mining Industry Act, which implemented some of the recommendations of the Samuel Commission. Advocates of cartelization were offered a departmental inquiry into co-operative selling, appointed in July 1926 and reporting in December. Neither legislation nor investigation bore fruit, however, largely because of the undiminished opposition of the owners to any interference in their affairs. For some eighteen months after the end of the mining lock-out the classical principles of Political Economy reigned once again in this industry; after which point the restoration so strenuously achieved was step by step abandoned by its erstwhile supporters.

The Mining Industry Act was a diluted version of the Royal Commission's report, which followed its recipe of encouraging voluntary improvements in the industry in preference to applying compulsion. Its principal clauses sought to facilitate the amalgamation of colliery enterprises, by empowering the Railway and Canal Commission to override minority opposition to schemes put forward by two or more owners for this purpose when they were held to be 'in the national interest'. But it ignored the proposal made by Samuel that in areas where concentration was deemed necessary, outside undertakings could be introduced in the absence of local initiatives. The other provisions of the Act strengthened the machinery for dealing with obstructive mineral owners (as an alternative to nationalizing mineral royalties), created a levy on their income to augment the miners' welfare fund, and authorized the Minister of Labour and the President of the Board of Trade, at their discretion, respectively to restrict the recruitment of new labour to the industry and to establish (after two years) statutory pit committees.[73]

Prior to mid-1928 the rate of colliery amalgamation increased slightly, but thereafter slackened once again. The Board of Trade reported that fourteen schemes had been carried through in the two years following the Mining Industry Act, involving 172 pits and

126,000 men. It seems doubtful, however, whether mergers made any impact on the areas where they were most likely to be beneficial: the two largest fusions took place in South Wales, already a region of high concentration. Moreover, only three of the amalgamations made use of the facilities of the Act – whose role otherwise was merely to afford a certain incentive to private effort. By 1930, a further twelve schemes involving just under 90,000 workers had been implemented; and in the next six years, following the passage of the supposedly more mandatory Coal Mines Act under the second Labour Government, thirty-two amalgamations covering 164,000 workers took place.[74] Whether this fairly gentle process of consolidation did much to increase the efficiency of the industry may well be doubted, though it did give rise to a number of relatively profitable combines which could afford to pay improved wages to their employees. Coal-mining, however continued to suffer from a large production surplus and an uneven technical performance, as well as much long-term unemployment, throughout the interwar years.[75]

The Lewis Committee on Co-operative Selling examined another possible remedy for the decline of coal – and, like others, reached moderate and somewhat tentative conclusions. Collaboration for marketing purposes, though found impractical on a national basis as yet, was desirable and possible at district level. It was not, however, to be imposed on unwilling owners unless they were in a distinct minority. Nor was it necessary to link such co-operation with general restriction of output: although a policy of 'unregulated expansion' *might* now be outdated, the Committee proposed instead (without defining) the goal of 'regulated growth'.[76]

Even this was too much for the mine-owners. Three of their four representatives on the Committee dissociated themselves from its findings, deploring any attempts artificially to raise prices or to limit production in any way – and the majority acknowledged that this reflected the dominant view within the Mining Association's ranks.[77] Faced with these objections, and apprehensive about the reception of legislation calculated to raise prices to other industries, the government decided against any immediate measure.[78]

From the end of 1926, therefore, the mine-owners sought to operate their own chosen policy of increasing output and lowering selling prices. As a means to recovery, this procedure proved wholly barren. Between 1925 and 1928, thanks largely to the lengthening of the working day, they were able to cut pit head prices by an average of 3s 6d a ton, and export prices by 4s 3d, despite the fact that both had been subsidized in the former year. But output actually declined slightly over this period, from 243 to 237 million tons. The share of total foreign coal consumption supplied by Britain fell from 6·9 per cent (11·2 per cent in 1923) to 6·5 per cent.[79] Although the industry enjoyed a slight revival in 1929 (when both national and world prices were rising), any further hope of prosperity was destroyed by the depression.

The fall in aggregate British output after 1925 can be explained by the contraction of home demand from iron and steel and manufacturing industries, themselves suffering from recession. But exports stagnated because the British coal trade, despite all its efforts, was incapable of recovering the markets lost during the 1926 stoppage. Between 1925 and 1926 German coal exports rose from 22½ million to over 38 million tons, and Polish from 8¼ to 14¾ million tons.[80] These gains, with the help of discriminatory price policies and indirect government subsidies, they were largely able to retain. Faced with the kind of 'unfair competition' which they had foresworn, British owners could and did cut costs to the point of near bankruptcy without significantly injuring anyone but themselves and their workers. But for a moderate expansion of total world demand in these years, the plight of the British industry would have been even worse.[81]

These circumstances were bound, eventually, to induce a change of outlook. From the spring of 1928 the principal coalfields all devised their own collective marketing arrangements. The most ambitious of these, the 'Five Counties' scheme of Yorkshire, Lancashire and the midlands, incorporated an output quota and a general levy to subsidize exports. South Wales also limited production levels, and the Scottish plan was intended to raise funds to allow the closure of unwanted pits. The north-east were content to fix minimum prices in order to curtail intra-district competition. In 1930 these voluntary district agreements were in effect given statutory force by Labour's Coal Mines Act, passed with little or no opposition on this count from mining interests.[82]

Henceforth the coal industry was run on lines far removed from those maintained by the Mining Association in 1926. Seeking to bolster prices rather than reduce them, to curtail instead of to foster competition, the owners evolved a form of incomplete dependence on the state which in earlier years had been thought inimical. Though attempting still – with greater success, indeed, than during the 1920s – to raise productivity and efficiency, they now accepted the corollary of extensive pit closures.[83] In almost all respects, therefore, employers came close to adopting the mode of operation recommended by the miners' leadership (once nationalization had been ruled out) prior to the General Strike. But since this *bouleversement* was the product of piecemeal and unplanned adjustments of policy, neither capitalists nor governments ever shaped it into a logical programme. The miners, though returning to a seven-and-a-half hour day under the 1930 Act and reviving national wage settlements in the mid-1930s, continued to suffer from heavy unemployment caused by rationalization and the lack of an effective regional policy, just as they had suffered from deteriorating conditions of work during the previous decade. Neither admitted to power not acknowledged as prophet, the Miners' Federation, for all its faults, was the victim of injustices it had done little to deserve.

XII The Reckoning, 1926-7

The expressions of outrage which greeted the end of the General Strike had been fully and fearfully anticipated. 'We shall be told we have betrayed the miners. We will get it in the neck, sure', Tillett told Herbert Samuel on the eve of its termination.[1] When the news was relayed to the strikers in the country, Eccleston Square was exposed to a barrage of phone calls and messages from local organizations, at first apprehensive, then increasingly accusatory. The fierceness of the reaction was greater because, in some cases, the conclusion of the stoppage had been interpreted as a sign that a victory had been secured.[2] When the worst news was confirmed, deputations were sent to London from as far away as Newcastle to confront those responsible for the capitulation.[3]

Widespread and emotional as this popular condemnation was, however, it was not clearly focussed nor without certain qualifying nuances. In the first place criticism did not usually lead – except from Communist sources – to a demand for the renewal of the General Strike. The firm allegiance of local strike bodies to the TUC was, to this extent, unaffected by the decision of the latter to call off the stoppage. The miners' leadership did not attempt to resist the resumption of work, and while their lodges across the country might have been more disposed to urge an unofficial prolongation of sympathetic action, the geographical isolation of the miners' organizations curtailed the possibility of their influencing other workers. Moreover, the circumstances in which the stoppage had ended diverted attention from the General Council itself to its constituent unions, who were made responsible for the return to work – and thus from the desertion of the miners to the terms and conditions imposed upon strikers by their own employers. Union branch meetings were apt to direct their displeasure against their own leadership rather than against the TUC. Significantly, too, the protests reaching the General Council itself, which were partially analyzed by its research department, were found to be levelled more frequently at its failure to secure guarantees against victimization than at any other alleged delinquency.[5] The rank and file of his own union, Bevin asserted later, were not much concerned about 'who was right and who was wrong at the General Council [but] . . . whether we could have got them back better'.[6]

Few union executives joined the chorus of denunciation – most preferring to observe, as long as possible, a diplomatic silence on the circumstances of the strike's conclusion. The principal exception was the Amalgamated Society of Woodworkers, which adopted a resolution on 13 May, circulated subsequently to all the affiliates of the TUC, expressing 'grave concern at the instruction received from the Trades Union Congress that the General Strike initiated by that body with the full approval of the affiliated unions had been called off without the consideration of the unions concerned', and demanding an immediate reconvention of the special executive conference.[7] This view was endorsed by the Electrical Trades Union and NATSOPA, but by no other organization of importance.

The General Council and its critics

The indictment of the General Council depended primarily, of course, on the strength of the miners' case. But their attack was also, for various reasons, inconsistently pursued and relatively ineffectual. Its conduct was left, at least initially, largely in the hands of Arthur Cook, whose outspoken public speeches after the stoppage were supplemented by the publication, early in June, of his own account of the strike in the pamphlet, *The Nine Days*.[8] Cook's denunciatory rhetoric exposed him, however, to counter-charges of distortion, self-contradiction and personal animus, discrediting his argument at least in official quarters. But the other miners' leaders, like their fellow-executives, were reluctant to engage in open recriminations – though their word might in some cases have carried more weight – both because of the damage likely to be sustained by the movement in the process of internal conflict, and more particularly because of their continued dependence on the TUC and its constituents for a measure of financial and moral support during the lock-out.[9] The Federation's council did not finally publish their own statement on the crisis until immediately before the conference of union executives in January 1927. Even in making this belated submission, moreover, they still revealed a certain uncertainty over whether to fashion their criticisms to appeal to the prejudices of the officers of other organizations – which implied emphasizing the largely constitutional issue raised by the woodworkers of the impropriety of the method by which the strike had been ended – or to concentrate upon their own sectional grievances, especially the unacceptability of the Samuel memorandum, at the risk of appearing unduly self-interested. In the end their case was weakened by the element of ambiguity, even of disingenuousness, which it displayed.

It was however the miners' delay in launching their attack, not its inherent lack of conviction, which did most to diminish its force. Faced with the popular outcry against its treachery and incompetence after the strike, the General Council itself favoured recalling the conference of executives without delay to endeavour to rebut the accusations directed against it. As soon as the reports of its various subcommittees had been drafted and approved, therefore (and a document prepared, based on that of the Negotiating Committee, for distribution to the executive delegates) the Council summoned the meeting of its constituents for 25 June. But at its session on the seventeenth the MFGB representatives, Smillie and Richards, urged their colleagues that the issue of the TUC statement at this point 'would be most damaging to the Miners' cause'. The date of the conference was discussed again on 22 June, when a considerable section of the Council still wished to see it take place and a motion to send out the official report was declared 'not carried' after twelve votes had been cast for and against. That evening the Council eventually agreed with the miners' officials to postpone the conference, on condition that Cook's pamphlet was withdrawn from sale, that public attacks on their own members ceased and that the Federation refrained from advocating further an embargo on coal or a financial levy without the consent of other unions.[10]

The rule of silence thus enacted was not wholly observed. At the TUC in September, for example, miners' and left-wing delegates shouted down John Bromley, the ASLEF secretary, who had written a fierce attack on the MFGB leadership and policy in his union journal.[11] But further controversy was successfully damped down both by Pugh's circumspect presidential address and by the General Council's insistence that any debate on the strike be left to the delayed conference of executives. A Communist motion objecting to this decision, unsupported by the miners, received only three quarters of a million block votes.[12]

By the time the trade-union executives assembled to consider the

General Strike (and the General Council's activities during the mining lock-out which followed) there was a natural inclination to avoid opening old wounds. Except in the coal industry itself the effects of the struggles of the past year had been less drastic than previously feared. A broad 'capitalist offensive' still showed no signs of materializing; even the unemployment and victimization which had followed the General Strike had been reduced to modest proportions. On the other hand both the necessity of concerting resistance to the apprehended Conservative legislation on trade disputes, and equally the anxiety not to dissipate the political success which recent by-election gains promised to the Labour Party, sustained a desire for unity.[13] The miners' executive, for its part, were increasingly reluctant to associate themselves with the more extreme viewpoint of Communist critics who had lambasted the Federation's own retirement from the battle with the mine-owners the previous month[14] Nor, of course, was it any longer apparent what tangible benefit the miners themselves would gain from the inquisition which they now chose to advocate.

The miners' attack on the General Council can be broken down into a number of separate charges, at least three of which had also been made by the woodworkers and other disaffected members of Congress:

(i) That the TUC leadership had failed to undertake the preparations necessary to ensure the effective organization of the General Strike.

(ii) That the Council had exceeded its authority in accepting the terms of settlement without referring them to the conference of executives for approval.

(iii) That it had failed to obtain guarantees protecting the strikers against victimization.[15]

For those accusations concerning their own maltreatment by the General Council, the miners had little overt support except from the unofficial left:

(iv) That the MFGB representatives had been insufficiently consulted during the Council's negotiations with the government immediately before the stoppage, or the talks with Samuel during it.

(v) That the Samuel memorandum had been accepted without any assurance of the government's readiness to observe its terms.

(vi) That those terms, in acquiescing in the necessity of wage reductions, were themselves inconsistent with the resolution empowering the Council to order a general strike.[16]

The General Council's own report to the conference, much longer than the Federation's statement, consisted chiefly of a detailed narrative of its various diplomatic activities between 1 and 12 May. It afforded *explicit* answers only to the last two of the charges set out above, though the defence it offered on other counts was either implicit in its rendering of the history of the negotiations, or else was provided by its spokesmen in the course of the conference debate. To the six articles of indictment, the response, direct or indirect, was thus as follows:

(i) Elaborate preparations for a general strike were impractical in view of the limited constitutional authority and financial resources of the General Council; to have undertaken them would simply have led to further counter-measures on the government's part and impeded negotiations.[17]

(ii) The General Council regarded the first conference of union executives as having given it full powers to negotiate a settlement provided it respected the main principles of the memorandum submitted to them (*The Coal Crisis*), and treated the withdrawal of the mining lock-out as a *sine qua non*. In effect this charge was thus met by the defence of the Samuel memorandum. The Council also argued that 'If . . . the strike was to be terminated with a maximum of advantage to the miners and the other unions, a decision [had to be] reached whilst the unions remained both strong and disciplined'; procedural delays were clearly undesirable.[18]

(iii) The avoidance of victimization, like the implementation of the orders to strike in the first instance, was, according to Arthur Pugh, a responsibility which individual unions could not constitutionally delegate. Furthermore, only a handful of replies were received to Citrine's telegram of 13 May instructing affiliated organizations to seek negotiations with their employers 'and report forthwith'. It was to ease the problem of reinstatement, Thomas noted, that the Council had urged the miners, without effect, to resume work alongside other unions.[19]

(iv) The Council did not meet the miners' specific complaints, that they had no representatives present at its meetings during the strike, or at the majority of the conversations with Sir Herbert Samuel. But this issue hinged on a larger one: by turning down successive 'bases of negotiation' worked out with Samuel, the Federation had asserted a *de facto* power to decide collective policy on behalf of the TUC which it did not rightfully possess. An absolute veto, indiscriminately exercised, made 'consultation' futile.[20]

(v) The Council, as has been shown, maintained that the acceptance of the Samuel memorandum by the miners would have brought about a situation in which the government would have felt obliged to adopt it; but they did not answer the miners' further point, that since they were aware of the Federation's objections to the memorandum on 12 May, they were dishonest in claiming to other unions that an understanding involving the withdrawal of the lock-out had been reached and remained intact.

(vi) The Council admitted, as it was bound to do, that it had agreed in principle to a reduction in the miners' wages. 'Every Executive here has always set out, and always will set out, in wage negotiations with a certain programme', said Thomas, 'but every Executive . . . knows perfectly well that they must and do reach a point where they have got to determine on balance what is best.'[21] At the same time, it was contended that the terms of the Samuel memorandum were consistent in all essentials with the statement submitted to the union executive conference on 29 April (*The Coal Crisis*), and with the proposals drafted by the Council's sub-committee in co-operation with the miners' officials on 3 May. *The Mining Dispute* contained an elaborate appendix setting out in parallel columns the corresponding clauses of the three documents (together with those of the government offer of 14 May). The willingness of the Council to require the miners to accept a revision in wages was justified partly by reference to the jointly devised terms of 3 May, and partly, once again, by Herbert Smith's eve-of-strike statements on his attitude to the Royal Commission report.[22]

Manifestly the General Council could not acquit itself fully of charges of betraying, or at least misleading, both the miners and its own constituent unions. It omitted to mention the discussions which had taken place in the Negotiating Committee on the subject of strike preparations; gave only the briefest indication of the concern which it had felt about the durability of the stoppage and none of its fear of indiscipline; and not surprisingly disguised its own confusion over the status of the Samuel memorandum. If its arguments nonetheless prevailed, this was probably for two overriding reasons. Firstly, most union executives accepted its view, without need of elaborate demonstration, that a continuation of the General Strike would have brought it no nearer to success, but rather entailed its defeat 'by a process of attrition which would have disorganised the Trade Union movement . . . completely established the reactionary elements in the country, and damned any possibility of getting a fair consideration of the miners' case'; and that in these circumstances the terms of the Samuel memorandum, however unofficial, represented a reasonable basis of negotiation.[23] Secondly, what rested on the endorsement of the Council's judgements was not just its prestige, but its legitimacy as a representative organ of the movement. The miners were regarded as having denied its powers of determining the general interest, and their claim to have done so in the name of some higher court, or in accordance with some original and binding contract, were in the end seen to be untenable.

Such hopes as the miners may have entertained of carrying the conference with them were dispelled by the character and course of the debate. The chairman, George Hicks, appealed to the participants to avoid a display of animosity, and his plea was uniformly obeyed. There was on this occasion none of the visible ill-feeling seen at the meeting of Congress four months earlier. Arthur Pugh, opening the case of the General Council, created an atmosphere of sobriety, and even of torpor, by reading the whole of the official report to the delegates. In the exchanges which followed, the contrasting dialectical skills of Bevin, Thomas and Citrine far excelled those of Smith and Cook. But since more attention was devoted on both sides to the course of the conversations at Eccleston Square and Downing Street during the nine days, than to the major issues allegedly in dispute, the union representatives present were unlikely to have been swayed from an initial predisposition to vindicate the Council and to put an end to an unwanted controversy. The miners' proposal to refer the General Council's report to the membership of its affiliated organizations for further discussion offered no resolution, and cast doubt on the capacity of the executives to make up their own mind. It received the support of the woodworkers and a few small unions, but was easily defeated, soon after the conference had entered its second day, by 2,840,000 votes to 1,095,000.[24]

The General Strike interpreted

In retrospect, and to the detached observer, the discussion which followed the General Strike appears irritatingly superficial and the lessons drawn from this experience disappointingly unperceptive. Most union leaders remained, in the aftermath, unwilling to admit the inherent deficiencies of this industrial weapon or their own error in resorting to it. The stoppage continued to be measured as a triumph of solidarity and organization without regard to its tactical and industrial objectives.[25] Within a few weeks of its termination, two of the General Council's members, Hicks and Purcell – endeavouring perhaps to restore their reputation as left-wingers – were writing that the rank and file response to the strike call represented a union victory in itself, and that the continued concentration of capitalist forces might necessitate a repetition of the effort.[26] Even those more noted for their moderation expressed similar opinions. In his presidential address to the Bournemouth TUC Pugh suggested a view of the General Strike little altered by the experience:[27]

> When the unions combined their forces last May, they were not invoking any new principle of industrial action, but simply asserting more effectively on a large scale the traditional Trade Union refusal to accept dictated terms of employment whether from employers or the Government. As a means of resisting such settlements in industrial disputes, the weapon used by the unions last May will not be left unused when it is sought to enforce upon any section of the workers terms which have not been made the subject of negotiation and collective agreement.

The expression of these sentiments no doubt reflected a wish among leading trade unionists to undo the psychological damage of defeat, but they were not for that reason insincere. And the explanation of the failure of the General Strike which may be distilled from them, facile though it was, suffered no private or retrospective criticism. According to this interpretation, the unhappy outcome of the stoppage was to be attributed, firstly to the obstinacy of the miners, and secondly to the prominence given by the government to the factitious question of constitutional security. The Conservative administration, according to *The Mining Dispute*, 'ingeniously obscured their own position as a third party in the dispute by raising constitutional issues and treating a sympathetic strike on industrial issues as a political movement'.[28] At the September Congress Arthur Pugh had earned applause from his audience for making this same point: 'It was not the unions but the Government which endeavoured to convert an industrial struggle into a political conflict, and sought to make party capital out of it. Nothing but the restraint, forbearance and good sense of our members prevented the agents of the Government fomenting a revolutionary temper and plunging the country into conditions of civil war.'[29] Even some of those who claimed to have opposed the declaration of a general strike, like J. H. Thomas, appear to have subscribed to the same view, that the fate of the stoppage was sealed by the 'constitutional issue' being 'falsely raised' and 'unfairly used'.[30]

For a greater logic and a more decisive verdict it is necessary to look outside the trade-union movement, to socialist politicians of left and right. After the event, and from their differing vantage points, both Labour and Communist Party leaders affirmed that the General Strike was *inherently* a polical act; that the General Council's enduring assumption that 'industrial' and 'political' objectives would be rigidly separated was fundamentally mistaken; that, accordingly, *any* government faced by an attack of this kind would be bound to adopt an unyielding stance. To the spokesmen of the Parliamentary Labour Party this conviction precluded any resort to a general strike for conventional union purposes. 'We learned', avowed J. R. Clynes, 'that a national strike could not be used as a weapon in a trade dispute.... There is one way, and one only, to alter unfair conditions in Britain. It is through the ballot box, and not through violence or resistance.'[31] And MacDonald, in the *Socialist Review*, wrote in similar vein:[32]

> The General Strike is a weapon that cannot be used for industrial purposes. It is clumsy and ineffectual. It has no goal which when reached can be regarded as victory. If fought to a finish as a Strike, it would ruin Trade Unionism, and the Government in the meantime could create a revolution; if fought to a finish only as a means to an end, the men responsible for decisions will be charged with betrayal.... The real blame is with the General Strike itself and those who preached it without considering it and induced the workers to blunder into it. It was not (because of its nature it could not be) of help to the miners.... I hope that the result will be a thorough reconsideration of Trade Union tactics. Large industrial operations of either offence or defence cannot be planned by platform speeches. If the wonderful unity in the Strike which impressed the whole world with the solidarity of British labour would be shown in politics, labour could solve mining and similar difficulties through the ballot box.

The Communist *Theses on the General Strike*, presented to their October Congress, were *mutatis mutandis* equally definite about the futility of the General Council's conception of it.[33]

> The fact that every mass strike is a political strike was clearly revealed in spite of the denials of the General Council. The basic industries were stopped, not to coerce the mineowners, but to coerce the Government. The General Council was objectively decreeing that no newspapers should be printed, that no food should be transported without its permission, or that of its local organizations, that no person could travel to or from work by the recognized

public means. To render these prohibitions effective, its local organs had to enter into conflict with the emergency organizations of the Government. It had to call upon the workers to be loyal to their unions, which was in effect to be disloyal to the Government, which was locked in conflict with those unions. The germs of alternative Government were apparent. . . .

The technical weakness of the strike plan followed from the General Council's attitude. They believed that the Government in the existing situation was impregnable and sought for an excuse to call off the strike. When the Government raised the cry of 'The Constitution in danger', they weakly denied that they were challenging the Government (which, if true, would have made the strike purposeless). The strike was either aiming at coercing the Government, representing the capitalists as a whole, or it was nothing.

Whilst these strictures had an undoubted plausibility, however, such post hoc wisdom did nothing to *explain* the confusion which it discerned in the behaviour of the General Council, still less to demonstrate an alternative course of action which would obviously have brought greater success.[34] The TUC leadership was indeed vacillating and confused. But its critics failed to appreciate that the economic and political situation to which it was responding was itself obscure and ambiguous. Thus on the one hand the memory of a 'capitalist offensive' against organized labour during the post-war depression was still fresh in the minds of the union leadership, whilst on the other, outside the mining industry, the evidence of an immediate threat to working-class standards in 1926 was slight; the General Strike was the echo rather than the voice of class war. This receding memory also explains why the General Council were on the one hand impelled to resort to a general strike by rank-and-file enthusiasm for and faith in this tactic, but on the other hand lacked the means of sustaining that enthusiasm. There may have been 'a great wave of emotion and resentment against the attempt to use the weapon of [the] lock-out to starve the miners into submission';[35] but unending sacrifices could not be demanded from sympathy and nothing more. By the very act of involving other unions in the conflict the Council highlighted differences of interest, for not all organizations were equally involved nor all combatants equally resilient, nor all wage-earners equally assured of reinstatement. Finally, whilst on the one hand the Conservative government did display some partiality for the views of the mine-owners during the crisis, on the other hand it could not credibly be portrayed as an administration of pure reaction, nor even of blatantly capitalist sympathies; in consequence, its overthrow could never be seen by the majority as a *sine qua non* of the winning of concessions on the mining question. In short, it is obvious that the General Strike had specific and substantial causes more potent than the 'muddled philosophy' of its leadership;[36] but that these causes were, of their very nature, certain to moderate the goals in view and to inhibit the manner of its conduct. Only in the light of these complex circumstances can one understand the paradox, that the General Council entered the strike with the utmost reluctance yet remained, after the event, sure that the enterprise had been morally justified.

The Trade Disputes Act

The Conservative government's legislative response to the General Strike – like its policy on the reinstatement of government employees – seemed to cast considerable doubt on its previous claims to industrial neutrality. The Trades Disputes Act, put through when the union movement was at its most vulnerable, appeared designed to prolong its injuries. The ill-feeling the law aroused among labour spokesmen was deep and lasting.[37] The enthusiasm it stimulated amongst Conservatives, on the other hand, was short-lived, not least because of its apparent inefficacy. It has thus gained the reputation of a vindictive and essentially ill-considered measure, the product of Baldwin's temporary abdication from true political leadership. 'With the laying of the Trades Disputes Bill', wrote his first biographer, 'the Disraelian make-believe rolled away like a morning mist and revealed the Conservative Party armed and accoutred to keep the unions in their places and arrest the growth of the Parliamentary Labour Party.'[38] His more recent portraitists, though crediting the Prime Minister with a larger responsibility are scarcely kinder to the work:[39] 'The Trade Disputes bill . . . remained primarily restrictive and repressive, and it must be concluded that, if Baldwin had wished it otherwise, he would have tried harder to amend it.'

As has recently been shown by Alan Anderson, however, the intentions underlying the Trade Disputes bill were at its origin less simple, even if the accepted verdicts on its achievement are not altogether unjust.[40] The measure was not merely a concession to backbench and constituency atavism; the role of the tory rank and file was in some respects a moderating one. The final shape of the measure was influenced by pressure from several other sources besides, and by the predilections of various government ministers. In the end the resultant legislation was a good deal less draconian than some lobbies had wanted. If it were negative in character this was, in large part, because conflicting interests had vetoed more positive proposals.

The government's initial determination to legislate on the subject of trade disputes arose from two considerations. Firstly, it was felt necessary to clarify the law relating to general strikes, which neither Simon nor Astbury had authoritatively accomplished. The first draft of such a declaratory act was discussed by the Cabinet while the stoppage was still in train, and though eventually postponed on 11 May, it was not abandoned. Secondly, the administration had committed itself during the crisis to ensuring the rights and security of those workers who had defied their unions' orders and remained at their posts, and one version of the government's pledge to these non-strikers, on 8 May, had specifically promised legislation to this end. Both the Solicitor-General and the Lord Chancellor asserted, during or after the strike, the need for a bill to fulfil this purpose.[41]

Neither of these objectives, when reflected on, constituted a very adequate basis for legislative action. Having omitted to outlaw the General Strike when it was in being, the government scarcely seemed required to do so when it was over and its defeat accomplished without the help of the law. Considerable problems were experienced, moreover – to be left deliberately unsolved – in defining what exactly was being prohibited. As for affording safeguards to non-participating trade unionists, this responsibility proved to be of miniscule proportions. On 19 November Steel-Maitland reported that only ninety-eight cases of workers facing disciplinary penalties from their organisations were known to the Ministry of Labour, that all of these were subject to appeal, and that forty-seven of them had already been effectively dismissed.[42] When Lord Cave had first recommended the framing of legislation, on 17 May, however, he had suggested that other desirable goals might thus be secured, including the revision of the Trade Disputes Act of 1906, the enforcement of union ballots prior to strike action, and possibly clauses to limit the right to strike in essential services and to deal with the unions' political levy. The Cabinet Committee appointed to draft a bill adopted a similarly wide perspective on its prospective contents.[43]

Whereas Cave had been inclined to favour legislation restrictive in emphasis, the committee's first report, at the end of June, put forward an ambiguous but seemingly more generous principle: 'any legislation which may be introduced in the near future should be such as will command the support of the great mass of public opinion, including that of the moderate trade unionist, and it [should] not be capable of being represented as having a party character'. Its chief constructive proposal was for the registration of all trade unions, the compulsory submission of their rules to official scrutiny, and the requirement that they should make provision for strike ballots. It discountenanced any alteration of the immunities granted in 1906 as politically inexpedient, and was doubtful of the practical value of tighter regulation of picketing. On the other hand, at Neville Chamberlain's behest, it recommended that unions in the civil service be prevented from affiliating to outside organizations like the TUC, and that local authorities should not have the right to demand union membership as a condition of employment.[44]

Nine months were to elapse from the submission of this report to the government's approval of its Trade Disputes bill. The Cabinet failed to reach unanimity on the committee's suggestions at its meeting of 7 July, and its continued differences about what should or should not be incorporated were the main cause of the long delay. Backbench MPs, constituency organizations and employers' representatives were asked for opinions which proved mutually contradictory. Other nostrums were put forward by individual ministers and provoked new debates and disagreements.[45] It seems evident, moreover, that Baldwin welcomed a postponement. Perhaps as G. M. Young suggests, 'he was in one of those moods of exhaustion and collapse which followed on the hour of decision, resolve, success'.[46] But he may have hoped that the pressure for a large-scale and punitive measure, which built up to a peak in the two or three months before the Unionist Party conference of October 1926, would tend to recede with time. He told Cave well in advance of the conference that there was no chance of legislation during the present year. And certainly the Minister of Labour, Steel-Maitland, was urging the advantage of procrastination at this juncture, partly because he disliked the tendency of the proposed bill to get longer and tougher and partly because he wished to make informal approaches to the unions to obtain an 'industrial concordat', involving temporary abrogation of industrial stoppages.[47] Other ministers were in no hurry unless and until they got their own way.

In the end the bill changed very little during this interval. Of the Cabinet committee's original proposals, those on the proscription of general strikes and the protection of individual union members who disobeyed unlawful orders were never contentious; those on civil service unions and local authority employees were also eventually included without objection. The issue of picketing was settled by a weak compromise formula, preventing the practice at private dwellings and redefining 'intimidation'; the 1906 Act was left untouched. Only two significant revisions thus occurred as a result of the delay: the exclusion of the 'constructive' clauses on union registration and compulsory strike ballots; and the inclusion of the clause allowing unions to charge subscriptions for their political funds only to members who had 'contracted in' to this levy – not, as previously, to all but those who had 'contracted out'. The former were controversial items on which disagreement had proved impossible to overcome; the latter amendment was arguably bound to be introduced at some stage in view of the Conservatives' election promises, and caused dissension only in so far as its relevance to this bill was in question.

Why the bill remained largely unaltered is readily apparent if the wishes of the various outside bodies who sought to influence it are examined together. Employers' spokesmen wanted the amendment of the 1906 Trade Disputes Act to make unions liable for damages where their orders gave rise to tortuous acts and breaches of contract; the restriction, or even the total prohibition, of picketing; and in some cases a more rigorous law preventing lightning strikes in public services. On the other hand the majority opposed compulsory strike ballots and union registration.[48] The labour advisory committees of the Conservative constituency organizations, in contrast, supported strike ballots but opposed both the amendment of the 1906 measure and other penalties on stoppages. The trade-union subcommittee of the 1922 Committee joined the employers in objecting to compulsory ballots and registration and favoured a less drastic reduction of the unions' legal immunity. Amid this discord even the partial agreement on the desirability of new provisions on picketing was of little help, for there was no unanimity about whether prohibition or merely restriction should be attempted, and no specific proposal about how to achieve the latter.[49]

The one subject on which all lobbies proved to concur was the reform of the political levy. And this, as has been seen, became the single significant addition to the bill during its gestation. The idea of replacing 'contracting out' by 'contracting in' had been floated but not pressed by Cave when he first outlined his legislative proposals, and had not been mentioned by the Cabinet committee's first report. At the end of October, however, following the submissions of the constituency parties, the cause was taken up by Churchill: 'This is a real and dangerous abuse, and, as we shall in any case encounter the violent hostility of the Labour Socialist Party, it is surely worth our while to do our work thoroughly in the general interest.'[50] The inclusion of this clause in the Trade Disputes bill was strongly opposed by Steel-Maitland, who argued, with considerable force, that it contradicted what had been taken as the guiding principle of the Cabinet committee, the composition of a non-partisan measure.[51] But the Conservative leadership had promised action on this long-standing issue at the 1924 election, and though Baldwin had been able to evade the commitment on the introduction of the Macquisten bill the following year, backbench and constituency opinion was running too high by 1926 to be further resisted. By the beginning of December the majority of the Cabinet committee had consented to the proposal.[52] No other additions were accepted subsequently, however. The bill was completed by the final acceptance of the clause on picketing. The measure was at length published in March 1927 and got its second reading at the beginning of May.

The Trade Disputes Act remained, as it had begun, a legal *pot-pourri*.[53] Only three of its eight clauses were directly related to the prohibition of general strikes which formed its ostensible justification. Of the other sections the restraint on picketing represented a modest concession to the employers, the amendment of the political levy a major one to the Conservative Party. The sanctions against civil service unions and local authorities had no particularly strong advocates, and were evidently left in because they aroused no strong opposition. Taken as a whole, however, the Act which emerged from this long discursive process was the complete antithesis of what the Cabinet committee had claimed to be seeking; it was an effective rallying point for party opinion, but had little chance of winning wider political support. 'The bill', Birkenhead wrote to the Indian Viceroy in February, 'will naturally make a great row, but it was right and necessary,' and 'our party, both in the House of Commons and in the country is inflexibly determined, whatever the risk may be, that we shall adopt this course'. Its relevance to current industrial issues and its appeal to 'moderate workmen' were negligible.[54]

Labour and the Trade Disputes Act

The reaction to the legislation from the labour movement was as pronounced as Birkenhead had forecast. For all its lack of real ambition, the bill could not have been more calculated to unite its potential enemies. The Parliamentary Labour Party, its constituency organizations, local councillors and the trade unions were alike affected and antagonized. The fact that the unions and the party were already in a weakened condition as a result of the General Strike helped to foster a siege mentality. And the deliberate vagueness of the provisions concerning the legal limits of strikes and picketing created the impression that the bill was more threatening than it proved to be.[55] The unity it thus imposed on the labour movement, at least temporarily, following the ructions caused by the nine days, was perhaps its most important consequence – going some way to justify Steel-Maitland's prediction that it would 'be a boomerang that will inflict more hurt on the attackers than on the object of attack.'[56]

Opposition was not as formidable, however, as the energy spent upon it seemed to promise. At the beginning of April 1927 the National Trade Union Defence Committee was instituted, representing the Scottish and English General Councils, the Labour Party executive and MPs, and the Co-operative Union – 'as authoritative and all-embracing a body as the labour movement has ever known'. More than 1,100 meetings were held under its auspices, and its campaign was 'the most extensive ever undertaken by the Labour Movement, reaching corners of the country . . . which, it is believed, have never been touched before'.[57] But both as a publicity and a recruiting exercise its success was very limited. Labour activists, like the Conservatives, had almost certainly overestimated the importance of the controversy for those outside their ranks.[58] Nor did the resistance offered by the bill's opponents go beyond these propagandist bounds. The Parliamentary Labour Party discussed, but decided against, an organized boycott of the House of Commons. Talk of strike action upon this political matter was confined to the extreme left. Once the statute was enacted, the General Council advised its affiliates to comply with it by altering their rules to allow 'contracting out'.[59] And if trade-union leaders remained more antipathetic to the Conservative government than might otherwise have been the case (a disputable point), they were soon to appear actively willing to be reconciled to industrial employers – both prominent individual representatives like Lord Weir and Sir Alfred Mond, and even organizations like the National Confederation – regardless of the fact that they had advocated legislation more penal or more restrictive in character. The election of the second Labour Government on the one hand, and the Mond-Turner talks on the other, served to emphasize how ephemeral was the conflict precipitated by the Trade Disputes Act, and how marginal its impact on the conduct of politics or industrial relations.

XIII The Aftermath

Any event as dramatic in character as the General Strike can readily be viewed as a historical watershed. The difficulty of seeing the crisis of 1926 in this light has, however, already been indicated. In the first place the strike was itself the outcome of developments in the structure of the labour movement which originated two generations before, and in relation to which it stands as an effect only partly foreseen and intended. Secondly it has been suggested that the temperament of union leaders and the circumstances in which the strike was ended alike conspired against the extraction of political and tactical lessons from it. Though the men responsible may have conducted themselves differently following this experience, they did not explain their changed behaviour by reference to it – preferring, on the contrary, to claim a consistency for their opinions which tended to depreciate its importance. And while this apparent indifference may contain a measure of deception, it also affords a marked contrast with the much more explicit and unambiguous response to the failure of Black Friday, five years earlier.

As far as 1926 is concerned, it is often impossible to separate the results of the General Strike *per se* from those of the miners' lock-out which continued thereafter. If the two episodes are conflated, however, certain provisional conclusions may be drawn. The dispute had, to begin with, a significant short-term effect upon union strength – measured primarily in terms of membership and its distribution – but almost no lasting consequences. On industrial tactics, and especially on the use of the strike weapon, their impact was rather to provide a further restraining influence where inhibiting factors were already in evidence, than to initiate any change of conduct. Similarly, though the broad political and economic outlook of union leaders, and especially the members of the General Council, was doubtless modified by what happened in 1926, what transpired was a rediscovery or a bolder re-assertion of familiar principles more than a formulation of original ones.

More accurately, perhaps, it may be said that the reverses of this year simplified a previous ambivalence, without giving birth to new values.

The General Strike and union membership

Aggregate trade-union membership fell steadily in the years 1925–8, at a significantly faster rate than it had fallen in 1922–5 but far less rapidly than in the first years of the post-war depression, between 1920 and 1922.

TABLE 14. *Total union membership and rate of unemployment, 1920–39*

	membership (000s)	*rate of change* (%)		*unemployment* (%)
1920	8,348	1920–1	−20·55	7·9
1921	6,633			16·9
1922	5,625	1922–5	+2·12	14·3
1923	5,429			11·7
1924	5,544			10·3
1925	5,506	1925–8	−12·71	11·3
1926	5,219			12·5
1927	4,919			9·7
1928	4,806			10·8
1929	4,858	1929–3	−9·59	10·4
1930	4,842			16·1
1931	4,614			21·3
1932	4,444			22·1
1933	4,392	1933–9	+43·39	19·9
1934	4,590			16·7
1939	6,298			10·5

Source: British Labour Statistics, 1886–1968, Tables 196 and 160. The unemployment figure for 1920 is the rate for December only; for other years, a twelve-month mean.

Most, if not all, of the decline between 1925 and 1928 must be attributed to the effects of the General Strike. In 1926 and 1927 there was an underlying improvement in the labour market. In the former year this was concealed by the repercussions of the mining lock-out; but under normal circumstances it would have produced at least a modest expansion of labour organization. Indeed the proportion of the insured labour force out of work in April 1926 was the lowest for that month throughout the years 1920–40 (though some part of this additional employment may have resulted from industrial preparations for the coal stoppage). Only in 1928 was the unemployment trend clearly, if slightly, upwards. In the absence of the defeat of 1926, there seems no reason why the unions should not have retained their strength at about the level of 1924, at least up to the inter-war depression. Manifestly, however, they would have preserved it no longer.

The impact of the General Strike in this regard is more marked, however, when particular industrial groups are considered. Table 15 shows those industries where the rate of decline of union membership increased after 1926 in comparison with the preceding period, and those in which the shift was in the reverse direction. It is apparent that the stoppages of 1926 did render the most severe damage to the unions heavily involved in the conflict, but did not affect them equally. The relatively slight losses sustained by the engineering and shipbuilding organizations may be explained by their late and brief participation in the strike; but more probably they, like the building unions, contracted less sharply now precisely because they had been brought nearer to bedrock by earlier defeats. What characterizes the unions that were most adversely affected by the General Strike, as Professor Clegg has pointed out, was not just their exposure to the full brunt of the struggle on this occasion, but their relative immunity to industrial reverses in the immediately preceding years of 1921–5.[1] For the most part sheltered from the economic effects of depression, they had also escaped major industrial defeats. Some, but by no means all, printing workers, and engine drivers in ASLEF but not NUR members, had been engaged in unsuccessful conflicts in 1922 and 1924 respectively.[2] But their losses had been minor in comparison with those suffered by the engineers in 1922, the boilermakers in 1923, the builders and some shipyard workers in 1924.[3] The general unions, for their part, had mostly avoided national stoppages during the depression, and the dockers had managed to win a clear and fairly bloodless victory by their strike in 1924.[4]

The two apparent exceptions to this general pattern are the coal-miners and the iron and steel workers. The miners had lost relatively few members in the early 1920s despite their heavy defeat inflicted on them in 1921; and their organization must simply be counted as extraordinary, on grounds of resilience as well as of militancy. The iron and steel workers, on the other hand, had avoided unsuccessful strikes prior to 1926, but had not avoided the rapid loss of membership

TABLE 15. *Union membership by industry/occupation, 1921–39 (end of year)*

(a) Unions with increasing rate of membership loss, 1921–8

	1921	*1925*	*% change 1921–5*	*1926*	*1928*	*% change 1925–8*	*1932*	*% change 1928–32*	*1939*	*% change 1932–9*
coal-mining	936,653	885,789	−5·44	762,916	592,379	−33·12	554,015	−6·31	707,012	+28·05
paper and printing	201,614	207,151	+2·75	185,975	180,878	−12·68	184,218	+1·85	224,188	+21·69
railways	506,875	528,764	−4·32	491,861	412,037	−22·08	399,184	−3·14	470,033	+17·75
transport and general labour	1,086,783	919,172	−15·42	860,485	769,483	−16·29	660,180	−22·0	1,218,911	+84·64

(b) Unions with decreasing rate of membership loss, 1921–8

	1921	*1925*	*% change 1921–5*	*1926*	*1928*	*% change 1925–8*	*1932*	*% change 1928–32*	*1939*	*% change*
furniture and woodwork	73,422	67,063	−8·66	63,785	63,286	−5·63	53,717	−15·12	420,105 (furniture and woodwork, and building)	+27·89
building	460,998	334,528	−27·43	328,970	308,697	−7·72	274,752	−11·0		
water transport	140,532	86,351	−38·55	97,800	105,796	+22·52	77,441	−26·8	74,277	−4·09
textiles	730,895	626,973	−14·22	620,105	591,620	−5·64	492,473	−16·76	419,559	−14·81
engineering and shipbuilding	895,043	594,568	−33·57	573,083	540,805	−9·04	472,251	−12·58	936,125 (engineering and shipbuilding, and iron and steel)	+77.89
iron and steel	131,661	86,911	−33·99	83,851	66,498	−23·49	53,983	−18·82		

Source: *Abstract of Labour Statistics*, vol. 21, 1933; *Ministry of Labour Gazette*, October 1940, p. 262. In the 'transport and general labour' group, 'transport' signifies dock and road vehicle workers; 'general labour' means the membership of 'general' unions only.

which was the normal consequence of such setbacks. Moreover their numerical strength continued to decline after the General Strike, despite their large involvement in it, at roughly the same rate as before. In this case, therefore, the decline of trade unionism must be attributed to other factors: to the level of unemployment in the industry – higher than in any other except shipbuilding and port transport in the years 1923–9 – and to the fact that its workers suffered regular wage cuts under the automatic sliding scale arrangements maintained with the co-operation of the Confederation.[5] In these circumstances, where union membership seemed to offer such dubious protection, it was unlikely that the 1926 dispute would have the same critical impact as it did in the case of the miners and transport unions.

The 'transport and general' group of unions might also be regarded as a somewhat ambiguous case on this evidence. Their membership contracted immediately after the General Strike only slightly faster than it had done at the onset of depression in 1921, and significantly more slowly than it was to do during the interwar slump. In order to obtain a more revealing picture of their fortunes, however, it is necessary to examine the discrepant membership fluctuations of the major organizations concerned. It is evident from Table 16 that the union most heavily involved in the General Strike was also that which, in the short term, registered the largest defections.

TABLE 16. *Membership of principal 'general' unions, December 1925–8*

	1925	*1926*	*1927*	*1928*
T&GWU	376,251	335,791	319,533	316,454
NUG&MW	313,981	322,345	308,305	283,906
Workers' Union	152,000	151,200	140,000	122,882

Source: Report of the Chief Registrar of Friendly Societies, 1927, Part 4.

Between 1922 and 1925 the Transport and General Workers had recorded a net gain of some 75,000 members; in 1926 it suffered a net loss of 40,000, despite absorbing the Enginemen and Firemen's Union (some 22,000 strong) during the year. The General and Municipal Workers and the Workers' Union, less embattled in 1926, continued to show themselves more sensitive to changes in unemployment rates than to the effect of industrial disputes – and the latter especially had lost far more of its numerical strength in the early 1920s. It is, however, worth adding that this organization suffered irreparable financial losses as a result of the General Strike, which may well have restricted its subsequent recruiting activities in the more favourable circumstances of 1928–9.[6]

After 1929 the incidence of union membership loss in different industries formed another new pattern. During the depression the principal determinant of relative rates of decline was once again the extent to which particular organizations were sheltered from, or exposed to, the trade slump. For this reason railway, building and printing unions fared better than those in the 'transport and general' section, shipping, textiles and metal. Mining unionism again occupies an anomalous position, suffering heavy unemployment but little further numerical erosion. After 1933 it was to be the general unions and the engineers which grew most rapidly, thanks to breadth of recruitment and flexibility of organization on the one hand, and the direction taken by economic recovery on the other. These two groups contained about thirty-five per cent of total union membership by 1939, as against some twenty-nine per cent in 1925.[7]

As far as the distribution of union membership was concerned therefore, the conflicts of 1926 had visible short-run effects on a limited number of organizations, but made little or no difference to long-term trends. The main victims of the General Strike were the miners, the Transport and General Workers' Union, and the railway and printing societies, which by one means or another had escaped the damage suffered by other unions in the period 1921–4, but now lost that relative advantage. No other organization except the iron and steel workers lost as high a proportion of its membership in 1925–8 as they did. Only the miners, however, failed to undergo a full recovery, in numerical terms, by the outbreak of the second world war – and the permanence of their loss was, of course, primarily the result of the rationalization of the coal industry after 1929. The railwaymen and the printers, on the other hand, maintained their strength more successfully than most during the depression of 1929–33; and the T&GWU, like the other general unions, significantly improved their position during the mid- and late-1930s. Only in so far as the *overall* reduction in unionization in certain industries enhanced – to a very limited extent – the organizing potential of the large and multi-industry general unions during the economic recovery, can the conflict of 1926 be said to have had a more lasting influence on the profile of the movement.

Industrial stoppages after 1926

On the development of collective bargaining, and especially the unions' use of the strike weapon, the General Strike and mining lock-out again had only a modest effect. The events of 1926 did not issue in an era of industrial peace, any more than they permanently altered the pattern of union membership; but in the former context they did serve to reinforce an existing trend. The number of working days lost as a result of strike action had been moving downwards, with only one irregularity, since 1921. It dropped still further in 1927–8, and the abnormally small scale of the disputes occurring in these two years can plausibly be ascribed to the moral and financial consequences of the previous year's conflicts. But by 1929 accumulated union funds had been restored almost to the level of 1924 (and above that of 1921); and it has been seen that membership, too, began to revive after 1933.[8] Thus the absence of any renewed union militancy either in the period of the inter-war depression or the subsequent recovery is more credibly to be attributed to the cautious and restrained policies followed by industrial employers. In 1921–3 the concentration of disputes had reflected union response to the imposition of widespread and penal wage cuts in a period of rapid deflation, which in some cases appeared to threaten the safety of bargaining rights. No such extensive attack on standards of pay accompanied the slump of 1929–33, however, and even in the worst year of the crisis, 1931, wage cuts amounted to only one fifteenth of the level of ten years earlier; while throughout the four years 1930–3 only one-eighth as much was taken from the net weekly wage bill as in the single year 1921.[9] Moreover nearly half of these changes were made under sliding scale agreements linking pay to indices of the cost of living, the price of industrial products or the proceeds of industrial output – forms of adjustment which the unions, whether or not willingly, had agreed by negotiation.[10]

The increasingly moderate behaviour of employers was not, in all probability, the result of the General Strike, whose imminent recurrence appeared inconceivable. It may have been more markedly influenced by the memory of the sectional conflicts which took place in the early 1920s, which had in many cases been more costly to the firms involved, and which certainly seemed a likelier mode of resistance to a further attack on wages now. In addition, however, the pressure on employers to reduce costs was less intense because the rate of decline of wholesale prices was on this occasion slower; in the financial year

TABLE 17. *Number of workers directly and indirectly involved in, and working days lost through, industrial stoppages, 1920–39*

	workers	days lost		workers	days lost
1920	1,932,000	26,568,000	1931	490,000	6,983,000
1921	1,801,000	85,872,000	1932	379,000	6,488,000
1922	552,000	19,850,000	1933	136,000	1,072,000
1923	405,000	10,672,000	1934	134,000	959,000
1924	613,000	8,424,000	1935	271,000	1,955,000
1925	441,000	7,952,000	1936	316,000	1,829,000
1927	108,000	1,174,000	1937	597,000	3,413,000
1928	124,000	1,388,000	1938	274,000	1,334,000
1929	533,000	8,287,000	1939	337,000	1,356,000
1930	307,000	4,399,000			

Source: *Abstract of Labour Statistics 21, 1919–33*; *British Labour Statistics 1886–1968*, Table 197.

1921–2 wholesale prices had been halved, whilst between 1929 and 1933 they fell, in all, by only one-third.[11] Improvement in the terms of trade, price inelasticities of demand for many industrial commodities and increases in the rate of manufacturing productivity all played a part in permitting employers to forgo large wage reductions, or at least to regard the cost of attempting to impose them as too high.

If a large part of the responsibility for preserving industrial peace after 1929 can be ascribed to industrialists, it is nonetheless apparent that most trade unions were increasingly reluctant to resort to the use of national strikes, whether to resist such wage cuts as were exacted during the depression or to secure increases of pay during the recovery of the mid-1930s. But again it is rarely necessary to cite the General Strike as the main explanation for this lack of militancy. Most organizations could calculate the odds on the successful outcome of such industrial action from their own experience of sectional stoppages, which usually indicated that long-drawn-out strikes in conditions of heavy unemployment were futile as a means of self-defence, and that the maintenance of effective bargaining machinery was more advantageous in the long run than gains made at the expense of its disruption by policies of open aggression.

The events of 1926 should not be completely disregarded, however, as a contributory factor in the decline of labour stoppages. The minority of unions which lost membership most heavily as a result of those conflicts were obviously more likely than others to readjust their industrial tactics subsequently, particularly because their previous organizational durability had been the result in part of their avoidance of serious defeats. For the miners, therefore, it is clear that the 1926 lock-out does mark a turning point in this respect. Even so, miners were responsible for at least one-third of working days lost through stoppages in every year between 1933 and 1939, and for more than half in the relatively strike-affected years of 1936–8. The case of the railwaymen is more difficult; the moderate leadership of the NUR had shown no disposition to attempt to repeat the success of the national strike of 1919 and had refused to support the footplatemen's stoppage in 1924. But the pressure for a more belligerent policy from the elected members of the executive and to some extent from the rank and file – hitherto not inconsiderable – was probably diminished by the defeat of 1926. The dockers, organized principally by the T&GWU, had conducted an industry-wide strike with good effect in 1924. Here, too, the General Strike was perhaps most significant in shifting the balance of forces within the union towards national officials always cautious in their use of the strike weapon. The effect of the nine days and the mining lock-out should be not exaggerated, even in these instances; but neither was it politically negligible. And it is notable that the one industrial group in which national stoppages remained conspicuous in the years between 1929 and 1933 – the textile trades – had avoided involvement either in the conflicts of the early 1920s or in the crisis of 1926.

Union ideology and the Mond–Turner talks

If the General Strike had little effect on the industrial behaviour of union leaders, it might still have modified their ideas. At the very least it can be argued that the principal spokesmen of the movement became less prone to assert radical objectives, or to employ left-wing rhetoric. One obvious indication of this reorientation was the emergence of a more open hostility towards the activities of Communists within the unions. Prior to the General Strike the National Minority Movement, though widely distrusted and disliked by most established officials, was neither publicly criticized nor obstructed. The General Council did warn Trades Councils against associating with it during 1925, and one or two other conservatively-inclined organizations uttered their own admonitions. But it was not until after 1926, when the MM itself changed from 'a comparatively unstructured propaganda campaign into an organized electoral pressure group', that more determined measures were adopted.[12] In November 1926 the General Council resolved that the affiliation of Trades Councils to the Movement was 'not consistent with the policy of the Congress and General Council', and in February 1927 it decided to withdraw recognition from those that remained attached. At the meeting of the TUC that year an official inquiry was authorized, primarily at Citrine's instigation, into Communist disruption within the unions. A number of organizations sought, with varying success, to prohibit or discourage Communists from securing official or representative positions.[13] Finally, the campaign to reunite the International Federation of Trades Unions with the Red International of Labour Unions, which had commanded widespread support within Congress prior to 1925, was tacitly abandoned, and the Anglo-Russian Joint Committee itself dissolved in 1927.[14]

Whilst the far-left was being outlawed and ostracized, furthermore, those causes and slogans with which it had successfully identified itself were also coming under fire. In the 1926 TUC a resolution to strengthen the authority of the General Council to propose joint strike action and levy financial assistance from its constituents was openly opposed and decisively defeated.[15] The other radical *eldorado banal*, industrial unionism, took somewhat longer to disappear, being once again upheld, on a narrow vote, at the Bournemouth Congress. But the following year the report of the organization committee of the General Council, appointed as a result of the resolution at Hull in 1924 – and still more the debate upon it – exposed the inadequacies and impracticalities of the dogma. It was never again to enjoy its former vogue.[16]

It should not, of course, be concluded that the position of the General Council or the prospects of union amalgamation were much affected by the outcome of these debates. The passage of motions on such subjects had had little import in the past. The one discernible effect of the altered posture here remarked was the cessation, after 1926, of ill-fated attempts to form strategic union coalitions like the Industrial Alliance. Otherwise, what is being noted is a change in the tone and style in which union leaders presented their objectives – more conspicuous, certainly, than a change in the objectives themselves.

Undoubtedly the most widely-publicized and seemingly profound shift of opinion in the union movement following the General Strike, however, was that which led to the 'Mond-Turner talks'. To its critics, the General Council's participation in a national conference together with prominent industrialists signified an indifference to socialist principles, a belief in the compatability of working-class and capitalist interests, even a denial of the necessity for a distinct form of labour politics. 'Mondism', writes Mr Griffin, entailed an insistence on 'the rigid division between industrial and political matters', the former to be settled between employers and employed, the latter left entirely to an elected parliament.[17]

This left-wing view of the discussions which began in 1928 does have a certain plausibility. The General Strike caused a marked deterioration in relations between the TUC leadership and the Labour Party – and historical accounts which see 1926 as the origin of a renewed union faith in 'parliamentarism' are to this extent misleading. Ramsay MacDonald's attitude to the strike, which provoked a violent attack on him by Bevin, was probably widely resented.[18] The party leader's sensitivity to this ill-feeling caused him, in December 1926, to decline George Hicks' proposal for a general congress of the labour movement with the observation that an improved understanding between the General Council and the parliamentary party was a more urgent need.[19] Better collaboration was briefly achieved in opposition to the Trade Disputes bill the following year, but it was not to endure beyond the formation of the second Labour government. It is also apparent that the Conservative support for the idea of an industrial conference in 1927–8 reflected more than a simple desire to promote industrial peace. Mond, himself a Conservative MP, received encouragement and a measure of practical help from Baldwin and Steel-Maitland, no doubt with an eye to the electoral advantages to be derived from such a display of industrial goodwill.[20] And if the ministers did not expect to bring about an open schism in labour's ranks, the drafting of the Trade Disputes bill suggests that they did at least hope to strengthen the forces of 'moderate', non-political unionism.

To see in the Mond–Turner talks the conversion of the General Council itself to a kind of consensus politics is, however, to exaggerate both the novelty of the idea and the extent of the obligations to which it gave rise. Many unions, though not all, had approved in principle of the creation of some kind of national forum with employers' representatives before 1928 (or 1926). The National Industrial Conference convened by the government in 1919 had obtained general support for the establishment of a permanent body drawn from both sides of industry. Depression and resultant conflicts had caused this to miscarry.

But an institution on such lines still seemed a logical extension of the joint industrial councils formed in individual industries on the recommendations of the Whitley report on industrial relations, published in 1917. In 1921 a national association of these councils was in fact set up.[21] To the General Council, therefore, the Mond talks were no more prejudicial to the ideas of the movement than the existence of negotiating structures already common on a sectional basis. The most far-reaching purpose conceived for these meetings was, indeed, to broaden the scope and enhance the usefulness of established negotiating procedures for the unions' benefit. But they were also seen as having an immediate and specific objective: to discourage employers as a whole from seeking wage cuts and imposing measures of rationalization detrimental to their workmen while the unions were so ill-equipped to offer opposition. Finally, in taking this course, the TUC leadership felt safeguarded by the fact that the conversations with the Mond group were binding on neither side, no prior conditions or recommendations having been accepted. The Council consented to take part because, as Pugh told his colleagues, 'we cannot possibly do harm'.[22]

The suggestion that Mondism represented a lurch in the direction of 'non-political' unionism is equally difficult to sustain. If the talks rested on the premise that 'industrial' and 'political' questions could be segregated, this had been a long-standing belief of union leaders, upholding the strategy of the General Strike itself. If the result was to emphasize the breach between the TUC and the Labour Party, this breach had appeared mainly because the party was insufficiently militant, not because the unions were insufficiently socialist. It should be noted, too, that a move towards autonomy had been made by the TUC in 1925, with the dissolution of the system of policy committees formerly staffed jointly with the party.[23] In short, it is no more possible to see the Mond–Turner talks as part of a consistent progression to right-wing politics than it is to see the unions before 1926 as consistently wedded to a radical, anti-capitalist programme.

It is true that the Council hesitated for some time before embracing the proposal for an industrial conference. When first suggested by Lord Weir in December 1926 the idea was discussed and then for a time shelved.[24] But it was the timing of the proposal rather than its content which necessitated this delay, for the introduction of the Trade Disputes bill shortly afterwards caused too much antagonism towards the employers' side to allow any immediate *rapprochement*.[25] In addition the nature of this legislation gave rise to suspicions, fostered by both the Labour and the Tory press, that what was being sought for at this juncture was a restriction of the right to strike. It was partly to try and dispel this impression, no doubt, that the General Council insisted that the first topics discussed with the employers' group in the spring of 1928 should be trade-union recognition and victimization. And whilst it was subsequently agreed that a permanent national industrial council should establish its own appeals machinery for use in industrial disputes, the prime function of this device was investigative, and its ability to postpone stoppages for the purpose of inquiry was made wholly dependent on the voluntary consent of the parties concerned.[26]

Promises of constructive cooperation did not cause the unions to lower their guard; nor, indeed, should their belief in cooperation be overstated. The vision of a national bargaining apparatus which comprehended large new fields of management and social policy may have been clearly perceived by Bevin and Citrine; but others followed more falteringly or less purposefully in their wake. [27] There was, besides, always a significant minority of the General Council and the TUC who were anxious to bring the enterprise to an end. This consisted not just of A. J. Cook, voicing the opinions of the left, but of the engineering union, whose President asserted at the 1928 Congress that the Council had exceeded its powers in entering the talks and that 'the whole action is an attempt by certain individuals to interfere with the affairs of unions other than their own'; and also the builders, on whose behalf George Hicks (despite his support for the idea of national consultations with employers the previous year) objected now to any standing industrial council, and claimed that mutual agreement on rationalization 'will undermine the position of the craftsman'.[28]

It was this last issue which eventually aroused most widespread misgivings in the movement as a whole. In July 1928 the Council had endorsed the resolution which, from the employers' point of view, stated the *raison d'être* of the talks:[29]

> The tendency towards a rational organization of industry and trade including the grouping of individual units within an industry into larger units is recognized, and this tendency should be welcomed and encouraged in so far as it leads to improvements in the efficiency of industrial production, services and distribution, and to the raising of the standard of living of the people.

By 1930 almost all union leaders were becoming more dubious about the acceptance of such industrial innovations under conditions of rising unemployment. Even those previously most inclined to preach cooperation, like Bevin and Pugh, appeared increasingly sceptical about whether meaningful agreement could be reached to permit rationalization whilst safeguarding the interests of their members.[30] At the end of 1930 the General Council prevailed upon the National Confederation of Employers' organizations to discuss the subject of 'displacement of labour due to rationalization' under the arrangements for national consultation on an official basis made after the Mond conversations had taken place. But by the summer of 1931 these talks had been found barren and were quietly abandoned.[31] Their failure preceded the framing of any agreed policy on this question by the TUC – whose ability to achieve a consensus among its own members was thus left in considerable doubt.

Whilst it is possible to regard the Mond–Turner talks as an outcome of the General Strike, therefore, so far as the union leadership were concerned their value was limited and short-lived. They created an atmosphere of goodwill at a time when employers were strong and labour felt vulnerable to wage cuts and loss of bargaining rights. They led to the formulation of some vague platitudes about industrial progress which had no evident or lasting effect on the policy of any union. They encouraged Bevin, and perhaps Citrine, to take an interest in wider questions of economic and financial policy – but this interest was not shared to the same extent by others. The policy documents produced with the employers' group during 1928 were not advocated with any determination subsequently. The TUC failed to formulate an agreed and distinctive programme to deal with unemployment after 1929, and even its belated opposition to the retrenchment measures proposed by the Labour government in 1931 disguised major internal disagreements on the issue of tariff reform in particular.[32] Not until the advent of the National Government, when relations between the General Council and the Labour Party developed a greater intimacy, did the former begin to take an effective part in the devising of national economic policies. And not until 1940 did they gain access to the ear of a government in power.

Conclusion

Only in a very modest and unspectacular fashion, therefore, did the General Strike alter the ideas or the behaviour of the union movement. It reinforced a trend towards industrial peace that was already under way, and it confirmed a long-established faith in a regulated system of voluntary collective bargaining. Its chief effect, however, was simply to change the movement's rhetorical style, the tone of its public discourse. This meant that to some extent the unions presented a different and more acceptable image to the outside world. It also entailed an adjustment, more significant but more difficult to assess, in the relations of the union leadership with its rank and file. The attention now given to maintaining the morale of the membership, and perhaps to encouraging their active involvement in organizations that were democratic at least in aspiration, appears to have diminished. Even so, the degree of alienation which resulted is demonstrable only in the case of that organized left-wing movement within the unions whose criticisms of officialdom were probably too extreme to be widely accepted and whose militancy was too undiscriminating to be generally popular. In the long run it is possible that the decline of a conspicuous idealism, the loss of a radical aura, did affect the motives which caused men to join trade unions and the extent to which members participated in their affairs. Yet so broad a judgement is not only resistant to proof, but risks doing injustice to the diversity of character and outlook which the movement still accommodated.

In the end the General Strike merits historical study less for what it changed in the labour movement, than for what it revealed of the unchanging. It was the product of a trade unionism which, though it seemed to contain many inconsistent features, was still too stable a compound to be transformed by so short a process. The union movement was so durable in its make-up, as it revealed on this occasion, because it was predominantly defensive in its objectives, disinclined to state its purposes in ideological terms, concerned primarily with the achievement of an effective organization and internal discipline, not with any long-term programme of social and political reconstruction. Not only was the General Strike justified by reference to these relatively unambitious standards in the first instance; it could also be reckoned subsequently, on the same basis, by no means a total failure. The relations of the unions with the social system of which they were part were similarly difficult to disturb. The conditions to which the organized working class were subject were far from uniform and the social resentments they created were equally variable. But in every case – even in the coal industry – hostility to the capitalist order was moderated by the very fact of the survival of a powerful trade union organization. Moreover the crisis of 1926 served to indicate how far the leaders and members of these institutions shared, especially in the political sphere, the values of their fellow-citizens: the belief in constitutional modes of government, in the virtues of legality, in a pragmatic and conciliatory approach to potentially disruptive social issues. Neither the grievances which had brought about the General Strike nor the inhibitions which had limited its scope and shortened its course were much affected by the experience of it; one or even two generations later they were scarcely less in evidence.

Appendix I

Wages and Hours in the Coal Industry

The miner's wage, both before 1917 and after 1921, was made up of two elements:
(i) The *basis rate*, which was negotiated locally at each colliery and consisted of a time or piece rate corresponding to the grade of worker, the jobs performed and in some cases to the seam or shaft where he was working. Such rates, once fixed, were rarely altered to any substantial degree, although they tended to be subject to small cumulative changes over a period of years.
(ii) The *district percentage*, which was the proportion added to the basis rate by negotiation throughout each district or county. Each worker thus received the same percentage addition, but in cash terms the amount depended on their earnings on basis. Under the 1921 agreement the percentage was determined by the division of the net proceeds of the collieries in the district concerned in an agreed ratio between wages and profits.

The amount of the wage thus realized was safeguarded after 1921 by two guarantees. (a) In each district a 'subsistence wage' was specified for the lowest-paid workers, who received this rate whenever it was higher than their basis plus percentage. (b) The National Wages Board fixed a national minimum percentage, payable to workmen of all grades in all districts whose earnings under the proceeds-sharing agreement failed to reach this level. It was expressed as a percentage to be added to the 'standard' wage – the wage received by each class of workmen in each district in July 1914.

Changes in wages and hours, 1914–24

From 1919 hours of work for men underground were governed by the Seven Hours Act. The working day thus established excluded 'winding time', which added on average about half an hour to the period of attendance. It included time spent travelling underground and mealtimes. Time spent working at the face under the Act was estimated to be about five and a half hours.

TABLE 18. *Average earnings per shift of various grades of workmen in coal mining, November 1918*

piecework coal-getters	16s 4d	enginemen	12s 1d
stonemen and rippers	15s 4d	surface mechanics	10s 7d
deputies and firemen	13s 5d	screeners	9s 10d
mechanical hauliers	10s 2d	pithead men	9s 11d
all underground men	13s 6d	all surface workers	9s 5d

Source: R. H. Tawney, *The Nationalization of the Coal Industry* (1920), p. 10.

Wage rates and earnings rose steadily from 1910 to 1920, fell sharply in 1920–2, but rose again as a result of the 1924 agreement. Real earnings are difficult to assess, for a number of reasons. Firstly, they were affected by the rate of unemployment and short-time work, so that average individual earnings per shift worked were, especially after 1921, significantly higher than weekly or yearly average earnings per man employed. Secondly, a composite average of earnings for all workmen in the industry does not reflect the changing structure of the labour force, which tended to increase the proportion of wage earners away from the coal-face. Since hewers were highly paid relative to other grades, a wage index based on the 1914 pattern of labour distribution overstated the level current in the 1920s by three or four per cent. Thirdly, the assessment of real wages requires the use of a cost-of-living index which in itself is unreliable, because of the changes of consumer behaviour resulting from the first world war. Finally, real income might be marginally affected by changes in the value of payments in kind – principally subsidized housing and free coal.

The main argument concerning real wage statistics, however, centred on the base year to be used in their calculation. The miners habitually compared their post-war standard of living with that of July 1914, when the industry was at the height of its prosperity. By any estimate this showed a decline in real wages during the subsequent ten years. The Samuel Commission in 1925 argued that earnings in the depression should be related to those received during the whole pre-war trade cycle of 1909–13, and concluded on this assessment that no appreciable gain or loss had occurred up to 1924.

Below are given three indices of money earnings and the cost of living. Bowley's figures do not reflect the declining proportion of coal-getters, but his cost-of-living series attempts to make allowance for new wartime and postwar consumption patterns (*Prices and Wages in the United Kingdom, 1914–20*, p. 150). The Miners' Federation series makes allowance for unemployment, the Samuel index for changes in the composition of the labour force. Both use official Board of Trade figures on retail prices, but the Samuel Report makes slight corrections to eliminate seasonal influences (Samuel Report, p. 283; Mins. of Evidence, pp. 387–94).

	Earnings per shift			*Cost of living*		
	Bowley	*MFGB*	*Samuel*	*Bowley*	*MFGB*	*Samuel*
1909–13			100			100
1914	100	100		100	100	
1918	195			180		
1920	260			220		
1925		153*	176·5†		173*	175†

* April–June.
† July–December.

What is not in dispute, on any calculation, is the substantial fall in the miners' real earnings between 1920 and 1925. Taking Bowley's computation of money wages in 1920 and comparing it with the two estimates of earnings in 1925 yields the following results (set against the official Ministry of Labour cost-of-living index):

	Bowley/MFGB	*Bowley/Samuel*	*cost of living*
1920	100	100	100
1925	58·8	67·9	76·3

This method of conflating different wage indices is somewhat unsatisfactory, but the outcome may be checked against two other indices beginning in 1920, applying to all forms of employment in mining and quarrying. E. C. Ramsbottam computes average weekly wage rates over each full year (which fell more rapidly than earnings in this period).[1] Agatha Chapman provides two series, the first referring to *possible* earnings per man year, assuming full employment in pits at work and no other irregular interruptions of production; the second measuring changes in actual earnings, affected by unemployment, short-time, trade disputes and abnormal absenteeism.[2]

	Ramsbottam	*Chapman* (1)	*Chapman* (2)
1920	100	100	100
1925	52·1	62·2	59·6

Source: E. C. Ramsbottam, 'The Course of Wage Rates in the United Kingdom, 1921–34', *JRSS*, 1935, cited also in Mitchell and Deane, *op. cit.*, p. 351; A. L. Chapman, *Wages and Salaries in the United Kingdom, 1920–38* (Cambridge 1953), p. 68.

Appendix II

The *Daily Mail* dispute

The *Daily Mail* stoppage on 2 May was not the first case of unofficial action by printing workers in anticipation of the General Strike, nor the first to have been brought to the government's attention. The OMS posters with which the Negotiating Committee confronted Baldwin on 30 April were (unbeknown to him) supplied by Odhams employees who had refused to print them.[1] On the same day the chapel fathers at the *Sunday Express* declined to insert official advertisements for volunteers. The proprietor, Beaverbrook, took Birkenhead's advice to negotiate a compromise rather than Churchill's to close down – and production was resumed.[2] There may have been other incidents of the same kind, for the following afternoon Lord Burnham, President of the Newspaper Proprietors' Association, agitatedly told J. C. C. Davidson, the deputy Chief Civil Commissioner, that it would be impossible to print any London papers on 3 May, since the unions were 'introducing the Soviet system into all newspaper offices so that their officials could act as self-constituted censors'.

In the case of the *Daily Mail* the dispute of Sunday evening concerned the proposed editorial, 'For King and Country'. According to George Isaacs, the General Secretary of NATSOPA, a deputation representing various printing unions had asked the editor, Marlowe, to omit one paragraph which read: 'A general strike is not an industrial dispute. It is a revolutionary movement intended to inflict suffering upon the great mass of innocent persons in the community and thereby to put forcible constraint upon the Government.' They did not, however, demand the removal of the article.[3] Marlowe phoned Downing Street, where the message delivered to the Cabinet, through Baldwin's secretary, Gower, and Joynson-Hicks, suggested that the newspaper had 'ceased to function'.[4] If Isaacs is to be believed, the editor sent his workers home only after a further delay of about half an hour, though there is no direct evidence that he received any advice from the Cabinet.[5]

The following day the dispute spread. The *Evening News* attempted to print an article including quotations from the offending editorial of the *Mail*, but was stopped by members of NATSOPA and the machine managers. According to the report of *The Times* the executive of the former union was appealed to, but declined to give guidance. On the *Evening Standard* printers, stereotypers and packers made objections to an account of the recruiting of volunteers in Whitehall. No afternoon edition of either paper was published. The later editions of the *Star* were likewise scrapped after interference on the same count.[6]

It appears, therefore, that the Cabinet obtained an exaggerated impression of the scale of the dispute at the *Daily Mail* – but that its view of the significance of this episode was fortuitously confirmed by events. It is not clear whether Marlowe or Joynson-Hicks was responsible for the initial distortion, but the majority of ministers not surprisingly felt justified, as a result, in stressing the importance of the incident in their revision of the ultimatum to the TUC. It is still unlikely, on balance, that negotiations with the General Council would have been resumed but for this development – but the question remains an open one.

Appendix III

Samuel Memorandum and Accompanying Correspondence

(1) Samuel to Pugh, 11 May 1926

Dear Mr. Pugh,

As the outcome of the conversations which I have had with your Committee I attach a memorandum embodying the conclusions that have been reached.

I have made it clear to your Committee from the outset that I have been acting entirely on my own initiative, have received no authority from the Government, and can give no assurances on their behalf.

I am of opinion that the proposals embodied in the memorandum are suitable for adoption and are likely to promote a settlement of the differences in the Coal Industry.

I shall strongly recommend acceptance by the Government when the negotiations are renewed.

(2) The memorandum

1. The negotiations upon the conditions of the coal industry should be resumed, the subsidy being renewed for such reasonable period as may be required for that purpose.
2. Any negotiations are unlikely to be successful unless they provide for means of settling disputes in the industry other than conferences between the mine-owners and the miners alone. A National Wages Board should, therefore, be established which would include representatives of those two parties with a neutral element and an independent chairman. The proposals in this direction tentatively made in the Report of the Royal Commission should be pressed and the powers of the proposed Board enlarged.
3. The parties to the Board should be entitled to raise before it any points they consider relevant to the issue under discussion, and the

Board should be required to take such points into consideration.

4. There should be no revision of the previous wage rates unless there are sufficient assurances that the measures of re-organisation proposed by the Commission will be effectively adopted. A Committee should be established as proposed by the Prime Minister on which representatives of the men should be included, whose duty it should be to co-operate with the Government in the preparation of the legislative and administrative measures that are required. The same Committee, or alternatively the National Wages Board, should assure itself that the necessary steps, so far as they relate to matters within the industry, are not being neglected or unduly postponed.
5. After these points have been agreed and the Mines National Wages Board has considered every practicable means of meeting such immediate financial difficulties as exist, it may, if that course is found to be absolutely necessary, proceed to the preparation of a wages agreement.
6. Any such agreement should
   (i) if practicable, be on simpler lines than those hitherto followed.
   (ii) not adversely affect in any way the wages of the lowest paid men.
   (iii) fix reasonable figures below which the wage of no class of labour, for a normal customary week's work, should be reduced in any circumstances.
   (iv) in the event of any new adjustments being made, should provide for the revision of such adjustments by the Wages Board from time to time if the facts warrant that course.
7. Measures should be adopted to prevent the recruitment of new workers, over the age of 18 years, into the industry if unemployed miners are available.
8. Workers who are displaced as a consequence of the closing of uneconomic collieries should be provided for by
   (a) The transfer of such men as may be mobile, with the Government assistance that may be required, as recommended in the Report of the Royal Commission.
   (b) The maintenance, for such period as may be fixed, of those who cannot be so transferred, and for whom alternative employment cannot be found; this maintenance to comprise an addition to the existing rate of unemployment pay under the Unemployment Insurance Act, of such amount as may be agreed. A contribution should be made by the Treasury to cover the additional sums to be disbursed.

(c) The rapid construction of new houses to accommodate transferred workers. The Trades Union Congress will facilitate this by consultation and co-operation with all those who are concerned.

(3) Pugh and Citrine to Samuel, 12 May

Dear Sir

The General Council having carefully considered your letter of today and the memorandum attached to it, concurred in your opinion that it offers a basis on which the negotiations upon the conditions in the Coal Industry can be renewed. They are taking the necessary measures to terminate the General Strike relying upon the public assurances of the Prime Minister as to the steps that would follow. They assume that during the resumed negotiations the subsidy will be renewed and that the lock-out notices to the miners will be immediately withdrawn.

Note. A copy of the memorandum, and of Samuel's letter (dated 11 May) is to be found in P.R.O. Lab 27/4. The letter was published in the press, like the TUC reply, under the date 12 May.

Notes

NOTES TO CHAPTER I

1 G. Woodcock, *Anarchism* (1962); F. Ridley, *Revolutionary Syndicalism in Modern France* (Cambridge 1970); P. Nettl, *Rosa Luxemburg* (1966); P. Renshaw, *Wobblies: The Story of Syndicalism in the United States* (1967).

2 W. H. Crook, *The General Strike* (Chapel Hill 1931), pp. 107–44; E. Vandervelde, L. de Brouckère and L. Vandersmitten, *La Grève Générale en Belgique* (Paris 1914); S. Schwarz, *The Russian Revolution of 1905* (Chicago 1967); S. Backlund, 'The General Strike in Sweden in 1909', *Labour Magazine*, August 1923.

3 D. Chewter, 'The History of the Socialist Labour Party of Great Britain from 1902 until 1921' (Oxford University B.Litt. thesis, 1966); E. Burdick, 'Syndicalism and Industrial Unionism in England until 1918' (Oxford University D.Phil. thesis, 1950).

4 J. Joll, *The Second International* (1955), pp. 140–42; National Transport Workers' Federation, Ann. General Council *Report* 1913, pp. 31–2.

4a See p. 9.

5 R. Challinor and B. Ripley, *The Miners' Association: A Trade Union in the Age of the Chartists* (1968); H. Clegg, A. Fox and A. F. Thompson, *A History of British Trade Unions since 1889* (Oxford 1964), pp. 3, 15–20.

6 P. Bagwell, *The Railwaymen* (1963), pp. 128–33; G. Alderman, *The Railway Interest* (Leicester 1973), chaps 8 and 10.

7 E. J. Hobsbawm, 'General Unions, 1889–1914', in *Labouring Men* (1964); J. Saville, 'Trade Unions and Free Labour', in A. Briggs and J. Saville (eds), *Essays in Labour History* (1967); J. Lovell, *Dockers and Stevedores* (1964); R. Hyman, *The Workers' Union* (Oxford 1971).

8 B. Pribecevic, *The Shop Stewards' Movement and Workers' Control, 1910–22* (Oxford 1959), pp. 12–15.

9 R. Hyman, *op. cit.*, p. 69.

10 H. A. Clegg, *The System of Industrial Relations in Great Britain*, 2nd edn (Oxford 1970), pp. 124–7; J. B. Jefferys, *The Story of the Engineers* (1945), pp. 143–8.

11 B. Tillett, *A Brief History of the Dockers' Union* (1910); J. Lovell, *op. cit.*, pp. 143–5, 148.

12 H. Pelling, 'The Labour Unrest, 1911–14', in *Popular Politics and Society in Late-Victorian Britain* (1968).
13 E. H. Phelps Brown, *The Growth of British Industrial Relations* (1959), pp. 294 ff.; Lovell, *op. cit.*, pp. 150–79.
14 Burdick, *op. cit.*, vol. II, p. 59.
15 Burdick, *op. cit.*, II, pp. 43–7; B. C. Roberts, *The Trades Union Congress, 1868–1921* (1958), pp. 251–4.
16 See, for instance, Tom Mann's role in the Merseyside stoppages of 1911 (H. R. Hikins, 'The Liverpool General Transport Strike of 1911', *Lancs. and Cheshire Hist. Soc. Trans.*, 113, 1961); and, of course, *The Miners' Next Step* of the South Wales Unofficial Reform Committee (1912), for which esp. M. G. Woodhouse, 'Rank and File Movements among the Miners of South Wales' (Oxford University D.Phil. thesis, 1969, p. 75 f.).
17 G. A. Phillips, 'The Triple Industrial Alliance in 1914', *EcHR*, Ser. II, vol. 24, 1971.
18 G. A. Phillips, 'The National Transport Workers' Federation, 1910–27' (Oxford University D.Phil. thesis, 1968, pp. 285–7); S. R. Graubard, *British Labour and the Russian Revolution* (1956), pp. 73–80; P. Bagwell, *op. cit.*, pp. 400–1; R. Page Arnot, *The Miners, Years of Struggle* (1953), p. 218.
19 A. Bullock, *Ernest Bevin* (1960), vol. I, pp. 135–40; B. Macfarlane, ' "Hands off Russia" in 1920', *P. & P.*, 38, 1967.
20 Bagwell, *op. cit.*, pp. 400–1; also Bagwell, 'The Triple Alliance', in A. Briggs and J. Saville (eds), *Essays in Labour History, 1886–1923* (1971).
21 Page Arnot, *op. cit.*, pp. 218–19.
22 A. Clinton, 'A history of trades councils from the beginning of the twentieth century to the Second World War' (London University Ph.D. thesis, 1973, pp. 204–6).
23 The best published account of Black Friday is by Bullock, *op. cit.*, I, pp. 167–79.
24 See below (Marchbank); also R. Williams in *Labour Monthly*, August 1921.
25 *Labour Magazine*, May 1922, p. 7.
26 See S. T. Glass, *The Responsible Society* (1966). As an instance of prevailing attitudes to workers' control in the mid-1920s, see Citrine's remarks in his report on trade-union structure to the 1925 TUC: 'It is being recognised by thinking Trade Unionists that to secure the maximum result for their members some measure of control of industry is desirable. A few unions have declared that as part of their objects, and most progressive Trade Unionists are convinced of its necessity. . . . But control of industry of itself implies a greater object to be achieved. Within the limits of the capitalist system only a restricted elevation of working class standards is possible. Some time or other the moment will arrive when the Trade Union Movement as an organic whole will have to take its part in

functioning actively against capitalism as an institution.' (*General Council Repcrt*, TUC 1925, pp. 228–9. See also George Hicks in *Labour Magazine*, November 1922, p. 303).

27 MFGB Proceedings, p. 415: 'The irresistible conclusion to be drawn from this episode is, that the Triple Alliance could not function and never will function until each party is affected simultaneously by the same questions or have the same claims maturing at the same moment or are attacked by joint organised capitalism at the same moment; but capitalism is far too astute to allow such common grievances to mature at the same moment.'

28 Bullock, *op. cit.*, I, pp. 152, 179.

29 J. Klugmann, *History of the Communist Party of Great Britain* (1968), vol. I, pp. 94–5.

30 Bagwell, *Railwaymen*, pp. 397–98; Bullock, *op. cit.*, I, pp. 110–11; V. L. Allen, 'The Reorganisation of the TUC, 1918–27', *British Journal of Sociology*, 1960; B. C. Roberts and J. Lovell, *A Short History of the TUC* (1968), pp. 65–6.

31 TUC *Report*, 1920, p. 318; TUC, *The General Council of the TUC* (1925).

32 TUC Standing Orders, 1921.

33 TUC *Report*, 1922, p. 396.

34 TUC *Report*, 1922, pp. 403–4. A motion more clearly designed to inhibit sectional strikes had been proposed, unsuccessfully, by Arthur Pugh of the steel workers the previous year (TUC *Report*, 1921, p. 381). Earlier in 1922 the General Council had refused to call a special conference to discuss the engineering lock-out, and the AEU also now opposed increasing its authority (Lovell and Roberts, *op. cit.*, p. 74).

35 *Workers' Weekly*, 11 April 1923.

36 G. Hardy, *Those Stormy Years* (1936), p. 173. Cook's ideas on appropriate strike preparations exemplified by his mother-in-law, were apparently influenced by Mann; for the 'British revolution on a tin of salmon', see J. H. Thomas, *My Story* (1937), pp. 105–6.

37 TUC *Report*, 1923, pp. 378–82.

38 Lovell and Roberts, *op. cit.*, pp. 79–81; Lord Citrine, *Men and Work* (1964), pp. 75–7; Clinton, *op. cit.*, p. 193; TUC *Report*, 1924, pp. 126–35.

39 TUC *Report*, 1924, *passim*, esp. pp. 311 f, 338, 439; Lovell and Roberts, *op. cit.*, p. 83; see also Bullock, *op. cit.*, I, pp. 261–2; C. Farman, *The General Strike* (1972), pp. 14–15.

40 The National Union of General Workers had merged with two other labourers' unions to form the General and Municipal Workers in 1924; this may conceivably have affected its attitude.

41 When this recommendation had first been put forward, by the Council's Joint Defence Committee, in January 1922, only 553,600 block votes had been recorded as wholly in favour, and over two million as wholly

opposed (TUC *Report*, 1922, p. 162). For Bevin's initial objections to the resolution, see *ibid.*, p. 407.

42 I.e. the T&GWU by Tillett and Mary Quale; the AEU by Swales; the NUR (in Thomas's absence) by Marchbank, its president, rather than Cramp, its industrial secretary. Though Thorne, the secretary of the NUG&MW, was a member of the Council, he took a much less active part in its affairs than his district official, Arthur Hayday.

43 TUC *Report*, 1924, p. 82.

44 TUC *Report*, 1922, pp. 405–6.

45 P. Johnson, *A Land Fit for Heroes* (Chicago 1968); S. Armitage, *The Politics of Decontrol of Industry*, 1918–21 (1969).

46 R. H. Desmarais, 'The British Government's Strike-Breaking Organization and Black Friday', *JCH*, 6, 1971; Bagwell, 'Triple Alliance', *loc. cit.*

47 G. Glasgow, *General Strikes and Road Transport* (1926), p. 12 and Appendix; Desmarais, *loc. cit.*,; 10 and 11 Geo. V ch. 55. The sixteen divisions of 1919 were reduced to 15 after 1923.

48 For the Labour government see R. Lyman, *The First Labour Government* (1958), pp. 217–23, and R. H. Desmarais, 'Strike-Breaking and the Labour Government of 1924', *JCH*, 8, 1973.

49 Phillips, *op. cit.* (thesis), pp. 503–4; Desmarais, 'Strike Breaking Organization and Black Friday', *loc. cit.*; Glasgow, *op. cit.*, Appendix.

50 A. Mason, 'The Government and the General Strike', *International Review of Social History*, 14, 1969; R. R. James (ed.), *Memoirs of a Conservative: J. C. C. Davidson's Memoirs and Papers, 1910–37* (1969), pp. 178–80, 228.

51 R. K. Middlemas and J. Barnes, *Baldwin* (1969), pp. 294–5; S. Baldwin, *On England* (1926), pp. 31, 39.

NOTES TO CHAPTER II

1 G. Routh, *Occupation and Pay in Great Britain, 1906–60* (Cambridge 1965), p. 86; S. B. Saul, 'The Export Economy, 1870–1914', *Yorks. Bull.*, 17, 1965; B. Mitchell and P. Deane, *Abstract of British Historical Statistics* (Cambridge 1962), pp. 118–21.

2 Department of Employment and Productivity, *British Labour Statistics 1886–1968* (1970), Tables 163, 164; Mitchell and Deane, *op. cit.*, pp. 352–3. Iron and steel and shipbuilding were the only industries where a larger fall in real incomes occurred.

3 *Royal Commission on the Coal Industry*, Cmd. 2600, 1926 (Samuel), *Report*, p. 218.

4 R. A. S. Redmayne, *British Coal Mining Industry during the War* (1923), p. 263.

5 W. H. B. Court, 'Problems of the British Coal Industry between the

Wars', *EcHR*, 15, 1945; G. C. Allen, *British Industries and their Organisation* (1933), p. 35; International Labour Office, *The World Coal Mining Industry* (Geneva 1928), p. 76.

6 J. H. Jones, *et al*, *The Coal Mining Industry* (1939); A. M. Neuman, *Economic Organisation of the British Coal Industry* (1934).

7 The League of Nations Economic Committee estimated the surplus capacity of the German industry in 1925 at 25 per cent, of the Polish at 50 per cent, of the British at between 25 and 33 per cent (ILO, *op. cit.*, p. 74).

8 For a discussion of the effects of reparations on the coal trade, see *Royal Commission on the Coal Industry*, vol. II, *Mins. of Evidence* (1926), pp. 89–96.

9 A. J. Taylor, 'Labour Productivity and Technological Innovation in the British Coal Industry, 1850–1914', *EcHR*, 14, 1961–2.

10 Samuel *Report*, p. 266.

11 Neuman, *op. cit.*, pp. 27, 43; *Coal Mining*, *Report of the Technical Advisory Committee* (Reid), Cmd. 6610, 1945.

12 A. Beacham, 'Efficiency and organisation of the British coal industry', *Econ. J.*, 55, 1945.

13 323 companies produced 84 per cent of British output in 1923, according to the Samuel Commission (*Report*, p. 47). It also stated that 715 firms employed 100 men or more; but this figure was reduced to about 500 by the Lewis Committee, on the grounds that some undertakings could not be counted as financially autonomous (*Report of Departmental Committee on Cooperative Selling in the Coal Mining Industry*, Cmd. 2770, 1926, p. 19).

14 N. Buxton, 'Entrepreneurial Efficiency in the British Coal Industry between the wars', *EcHR*, 33, 1970.

15 Lewis Committee *Report*, pp. 9, 23, and *Minority Report* by J. R. D. Bell *et al.*; M. W. Kirby, 'The Control of Competition in the British Coal Industry in the Thirties', *EcHR*, 24, 1973.

16 By then, according to Kirby (*loc. cit.*) cartelization for selling purposes had become, as a result of legislative enforcement, a restraint on industrial concentration.

17 Buxton, *loc. cit.*; J. J. Astor, *et al.*, *The Third Winter of Unemployment* (1923).

18 Londonderry Papers, D/Lo/C 277: Dillon to Londonderry, 29 April 1926.

19 MAGB/MFGB, Proceedings of Joint Committee of Inquiry into the Coal Industry, 1925, Appendix L; P.E.P., *Report on the British Coal Industry* (1936), p. 152.

20 Page Arnot, *The Miners: Years of Struggle*, pp. 127–9; S. T. Glass, *The Responsible Society*, p. 11. Keir Hardie put forward a bill with the support of the Scottish miners in 1893.

21 See B. Pribecevic, 'The Demand for Workers' Control in the Railway,

Coalmining and Engineering Industries, 1910–22' (D.Phil. thesis, Oxford University, 1957).

22 For the syndicalists see Pribecevic, *op. cit.*; M. G. Woodhouse, 'Rank and File Movements among the Miners of South Wales, 1910–26' (D.Phil. thesis, Oxford University, 1969); R. Challinor, *The Lancashire and Cheshire Miners* (Newcastle 1972); W. R. Garside, *The Durham Miners, 1919–60* (1971). For the Guild Socialists, see Glass, *op. cit.*, and M. I. Cole, 'The Labour Research Department', in A. Briggs and J. Saville (eds), *Essays in Labour History, 1886–1923*. For the Fabians, see R. H. Tawney, *The Nationalisation of the Coal Industry* (1920); Pribecevic, *op. cit.*, p. 96; Page Arnot, *op. cit.*, p. 204; *Coal Industry Commission*, Cmd. 360, 1919 (Sankey), vol. II, pp. 481–2. Tawney and Webb (together with Leo Chiozza Money) were members of the Sankey Commission; Webb was also a participant in the joint committee of 1925, and Tawney was the miners' principal spokesman on the nationalization question before the Samuel Commission.

23 Parl. Proc. (HoC) 5th ser., vol. 173, *c.* 1711 f.; Labour Party Conference 1925, *Report*, p. 45; Labour Party and General Council, joint committee on nationalization, minutes 2 and 17 December 1925. The committee failed to reach agreement on the question of whether to compensate the owners of royalties in the event of public ownership.

24 Samuel Commission, vol. II, pp. 1020–5; Samuel *Report*, pp. 64–73.

25 See, for instance, F. Hodges, *Nationalization of the Coal Industry* (1920).

26 Sankey Commission, vol. II, p. vii; J. P. Dickie, *The Coal Problem* (1936), pp. 315–16; Lloyd George (ed.), *Coal and Power* (1924), pp. 24–6.

27 See especially Samuel Commission, vol. II, Qs. 16941–2, 17148–58.

28 Gainford papers: Mins. of meeting of MAGB Central Cttee and MFGB EC, 5 March 1925.

29 Sankey Commission, vol. II, pp. xxv–vii; Armitage, *op. cit.*, pp. 125–6.

30 The Liberals were allegedly influenced by *The Problem of the Coal Industry*, a pamphlet published by the former secretary of the Sankey Commission, A. D. McNair, in 1924. Their committee also included Sir Richard Redmayne, formerly chief adviser to the Coal Controller, whose evidence to Sankey had contributed substantially to Duckham's proposals, and who also gave evidence to the Samuel Commission (R. A. S. Redmayne, *Men, Mines and Memories* (1942), pp. 209–10). Note also J. R. MacDonald's comment on the personnel of the Samuel Commission, below, p. 75.

31 For the miners' attitude to the government proposals of 1919 see Page Arnot, *op. cit.*, p. 337; G. D. H. Cole, *Labour in the Coal Mining Industry, 1914–21* (Oxford 1923), pp. 130–5.

32 The owners' representatives on the Sankey Commission had approved the proposal to nationalize royalties, but this measure was not endorsed

by the Mining Association, and was consistently opposed by it once the Mining (Working Facilities and Support) Act of 1923 had given some redress against the abuse of mineral rights. See Sankey Commission vol. II, pp. xx, 810; MAGB, *What Mr. Lloyd George was not Told* (1924), p. 10.

33 See below pp. 108–9. The most authoritative statement of this general view was made after the General Strike, by the Lewis Committee on Cooperative Selling (*Report*, p. 21, see below, p. 260): 'It may confidently be hoped that when trade revives the British coal mining industry can get back to its historical basis of a freely expanding output, without undue sacrifice in price. But it seems to us there can be no certainty that this will be the case . . . It would seem prudent for the British coal mining industry to be prepared to meet the contingency that its unregulated expansion may result in evils of over-production which a regulated growth would avoid.' Even this judgement does not, of course, admit the likelihood of actual contraction.

34 Samuel Commission, vol. II, pp. 929–35; MAGB, *What Mr. Lloyd George was not Told*; W. A. Lee, *Thirty Years in Coal* (1954), pp. 10–13.

35 Sankey Commission, vol. II, p. 810.

36 MAGB, *The Case for the Mine Owners* (1925), p. 5.

37 Gainford papers, box 51, draft letter to local press (unpublished?), 8 March 1926. See also the comments of Finlay Gibson, Secretary of the South Wales Coal Owners' Association, to Ministry of Labour officials in April 1925: 'So far as the future was concerned . . . provided that . . . they could obtain a reduction in working costs equivalent to 2/6d a ton, his considered judgement was that within six months the South Wales field could be producing over 50 million tons of coal and that the absorption of practically the whole of the existing live register could be contemplated within the period of twelve to eighteen months.

'He did not agree that there was any "surplus" labour to any appreciable extent in South Wales.' (Bald. 13, memo of interview, 23 April 1926).

38 H. A. Clegg, A. Fox and A. F. Thompson, *History of British Trade Unions*, vol. I, 98–111, 123–5, 407; G. D. H. Cole, *Labour in the Coal Mining Industry, 1914–21*, pp. 2–5.

39 H. A. Turner, *Trade Union Growth, Structure and Policy* (1963), pp. 185–92; S. and B. Webb, *The History of Trade Unionism* (1920 edn), pp. 513–14, 549–50. For the earnings of various grades, see below, p. 298.

40 Page Arnot, *op. cit.*, pp. 81, 87–9.

41 J. E. Williams and B. McCormack, 'The Miners and the Eight Hour Day', *EcHR*, II, 12, 1959; Clegg, Fox and Thompson, *op. cit.*, p. 98; S. and B. Webb, *Industrial Democracy* (1902), p. 589.

42 Clegg, Fox and Thomson, *op. cit.*, pp. 110–11.

43 For details see the regional studies of miners in this period: R. Page Arnot, *The Scottish Miners* (1955) and *The South Wales Miners, 1898–1914*

(1967); E. W. Evans, *Miners of South Wales* (Cardiff 1961); F. Machin, *The Yorkshire Miners* (Barnsley 1958).

44 G. D. H. Cole, *Labour in the Coal Mining Industry, 1914–21.*

45 *Ibid.*, pp. 160–1, 172–6; Page Arnot, *op. cit.*, chap. X.

46 H. A. Clegg, *System of Industrial Relations in Great Britain*, p. 121; J. R. Raynes, *Coal and its Conflicts* (1928), p. 41; I. G. Sharp, *Industrial Conciliation and Arbitration in Great Britain* (1950), p. 21; D. H. Robertson, 'A Narrative of the Coal Strike, 1912', in *Economic Fragments* (1931).

47 Tom Jones, *Whitehall Diary* (1969), vol. II, p. 12; Bald. 21: Mond to Baldwin, 26 April 1926.

48 Industrial Council, *Inquiry into Industrial Agreements*, Cd. 6953, 1913, Qs. 15536–8.

49 For the Whitley Report, see J. B. Seymour, *The Whitley Councils Scheme* (1932). For the Coal Mines Act, 1920, see Cole, *op. cit.*, pp. 130–4.

50 Armitage, *op. cit.*, p. 140.

NOTES TO CHAPTER III

1 *Report of a Court of Inquiry concerning the Wage Position in the Coal Industry* (Buckmaster), Cmd. 2129, 1924, p. 9; MAGB and MFGB Joint Committee on the Coal Industry, Proceedings, Appendix D.

2 R. Martin, *Communism and the British Trade Unions 1924–1933* (Oxford 1969), pp. 57–9; M. G. Woodhouse, 'Rank and File Movements among the Miners of South Wales' (thesis), pp. 277–80.

3 His nomination for South Wales was not approved without considerable opposition in the MMM (Woodhouse, *op. cit.*, pp. 290–1).

4 Citrine, *Men and Work*, pp. 155, 210; B. Turner, *About Myself* (1930), p. 307; T. Jones, *Whitehall Diary*, vol. II, pp. 16, 23; Lee, *Thirty Years in Coal*, p. 43; Woodhouse, *op. cit.*, pp. 259–62; MFGB Special Conf. 21 May 1925, *Report*, p. 40; R. H. Desmarais, 'Charisma and Conciliation: a sympathetic look at A. J. Cook', *Societas*, 3, 1973.

5 J. Lawson, *The Man in the Cap* (1941), pp. 148–9.

6 Martin, *op. cit.*, p. 33; Woodhouse, *op. cit.*, p. 335; Buckmaster *Report*, p. 10; Page Arnot, *Miners 1910–26*, pp. 345–8.

7 MAGB and MFGB, Joint Committee on the Coal Industry, Appendix D; *Statement of Colliery Undertakings showing Credit Balances and Debit Balances, January 1924–March 1925*, Cmd. 2454, 1925.

8 MFGB EC mins 22 January 1925; MFGB Special Conference, 21 May 1925, *Report*, p. 36; MAGB and MFGB, joint meetings, 29 January, 19 February 1925.

9 MAGB and MFGB, joint meeting 29 January 1925, *Report*, p. 5.

10 Parl. Proc. (HoC), 5th series, vol. 187, *c.* 1631. Evan Williams, the

President of the Mining Association, claimed afterwards that he had told the Board of Trade as early as March 'how little, if any, hope there was of our being able to get through this difficult question without a suspension of operations in the coal industry and very likely in other industries as well' (Lab. 27/3, proc. of interviews between Prime Minister and coal owners, 31 July 1925). This looks like an unwarranted claim to prescience, but it is reasonable to suppose that Williams did tell Cunliffe-Lister that reduced conditions of work would be demanded.

11 J. B. Jeffreys, *The Story of the Engineers*, pp. 230–2; A. Pugh, *Men of Steel* (1951), pp. 388–9.

12 R. Page Arnot, *The General Strike* (1926), pp. 77–8; H. J. Fyrth and H. Collins, *The Foundry Workers* (Manchester 1959), pp. 179–80; A Hutt, *The Post-war History of the British Working Class* (1937), pp. 121–2.

13 Page Arnot, *op. cit.*, pp. 80–2; MFGB Annual Conference, July 1924, *Report*, pp. 106–7; T&GWU Finance and Emergency Cttee Mins., 26 March 1925.

14 T&GWU Bienn. Deleg. Conf., 23 July 1925, *Report*, p. 5.

15 *T&GW Record*, July 1925, p. 277; T&GWU GEC Mins., 4 June, 17 July.

16 H. A. Clegg, 'Some Consequences of the General Strike', *Manchester Statistical Soc. Papers*, 1954.

17 See W. H. Crook, *The General Strike*, p. 288, for the MFGB's continued reluctance to abandon the practice of strike ballots. The NTWF decided against joining the Alliance in February 1926 (NTWF Nat. Council 1926, *Report*, p. 20).

18 *AEU Monthly Journal*, December 1925, p. 12; Bagwell, *op. cit.*, p. 466; according to the ETU, the block votes eventually cast on the Alliance's constitution were: in favour, 1,741,000; against, 905,000. Some supporters had done no more than give a nominal approval 'in principle': see MFGB Spec. Conf. 5 September 1925, *Report* (MFGB Proc., 1925, p. 725).

19 MFGB Spec. Conf., 19 August 1925, *Report*, pp. 1, 8. It is worth noting in this connection that the NUG&MW withheld approval of the Alliance constitution until the powers of the General Council to handle the mining dispute in 1925 had been clarified. But there were other influences working within this union against the Alliance (H. A. Clegg, *General Union in a Changing Society* (Oxford 1964), pp. 117–18).

20 See their own proposals for the formation of an Industrial Alliance, described in L. J. Macfarlane, *The British Communist Party* (1966), p. 154.

21 GC box 123, SIC Mins., 23 July 1925. Rule 4 of the draft constitution required the executive of the Alliance to 'keep the General Council of the Trades Union Congress informed of all developments, and where necessity arises endeavour to secure their cooperation in the co-ordination of the whole Trade Union Movement.' An article by a left-wing engineer,

W. H. Hutchinson, though critical of the Council, made a similar proposal. According to him the TUC was 'fettered in any comprehensive strike by the hesitancy and conservatism of isolated unions which are disinclined to join in any movement which does not affect their interests at a given moment. Obviously some degree of consolidation of groups of unions is vitally necessary to any genuine functioning of the General Council. . . . In the present position of Trade Unionism, the extra powers needed by the Council cannot be obtained, and could not be used in the ultimate issue even if they were specifically conferred on that body. If, however, the necessary coordination of the craft units were achieved, the Council would function with efficiency and executive authority.' (*Labour Monthly*, March 1926).

22 *Macmillan Report*, pp. 10–11; *Statement on Colliery Returns 1924–25*.

23 MFGB EC Mins. 19 June 1925; MFGB, *Copies of all Reports, Communications and Minutes received and issued in connection with the recent Wages Crisis, 1925* (henceforth, *Wages Crisis*), p. 6.

24 TUC *Report*, 1925, pp. 173–4; MFGB, *The Coal Crisis*, 22 July 1925, pp. 4–5; MFGB Spec. Conf. 3 July, *Report*, p. 6.

25 TUC *Report*, 1925, p. 175.

26 MFGB, *Coal Crisis*, p. 14.

27 Citrine, *op. cit.*, 133–4; GC 16 1924–5, 10 July. They issued a press statement afterwards, calling on the union movement to place themselves 'without qualification and unreservedly at the disposal of the Miners' Federation to assist the Federation in any way possible.' (*Wages Crisis*, pp. 7–8.)

28 Its other members were Bromley, Hicks, Hayday, Marchbank, Poulton, Tillett, Walkden, and Citrine.

29 *Wages Crisis*, pp. 7–11; Jones, *op. cit.*, I, p. 322. Bridgeman, formerly Secretary of Mines was chosen by Baldwin in preference to Cunliffe-Lister, President of the Board of Trade, who had previously reported on the development of the dispute to the Cabinet, because the latter held himself to be an interested party by virtue of his wife's colliery holdings. Cunliffe-Lister had offered his resignation on these grounds, declined by Baldwin on 1 July (Bald, 18: Lister to Baldwin, 1 July; see also same to same, 13 August, 26 August 1925).

30 MFGB Annual Conference 1925, *Report*, p. 42.

31 MFGB Annual Conference *Report*, p. 39; *The Coal Crisis*, p. 6.

32 Cab 23/50 39 (25) 22 July; Lee, *op. cit.*, pp. 42–3; A. Scheps, 'Trade Unions and the Government 1925–7, with special reference to the General Strike' (Oxford University D.Phil. thesis 1972 p. 105).

33 *Macmillan Report*, pp. 12–13, 18; *Colliery Guardian*, 31 July 1925.

34 *Macmillan Report*, p. 19.

35 See, for example, *The Times*, 27 July 1925.

36 *TGW Record*, August 1925, p. 7; GC box 123 13/6/12, SIC Mins, 23 July.

37 GC mins. 23–24 June, 10 July; United Society of Boilermakers, *Monthly Report*, August 1925.

38 In fact fewer workers were to be affected by wage changes in 1925 than in any previous year since 1914, and significantly more received wage increases than wage reductions. The employers in the woollen industry imposed a general lock-out early in August, but subsequently agreed to a Court of Inquiry which stabilised wage rates at their existing level. The other demands for cuts mentioned above were not pressed (*Min. of Labour Gazette*, January 1926, pp. 3–4).

39 Subsequently published as *The Economic Consequences of Mr Churchill*. See Citrine, *Men and Work*, pp. 136–8.

40 Sir Josiah Stamp blamed the deterioration in the coal trade on the gold standard in an addendum to the Macmillan Report published on 28 July (pp. 21–23). The *Daily Herald* of 31 July gave great play to a statement which Baldwin had allegedly made to the miners the previous day: 'all the workers of this country have got to face a reduction in wages in order to put industry on its feet.' The Central Office afterwards claimed rather ineffectually that he had been misrepresented (see Lab 27/3; Bald. 13: Wilson to Gower, n.d.; Parl. Proc. (HoC) vol. 200, cs. 2145–6). It is instructive to compare the miners' own passing reference to this subject in *The Coal Crisis*, published on 22 July: 'The situation in this country has been further aggravated by the interference with our normal markets by German Reparation coals, the loss of the Russian market, and the premature return to the gold standard' (p. 4) – with Herbert Smith's much more pointed comment in his foreword to the General Council's pamphlet on *The Mining Dispute*, published in mid-September: 'What the Trade Unions have yet to realise is that a policy of wage reductions is a necessary consequence of the Government's action in undertaking, at the bidding of the banking and financial interests which control currency and credit, to restore the gold standard.' The only union leader who showed evident awareness of the significance of the gold standard issue before Red Friday was Ernest Bevin, who discussed its repercussions on employment (but not directly on wages) in May 1925 (*A Review of Trade Conditions and Their Effect on Unemployment*).

41 See *Colliery Guardian*, 29 May 1925; and Citrine, *op. cit.*, p. 142.

42 GC box 123, SIC, 23 July.

43 GC 123, SIC, 25 July.

44 For its official determination, see especially the press statement issued on 25 July (*ibid.*).

45 GC 122, 13/6/8.

46 TGWU GEC Mins., 30 July 1925.

47 GC, *Report of Special Conference on Coal Dispute*, 30 July, p. 14; TGWU GEC Mins., 31 July.

48 GC 123, SIC, 23 July.

49 Trade Union Conference of Executives, 30 July 1925, *Report*, p. 13.

50 Parl. Proc. (HoC), 5th ser., vol. 182, c. 2011 and 2558–9; Cab 23/50 27 (25).
51 Middlemas and Barnes, *op. cit.*, p. 384.
52 *The Times*, 25 July 1925.
53 GC 123, SIC, 27 July.
54 Cab 23/50 40 (25).
55 Lab 27/3: Gowers to Baldwin, 28 July 1925.
56 MFGB *Wages Crisis* p. 52; TUC *Report*, 1925 p. 178; GC 123, SIC 29 July.
57 MFGB, *loc. cit.*, pp. 52–3; Jones, vol. I, p. 324. A minimum had in fact been proposed in the 'federated area' but not elsewhere.
58 TUC *Report*, 1925, p. 179; GC 123, SIC, 29 July; Jones, *op. cit.*, I, p. 325.
59 TUC *Report*, 1925, pp. 179–180.
60 MFGB, *Wages Crisis*, p. 55.
61 Cab 23/50 42 (25); Scheps *op. cit.*, p. 114. Salisbury gave his reasons in a memorandum of 4 August: 'who will believe us, after the experience of the last few days, when we say we will die in some ill-defined last ditch rather than accept the nationalization of the coal industry, and inferentially, the nationalization of every other distressed industry' (CP 383 (25)).
62 MFGB, *Wages Crisis*, p. 58.
63 See Bullock, *Bevin*, I, p. 279; Symons, *General Strike*, pp. 19–20; C. Farman, *The General Strike* (1972), pp. 26–7; Middlemas and Barnes, *op. cit.*, pp. 387–8; A. Mason, 'The Government and the General Strike', *IRSH*, 14, 1969.
64 Cab 23/50 42 (25).
65 Middlemas and Barnes, *op. cit.*, p. 387.
66 Cab 23/50 42 (25).
67 G. M. Young, *Stanley Baldwin* (1952), p. 99.
68 James *Memoirs of a Conservative*, p. 230; CP 492 (25), 24 November 1925.
69 Lab 27/3: Proceedings of interviews between Prime Minister and coalowners, 31 July.
70 Parl. Proc. (HoC), vol. 189, c. 233.
71 Mason, *loc. cit.*; Cab 27/261 ST (24) 4th meeting.
72 Cab 27/261 ST (24) 3.
73 Cab 27/260 ST (24).
74 CP 356 (25).
75 Power 16/22 1925.
76 Cab 23/50 42 (25).
77 CP 390 (25).
78 CP 356 (25).
79 CP 390 (25); CP 462 (25); Cab 23/50 43 (25).
80 Lab 27/3: proceedings of interviews etc., 31 July.

81 *Explanatory memorandum of the Terms of Settlement of the Dispute in the Coal Mining Industry*, Cmd 2488, 4 August 1925.
82 Parl Proc. (HoC), 5s., vol. 187, cs. 1605–12.
83 Jones, *op. cit.*, I, p. 325.
84 Parl Proc. (HoC) vol. 187, cs 1591–2.
85 Parl Proc. (HoC) vol. 189, c. 733 f.
86 GC mins., 30 July 1925; *The Nation* (New York), quoted in Crook, *op. cit.*, p. 294.
87 Symons, *op. cit.*, p. 19.
88 *Labour Magazine*, August 1925, p. 199.
89 GC 123, SIC, 23 July; *TGW Record*, August 1925.
90 TUC *Report*, 1925, p. 183; *The Mining Dispute*, p. 3; GC 123, SIC, 6 August.
91 For the contrary view see, for example, Lovell and Roberts, *op. cit.*, p, 86.
92 *Answers*, 22 January 1927.
93 *Labour Magazine*, August 1925, pp. 198–200.
94 TUC *Report*, 1925, pp. 386, 387.
95 GC 123, SIC, 27 July.

NOTES TO CHAPTER IV

1 Bald. 13: Lane-Fox to Baldwin, 12 August; Middlemas and Barnes, *Baldwin*, p. 389.
2 Bald. 13: Salisbury to Baldwin, 10 August 1925.
3 Bald. 13: Grey to Baldwin, 12 August; Viscount Samuel, *Memoirs* (1945), pp. 183–4; Cab 23/30 44 (25).
4 Lee had advised the Liberal Party on matters of industrial policy (Scheps, 'Trade Unions and the Government 1925–7' (thesis), p. 168); for Beveridge, see his autobiography, *Power and Influence*.
5 Lord Robbins, *Autobiography of an Economist* (1971), p. 136; R. A. S. Redmayne, *Men, Mines and Memories*, p. 290.
6 Beveridge, *op. cit.*, p. 218.
7 MFGB deputation to Prime Minister, 23–4 September 1925, *Report*, p. 23.
8 MFGB Spec. Conf., 8 October 1925, *Report*, pp. 59–60; *The Times*, 5 January 1926.
9 MFGB EC mins., 27 November 1925.
10 CP 492 (25) 24 November; MFGB Proc., 1926, p. 19.
11 See Martin, *Communism and the British Trade Unions*, p. 68; Klugmann, *History of the Communist Party of Great Britain*, vol. II, pp. 44–51, 93–6; G. Spencer at MFGB Spec. Conf., 19 August 1925, *Report*, p. 24.
12 CP 492 (25), 'Position of the Coal Mining Industry, 24 November'. Lane-Fox did not relish remaining in his post, and offered his resignation

to Baldwin in September, inferring that 'you may well be thinking you want a really able man for Secretary of Mines and that you can well improve on what you have got.' (Bald. 18: Lane-Fox to Baldwin, 16 September.)

13 Symons, *General Strike*, p. 33; Bullock, *Bevin*, vol. I, p. 293; Farman, *General Strike*, pp. 55–61.

14 Samuel, *op. cit.*, p. 185; Scheps, *op. cit.*, pp. 191–4.

15 Samuel *Report*, pp. 162–3.

16 *Socialist Review*, April 1926, p. 4.

17 Bald. 13: Gowers to Waterhouse, 19 December 1925; W. H. B., Coal Commission XVI, Gowers to C. S. Hurst, n.d.

18 Samuel *Report*, pp. 13–14, 39–44, 60–3, 83–4, 104–7.

19 J. H. Jones, 'The Report of the Coal Commission', *Econ. J.*, 6, 1926; see also J. M. Keynes, 'Back to the Coal Problem', *The Nation*, 15 May 1926: 'The Royal Commission left untouched the most ticklish part of the problem, namely, the new equilibrium points of prices, output and wages.'

20 Samuel *Report*, pp. 126–9, 173–5, 227.

21 Lane-Fox, the Secretary for Mines, commented that 'by comparison with the "Duckham" scheme which the Government of the day accepted in 1919, they certainly do not err on the side of being too drastic' (Cab 24/179 CP 106). Lord Bledisloe, Parliamentary Secretary to the Minister of Agriculture, and himself a mine owner in the Forest of Dean, told Baldwin, 'This problem [of small-scale enterprises] is never going to be solved in such an area as this (as the Royal Commission appeared to imagine) by local effort and encouragement without definite and emphatic pressure under statutory authority by the Government itself.' (Bald. 18: Bledisloe to Baldwin, 6 May 1926).

22 Samuel *Report*, pp. 61–2.

22a WHB CC, I, ff. 31–2.

23 WHB CC, II, ff. 62–98; III, ff. 17–18, 41–49, 53–84, 131–2; WHB Hc 157: Gowers to Beveridge, 3 February 1926.

24 Cab 24/179 CP 107 (26); Samuel *Report*, pp. 63–73.

25 Samuel *Report*, pp. 228, 294.

26 *Ibid.*, p. 236. See also pp. 148–9, 152–3, 164.

27 J. W. F. Rowe, *Wages in the Coal Industry* (1923), pp. 138–41. The report did suggest, to offset this tendency, that the poorer pits should be excluded from the district ascertainments (p. 143), but without specifying any measure of poverty. If a purely relative measure were used, of course, then as poor pits closed so other collieries would be designated 'poor', with peculiarly drastic consequences. The Commission also recognised but did nothing to avert, the danger that men in condemned pits would accept rates lower than those agreed in order to escape unemployment (p. 231).

28 Beveridge, *op. cit.*, pp. 219–21.

29 Samuel *Report*, pp. 164, 178–9, 208–10, 215–16.

30 Samuel *Report*, pp. 223–4; WHB CC XV, 'machinery for fixing wages'.

31 Samuel *Report*, p. 164.

32 *Ibid.*, p. 237. For criticism see J. R. MacDonald in *Socialist Review*, May 1926, p. 6; Jones, *Whitehall Diary*, vol. II, pp. 9–10.

33 Cab 27/316 CP 122 (26); Cab 23/52 9 (26).

34 Cab 27/286 MR (25); CP 374 (25).

35 Bald. 13: Niemeyer to Baldwin, 14 March 1926; Cab 27/317 RCC (26) 7.

36 Cab 27/316, CP 122 (26); Cab 23/52 12 (26); Bald. 18: Salisbury to Baldwin, 24 March 1926. For Salisbury's views see Cab 24/179 CP 119.

37 Cab 23/52 12 (26).

38 MFGB Proc. 1926, report of deputation of MAGB and MFGB to Prime Minister, 24 March.

39 *Ibid.*; Cab 24/179 CP 108 (26). In a Cabinet memorandum, Lane-Fox argued that 'Given the will, a new wages agreement could be made in six weeks; if the will is not there, six months would be insufficient; and if the subsidy is continued, the will would certainly not be there.' See also Cab 23/52 15 (26).

40 The government did prepare, prompted by the miners, a list of those recommendations – the 'fourteen points' – of the Samuel Report which required state action. But the only bill reaching even a provisional draft before 3 May was one on local authority trading in coal (see below, p. 131).

41 Cab 27/317 RCC (26) 4.

42 MAGB/MFGB deputation to Prime Minister, 24 March 1926, *Report*, p. 6; MAGB/MFGB mins. of joint meeting, 25 March.

43 MFGB Special Conference, 12 March, *Report*, p. 5. Cf. also Tom Richards, p. 12: 'Suppose that the Government are prepared to accept the recommendations this Committee has made, I think the position is rather stronger than after the Sankey Commission.'

44 *Daily Chronicle*, 12 March; MFGB Spec. Conf. 12 March, *Report*, pp. 15–16. For the M.M., see Klugmann, *op. cit.*, II, pp. 99–102.

45 GC box 123, 13/6/13A, SIC Mins, 11 March 1926.

46 MFGB Spec. Conf. 12 March, *Report*, p. 13.

47 Middlemas and Barnes, *op. cit.*, p. 397.

48 GC 123, SIC Mins, 11 March.

49 TUC *Report*, 1925, p. 380.

50 R. W. Postgate, *Life of George Lansbury* (1951), p. 236; Martin, *op. cit.*, pp. 68–9; Klugmann, *op. cit.*, II, pp. 107–9.

51 TUC *Report*, 1925, pp. 384–7.

52 GC box 123, 13/6/9A; TUC *Report*, 1926, p. 92.

53 TUC *Report*, 1924, pp. 181–2; TUC *Report*, 1925, pp. 213–4; A. Clinton, Trades Councils from the beginning of the Twentieth Century to the Second World War' (thesis), pp. 182–94.

54 GC 123 13/6/12, SIC, 28 July 1925.

55 *The Times*, 20 February 1926; *Labour Magazine*, March 1926, pp. 486–9.

56 This version is reprinted in *Men and Work*, pp. 146–53.
57 GC box 123, 13/6/13, SIC mins. The miners' subcommittee continued to act as an intermediary between the SIC and the full executive during the subsequent industrial negotiations of March and April.
58 Citrine, *op. cit.*, pp. 144, 148, 154.
59 *Ibid.*, pp. 150–1, 153.
60 GC 123 13/6/13A, SIC, 19, 29 January 1926.
61 SIC, 12 February 1926. See also the report of the conversation between Citrine and other members of the TUC and Labour Party staffs on 18 February (GC 121 13/6/2A).
62 SIC, 19 February.
63 GC 123, 13/6/13, SIC, 19 February, official minutes.
64 *The Times*, 20 February 1926.
65 It read: 'The Industrial Committee has been in constant consultation with the Miners' Federation, and whilst it would be premature at the present stage to attempt to formulate any detailed policy which may have to be pursued, the Committee has already reaffirmed the attitude of the Trade Union Movement as expressed in July last, namely. . . .' (*The Mining Dispute*, GC box 123).
66 GC 123 13/6/13A, SIC, 26 February.
66a Citrine, *op. cit.*, pp. 148–50.
67 GC 123 13/6/13A, SIC, 19 January, 12 February.
68 The main reason for this opinion given to his staff colleagues on 18 February was simply that 'the Trade Union Movement had only 4½ million people and when at least one-third of trade union membership was idle in the first few days and increasing in number as each industry was affected, soon there would be no funds to draw' (GC 121 13/6/2A).
69 GC 123 13/6/9A.
70 GC 121, 13/6/2A.
71 GC 123, 13/6/13A, SIC, 8 April.
72 SIC, 18 December 1925, 19 January, 26 February 1926.
73 Citrine, *op. cit.*, p. 152; Ernest Bevin papers (Bev.) Series C box 4, 'Essential Services during Trade Disputes', 3 March 1926. The Co-operative movement comprised 1,314 retail societies at the end of 1923, with reserve funds of £5,047,736 (British Isles). See Cooperative Congress 1924, *Report*, pp. 471, 477.
74 SIC, 25 March, 8 and 23 April 1926; GC mins. 27 April.
75 Bev. Ser. C box 4.
76 Labour Party Conference 1925, *Report*, p. 193: Labour Party: NEC and GC mins., 17 December 1925; NJC mins. 21 January 1926. The members were Pugh, Citrine, Smillie, Robert Williams and Arthur Henderson.
77 'The maintenance of Essential Supplies': incomplete typescript in the file of documents relating to the general strike collected by Iron and Steel Trades Confederation (I&STC/45).

78 T&GWU *Annual Report 1926*, p. 7.

79 Cab 23/50 44 (25); MT 45/244, weekly report on emergency arrangements, 19 September 1925.

80 Cab 27/260 ST (24).

81 It had already by then set up twenty-two local committees in metropolitan boroughs (Symons, *op. cit.*, p. 21).

82 Previously Under-Secretary for Foreign Affairs, ambassador in Leningrad and Paris and Viceroy of India (cf. his memoirs, *The Old Diplomacy*, published in 1947). For the other leading members of the OMS see Page Arnot, *General Strike*, pp. 50–2.

83 CP 390 (25).

84 Quoted in Page Arnot, *General Strike*, pp. 54–5.

85 Farman, *op. cit.*, p. 42; Cab 27/261 ST (24), 7 December 1925; Cab 23/51 53 (25), 18 November.

86 Cab 27/261 ST (24) 12; Cab 27/260 ST (24), 30 October.

87 CP 462 (25), 6 November; Cab 27/261 ST (24) 14.

88 Earl of Scarbrough, *English Review*, 1926, p. 230; Londonderry D/Lo/C 277. A 'constitutionalist' group seceded from the British Fascists immediately before the general strike, proposing to join the OMS (*Manchester Guardian*, 28 April 1926).

89 HO 45 12336.

90 *The Times*, 5 October 1925 (he wrote again on the 8th); Citrine, *op. cit.*, p. 159.

91 Parl. Proc. (HoC), 5th ser., vol. 191, c. 2104–5.

92 Cab 23/51 53 (25), 18 November; Cab 27/179 CP 163 (26); MT 45/244, Ashley to Joynson-Hicks 25 January 1926; Glasgow, *General Strikes and Road Transport*, Appendix.

NOTES TO CHAPTER V

1 MFGB Proc. 1926, pp. 177–83.

2 MAGB and MFGB, report of meetings, 31 March–1 April 1926, pp. 35–8, 86–8; MFGB Proc. 1926, p. 179.

3 Lon. D/Lo/B 18: Durham and Northumberland Coal Owners' Association, report of Secretary, 12 March.

4 MAGB and MFGB, 31 March–1 April, p. 28; Cab 27/317 RCC (26), 11 and 14, 21 and 23 April.

5 Lon. D/Lo/C/277: Dillon to Londonderry, 15 March; see also same to same, 8 and 20 April.

6 *Manchester Guardian*, 24 April 1926; Lon. D/Lo/B 18, D&NCOA, report of meeting, 24 April.

7 Those making their criticism known through the press (primarily the *Daily Mail*) included Lord Londonderry, Sir Alfred Mond MP, Sir

Tudor Walters, Sir Samuel Instone, Sir Beddoe Rees MP and Sir Hugh Bell. Two members of the government, Lord Bledisloe and Philip Cunliffe-Lister, also had interests in the coal industry and supported a conciliatory line (see n.21 p. 319 and p. 259). Sir Richard Redmayne provided the government with a list of owners sympathetic to his own schemes of trustification, including Sir A. F. Pease and Montagu McLean (Redmayne, *Men, Mines and Memories*, p. 243). Those invited to a (more widely representative) dinner by Mond to discuss cooperative selling arrangements included Lord Aberconway, Sir John Beynon and Sir Alfred Cope (*Colliery Guardian*, 30 April). Mond summoned a further meeting, somewhat differently constituted, on 7 May (see below, p. 223).

8 Jones, *Whitehall Diary*, vol. II, p. 16; Lon. D/Lo/C 277: Londonderry to Dillon, 15 and 16 April, 1 May 1926.

9 *Daily Mail*, 26 and 27 January 1926; *Manchester Guardian*, 24 April.

10 MFGB Spec. Conf., 9 April, *Report*, pp. 11, 16, 18. The final clause was probably included to rule out reductions in basis rates like those threatened the previous year.

11 MFGB Proc., 1926, pp. 1123–9; MAGB and MFGB, report of meeting, 13 April, p. 18.

12 Lon. D/Lo/B 18, Durham Coal Owners' Assoc., Gen. Meeting, 12, 16 April; report of Secretary on position in Mining Industry, 16 April.

13 MFGB Spec. Confs., 9 April, *Report*, p. 13; 28 April *et seq.*, *Report*, pp. 4, 15.

14 GC 123, 13/6/13A, SIC, 8, 22 April.

15 Jones, *op. cit.*, II, p. 16.

16 Lab. 27/4, 24 April; see also Citrine, *Men and Work*, p. 154.

17 MAGB and MFGB, joint meeting, 31 March–1 April, *Report*, p. 78; A. J. Cook, 'The Coal Crisis and the Way Out', *Labour Monthly*, March 1926, p. 161.

18 MFGB EC mins., 8 April 1926; GC 123, 13/6/13A, SIC, 8 April.

19 SIC, 23 April; TU Conf. of Executives, 29 April 1926.

20 SIC, 8 April.

21 SIC, 15 April.

22 Lab 27/4; Jones, *op. cit.*, II, p. 12; GC 123, 13/6/13, SIC, 13 April.

23 SIC, 13 April.

24 Cab 23/52 15 (26), 14 April. According to Jones it was only now that Baldwin sought to familiarise himself with the nature of the wages dispute, from a 'Child's Guide . . . prepared by the Ministry of Labour' (*op. cit.*, II, pp. 14–15).

25 Middlemas and Barnes, *op. cit.*, p. 399; MFGB, *Report of meeting with Prime Minister, 15 April*, p. 6.

26 Lab. 27/4; MFGB Spec. Conf., 28 April, *Report*, p. 7. There are some slight discrepancies between these two sources: in these cases the higher figure has been shown.

27 MFGB EC Mins., 21 April; TU Conf. of Executives, 29 April, *Report*, p. 7.

28 Bald. 18, Worthington-Evans, 'Coal Position of 19 April'; Lister to Baldwin, 17 April; Cab 27/317, RCC, 11, 13, 23 (26). This formula was included as one possibility in the settlement Baldwin put before the owners on 28 April (see below p. 110).

29 Jones, *op. cit.*, II, p. 16; Cab. 27/317, RCC (26), 11. Steel-Maitland told Tom Jones as early as 13 April that the Ministry of Labour were drafting legislation to allow a lengthening of hours if it proved necessary (Middlemas and Barnes, *op. cit.*, p. 399).

30 Middlemas and Barnes, *op. cit.*, p. 400.

31 *Daily Mail*, 19–21 April. Among the districts which had posted their wage proposals on 21 April, Lancashire, Scotland and South Wales had offered a higher minimum on an eight hours basis (MFGB Proc., 1926, Appendix). Frank Hodges, the Secretary of the International Miners' Federation, had also argued that longer hours were the better alternative, in a speech at Nottingham on 9 April (*Daily Mail*, 10 April). Baldwin's view is quoted by Jones, *op. cit.*, II, p. 24; see also p. 22.

32 *Colliery Guardian*, 14 August 1925, 31 April 1926; Bald. 13; Jones, *op. cit.*, II, p. 16.

33 Jones, *op. cit.*, II, p. 19; Cab 27/317, RCC, 19 (27 April).

34 Jones, *op. cit.*, II, pp. 22–3; Cab 27/317, RCC, 16 and 22.

35 Cab. 27/317, RCC, 14 and 17.

36 Jones, *op. cit.*, II, p. 24.

37 Cab 27/317, RCC, 19.

38 Cab 27/317, RCC, 23.

39 Lon. Durham Coal Owners' Assoc., Secretary's report, 29 April; DCOA *Annual Report 1926*, p. 10.

40 Cab 27/318, RCC, 26; DCOA *Annual Report 1926*, p. 12; MFGB Spec. Conf., 30 April, *Report*, p. 29.

41 Lon. D/Lo/C 277, Londonderry to Dillon, 1 May; Cab 27/318, RCC, 27.

42 Baldwin did fill out the government's originally vague proposal on financial assistance, for the miners' benefit, on 29 April, stating that £3m. would be available both to support wages and to help transfer labour (Cab 27/318, RCC, 27). Birkenhead gave his interpretation of the report of the Samuel Commission on the issue of national negotiations in a note of 26 April, to the effect that the national board was to have 'the final say' on district wage proposals (Cab 27/317, RCC, 15; Jones, *op. cit.*, II, p. 19).

43 Cab 27/317, RCC, 17, 19; Cab 27/318, RCC, 29, 31.

44 GC 123, 13/6/13A, SIC, 8 April; see also 21 April.

45 GC 125, 13/6/33. In a conversation on the 23rd, Arthur Henderson suggested to Citrine that the government should provide a ten-year loan to serve both purposes (GC 121, 13/6/2A).

46 GC 125, 13/6/33; GC 121, 13/6/2A; Lab 27/4, note by Horace Wilson on conversation with Pugh and Citrine, 4 April.
47 GC 123, 13/6/13A, SIC, 21 April.
48 GC 125, 13/6/33. 'Mining Position, 13th April'.
49 GC 123, 13/6/13A, SIC, 23 April.
50 GC 123, 13/6/13, SIC, 27 April.
51 *Mining Situation*, paras. 4, 6, 9, 11, 12, 15.
52 Trade Union Conference of Executives, 29 April *et seq.*, *Report*, pp. 8–9, 12, 16; Turner, *About Myself*, pp. 306–8; H. H. Fyfe, *Behind the Scenes of the Great Strike* (1926), pp. 12–13.
53 MFGB Spec. Conf. 30 April, *Report*, pp. 33, 35; Cab 23/52, 20 (26); Jones, *op. cit.*, II, p. 17. In the final session Bridgeman and Salisbury joined the government side.
54 Cab 27/318, RCC, 32, 33, 35, 36; MFGB Spec. Conf., 1 May, *Report*, pp. 37–8.
55 On this point, too, the miners made considerable concessions, at least verbally. Their answer to the owners' offer had required that measures of reorganization should be allowed to take full effect before wages were discussed; this was modified subsequently to a demand that they be 'initiated'; and, finally, simply to a proposal that the joint advisory committee should be allowed to complete its inquiries, which Smith thought might take 'at the full extent . . . a month' (MFGB Spec. Conf., *Report*, p. 37; Cab 27/318, RCC, 36).
56 Cab 27/318, RCC, 36. Bridgeman's impression was that 'Thomas kept on trying to force a formula down Herbert Smith's throat which was steadily spat out by Mr. Smith' (Scheps, *op. cit.*, p. 224).
57 MFGB Spec. Conf. 14 May 1926, *Report*, p. 20; TUC GC, *The Mining Dispute: National Strike* (June 1926), p. 9; see also A. J. Cook, *The Nine Days* (1926), p. 8.
58 TU Conf. of Execs., *Report*, p. 33. The list of unions refusing support is not given. A number of organizations were absent, including the Scottish Horse and Motormen and the Scottish Typographical Association. The Sailors' and Firemen's Union delayed its reply, announcing that it would ballot its members.
59 *Ibid.*, pp. 35–6, 40; Bullock, *op. cit.*, I, pp. 305–6. Smith's second pronouncement ran: 'I did not mean to say . . . that I agreed to accept the Report. What I did intend to imply was that I am prepared to examine that Report from page one to the last page, and to stand by the result of the inquiry.' According to J. H. Thomas this statement was made at Cook's insistence, to clarify that the Federation did not accept the report unconditionally; but it was taken by the TUC Negotiating Committee to indicate that a settlement 'on the lines of the Report' was feasible (NUR AGM 6 July 1926, *Report of Proceedings on the General Strike*, pp. 8–9; see below, p. 118).
60 MFGB Spec. Conf., 30 April, *Report*, p. 34.

61 MFGB Proc., 1926, pp. 204–5; Parl. Proc. (HoC), 5th ser., vol. 195, cs. 343–4.

62 Citrine, *op. cit.*, p. 197; Scheps, 'Trade Unions and the Government 1925–27' (thesis), p. 252; Turner, *op. cit.*, p. 309.

63 *The Mining Dispute: National Strike*, p. 10.

64 *Ibid.*, pp. 8–9; GC 125, 13/6/22, Negot. Cttee report to GC, 16 June 1926; NUR AGM 1926, *Report*, p. 8; Cab 27/318, RCC, 37; Citrine, *op. cit.*, pp. 164–5. Horace Wilson was told of Smith's statements to the conference of executives during Saturday night, but it is not clear that he informed the members of the Cabinet (Jones, *op. cit.*, II, p. 26).

65 GC 124, 13/6/18, NC, 11 May.

66 Cab 27/179, CP, 186; Jones, *op. cit.*, II, p. 36. Pugh himself admitted that 'we cannot negotiate independently of them [the miners] absolutely .... we cannot take the decision' (Cab 27/318, RCC, 37.) See also the comments of Steel-Maitland and Neville Chamberlain, Parl. Proc. (HoC), vol. 195, cs. 417–19 (5 May).

67 Citrine, *op. cit.*, pp. 165–6.

68 Jones, *op. cit.*, II, p. 27; Cab 23/52, 21 (26).

69 Citrine, *op. cit.*, p. 165; Jones, *op. cit.*, II, p. 27.

70 GC mins., 2 May.

71 GC 124, 13/6/18, NC 4, 2 May; Citrine, *op. cit.*, pp. 166–7.

72 GC 124, NC 5, 2 May.

73 GC mins., 2 May; Citrine, *op. cit.*, p. 167; Bev. C5, C2/3/33, statement to area secretaries, 27 May; Bullock, *op. cit.*, I, p. 309.

74 Cab 23/52 21 (26).

75 Scheps, *op. cit.*, p. 241.

76 Jones, *op. cit.*, II, p. 27–9; Scheps, *op. cit.*, p. 241.

77 J. H. Thomas recalled afterwards the cool reception which he and his colleagues received that evening (NUR AGM 1926, *Report*, p. 10).

78 Cab 23/52 21 and 22 (26); Jones, *op. cit.*, II, p. 30.

79 Jones, *op. cit.*, II, pp. 32, 35.

80 Citrine, *op. cit.*, pp. 169, 184; Jones, *op. cit.*, II, pp. 32, 35.

81 Citrine, *op. cit.*, pp. 169–70.

82 MFGB Proc. 1926, p. 205; GC mins., 3 May.

83 Bev. Ser. C. Box 5, C2/3/33. This account is supported by an unsigned typescript report, dated 11 May, 'The British General Strike – from the Inside', almost certainly by Milne-Bailey (GC 131, 13/7/10); and also by the report of the Negotiating Committee to the General Council (GC 125, 13/6/22).

84 Bev. Ser. C. Box 3, C2/2/15 and 16. In a further, undated memorandum written between 27 and 30 April Bevin suggested, rather imprecisely, that his national wages board be made part of the scheme of the TUC and the miners (C2/1/6).

85 Bullock, *Bevin*, I, pp. 311–12.

86 Cab 23/52 23 (26); Scheps, *op. cit.*, p. 247.

87 Cab 23/52 23 (26); James, *Memoirs of a Conservative*, p. 235.
88 GC, *Mining Dispute*, pp. 11–13; Citrine, *op. cit.*, p. 171; GC mins., 2–3 May; GC 131, 13/7/10, 'The General Strike – from the Inside'.
89 GC 125, 13/6/22, report of Negotiating Cttee to General Council; GC mins., 2–3 May.
90 *Mining Dispute*, pp. 13–14. There were, not surprisingly, many ambiguities in the wording of this scheme. The board was to have an independent chairman, but to agree its own rules of procedure. The word arbitration was not used, though all parties were to agree in advance to accept its findings. The government was to submit legislation to it, but the board's constitutional position was unclear. Whilst its first duty was to agree on measures of reorganisation, evidently neither the presentation of legislation nor the proposed official inquiry into co-operative selling was to take precedence over the fixing of wage rates.
91 Citrine, *op. cit.*, p. 174; MFGB Proc. 1926, p. 207, *Mining Dispute*, p. 15.
92 Lab 27/7, 'Memorandum on the events of 3 May'.
93 Bev. C5, C2/3/33; Citrine, *op. cit.*, p. 174.
94 Lab 27/7, Wilson.
95 Parl. Proc. (HoC), 5th ser., vol. 195, cs. 73–82, 104–16; GC 124, 13/6/13, NC 7, 3 May; MFGB Proc. 1926, pp. 207–8.
96 Lab 27/7, Wilson. Citrine mentions his phone call to Bevin but does not recall this message. He does, however, recall that the General Council had been suspicious of his own absence from Eccleston Square, and 'had evidently got some wrong impressions as to what had been happening' (*op. cit.*, p. 175).
97 Citrine, *op. cit.*, pp. 175–6.
98 *Ibid.*, p. 167.
99 Bev. C5, C2/3/33.
100 NUR AGM 1926, *Report*, p. 16; TU Conf. of Execs., 21 January 1927, *Report*, p. 17.
101 GC 125, 13/6/22, Neg. Cttee report to G.C.
102 Jones, *op. cit.*, II, p. 8.
103 Cab 27/179 CP 183.
104 R. R. James, *op. cit.*, p. 250.
105 Cab 23/52 21 (26).

NOTES TO CHAPTER VI

1 The Powers and Orders Committee consisted of Bevin, Purcell, Findlay, Rowan, Turner, Walker and A. S. Firth. The Ways and Means Committee had probably had much the same membership, but had included Citrine.

2 TUC/GS/Powers and Orders Committee, report, 1 May, MD 84; TUC/GS/W&MC 1; GC 132, SOC report 22 June 1926.
3 Bev. Ser. C5 C2/3/33; Citrine, *Men and Work*, pp. 179–80. See also the comment of the AUBTW, below, p. 141.
4 Bev. C5 C2/2/19, 'The Coal mining crisis 1926: Position of the T&GWU'; Bev. C5 C2/3/33.
5 GC 131 13/7/11, W&M Cttee mins, 28 April.
6 *Operative Builder*, June 1926.
7 GC W&M Cttee mins, 28 April.
8 TUC/GS MD 26A, Committee Arrangements, 1 May; MD 30, Supplementary list of General Council and Committee decisions, 1–4 May; GC 14/5/ 1925–6, mins, 3 May, item 26.
9 TUC/GS/F&ESC, 2 May.
10 TUC/GS/W&MC 1 MD 4.
11 Bev. C5 C2/3/33.
12 Citrine, *op. cit.*, p. 178.
13 GC 131 13/7/11, Powers and Orders Cttee mins, 3 May; TUC/GS/MD 30, Supplementary list of decisions etc. For accounts of the stoppage, see below pp. 214–15. The Strike Organization Committee appears later to have assumed direct responsibility for issuing orders concerning power workers outside London.
14 GC 131 13/7/11, Gen. Purps. Cttee mins, 4 May; GC 132 13/7/19, report of Gen. Purps Cttee to General Council, 18 May. Elvin's appointment was 'a disaster' according to Bevin (Bev. C5 C2/3/33).
15 TU Conf. of Execs., 29 April *et seq.*, *Report*, pp. 34–5; TUC/GS/MD 25 and 29, Decisions of G.C. and Committees.
16 TUC/GS/MD 13, F&ESC mins, 2 May.
17 TUC/GS/MD 14 and 19, F&ESC mins, 2–3 May.
18 GC mins, 3 May; TUC/GS/MD 25 and 29, circular 27, 4 May.
19 TUC/GS/MD 35, F&ESC mins, 4 May.
20 Citrine, *op. cit.*, p. 178.
21 GC 125, 13/6/29, Decisions on Mining Dispute by G.C. and sub-committees; GC 132, 13/7/19, SOC report, 22 June; Citrine, *op. cit.*, pp. 179, 183.
22 Ben Turner's phrase: *About Myself*, p. 314. Some of the more obvious supernumeraries were assigned to speaking tours during the weekend of 7–9 May: Margaret Bondfield, Ben Tillett and Ben Turner (M. Bondfield, *A Life's Work* (1948), pp. 266–9; Turner, *op. cit.*, p. 297; Lab. Party NEC 39, 1926, report of Propaganda Cttee to G.C.).
23 Citrine, *op. cit.*, pp. 157–8, 172, 182–3.
24 GC 131, 13/7/11, SOC mins, 6–9 May; GC 132, 13/7/19, draft report of Public Services and Electrical Advisory Cttees; GC 129, 13/7/1, Hayward to Citrine, 10 May.
25 AUBTW *Trade Circular and General Reporter*, June 1926; *Operative Builder*, June 1926; TUC/GS/MD Circular 69.

26 Citrine, *op. cit.*, pp. 179–80.
27 GC 131, 13/7/11, SOC mins, 7 May.
28 GC 139, file 19, Citrine to AEU General Secretary, 11 May.
29 NUR/GS Head Office circulars 1926; GC 131, 13/7/11, SOC mins, 7 May; TUC/GS/Nat. Transport Cttee, Report No. 4, 9 May. The Cooperatives had hoped for a more general exemption: see below, p. 158.
30 GC 131, 13/7/19, F&ESC report, 18 May.
31 Citrine, *op. cit.*, pp. 182, 184.
32 GC 132, 13/7/19, Intelligence Cttee report to G.C., June 1926; printed in Farman, *The General Strike*, Appendix IV; TUC/GS/Intell. Cttee, circular to speakers, 6 May.
33 Citrine, *op. cit.*, p. 184; Bev. C5 C2/3/33.
34 GC 131, 13/7/11, SOC mins, 7 May. The allegations concerning Newcastle had already been given prominence by Michael Connolly in the House of Commons the previous evening (Parl Proc. (HoC), ser. v, vol. 195, cs. 486–7). For other alleged instances, see p. 199.
35 *About Myself*, p. 297.
36 Citrine, *op. cit.*, p. 188.
37 TUC/GS/MD 28; GC 123, 13/6/9A; Fin. and Gen. Purp. Cttee mins, 13 May 1926.
38 GC 139, file 34. Only two organizations appear to have responded officially to the appeal: the Boot and Shoe Operatives and the National Union of Clerks both called for a levy of 1s per week from their members. The AEU Executive later refused to handle branch collections (*Monthly Journal*, June 1926, p. 14).
39 F&GPC mins, 13 May. The contributions included £5,000 from the Post Office Workers (who gave another £1,000 shortly after the strike); £2,000 from the Shop Assistants; £1,000 each from IFTU and the Post Office Engineers; and £2,400 from private donors.
40 SOC mins, 12 May; C. J. Bundock, *The Story of the National Union of Printing, Bookbinding and Paper Workers* (Oxford 1958), pp. 336–7; F&GPC mins, 14, 21 May, 6 July, 2 September 1926.
41 I&STC/GS circular 14, 11 May; *AEU Monthly Journal*, June 1926, p. 14. Citrine issued an appeal to affiliates after the strike not to poach members from unions in this position.
42 NUR Financial Statement, 1926; Hyman, *The Workers' Union*, pp. 136–7.
43 GC, *Supplementary report to T.U. Conference of Execs. 20 January 1927*. The largest grant, at least £7,300, went to the T&GWU. The principal loans went to the iron and steel workers (£15,000) and the footplatemen (£5,000).
44 GC 125, 13/6/29; GC 131, 13/7/23; *British Worker*, 8 May.
45 GC 131, 13/7/23; F&GPC mins, 14 May. The Cabinet afterwards formally complained to the Russian government about their support for 'an illegal, unconstitutional act'. And the first attack on the General

Council by the Russian trade union leadership concerned not the refusal of the donation but the alleged suppression of the fact of its prohibition (All-Russian Council of Trade Unions, *Red Money* (1926); *Sunday Worker*, 13 June 1926; GC 131, 13/7/23).

46 A deputation from the Sheffield Dispute Committee were told by an unnamed member of the Council that 'Eccleston Square might be raided, that the members of the General Council might be arrested, and that the end might mean utter ruin so far as the finances of the movement were concerned, yet withal the General Council felt . . . better utter defeat than surrender.' This example of braggadocio is undated.

47 H. Slesser, *Judgement Reserved* (1941), pp. 156–7; Parl. Proc. (HoC), ser. v, vol. 195, cs. 787–97. Slesser states (p. 155) that the union leaders he spoke to after the strike denied that Simon's speech had any effect on the decision to end it.

48 GC 132, 13/7/18.

49 He wrote to the President of the American Federation of Labor on 21 June: 'So far as I am aware the Astbury Judgement had no bearing on the decision to terminate the General Strike, and certainly at no time was it under consideration by the General Council. . . . As we are at present advised, neither the Astbury Judgement nor the opinions of Sir John Simon can be regarded as sound law in respect of the General Strike. None of the legal questions which may be said to arise from the Strike have been tested in the Courts here, nor, as far as I can see, is there any immediate likelihood of their being so tested.' The intellectual merits of this controversy are not here discussed: but A. L. Goodhart's refutation of Simon and Astbury has not since been questioned ('The Legality of the General Strike in England', *Yale Law Review*, February 1927, reprinted by Camb. Univ. Press).

50 The one possible source of information in the General Council on the government's intentions was J. H. Thomas; for his personal activities during the strike, see pp. 223–5.

51 GC 132, 13/7/19. The report was undated, but seems unlikely to have been written immediately after the strike. The SOC report was dated 22 June.

52 In its report to the Council, the Intelligence Committee observed, 'the calling out of further groups of workers could not have had as substantial an effect as would seem to have been the case, as numbers of those in the second group were already standing because of shortage of materials etc., and because in some places the men had [already] come out' (*loc. cit.*).

53 Bev. C6 C2/4/36, 22 July; Citrine, *op. cit.*, pp. 191, 197. Bevin changed his mind *after* the strike: his address to the T&GWU docks group continued: 'I have been about the country and find that the estimate and report that Alderman Purcell and I made about the three weeks was rather beyond a limit. As a matter of fact it would not have been saved in some sections that long – there was a big crack after the Monday. . . .'

54 Citrine, *op. cit.*, pp. 189, 196, 197; Turner, *op. cit.*, p. 313; Bagwell, *Railwaymen*, p. 479.
55 The 1911 strike had lasted less than two days, that of 1919, nine days.
56 Citrine, *op. cit.*, pp. 188–9, 195.
57 *Ibid.*, p. 189.
58 K. Martin, *Harold Laski*, p. 66. See also Pugh's remarks to the 1926 TUC, quoted below, p. 271.
59 Parl. Proc. (HoC), ser. v., vol. 195, c. 1056.
60 See the railway manager quoted in Crook, *The General Strike*, p. 396.

NOTES TO CHAPTER VII

1 Cab 23/52 24 (26); Cab 27/260 ST (24), 13th and 15th meetings; Bald. 22, S&TC mins, 27 April 1926; G. Glasgow, *General Strikes and Road Transport*, pp. 112–13.
2 *The All-British Campaign*, *Bucks. News Budget*, 14 May 1926, cited in K. C. J. C. Knowles, *Strikes* (Oxford 1952), p. 130. No figure is given for the Eastern Division.
3 Cab 29/260 ST (24), 23rd meeting; Lord Winterton, *Orders of the Day* (1953), p. 138. The figure for the Northern Division is identical with that given in the *Newcastle Chronicle* of 12 May, which added that only 1,000 had been given jobs (cited in A. Mason, *The General Strike in the North East* (Hull 1970), p. 48). The number of volunteers in South Wales may well have been larger in fact, since the OMS later reported that it had enlisted 6,830 in Cardiff alone. Their records contain the only figures on recruitment in Scotland, where they claimed to have had lists of 1,000 names in Edinburgh and 1,800 in Dundee (HO 45 12336, Hardinge to Joynson-Hicks, 21 May 1926). A low ratio of employees to volunteers was also found in Birmingham: 1,990 out of 11,786 (R. P. Hastings, 'Aspects of the General Strike in Birmingham', *Midland History*, 2, 1974).
4 MT 45/245, 247, 248, 249. The Electrical Power Engineers' Association ordered its members to stay at work in generating stations.
5 HO 45 12336, 17 May and 30 June 1926; MT 45/246, 247. The lorry drivers referred to were used initially to operate the Hyde Park milk scheme.
6 *Ibid.*, Hardinge to Joynson-Hicks, 21 May.
7 Bald. 22, 'Cambridge University Volunteers'; MT 45/248/6, Report of Road Commissioner, Eastern Division. A total of 3,350 volunteers was obtained.
8 *The Times*, *Strike Nights at Printing House Square* (1926); Symons, *General Strike*, pp. 96–107; Mepol 2/3135D; MT 45/247, Memo. to General Purposes Committee of S&TC, Appendix vii.

9 Cab 27/331 STC Bulletin, 6 May.

10 Cab 27/260 ST 24, 17th meeting; D. E. Baines and R. Bean. 'The General Strike on Merseyside', in J. R. Harris (ed.), *Liverpool and Merseyside*; Symons, *General Strike*, pp. 98–9; TUC/GS/Intell. Cttee, RCA circular to branches, 7 May; MT 45/245, summary of reports of Road Transport Commissioners.

11 Cab 27/331 STC Information Bull, 13 May.

12 Glasgow, *op. cit.*, p. 73; MT 45/248/6: report of North West Road Commissioner. There was only one recorded case of requisitioning: six tankers belonging to 'Russian Oil Products' were appropriated in Bristol (MT 45/245).

13 Glasgow, *op. cit.*, pp. 39–40, 76, 85–6; Cab 27/311 STC Bull., 11 May; Cab 27/260 ST 24, 24th meeting.

14 MT 45/246.

15 Glasgow, *op. cit.*, pp. 39–40; Baines and Bean, *loc. cit.*,; Cab 27/260 ST 24, 23rd meeting; A. Hurd, 'The Navy on Active Service', *Fortnightly Review*, 1 July 1926.

16 Page Arnot, *General Strike*, pp. 165–6.

17 Cab 27/260 ST 24, 16th meeting.

18 Cab 23/52 28 (26), 10 May; Cab 27/260 ST (24), 20th meeting.

19 Cab 27/331 ST Bull, 10 May. In the north-west the Manchester Society telegraphed the General Council (informing the Ministry of Transport of the fact) 'to enter emphatic protest' at the immobilization of perishable commodities by the railwaymen, 'and to express their surprise that your promise not to interfere with the distribution of foodstuffs is not being kept.' In this case, however, the readiness of local unionists to continue supplying bread and milk was apparently sufficient to discourage resort to the emergency machinery (Cab 27/321 ST Bull., 6 May).

20 Cab 27/260 ST 24, 18th meeting; Cab 27/331 ST Bull., 12 May; MT 45/247, Appendix ii; Glasgow, *op. cit.*, pp. 65, 78–9. The number of volunteers at work by 12 May was as follows: Liverpool 4,500; Southampton 1,400; Bristol 1,000; Glasgow 770; Leith 600.

21 Cab 27/260 ST 24, 20th meeting; Cab 27/331 ST Bull., 6 May; Bald. 22, memo. by E. F. Strange, 24 May; Winterton, *op. cit.*, pp. 139–40. Winterton was told by Moore-Brabazon that 'he was not alone in his complaints'.

22 Cab 27/260 ST 24, 19th meeting.

23 Cab 27/260 ST 24, 18th meeting, 20th meeting; Glasgow, *op. cit.*, pp. 43–4; MT 45/248/7; Cab 27/260 ST (24), 21st meeting. The principal increase in the tonnage of cargo moved, however, evidently occurred between 13 and 15 May, when a lighterage service was at length organized.

24 MT 45/248/6, MT 45/245 and 246.

25 Bald. 22.

26 See James, *Memoirs of a Conservative*, p. 251; MT 45/247, Appendix II.

The report of the Minister of Transport, however, suggests that Davidson probably exaggerated the importance of the canals.

27 See above, p. 148; Symons, *op. cit.*, pp. 194–5; Farman, *op. cit.*, pp. 197–9.

28 Cab 27/260 ST 24, 17th and 18th meeting; Cab 23/52 25 (26) and 26 (26); *Report of the Commissioner of Police for the Metropolis, 1926*, Cmd. 2882, 1927, p. 7.

29 Cab 27/260 ST 24, 21st–24th meeting; *Reports of His Majesty's Inspectors of Constabulary . . . 1926* (P.P. xi 1927): 'it is probable that in some districts more decided action in the early stages (of the general strike) would have shortened public inconvenience and would have saved the actual use of force later' (Sir Leonard Dunning). But see below, p. 203.

30 Cab 27/260 ST 24, 17th, 21st, 24th meetings; Mepol. 2/2135D.

31 *Reports of H.M. Inspectors of Constabulary . . . 1926*, Table I.

32 H. de Watteville, 'The Employment of Troops under the Emergency Regulations', *Army Quarterly*, July 1926; Mepol 2/1965, Police bull, 8 May; James, *op. cit.*, pp. 242–3. Troops were also used to guard some London petrol stores and the bus depot at Chiswick.

33 James, *op. cit.*, pp. 251–3; Hurd, *loc. cit.*; Cab 27/331 ST Bull., 5 May; MT 45 247, Appendix iv; MT 45/248/7.

34 In London, though 47 buses were put out of action by strikers on 5 May, one in four of the normal quota of buses was running by the 12th, but less than one in twenty of the electric trams (Cab 27/260 ST 24, 18th meeting; Glasgow, *op. cit.*, p. 46; MT 45/248/15. The figures were: buses, 1,272 out of 4,404; trams, 94 out of 2,269).

35 Several working-class boroughs in London – West Ham, Battersea, Bethnal Green, Walthamstow, Shoreditch and Poplar – tried to cut all power other than to homes and hospitals, but only Stepney proposed to close down its generating station entirely, until threatened by an order-in-council (MT 45/247, Appendix iv; Cab 27/260 ST 24, 17th and 25th meeting; Cab 27/331 ST Bull., 12 May). The Electricity Commission took over the St Helens plant on 11 May, when the local authority proposed to transfer its control to the ETU (Cab 27/260 ST 24, 21st and 24th meeting). For examples of non-cooperation in the north-east, see Mason, *op. cit.*, pp. 46–7.

36 See Hastings, *loc. cit.*

37 NUR/GS 118: LM&S Railway, *The General Strike and its Effects on the L.M.&S. Company, 2 June 1926*; Bagwell, *Railwaymen*, pp. 477–9; Symons, *op. cit.*, pp. 98–101; A. R. Williams, 'The General Strike in Gloucestershire', *Trans. of Bristol and Glos. Arch. Society*, 91, 1972.

38 MT 45/248/5.

39 James, *op. cit.*, pp. 243, 250–1; Citrine, *op. cit.*, p. 183.

40 Jones, *Whitehall Diary*, vol. II, pp. 13, 15, 36.

41 Lab 27/7: Emergency Powers Regulations para. 13A (1). The clause was dated 3 May, but the General Council was subsequently informed by the bankers of IFTU that it had been operative only since 9 May (see above, p. 146).

42 CP 236 (26), 11 June; CP 241 (26). On 8 May the Cabinet approved a further regulation preventing the Communist party from withdrawing Russian money from any British bank (Cab 23/52 26 (26)).

43 Cab 23/52 25 (26). Simon was afterwards consulted on the contents of the bill, and was one of those who advised against proceeding with it (Cab 23/52 28 (26)).

44 Cab 23/52 26 (26); Jones, *op. cit.*, II, p. 44; S. Roskill, *Hankey* (1972), vol. II, p. 425. According to Tom Jones, Churchill had already asked Montagu Norman to hold up payments of union funds from the Bank of England, but had been refused (Jones, *op. cit.*, II, pp. 45–6).

45 Jones, *op. cit.*, II, pp. 44–7.

46 *Ibid.*, pp. 46–7; Middlemas and Barnes, *Baldwin*, p. 142; Nicholson, *King George V*, pp. 540–1.

47 Cab 23/52 28 and 29 (26).

NOTES TO CHAPTER VIII

1 W. Mellor, 'The British Worker', *Labour Magazine*, July 1926, p. 111.

2 GC Box 132, 13/7/19, Report of Publicity Committee to General Council, June 1926.

3 F. Brockway, 'A Diary of the Strike', *Socialist Review*, June 1926; output had been 30,000 copies on 4 May, but had fallen to 7,000 on 7 May (Pub. Cttees Report).

4 GC mins, 3 May. The Federation also wished to avert the stoppage of Fleet Street; see below, p. 177.

5 H. Fyfe, *Behind the Scenes of the Great Strike*, pp. 25–6; GC 131, 13/7/11, Pub. Cttee mins, 4 May.

6 *Ibid.*, 6 May. See also H. Fyfe, 'The Freedom of the Press', *Labour Magazine*, July 1926, p. 108.

7 Fyfe, *op. cit.*, p. 26.

8 Pub. Cttee mins, 6 May.

9 GC 131, 13/7/9, meeting of Publicity Committee with Mellor and Newlands; 13/7/11, Pub. Cttee mins, 6 May; 13/7/9, Pub. Cttee report to G.C.

10 See Fyfe, *op. cit.*, pp. 34–5; Citrine, *Men and Work*, pp. 181–2. According to Tom Jones, the Home Secretary had personally ordered the closure of the *Herald* on 4 May, but was countermanded by Baldwin (*Whitehall Diary*, II, p. 38). There is no corroboration for this story,

however, which seems inconsistent with Joynson-Hicks' general restraint during the strike.

11 Fyfe, *op. cit.*, p. 44; Pub. Cttee mins, 10 May.

12 GC 131, 13/7/11, Soc mins, 8 May; TUC/GS/BW. Some supplies may also have been given secretly by Odhams Ltd (R. J. Minney, *Viscount Southwood*, p. 198).

13 Fyfe, *op. cit.*, pp. 83–4.

14 TUC/GS/BW, Fyfe to Tracey, Tracey to Fyfe, 6 May; Pub. Cttee mins, 6 May.

15 'Account of Proceedings of Northumberland and Durham General Council and Joint Strike Committee', *Labour Monthly*, June 1926, p. 370; see also A. Mason, *The General Strike in the North East* (Hull 1970), pp. 37–8; TUC/GS/Intell. Cttee, 'Report from Newcastle', n.d. (6 May?).

16 TUC/GS/Intell. Cttee; A. Tuckett, *The Scottish Carter* (Glasgow 1967), p. 178.

17 GC 132, 13/7/19, Pub. Cttee report; Burns, *General Strike*, p. 36; TUC/GS/Loc. Tracey to Barber, 11 May.

18 Separate Communist bulletins were published, for instance, at Liverpool, Sheffield, Barrow, Airdrie and Coatbridge, and various London boroughs; Klugmann, *op. cit.*, II, pp. 154–9.

19 GC 131, 13/7/11, Pub. Cttee mins, 6 and 7 May; TUC/GS/BW, Tracey to W. Stevens, 6 May; Brockway, *loc. cit.*

20 Brockway, *loc. cit.*; TUC/GS/BW, reports to Pub. Cttee on Manchester edition, 8 May.

21 *Ibid.*, final report, 17 May; Brockway, *loc. cit.*

22 TUC/GS/BW, report on north eastern edition, 27 May. Dawson subsequently obtained the help of a second small printing shop in Gateshead

23 Pub. Cttee report to G.C. They had been led to do so by a courier who misinformed them that the General Council wanted the local production of a counterpart to the *British Worker*.

24 Pub. Cttee mins, 8 May; TUC/GS/BW, Tracey to Armstrong.

25 TUC/GS/BW, report on South Wales edition, n.d.

26 *Ibid.*, fourth report on Manchester edition, 11 May; Pub. Cttee report to G.C.; W. Elger, 'The Scottish Worker', *Labour Magazine*, August 1926, pp. 162–3. Johnston was MP for Dundee and editor of the Glasgow *Forward*. The circulation of the *Scottish Worker* reached 70,000 on 15 May.

27 Pub. Cttee mins, 9 and 10 May; TUC/GS/BW, fifth report on Manchester edition.

28 Pub. Cttee mins, 11 May; Pub. Cttee report to G. C. Mellor (*loc. cit.*, p. 111) says that one issue was printed in Leeds, but not on what date.

29 TUC/GS/Loc, Tracey to W. E. Morris. *The Preston Strike News* was however regarded as an exceptional case by the Publicity Committee by

reason of the lack of any equipment for multigraphing there (Pub. Cttee report to G.C.).

30 Pub. Cttee mins, 9 May.

31 GC 131, 13/7/9.

32 See below, p. 214.

33 Mason, *General Strike in the North East*, pp. 40–3.

34 GC 14/5/1925–6, mins, 3 May. It seems that Bevin hoped to make some such bargain on the eve of the strike; see above, p. 135.

35 Pub. Cttee report to G.C.

36 James, *Memoirs of a Conservative*, p. 233–4; *British Gazette*, 13 May.

37 James, *op. cit.*, pp. 238–9.

38 *British Gazette*, 13 May.

39 Davidson papers, Davidson to Wood, 14 June 1926; James, *op. cit.*, p. 236.

40 Davidson papers, memo. on *British Gazette*; James, *op. cit.*, pp. 237–8; P. J. Grigg, *Prejudice and Judgement* (1948), p. 188; Minney, *op. cit.*, pp. 193–4, 198; HO 45 12431; *British Gazette*, 13 May.

41 HO 45 12431; James, *op. cit.*, p. 241. The circulation figures were given in the *British Gazette* of 13 May. For instances of the paper's makeshift quality, see the editions of 7 and 11 May, which reprinted substantial sections of the issues of previous days. The most striking example of editorial oversight was the publication in the first edition of the large will of a leading north-east coal-owner, J. A. Pease.

42 HO 45 12431; MT 45/247; Elger, *loc. cit.*

43 Parl. Proc. (HoC), 5th ser., vol. 195, col. 712 (10 May); *The Times, Strike Nights at Printing House Square*, p. 37.

44 Templewood papers, V/8, A. H. M. Hudson to Templewood, 11 May.

45 *Strike Nights*, p. 34 (Churchill to Dawson, 8 May); A. J. P. Taylor, *Beaverbrook*, p. 232.

46 *British Gazette*, 5 May; see also Parl. Proc. (HoC), vol. 195, c. 689.

47 Davidson papers, Davidson to Wood, 14 June.

48 *British Gazette*, 5 and 8 May. King George V protested at the latter announcement (H. Nicolson, *op. cit.*, p. 540).

49 Fyfe, *op. cit.*, p. 70; K. Martin, *The British Public and the General Strike* (1926), pp. 76–8.

50 James, *op. cit.*, pp. 242, 244–5; Parl. Proc. (HoC), vol. 195, c. 189–92, 711–12. It was a result of this pressure that Churchill agreed to print an account of the appeal, which appeared on 12 May, along with a résumé of Cardinal Bourne's anti-strike sermon.

51 HO 45 12431.

52 LSE, General Strike ephemera, Coll. Misc. 140 IV. See also *The Yorkshire Post and the General Strike* (1926), and A. Mason, 'The Local Press and the General Strike: an Example from the North East', *Durham University Journal*, June 1969.

53 Daily News, *Strike Fortnight*, Appendix II. It praised the churches' declaration calling for a resumption of negotiations. See also *Daily News*, 18 May; L. Masterman, *C. F. G. Masterman*, pp. 360–1.

54 *British Gazette*, 12 May. For the *Mail*'s editorial policy, see Martin, *op. cit.*, pp. 78–81.

55 *Strike Nights at Printing House Square*, p. 40; Parl. Proc. (HoC), vol. 195, c. 690; E. Wrench, *Geoffrey Dawson and Our Times* (1955), pp. 248–9.

56 *Strike Nights*, pp. 28–9; Davidson papers, 'Coal Strike'; James, *op. cit.*, p. 240. According to A. J. P. Taylor the *Daily Express* was exempted from the requisition as a result of Beaverbrook's influence with Joynson-Hicks (*Beaverbrook*, p. 232).

57 James, *op. cit.*, p. 246. The BBC also composed daily 'editorials' which followed the main evening news, and were likewise monitored by Davidson's civil servants.

58 S. Usherwood, 'The BBC and the General Strike', *History Today*, 22, 1972.

59 A. Briggs, *History of Broadcasting in the United Kingdom*, vol. i (1961), p. 362; Lord Reith, *Into the Wind* (1949), pp. 108–9.

60 Cab 27/260 ST (24) STC, 6 May; Davidson papers, Davidson to Wood 14 June; James, *op. cit.*, pp. 249–50; Cab 23/52 26 (26) and 28 (26). The cabinet minutes do not record a specific decision against taking over the BBC, but the proposed declaration of the illegality of the general strike, on which policy towards the Company had been made to rest, was abandoned on 11 May.

61 Briggs, *op. cit.*, vol. I, p. 379; R. K. A. Bell, *Randall Davidson: Archbishop of Canterbury* (1938), pp. 1307–8.

62 Briggs, *op. cit.*, I, pp. 376–7; Cab 23/52 28 (26).

63 Quoted in A. Scheps, 'Trade Unions and the Government 1925–7' (thesis), p. 303.

64 Briggs, *op. cit.*, I, p. 363; Reith, *op. cit.*, p. 112.

65 Briggs, *op. cit.*, I, p. 373.

66 Summaries of daily news bulletins were kept by the TUC Intelligence Committee, and filed as TUC/GS/Intell. MD 32 ff.

67 For other examples see Symons, *General Strike*, p. 179.

68 TUC MD 42, 61, 68, 71, 73.

69 Quoted in Usherwood, *loc. cit.*

70 After the strike, Baldwin wrote to Reith 'a special word of thanks for the great help and service which the BBC rendered to the Government and the country during the emergency' (Bald. 23, 17 May).

71 See Beatrice Webb, *Diaries 1924–31*, ed. M. I. Cole (1956), p. 90.

72 GC 132, 13/7/19, Pub. Cttee report to G.C.; GC 131, 13/7/11, Pub. Cttee mins, 4 and 10 May; TUC/GS/Intell. Cttee, Interviews Committee to Intelligence Committee, 9 May.

NOTES TO CHAPTER IX

1 GC W&MC 1, 30 April.

2 The principal source of the role of the Trades Council in the General Strike is an inquiry conducted by the Labour Research Department in 1926, compiled by Emile Burns: *The General Strike 1926: Trades Councils in Action.* 131 local strike organizations formed through their initiative sent replies to the LRD. The total number of Trades Councils affiliated to the TUC in March 1926 was 464. The number of strike organizations set up after 3 May was probably even larger than this, however. Eighty strike committees and Councils of Action in Northumberland and Durham for instance, attended a conference at Newcastle on 8 May, and there were said to be seventy such bodies in the Greater London area (A. Mason, *The General Strike in the North East*, p. 24; J. Klugmann, *History of the Communist Party of Great Britain*, vol. II, p. 158).

3 R. Martin, *Communism and the British Trade Unions, 1924–33*, p. 69, 72; R. Page Arnot, *The General Strike*, pp. 192–3.

4 Page Arnot *op. cit.*, p. 114; CPGB 8th Congress, 1926, *Report*, p. 4; A. Clinton, 'Trades Councils' (thesis), p. 216. Such bodies were set up in Glasgow, Edinburgh, Barrow, Doncaster and Sheffield (Martin, *op. cit.*, p. 69); in Preston and Hull (R. Postgate, E. Wilkinson and J. F. Horrabin, *A Workers' History of the Great Strike* (1927), p. 46); in Liverpool (D. E. Baines and R. Bean, 'The General Strike on Merseyside' in J. R. Harris (ed.), *Liverpool and Merseyside*); and in Birmingham and Coventry, where this step was taken in expectation of a national engineering stoppage (Burns, *op. cit.*, p. 112; Crook, *The General Strike*, pp. 371–2; Clinton, *op. cit.*, pp. 214–15). In Manchester a Council of Action had been formed in advance, but had to be reconstituted at the outbreak of the General Strike (Clinton, *op. cit.*, p. 215).

5 G. Hardy, *Those Stormy Years* (1956), p. 185.

6 The Labour Party, for instance, was represented in Birmingham, Sheffield and Stockton; the Cooperative Movement at Blaengarw, Merthyr, and Brighton. The only local committee on which the Communist Party sat officially, so far as the author has ascertained, was also that of Blaengarw – where even the Conservative working men's club was brought in (*Workers' Weekly*, 21 May).

7 Despite this, the Communist satellite organization, the National Unemployed Workers' branch, refused to join forces with the Council (C. Wrigley, 'The demand for Labour Representation in Battersea 1886–1922', in K. D. Brown (ed.), *Essays in Anti-Labour History* (1974)). Other significant Communist 'factions' were formed in, for example, Islington, Stepney, West Ham and Bethnal Green, and in Scotland at Methil, Coatbridge and Paisley. C. P. chairman were to be found at

Barrow and on the Lanarkshire District Committee. George Fletcher was vice-chairman of the Sheffield Central Dispute Committee, but this nonetheless refused the local Communists' offer of cooperation, leading to the creation of an unofficial party committee (N. Connole, *Leaven of Life* (1961), pp. 147–8).

8 The most clear-cut exception was Greenock, where rival Trades Councils and strike committees were formed (see Klugmann, *op. cit.*, II, pp. 154–5). But see also the cases of Glasgow and Leeds, referred to below, pp. 194, 197.

9 J. T. Murphy in *Workers' Weekly*, 30 April, quoted in L. J. Macfarlane, *The British Communist Party, 1920–29*, p. 162.

10 Hardy, *op. cit.*, pp. 187–8; Macfarlane, *op. cit.*, p. 163; Klugmann, *op. cit.*, II, pp. 134–5; CPGB 8th Congress, *Report*, p. 10.

11 Klugmann, *op. cit.*, II, p. 136; M. G. Woodhouse, 'Rank and File Movements among the Miners of South Wales' (thesis), p. 363.

12 Klugmann, *op. cit.*, II, p. 158; Burns, *op. cit.*, pp. 120–3.

13 See the example of the Durham miners in the north-east, below, n.22; and A. R. Griffin, *The Miners of Nottinghamshire* (1962), p. 127, for Mansfield. There are, it must be added, counter-examples of miners playing an active part in more representative bodies, at Nottingham, Blaengarw, and probably elsewhere in central Scotland and South Wales. The Northumberland miners were attached to the Newcastle joint strike committee.

14 Burns, *op. cit.*, p. 138; London Trades Council, *68th Annual Report 1926–27*, p. 17. Klugmann states definitely that the meeting was held only after the General Strike was over (*op. cit.*, II, p. 158).

15 Burns, *op. cit.*, p. 139.

16 A. Tuckett, *The Scottish Carter*, pp. 174, 180–2, Postgate *et al.*, *op. cit.* p. 45; R. A. Leeson, *Strikes* (1973), p. 90; Klugmann, *op. cit.*, II, p. 154., The authority of the Scottish General Council was itself at first denied by the NUR district officials (GC Box 129, 13/7/1, Elger phone message to Citrine, 5 May).

17 J. Corbett, *Birmingham Trades Council* (1966), pp. 125–9; R. P. Hastings, 'Aspects of the General Strike in Birmingham', *Midland Hist.*, 2, 1974; P. Wyncoll, 'The General Strike in Nottingham', *Marxism Today*, June 1972, pp. 172–80; D. Large and R. Whitfield, *The Bristol Trades Council, 1873–1973* (Bristol H.A. 1973), p. 21; N. Connole, *op. cit.*, p. 147; Crook, *op. cit.*, p. 411; 'Interview with Len Youle', *Bull. Soc. Study of Labour Hist.*, 20, 1970; TUC/GS/Loc, Bristol Cttee to Intell. Cttee, 7 May.

18 Baines and Bean, *loc. cit.*

19 Klugmann, *op. cit.*, II, p. 154; Clinton, *op. cit.*, p. 217.

20 See E. and D. Frow, 'The General Strike in Manchester', *Bull. of North West Society for Study of Labour Hist.*, 1, 1974. The Bolton Council of Action seems to have accepted some instructions from this

authority (Burns, *op. cit.*, p. 104). But the Oldham Trades Council reported to E. L. Poulton (of the TUC Publicity Committee) on 10 May that the regional council was a body 'with which we have had no communication whatever, nor have we had any communication with regard to the constitution and power of that Council' (TUC/GS/Loc).

21 A full account of the history of this organization can be found in A. Mason, *The General Strike in the North East*; see also R. Page Arnot, 'The General Strike in the North East', in L. M. Munby (ed.), *The Luddites and Other Essays* (1971). The official 'Account of the Proceedings of the Northumberland and Durham General Council & Joint Strike Committee', written by its Secretary, Charles Flynn, was printed in *Labour Monthly*, June 1926, but does not go beyond 9 May. The TUC General Strike Collection contains one set of minutes for the meeting of the Strike Committee on 9 May, which record the admission of delegates from Stockton & Thornaby, but also note complaints from Hartlepool at the refusal of the Newcastle pickets to recognize permits issued by the local committee.

22 GC Box 139, file 16 contains notes of two phone messages from Flynn, the secretary of the north-east General Council, to the Strike Organization Committee, conveying the decision of the Durham miners to set up their own Council. One or more members of the TUC contacted W. P. Richardson, the Durham President and MFGB Treasurer, and A. J. Cook, as a result. Whether by virtue of this intervention or Flynn's own efforts, the DMA finally resolved on 12 May that, though they would recommend the establishment of their own county strike committee, they would also arrange a mutual exchange of representatives with the North East Strike Committee (Garside, *Durham Miners*, p. 198; see also GC Box 131, 13/7/11, SOC mins, 11 May).

Even in London, it may be noted, the General Council agreed to appoint a liaison officer to the Central Strike Committee, but failed to do so. (G. Tate, *The London Trades Council, 1860–1950* (1950), p. 129.)

23 See Burns, *op. cit.*, pp. 77, 117, for the cases of Dartford and Hampshire; also C. Farman, *The General Strike*, pp. 156–7.

24 GC Box 139, file 23: J. V. Wills to Citrine. For other examples, see GC 130, 13/7/4, Barker to Citrine, 21 May (Bradford); *ibid.*, Barton to Citrine, 7 July (Liverpool).

25 Coventry claimed to have been appointed as such a centre for the area including Rugby, Warwick and Hinckley, for instance (Burns, *op. cit.*, p. 114). For instruction to other Trades Councils to form area committees, see above, p. 136.

26 Postgate *et. al.*, *op. cit.*, p. 46. It is difficult to be certain whether their report of four local organizations having been formed was exaggerated or not. A Council of Action had existed at Leeds since Red Friday, but it had little or no official status (Clinton, *op. cit.*, p. 214). A letter from J. Brotherton to Citrine on 9 May states that two Committees were

formed in Leeds on the 3 May, one by the Trades Council and the other on the initiative of the NUG&MW District Committee, and that the latter had been 'recognized' by the General Council. But the same G.C. file contains a circular from Leeds Trades Council, dated 7 May, saying that the Central Strike Committee had been reconstituted on the 5th – which may perhaps indicate that an amalgamation had taken place, possibly with the pre-existing Council of Action (GC Box 130, 13/7/4; see also *Leeds Citizen*, 8 May). To complicate matters further, the minutes of the Central Strike Committee of 7 May (presumably the Trades Council version) refer to a letter received from the local NUR refusing to recognize it until its status had been properly established. The relationship between the railwaymen and the General and Municipal Workers' body remains unclear. The undated minute of the deputation from the second committee to Eccleston Square does not mention its composition or authority (see below, p. 214).

27 See Clinton, *op cit.*, p. 219; TUC/GS/Loc., Hanson to Citrine, 9 May. The minutes of the committee of Birmingham railway unions are in the LSE Library (R. Coll. General Strike), but they were at least represented on the general municipal committee (Birmingham Trades Council and Labour Party, *Ann. Report and Year Book 1926*, p. 6). There were other similar cases of such division at Oldham, Nottingham, Darlington, Dunfermline, Glasgow and Crewe (Burns, *op. cit.*, pp. 15, 123, 154, 171; TUC/GS/Loc., speakers' reports from Frank Varley and Mary Quaile; Tuckett, *op. cit.*, p. 177; Clinton, *op. cit.*, p. 217).

28 The Swansea strike committee alerted the General Council on 8 May: 'telegrams are being received at intervals, cancelling one another and signed by leaders of different unions . . . is government concocting conflicting telegrams to mislead strike committee?' (quoted in Clinton, *op. cit.*, p. 218). For other instances see 'Account of Northumberland and Durham General Council', *loc. cit.*, p. 366; Burns, *op. cit.*, p. 187; M. Bondfield, *A Life's Work*, p. 267.

29 Burns, *op. cit.*, p. 171; J. Mendelson *et al.*, *Sheffield Trades and Labour Council, 1858–1958* (Sheffield 1958), p. 88; Mason, *op. cit.*, pp. 27, 31–2; Clinton, *op. cit.*, p. 217. See also TUC/GS/Loc., *Gloucester Strike Bull.*, 10 May; GC 130, 13/7/4, Barton to Citrine, 7 July 1926.

30 See, for instance, GC Box 131, 13/7/10, 'Descriptive Account of a tour during the general strike', by H. Croft.

31 Klugmann, *op. cit.*, II, p. 156; Mason, *op. cit.*, p. 55 ff; Leeson, *op. cit.*, p. 89 (R. E. Scouller); Corbett, *op. cit.*, p. 126; Garside, *op. cit.*, p. 199; 'Interview with Len Youle', *loc. cit.*; Crook, *op. cit.*, p. 411; Hastings, *loc. cit.*

32 Postgate *et al.*, *op. cit.*, p. 52; Wyncoll, *loc. cit.*; A. Moffatt, *My Life with the Miners* (1965), p. 45, above, p. 148.

33 Clinton, *op. cit.*, p. 232. The quoted phrase is Page Arnot's: see Mason, *op. cit.*, p. 17.

34 GC Box 139, file 21, Bevin to National Transport Cttee, 12 May; J. P. M. Millar, 'The 1926 General Strike and the National Council of Labour Colleges', *Bull. Soc. Study of Labour Hist.*, 20, 1970; Tuckett, *op. cit.*, pp. 181–2. The unions concerned were the United Road Transport Workers and the Scottish Horse and Motormen.

35 GC Box 131, 13/7/10 (Croft); GC 129, 13/7/1, note of phone call from Elger, 5 May; Tuckett, *op. cit.*, p. 181; B. Davies, *Pages from a Worker's Life, 1916–26* (CPGB, *Our History*, 1961).

36 TUC/GS/Loc., speaker's report by Mary Quaile, 11 May; Clinton, *op. cit.*, p. 217. Oldham had referred the controversy there to the Manchester strike committee.

37 Mason, *op. cit.*, pp. 57–65. A note on an undated typescript 'Report from Newcastle' in the files of the G.C. Intelligence Committee suggests that the north-east Strike Committee contacted TUC headquarters and were instructed to refuse cooperation with Wood 'on the grounds our national offer was ignored by Government'. An account to this effect is given in Postgate, *op. cit.*, pp. 67–8. Other versions, however, including the official 'Account of the Northumberland and Durham General Council etc.' indicate that an offer to assist the Civil Commissioner on condition that blacklegs were not used together with union members was actually made by the representatives of the north-east General Council and was rejected (*Labour Monthly*, June 1926, p. 367; also *AEU Monthly Journal*, June 1926, p. 27: report of J. C. Little; Mason, *op. cit.*, p. 56). For Connolly's speech in the House of Commons, see Parl. Proc. (HoC), 5th ser., vol. 195, cs. 486–87; and for Wood's reply, vol. 196, cs. 545–50.

38 'Account of Proceedings of Northumberland and Durham General Council, etc.', *loc. cit.*, p. 372.

39 Baines and Bean, *loc. cit.*; Crook, *op. cit.*, p. 405–6; Hastings, *loc. cit.*; Tuckett, *op. cit.*, p. 183; GC 130, 13/7/4, Barber to Citrine, 21 May. See also *Preston Strike News*, 7 May.

40 It is not clear whether permits were withdrawn in Nottingham, a centre where 'dual control' did apparently exist, at least for a time. The local Strike Bulletin on 6 May claimed that 'Mr. Harding, the area food controller, has undertaken to move no food except by permission of the Strike Committee. He does not recognise the O.M.S.'. Despite this, a separate service of road transport vehicles connecting Nottingham with London, Birmingham, Manchester and Liverpool was operated by the Chamber of Commerce under the aegis of the West Midlands Civil Commissioner (Wyncoll, *loc. cit.*). It was exactly this kind of circumstance, of course, which caused unions to refuse all assistance in other places.

41 'Account of Northumberland and Durham General Council etc.',

loc. cit., pp. 370, 373; Page Arnot, 'General Strike in the North East', *loc. cit.*, pp. 272–3; TUC/GS/Loc., Northumberland and Durham Joint Strike Cttee mins, 9 May; TUC/GS/Intell. Cttee, report from C. Flynn, 11 May.

42 Burns, *op. cit.*, pp. 55–6, 61; Crook, *op. cit.*, p. 405; minutes of the Birmingham joint railway union committee, LSE R.Coll./Gen. Strike.

43 Burns, *op. cit.*, pp. 55, 125, 170; GC 129, file 31; above p. 191.

44 GC 131, 13/7/11, SOC mins, 10 May.

45 GC 139, file 21; MT 45/248/6, north-west road commissioner's report. See also above, p. 199, for the uncontrolled permit policy of the United Road Transport Workers in this area; and also TUC/GS/Intell. Cttee, Progress of Strike, report 5, 10 May, which refers to a joint strike committee in the Ashton-Stalybridge district being disciplined by the north-west regional council for its continued issue of permits.

46 MT 45/245, Summary of Road Commissioners' reports, especially South Wales, South Western, North Midlands and Eastern. Even in Doncaster, an area of mass picketing, vehicles carrying bread and milk were being allowed through, on production of permits, up to the end of the stoppage (*Doncaster Gazette*, 14 May).

47 Symons, *op. cit.*, p. 142. Even the famous Plymouth football match was not wholly unique: in Battersea, pickets at the South Metropolitan power station and local police took part in a miniature shooting competition (Davidson papers, 'Coal Strike', 'Actualities from the Areas').

48 J. T. Murphy, *New Horizons* (1941), p. 225.

49 TUC/GS/Intell. Cttee., report 7 May. In other parts of London picketing was more peaceful; the members of the Stratford Branch of the NUR were given the following instructions: 'Pickets' duties are that they must not lay their hands on any one and they had best keep them in their pockets, they must not impede anyone, but they can converse with any one by being at their side or walking at their side but not in front of them. If at any time they are interferred with by the Police by (sic) carrying out the above duties, then they MUST not reply, but take the number of the Policeman and report at this committee room or to Chief Picket.' (Minute book, 8 May, TUC Library.)

50 Garside, *op. cit.*, p. 199; Mason, *op. cit.*, p. 66; Klugmann, *op. cit.*, II, p. 154; Crook, *op. cit.*, pp. 416–17; *Doncaster Gazette*, 14 May.

51 Burns, *op. cit.*, p. 70; Postgate *et al.*, *op. cit.*, pp. 43–4; Klugmann, *op. cit.*, II, pp. 153–4; Clinton, *op. cit.*, p. 228.

52 Clinton, *op. cit.*, p. 228; Farman, *op. cit.*, pp. 155–6. The Minority Movement itself ordered that members of the corps should be 'trade unionists of good character and under commanders who are trade union officials. Their duty is to protect trade union offices, printing presses, mass meetings, pickets, and trade union officials holding important positions, to maintain peace and order and prevent *agents provocateurs*

and spies, whom without doubt the Government and employers will engage to commit violence' (Hardy, *op. cit.*, p. 185).

53 Millar, *loc. cit.*; Burns, *op. cit.*, p. 108. See also Leeson, *op. cit.*, p. 90; L. Paul, *Angry Young Man* (1951), p. 87; R. Hyman, *Oxford Workers in the Great Strike* (1966), p. 5; Clinton, *op. cit.*, p. 229.

54 *Scottish Worker*, 10 May.

55 Mason, *op. cit.*, pp. 71–4.

56 Burns, *op. cit.*, pp. 103, 158; TUC/GS/Loc., Paddington strike cttee to Citrine, 10 May.

57 Page Arnot, *General Strike*, p. 185; Burns, *op. cit.*, pp. 108, 123, 178; *Hull Daily Mail*, 8, 10 May; *Doncaster Gazette*, 14, 21 May.

58 Parl. Proc. (HoC), vol. 196, cs. 823–5. In all, 7,960 offences were tried in England & Wales in connection with the General Strike and coal lockout, including 3,304 for breaches of the emergency regulations. If the proportion of 'ordinary' to 'emergency' prosecutions was the same during the General Strike as afterwards, rather more than 2,000 would have been charged with strike offences under the ordinary law between 1 and 12 May. It is perhaps reasonable to assume, however, that the emergency regulations were relatively more frequently utilized whilst the General Strike lasted (*Judicial Statistics, England & Wales 1926 (Criminal)*, Cmd. 3055, 1928, p. 5. There was no similar return for Scotland).

59 T&GWU GEC, Subcommittee report on General Strike.

60 See Klugmann, *op. cit.*, II, p. 163; CPGB 8th Party congress, *Report*, p. 13. The Communist estimate of the number of prosecutions took the Home Secretary's into account.

61 See Connole, *op. cit.*, pp. 148–9, 153–5 (Sheffield); Corbett, *op. cit.*, p. 128 (Birmingham); Frow, *loc. cit.* (Manchester); Burns, *op. cit.*, p. 110 (Castleford), p. 128 (Gorton), p. 145 (Middlesbrough), and p. 162 (Pontefract); Mason, *op. cit.*, p. 71 (Blaydon); TUC/GS/Loc., *Bradford Worker*, n.d. (Shipley).

62 For the Manchester incident, see Frow, *loc. cit.*

63 *Birmingham Strike Bull.*, 12 May; Leeson, *op. cit.*, p. 91 (Garrard); TUC/GS/Loc., T. Jackson to SOC, 11 May. The provenance of this report is an illuminating instance of the tenuousness of communications among strike organizations. It originated as a misprinted item in the *Cricklewood Workers' Gazette*, which was noted by a local railwaymen's committee in Coventry, passed to the joint transport committee in Birmingham, and thence to the emergency committee (Hastings, *loc. cit.*).

64 Mepol 2/3134; also Cab. 27/260 ST 24, 18th Meeting; Mason, *op. cit.*, p. 75; *Scottish Worker*, 10 May.

65 For Tredegar, see M. Foot, *Aneurin Bevan* (1962), vol. I, p. 70.

66 See above, p. 148; A. Williams, 'The General Strike in Gloucestershire' *Trans. of Bristol and Glos. Archeol. Soc.*, 91, 1972, p. 210; *Scottish Worker*, 11 and 12 May; *Doncaster Gazette*, 14 May.

67 For examples see Burns, *op. cit.*, pp. 72, 137 (Lincoln); *Manchester Guardian Bull.*, 5 May; B. Davies, *op. cit.*, p. 15 (St Helens); A. Tuckett, *Up With All That's Down* (Swindon 1971), p. 66.

68 'Account of Proceedings of Northumberland & Durham Gen. Council etc.', *loc. cit.*, p. 370.

69 *Lansbury's Labour Weekly*, 22 May; National Strike: Special Conference of Trade Union Executives, 20–21 January 1927, *Report*, p. 35; MFGB Conf., 14 May 1926, *Report*, p. 4. See also MFGB, *Statement on the General Strike of May 1926*, January 1927, p. 3.

70 See above, pp. 195–6; also 'Account of Proceedings of Northumberland and Durham General Council etc.', *loc. cit.*, p. 363; *Evening Times and Echo* (Bristol), 6 May.

71 See, especially, the case of car workers in the West Midlands (Burns, *op. cit.*, p. 115; Corbett, *op. cit.*, p. 127; *Birmingham Post*, 8 May). See also J. Whyman, 'The 1926 General Strike: Its Impact on the Medway Towns' *Cantium*, 3, 1971; and the policy statement of the Building Trade Workers, quoted above, p. 141. The Sheffield Central Dispute Committee sent a deputation to the General Council to ask permission to continue the stoppage among men called out in error (GC Box 130, 13/7/4); and on 11 May the Electrical Advisory Committee (presumably the most appropriately constituted authority) accepted as a *fait accompli* the stoppage of some 20,000 government workers at Woolwich and Enfield arsenals (GC Box 131, 13/7/11, SOC mins, 11 May).

72 It was primarily for this reason that the stoppage spread in many places to the flour millers and other general workers among the membership of the T&GWU (T&GWU GEC, report of sub-committee on General Strike; also R. Bean, 'The General Strike in Liverpool', *Bull. North West Society for Study of Labour Hist.*, 1, 1974). For the piecemeal extension of the power workers stoppage on this count, see below, p. 214.

73 See, for instance, Hull *Daily Mail*, 6 and 7 May; B. Davies, *op. cit.*, p. 15.

74 See for instance TUC/GS/Intell. Cttee, National Union of Vehicle Builders' report, 10 May; NUR Head Office Circulars 1926, M7/MC/491, 9 May.

75 Baines and Bean, *loc. cit.*

76 This was true of, for instance, Castle Cary, Llandudno, Lichfield, Bicester, Tring, and Glastonbury (Burns, *op. cit.*, pp. 109, 127, 136, 142; TUC/GS/Loc., Bicester strike cttee report, 7 May, Tring strike cttee report, n.d.).

77 TUC/GS/Intell. Cttee, 4 May. The report mentioned Barrow and Bristol as particularly weak points.

78 See Bagwell, *op. cit.*, pp. 473–6.

79 B. Mogridge, 'Militancy and Inter-union Rivalry in British Shipping, 1911–29', *Internat. Rev. of Social Hist.*, 6, 1961, p. 405, n. 2.

80 See above, p. 147; GC Box 132, file 91. The NSFU Assistant Secretary Henson, resigned in protest against his President's conduct.

81 After the General Strike Wilson wrote a long and rather jocular letter to Baldwin, commenting that 'when my agents ask seamen for observations regarding my character they describe me as the greatest robber that ever lived. I have committed every crime in the calendar and they seem very much disgusted and surprised that I have not been hanged years ago'; but he denied having misrepresented their opinion during this crisis (Bald. 21, 14 May 1926). See also G. Hardy, *op. cit.*, p. 175.

82 Baines and Bean, *loc. cit.*; 'Account of Proceedings of Northumberland and Durham General Council etc.', *loc. cit.*, p. 364; Mogridge, *loc. cit.*, p. 405; TUC/GS/Intell. Cttee, 'report from Newcastle' n.d.; Shinwell, *Conflict without Malice* (1955), pp. 57, 100.

83 Bean, *loc. cit.*; Turner, *About Myself*, p. 313.

84 Citrine, *Men and Work*, pp. 190–1.

85 Postgate *et al.*, *op. cit.*, p. 91; Burns, *op. cit.*, p. 133; TUC/GS/Intell. Cttee, Bevin to Publicity Cttee, 8 May; TUC/GS/Loc., G.W. Post to Citrine, 5 May; GC Box 132, 13/7/19: report of Intell. Cttee to G.C., June 1926.

86 Baines and Bean, *loc. cit.*; TUC/GS/Intell. Cttee, Bevin to Publicity Cttee, 6 May; *AEU Monthly Journal*, June 1926, p. 20.

87 GC Box 131, 13/7/10 (Croft); Postgate *et al.*, *op. cit.*, p. 93; TUC/GS/Loc., Birmingham Emergency Cttee report, 12 May; *Electrical Trades Journal*, May–June 1926, p. 83 (Glasgow); Burns, *op. cit.*, p. 99 (Aberdeen); *Yorks Post*, 10 May (Huddersfield); TUC/GS/Intell. Cttee, Progress of strike report, 10 May (Lancaster).

88 See above, p. 162; below, p. 245; also Burns, *op. cit.*, p. 100, Postgate *et al.*, *op. cit.*, p. 91; Hyman, *op. cit.*, p. 3; Whyman, *loc. cit.*

89 G. Routh, *Occupation and Pay in Great Britain, 1906–60*, p. 35. The exact number of union members is impossible to calculate, since many of them belonged to the general unions.

90 GC 132, 13/7/19, quoted in Farman, *op. cit.*, p. 276.

91 Burns, *op. cit.*, pp. 101, 165; TUC/GS/Intell. Cttee, Progress of Strike report, 10 May; see also Postgate *et al.*, *op. cit.*, p. 46 (Bradford). Another union which recruited some tramway and haulage workers was the General and Municipal Workers, whose attitude to the strike has also been said to be lukewarm (see Clinton, *op. cit.*, p. 219). The evidence for this opinion is inconclusive. It lies partly in the failure of some of the union branches to receive instructions, which may simply reflect a difficulty of communications afflicting many organizations; it was also the result of the reluctance of some local organizers – in Nottingham, St Helens and Carlisle, for instance – to see stoppages of members in manufacturing firms which were *not* called out, even when they were accused of blacklegging. But their behaviour likewise has parallels, in the textile and building industries especially. In general, there

seem to be insufficient grounds for supposing that the NUG&MW did not play the part required of it in the 'first wave'. But it does seem likely that the outlook of its district officers varied considerably: one, the Leeds Committee chairman, led a deputation seeking an end to the strike (see below, p. 216): another, James Tarbit, was among the founder-members of the celebrated Northumberland and Durham joint strike committee. (See Mason, *op. cit.*, p. 18.)

92 Postgate *et al.*, *op. cit.*, p. 93; Burns, *op. cit.*, pp. 126, 150; TUC/GS/Loc., Bristol Strike Cttee to Intell. Cttee, 11 May; TUC/GS/Intell. Cttee, 'Survey of Strike, 12 May', quoted in Farman, *op. cit.*, p. 270. See also TUC/GS/Loc., Stafford Trades Council to Publicity Cttee, 11 May; *Evening Times and Echo* (Bristol), 10 May.

93 TUC/GS/Intell. Cttee, Survey, 12 May; Farman, *op. cit.*, p. 271.

94 TUC/GS/Loc., T. J. Hayward to Bevin, 10 May. The 'unaffected' stations may be fewer in number, since they include ten cases where there was 'no information'. Ten stations were being worked under union permit, mainly by agreement with labour councils; and one was awaiting strike orders. Eleven were being run by naval ratings.

95 D. Large and R. Whitfield, *op. cit.*, p. 21; Garside, *op. cit.*, p. 192; GC Box 131, 13/7/11; Leeson, *op. cit.*, p. 88; TUC/GS/Loc., Bristol Strike Cttee to Intell. Cttee, 7 May. The Hull power workers were also brought out on the 11th (*Hull Daily Mail*, 12 May); at Gloucester and for a time at Swindon, agreements with the local authority to restrict the supply to industry prevented a stoppage (A. R. Williams, *loc. cit.*, p. 209; Tuckett, *Up with All That's Down*, p. 64).

96 *Electrical Trades Council*, May–June 1926, p. 83; TUC/GS/Intell. Cttee, Bevin to Publicity Cttee, 8 May.

97 TUC/GS/Intell. Cttee, report from Southampton, 10 May; TUC/GS/Loc., Progress of Strike report, 6 May; *Ibid.* Cambridge Trades Council to Publicity Cttee, 7 May; *Ibid.* G. W. Post to Citrine, 5 May; R. Bean, *loc. cit.*.

98 GC Box 131, 13/7/10 (Croft); TUC/GS/Loc., report from Birmingham, 12 May; Hastings, *loc. cit.* The *Birmingham Post* (12 May) said that the local ETU branch had voted 64–50 in favour of a stoppage on 11 May. Power workers in Stafford were also expected to disobey orders to strike (TUC/GS/Loc., Stafford Trades Council to Publicity Cttee, 11 May).

99 ETU *Ann. Report 1926*; see also *The Story of the ETU* (1953), p. 119.

100 TUC/GS/Intell. Cttee, Bevin to Publicity Cttee, 6 May; see also Burns, *op. cit.*, p. 106 (Bootle).

101 TUC/GS/Loc., 'Interview with M.S.', 10 May; Burns, *op. cit.*, p. 113.

102 J. B. Jeffreys, *The Story of the Engineers*, p. 233. Glenny, the AEU Assistant Secretary, wrote to Citrine on 11 May, 'We have heard a very strong rumour over the wireless that the Strike has been called off.

Is this official. . . .?' His letter was minuted at Eccleston Square, 'Answered by Instructions for all Unions' (GC 140, file 40).

103 What sketchy evidence there is suggests that the engineering stoppage had been fairly solid in south Lancashire, Glasgow, Derby and Sheffield; but press reports suggested a lower turnout in Cardiff, Lincoln and Teesside (*AEU Monthly Journal*, June 1926; *Electrical Trades Journal*, May–June 1926, p. 83; E. and R. Frow, *loc. cit.*; *Evening Times and Echo* (Bristol), 12 May.

104 The Bristol strike committee were aware and resentful of these imputations. They claimed to have doubled the number on strike there, to 36,000, even before the engineers were brought out; and it was suggested that they had themselves propagated the story of the weakness of the strike in order to obtain the General Council's permission to extend it – specifically to the gas workers (*AEU Monthly Journal*, June 1926). But in fact at least three sections – printers, tramwaymen and railway clerks – were certainly disloyal to the strike orders here. Ben Turner also referred to the shakiness of the Bristol docks, an allusion not in itself very authoritative, but reinforced perhaps by the difficulty which the T&GWU had in obtaining reinstatement for its waterside members after the strike (see below, p. 249). See also *Western Daily Press*, 12 May; and *Evening Times and Echo*, 10 May, the latter of which mentions the resumption of Bristol brewery workers.

105 GC Box 130, 13/7/4.

106 Burns, *op. cit.*, pp. 126, 167.

107 TUC/GS/Loc., A. Dunn to General Council, 11 May. It should be added that Dunn wanted the strike to be extended as a cure for these doubts.

108 *Socialist Review*, June 1926.

109 John Strachey, 'What has the Great Strike Done to Us', *ibid.*, July 1926, p. 28.

110 *Ministry of Labour Gazette*, January 1927, p. 5; GC 132, 13/7/19.

NOTES TO CHAPTER X

1 R. Jenkins, *Asquith* (1964), p. 514; F. Owen, *Tempestuous Journey* (1954), p. 704.

2 Parl. Proc. (HoL), 5th ser., vol. 64, cs. 16–22.

3 *British Gazette*, 8 May; Parl. Proc. (HoC), 5th ser., vol. 195, cs. 582–88, 870–1; J. Simon, *Three Speeches on the General Strike* (1926), Appendix III.

4 Parl. Proc. (HoC), vol. 195, cs. 82–8.

5 A. J. Sylvester, *The Real Lloyd George* (1947), pp. 148, 157; T. Wilson, *The Downfall of the Liberal Party, 1914–35* (1966), pp. 330–4; R.

Douglas, *The History of the Liberal Party, 1895–1970* (1971), pp. 195–6. The inconclusive evidence on Lloyd George's soundings of the Labour Party after the General Strike is summarized in James, *Memoirs of a Conservative*, pp. 260–1.

6 Parl. Proc. (HoL), vol. 64, cs. 49–51.

7 J. K. A. Bell, *Randall Davidson, Archbishop of Canterbury* (1938), p. 1306.

8 Bald. 20, Jones to Baldwin, 7 May; Bell, *op. cit.*, p. 1307.

9 M. Cole, *Life of G. D. H. Cole* (1971), p. 155; TUC/GS/Intell. Cttee; Bald. 20. The local councils which sent such resolutions included Newcastle, Caernarvon (county) and Huddersfield.

10 For extremes of opinion among the anglican clergy, see on the one hand the complaints made to Baldwin by Lord Derby and Archibald Salvidge, the Conservative Party leaders in Liverpool, about the radical addresses of Bishop David among Lancashire miners and businessmen (Bald. 18); and on the other the Bishop of Durham's protests about the appeal's encouragement to 'the tendency, already dangerously active, for many parochial clergymen . . . to substitute for religious teaching a declamatory sentimental socialism as far removed from sound economics as from Christian morality' (Bell, *op. cit.*, p. 1316). For the support given to the appeal by clergymen of various denominations in Birmingham, see *Birmingham Post*, 10 May 1926, and J. Corbett, *The Birmingham Trades Council*, p. 127. There were similar differences of view among the Catholic hierarchy; see G. P. McEntee, *The Social Catholic Movement in Great Britain* (New York 1927), Appendix B.

11 Bell., *op. cit.*, p. 1307, 1313–4.

12 Bald. 18, Davidson to Baldwin, 18 May.

13 Bald. 21; Jones, *Whitehall Diary*, vol. II, pp. 39–40. Smith proposed that the General Strike be resolved by a temporary uniform wage cut on the existing working day, to be followed by joint discussions on other aspects of the Samuel Report. He held the strike to be a purely industrial dispute, and not likely to end soon.

14 Lab 27/6. Those present included Lords Londonderry and Crawford, David Davies MP, Sir Robert Hutchinson and Sir David Llewellyn, and others who had attended his earlier meetings (see above, p. 108).

15 Formerly Ivor Guest and Rufus Isaacs (see biographical notes).

16 The only extant account of these meetings is by Osbert Sitwell, *Laughter in the Next Room* (1950 reprint edn.). Sitwell was a friend of Lady Wimborne, and another guest at the luncheon.

17 Sitwell, *op. cit.*, p. 228.

18 See below, p. 237. Whether Wimborne and Reading knew that negotiations were taking place with Samuel cannot be ascertained. Wimborne himself, according to Sitwell, had suggested early in the conversations that Samuel might be a suitable mediator; and of course both he and Reading were former political colleagues. On the other hand Reading was clearly

surprised by the publication of the Samuel memorandum on 13 May (Jones, *op. cit.*, II, pp. 53–4).

19 Sitwell, *op. cit.*, pp. 228–9; Sitwell suggests that Reading had expected the General Council to be arrested *en bloc* on 12 May. This prediction was reported to him second hand and recalled after a considerable lapse of time, whether it was made must be thought doubtful.

20 Citrine, *Men and Work*, p. 185. The book, *Belief and Action on Everyday Philosophy*, was published in 1937.

21 Bald. 21, Samuel to Baldwin, 3 May; Baldwin to Samuel, 4 May; Samuel, *Memoirs*, p. 186; Citrine, *op. cit.*, p. 185.

22 Lab. 27/4, Samuel to Baldwin, 11 May; MFGB Proc. 1926, pp. 209–10; Citrine, *op cit.*, p. 187. For the similar views of Sir Herbert Lawrence on these matters, see Bald. 15, Hogg to Baldwin, 3 May 1926.

23 Sam. A/66. Beveridge had had to be dissuaded from giving his views on the interpretation of the Royal Commission Report by Steel-Maitland two or three days earlier (Jones, *op. cit.*, II, p. 37).

24 G. Blaxland, *A Life for Unity* (1964), p. 198. The early meetings took place at the house of one of Thomas's race-course friends, Sir Abe Bailey. They were later transferred to that of Samuel's brother.

25 Sam. A/66, draft letter to H. Smith and E. Williams, n.d.; Jones, *op. cit.*, II, p. 42.

26 Citrine, *op. cit.*, p. 185. It was, of course, one of the provisions of the settlement drawn up by the joint subcommittee of 3 May.

27 Lab. 27/4, Samuel to Baldwin, 11 May; Citrine, *op. cit.*, p. 186.

28 Citrine, *op. cit.*, p. 187; see below, p. 236. In a letter to Steel-Maitland written on 9 May, Samuel himself said: 'In the discussions which I have had on the present situation I have made it perfectly clear that I have been acting on my own initiative and without any kind of authority from the government.' (Sam. A/66.)

29 See below, pp. 237–40. This may be the significance of the following, rather obscure, entry in Citrine's diary for 8 May: 'Should we tell them [the miners] all about what was happening? It was risky because they might say that they must consult their full Executive. They might even insist on calling their delegate conference.... We came to the conclusion that it was extremely unlikely that the Government could approach us and we decided to tell the miners so.' (Citrine, *op. cit.*, p. 187).

30 GC, *Mining Dispute*, pp. 18–20.

31 *Mining Dispute*, p. 20 (my italics).

32 *Ibid.*, pp. 16, 20.

33 Citrine, *op. cit.*, p. 188. The miners' report to the trade-union executives in January 1927 does not mention this phase of the negotiations at all.

34 The amendments are to be found in the Samuel papers, Vol. A/159. For Bevin's contribution, see Bev. Ser. C box 6, C2/4/36; and box 5 C2/3/33. There is also a document, not dated, headed 'Suggested terms of settlement', in Bev. Ser. C box 3, which may be the version of the proposals

given to Milne-Bailey at this juncture. It includes a very definite recommendation that the wage structure should be reformed: 'It is suggested that the right way to approach the problem is to reconsider the whole method of fixing wages in the Coal Industry. This is at present complex and confused, and largely out of date.' Bevin specifically proposed the creation of four new national 'standards', covering different grades of colliery employees – a process which he estimated would take three months. Milne-Bailey devised his own proposals for wage reform in a memorandum of 11 May, but regarded them as a very long-term project, requiring perhaps three years to take effect (GC box 125, 13/6/33).

35 *Mining Dispute*, pp. 20–1.

36 Bev., Ser. C, box 6, C2/4/36 (Tillett); Turner, *About Myself*, p. 311; Lab. 27/4, Samuel to Baldwin, 11 May.

37 Citrine, *op. cit.*, p. 194–5.

38 *Mining Dispute*, p. 21.

39 Lab. 27/4.

40 The letter was eventually forwarded to Steel-Maitland on 13 May, and by him to Baldwin on 17 May (Sam. A/66, Samuel to Steel-Maitland, 13 May; Steel-Maitland to Samuel, 17 May).

41 See below, pp. 303–5; *Mining Dispute*, pp. 22–3. The principal amendments from the first source comprised the addition of clauses on the restriction of labour recruitment in the industry, and the provision of special relief or removal expenses for displaced miners. I can find no grounds to credit Harold Laski's claim that 'the ultimate settlement was upon a draft I had written', though his activity as an aide at Eccleston Square had certainly prompted him to produce peace proposals, which he showed to Tom Jones on 8 May (*Holmes-Laski Letters*, ed. D. Howe, vol. ii, p. 839; Jones, *op. cit.*, II, p. 43).

42 Sam. A/159; Citrine, *op. cit.*, p. 197.

43 *Ibid.*, pp. 197–8; *Mining Dispute*, p. 23.

44 Citrine suggests (*op. cit.*, p. 198) that their objection was to the new 'managerial' powers of the National Wages Board, but this appears to have been a minor item. In a letter to Samuel the following day Beveridge did not mention the issue directly, though he did propose that it should be the official advisory committee which was made responsible for overseeing reorganization. On the subsidy, however, he said (speaking for his colleagues), 'None of us would criticise or oppose this, but in view of the definite recommendations of the Commission against a continuance of the subsidy, Lee at least feels that we ought to leave this matter to the responsibility of the Government' (WHB Hc 157, Beveridge to Samuel, 12 May).

45 *Mining Dispute*, p. 23; MFGB Proc. 1926, p. 210.

46 Bev. Ser. C, box 5, C2/3/33.

47 MFGB Proc. 1926, p. 211.

48 Bev. ser. 5 C2/3/33; Citrine, *op. cit.*, pp. 200–1.

49 Sitwell, *op. cit.*, p. 232.
50 Bev. C2/3/33.
51 MFGB Proc. 1926, p. 212; Bevin C2/3/33.
52 Bev. C2/3/33; Citrine, *op. cit.*, p. 202; Turner, *op. cit.*, p. 298. Lord Birkenhead claimed, however, to be simply embarrassed: 'It was so humiliating that some instinctive breeding made one unwilling even to look at them. I thought of the Burghers of Calais approaching their interview with Edward III, haltered on the neck.' (Birkenhead to Irwin, 30 May 1926, quoted in Lord Birkenhead, *F.E.* (1959), p. 533.
53 Lab. 27/9, Appendix K.
54 Citrine, *op. cit.*, p. 203.
55 MFGB Proc., pp. 214–15.
56 Citrine, *op. cit.*, p. 196.
57 Bev. Ser. C, box 5, C2/3/33; box 6, C2/4/36.
58 Citrine, *op. cit.*, pp. 182, 184.
59 It is thus impossible to say who were the dissentients to the policy pursued. But it seems safe to suggest Spencer and Varley of Nottingham, Straker of Northumberland, the Derbyshire delegates and perhaps those of Kent, Bristol and Leicestershire.
60 Bullock, *Bevin*, I, p. 331.
61 It is assumed that the copy of the letter from Samuel to Pugh filed at PRO Lab. 27/4, dated 8 May, initialled by Horace Wilson and minuted 'not sent' is the version which Samuel presented to the Prime Minister on this occasion.
62 Jones, *op. cit.*, II, p. 42; Cab. 23/52 27 (26).
63 Jones, *op. cit.*, II, p. 48.
64 *Mining Dispute*, p. 17.
65 *British Gazette*, 10 May 1926.
66 Lab. 27/9, Appendix K.
67 MFGB Proc. 1926, pp. 213–14.
68 J. H. Thomas's view is more obscure. According to Cook, he appealed to the miners' secretary during the night of 11 May, to 'accept the word of a British gentleman who has been Governor of Palestine' that the lock-out would be called off (A. J. Cook, *The Nine Days*, p. 20). This does not suggest that he was deliberately falsifying Samuel's credentials. But he *may* have understood more quickly than his colleagues the consequences of the miners' rejection of the memorandum. It is clear, at any rate, that he held no grudge against Samuel afterwards: he wrote, on 18 May, 'Please allow me to take this opportunity of saying to you how much I appreciate all that you have done toward averting what I am satisfied might easily have developed into a revolution' (Sam. A/66. Thomas to Samuel). This was in sharp contrast with Pugh's letter, below, p. 238.
69 Citrine, *op. cit.*, pp. 197, 202. Citrine had been told by Arthur Henderson that a minority of the Cabinet had forced Baldwin to break off negotiations on 3 May.

70 Sam. A/66, Pugh to Samuel, 18 May.

71 Harold Laski, who 'looked after' Pugh during the strike reflected his view almost exactly in a letter to Felix Frankfurter on 24 May: 'It [the strike] was called off on a gentleman's understanding, which the Cabinet broke. The Secretariat was perfectly definite to me that if a man of Samuel's standing intervened he could pledge his honour to the T.U.C. that the govt would honour his terms if the strike was called off first. The terms were hammered out, Samuel seeing Steel-Maitland throughout and informing the T.U.C. of his attitude. And I think on this we were entitled to assume that in all except four we were negotiating with the govt.' (Kingsley Martin, *Harold Laski*, p. 66.)

72 *Observer*, 23 May 1926.

73 Bev. Ser. C, box 5, C2/3/34, 28 May.

74 See A. Hutt, *Post-War History of the British Working Class*, p. 159; *Forward*, 29 May 1926; *Sunday Worker*, 23 May; *Electrical Trades Journal*, May–June 1926, p. 70.

75 *Socialist Review*, July 1926, p. 2; *About Myself*, pp. 311–12. In the letter which Samuel addressed to Pugh to accompany the memorandum, he stated decisively, 'I have made it clear to your Committee from the outset that I have been acting entirely on my own initiative, have received no authority from the Government, and can give no assurance on their behalf.' It must be assumed that this was not circulated with the memorandum itself; but it was published in the *British Worker* on 12 May.

76 Professor Bullock asserts that Bevin's behaviour, at least, was consistent, but this is far from the case. He told his area secretaries after the strike that it was the phone call from Downing Street on the night of 11 May which finally convinced him that Samuel was indeed a government emissary; but his unpublished circular indicated that he had believed the 'assurances' of the Negotiating Committee (Bev. box 5, C2/3/33, and C2/3/34). Moreover he supported the adoption of the final version of the memorandum when (according to Citrine) he expected the miners to reject it; but then pressed the Council to make a further appeal to the miners after his forecast had been validated (Citrine *op. cit.*, pp. 196–7). The importance which he attached to securing their adhesion, and his ability immediately afterwards to address Baldwin as if this were incidental so far as the ending of the lock-out were concerned, is in fact very typical of the General Council's common lack of direction and clarity.

77 *The Times*, 24 May 1926.

78 Page Arnot, *General Strike*, p. 227.

79 Sam. A/66, Samuel to Pugh, 19 May 1926.

80 Samuel wrote to Steel-Maitland on 13 May, 'I hope it is quite obvious that the action which I took was only an incident in the termination of the general strike, and that the cause was the self-helpfulness of the nation itself, under the resolute and efficient leadership of the Government' (Sam. A/66). In a letter to Baldwin on 16 May he was mildly critical of

the proposals put forward by the government to the miners two days earlier, but did not mention the memorandum (*ibid.*).

81 Citrine, *op. cit.*, p. 204.

82 Bev. Box 6, C2/4/3, 2 June.

83 *Mining Dispute*, p. 24.

NOTES TO CHAPTER XI

1 Parl. Proc. (HoC), vol. 195, c. 878.

2 H. Nicolson, *King George V*, p. 542.

3 TUC/GS/GC 13 May.

4 The Strike Organization Committee took 'the view that it is imperative that the General Council having called the General Strike off must maintain that position and avoid getting back on the constitutional issue' (GC 131, 13/7/11, SOC mins, 13 May).

5 Parl. Proc. (HoC), vol. 195, cs. 1043–6, 1053–6.

6 *Ibid.*, cs. 1047–8.

7 The only exception mentioned by Thomas was that of the London haulage firm of Carter Paterson, who were said to have demanded a wage reduction of 4s a week. The only other case discovered by the author was a Newcastle engineering firm, mentioned in *AEU Monthly Journal*, June 1926. The cancellation of pay owed to workers at the outset of the strike, and of seniority rights, were more genuine grievances, however – see below, p. 247.

8 *British Gazette*, 13 May.

9 Cab 23/53 32 and 33 (26).

10 Parl. Proc. (HoC), vol. 196, c. 530; Cab 23/53 33 (26).

11 R. Bean, 'The General Strike in Liverpool', *Bull. of North West Soc. for Study of Labour History*, 1, 1974.

12 P. Dollan, 'The Aftermath in Glasgow', *Forward*, 22 May 1926. The figure looks like an underestimate if credit is given to the ETU's claim that 228 of its own members employed on the Glasgow tramway system had been dismissed (*Electrical Trades Journal*, May–June 1926, p. 84).

13 H. A. Clegg, *General Union in A Changing Society*, p. 119; R. Postgate *et al.*, *A Workers' History of the Great Strike*, p. 91; *T&GW Record*, May–June 1926; *Hull Daily Mail*, 17 May 1926.

14 T&GWU *Annual Report* 1926; Lab. 27/9, Report on the General Strike by C. F. K. Macmillan, Appendix Q.

15 Parl. Proc. (HoC), vol. 195, c. 1054. There is no evidence that the company carried out this threat, but according to Postgate they did take such action in Brighton (*op. cit.*, p. 91).

16 GC 129, 13/7/1, Bevin to Firth, 29 May; T&GWU GEC mins, Report of Subcommittee on the General Strike.

17 *Ibid.*; *T&GW Record*, May–July 1926.

18 I&STC/GS, Printing Trades Joint Cttee, 'National Strike Aftermath'; Scottish Typographical Assoc., *90th Report 1926*, p. 28. The union wa hampered by its own closed shop rule, compelling it to expel members who worked with non-unionists (J. Child, *Industrial Relations in the British Printing Industry* (1967), p. 252). NATSOPA exercised a similar ban, and had 501 members on dispute pay at the end of June, mainly in Scotland, though also in Manchester, Cardiff, Plymouth and Sheffield (J. Moran, *NATSOPA: Seventy-five Years* (Oxford 1964), p. 81).

19 Printing and Kindred Trades Federation, *Annual Report 1926*, pp. 35–8. At the end of 1926 NATSOPA and the Electrotypers reached agreement with the *Guardian* allowing men in certain departments to hold two cards, which enabled them to re-establish almost complete unionization, though not bargaining rights. The Typographical Association objected to the relaxation of apprenticeship rules under the new regime, refused to seek an accommodation, and expelled some 200 of their local members. The house union operated as the first stage of the collective bargaining procedure, and outstanding issues were then referred to the Printing Joint Council.

20 Lab. 27/9, Macmillan Appendix Q; E. Howe, *The British Federation of Master Printers, 1900–50* (1950), p. 97; Child, *op. cit.*, pp. 249–50; J. Moran, *op. cit.*, pp. 78–9; A. Anderson, 'The Labour Laws and the Cabinet Legislative Committee of 1926–7', *Bull. Soc. Study of Lab. Hist.*, 23, 1971.

21 Child, *op. cit.*, p. 252; C. J. Bundock, *The Story of the National Union of Printing, Bookbinding and Paper Workers* (Oxford 1958), pp. 337–8.

22 Railway companies were instructed by the government to cut coal consumption to 50 per cent of normal levels following the General Strike (Power 16/23, Mins of Coal Cttee, 17 May 1926). In October 45,000 NUR members were unemployed and 200,000 working a three-day week (Bagwell, *Railwaymen*, p. 495).

23 Bagwell, *op. cit.*, pp. 485–6; Jones, *Whitehall Diary*, II, p. 46.

24 NUR/GS Head Office Circulars; R. A. Leeson, *Strikes*, p. 99; *Railway Pioneer*, May 1926, p. 155; NUR Stratford No. 1 branch minute book, 13 and 14 May 1926 (TUC Library).

25 NUR/GS, Head Office Circulars etc.; Pole to Cramp 13 May; Bagwell, *op. cit.*, pp. 487–8.

26 *Railway Review*, 21 and 28 May. 114 names were given to the unions by the LMS, LNER and GWR before 20 May; 94 were actually moved (Bagwell, *op. cit.*, p. 491).

27 Bagwell, *op. cit.*, p. 492; Turner, *About Myself*, p. 314; Cab 24/180; CP 290 (26).

28 *Railway Pioneer*, June–July 1926, p. 166.

29 GC 129, 13/7/1.

30 ETU EC mins, 12–13 June 1926 (TUC Library).

31 For these cases, see the various district reports in the *AEU Monthly Journal*, June 1926, especially Southampton, Edinburgh, Manchester, Coventry and Bristol.

32 *Operative Builder*, June 1926.

33 Bev. Ser. C, box 5, G. Harris to Bevin, n.d.; *T&GW Record*, May–July 1926; T&GWU GEC Subcommittee report; A. R. Williams, *loc. cit.*, pp. 211–12.

34 I&STC/GS Conf. with Iron and Steel Trades Employers' Association, 28 May 1926; *ibid.*, Special Meeting of Galvanizing Conciliation Board, 16 June; Lab. 27/9 (Macmillan Appendix Q); *The Story of the ETU*, p. 120. One exception, perhaps surprisingly, was Arthur Pugh, who told the Midland Iron and Steel Board that 'he was not prepared to sign his name to a document which required that they should refuse to stand by an organised movement and that they should desert that movement because of their obligations to the Board.' (I&STC/GS, mins of meeting, 21 June 1926.)

35 *Min. of Labour Gazette*, June 1926, p. 210 f.

36 *Ann. Report 1926*, p. 6. The National Union of Distributive Workers reported that of nearly 10,000 of their members involved in the General Strike, only about forty were unemployed by December 1926 (NUDAW *Annual Report 1926*, p. 4).

37 Lab. 27/4, 'Course of Action in Coal Dispute', 13 May.

38 Cab 23/53 31 (26), 13 May; Barnes and Middlemas, *Baldwin*, p. 416.

39 Cab 27/318 RCC (26) 38 and 39. See also MFGB Special Conference, 20 May, *Report*.

40 Parl. Proc. (HoC), vol. 196, cs. 666–7; also c. 2101 and vol. 200, cs. 2145–6. In fact the miners' delegate conference on 14 May simply thanked their fellow trade unionists for their support and resolved to await the government's proposals. Smith diverted a suggestion that the three 'cardinal points' be readopted with the argument that it would 'satisfy somebody outside, particularly the Government, that we have cut straight across the General Council' (*Report*, p. 31). Four days later he gave his own version of the meeting with Baldwin. When the Prime Minister asked the executive whether they had accepted the memorandum 'he wanted us to say "No".' But 'I have realised it is not a sin to tell a lie as far as politics are concerned.... We neither said "No" nor "Yes". What we did say is "Any proposition put down that means our men going home with some wages to live on, the miners will never hesitate, but they will fight against compulsory arbitration".' (MFGB Conf., 20 May, *Report*, p. 17).

41 Parl. Proc. (HoC), vol. 196, c. 667.

42 Cab 25/53 31 (26); CP 202 (26).

43 The Advisory Committee was a much larger body than the joint committee would have been. It was to be allowed to make its own recom-

mendations, but these, even if agreed, could be refused adoption by the Secretary for Mines provided he gave his reasons to Parliament.

44 Cab 23/53 31 (26).
45 Middlemas and Barnes, *op. cit.*, p. 422.
46 Lab 27/4.
47 Cab 27/318 RCC (26) 42; MFGB Conf., 20 May, *Report*, p. 7.
48 Cab 27/318 RCC (26) 42.
49 Lon. D/Lo/B18, Durham Coal Owners' Association, *Annual Report 1926*; also Durham and Northumberland Coal Owners' Association, Report of Secretary, 17 May.
50 CP 212, 213 1926; MFGB EC mins, 9 June 1926. The letter to the Mining Association was signed by Baldwin's private secretary, Ronald Waterhouse.
51 Bald. 15, Steel-Maitland and Lane-Fox, 'The Coal Dispute', 25 May 1926; Jones, *op. cit.*, pp. 60–1.
52 Middlemas and Barnes, *op. cit.*, pp. 431–3; A. Briggs, *Seebohm Rowntree* (1961), pp. 257–68 and Appendix; Jones, *op. cit.*, II, p. 61. For the 'bishops' memorandum, see MFGB EC mins, 15 July; St Loe Strachey papers, Beaverbrook Library, Box 20 f. 2; and Page Arnot, *The Miners 1910–26*, pp. 470–1.
53 Cab 23/53 38 (26); Bald. 18; see also Middlemas and Barnes, *op. cit.*, p. 427; Scheps, 'Trade Unions and the Government, 1925–7' (thesis), p. 361; Jones, *op. cit.*, II, p. 62.
54 C.P. 239 (26); Bald. 18, Churchill to Baldwin, 9 June; Jones, *op. cit.*, II, p. 61.
55 The north-east was especially antagonistic; see Garside, *Durham Miners*, pp. 208–9.
56 Middlemas and Barnes, *op. cit.*, p. 429.
57 About 100,000 tons of coal had been imported by 6 June; up to 400,000 more were expected during the following months (Power 16/23 Mins. of Coal Cttee, 4 and 7 June 1926). During August the level was to rise to around 1,000,000 tons per week (Power 16/525 memo. by Cunliffe-Lister, 31 October 1926).
58 Jones, *op. cit.*, II, pp. 68–9, 74; A. R. Griffin, *The Miners of Nottinghamshire*, pp. 167–8, 176; J. E. Williams, *The Derbyshire Miners*, pp. 714–5; Page Arnot, *op. cit.*, p. 481. For Cook's attitude, see Desmarais, 'Charisma and Conciliation: A Sympathetic Look at A. J. Cook', *Societas*, 3, 1973.
59 MFGB EC mins, 14 September 1926; W. A. Lee, *Thirty Years in Coal*, pp. 83–4; Jones, *op. cit.*, II, pp. 76, 80.
60 MFGB EC mins, 20–21 September; Cab 23/53 51 (26) and 52 (26); Lee, *op. cit.*, Appendix II; Jones, *op. cit.*, II, pp. 82–91; Page Arnot, *op, cit.*, pp. 488–93; Middlemas and Barnes, *op. cit.*, pp. 437–8. According to the last authority cited, Baldwin was willing to widen the terms of reference of the wages tribunal, but was overruled by the Cabinet.
61 Page Arnot, *op. cit.*, p. 494; Griffin, *op. cit.*, pp. 187–93.

62 GC mins, 3 and 23 November 1926; MFGB EC mins, 2 November.

63 MFGB EC mins, 12, 20 November 1926.

64 Griffin, *op. cit.*, p. 207.

65 Garside, *op. cit.*, p. 230.

66 *Min. of Lab. Gazette*, January 1927, p. 4, and January 1928, p. 4; Page Arnot, *op. cit.*, p. 527.

67 Bald. 15, 'Coal Dispute', 25 May.

68 Jones, *op. cit.*, II, p. 76.

69 Cab 23/53 51 (26), Appendix. One minor but revealing indication of this loss of determination is provided by the Cabinet's changing view of the method of proceeds sharing in the coal industry. In July, during the passage of the act suspending the seven-hour day, it had insisted that the West Yorkshire owners withdraw their proposal for an increase in the proportion of profits from 13 per cent to 15 per cent of total revenue, and delayed the passage of the Act in the House of Lords until satisfied. In November it was prepared to allow any owners to claim the higher ratio (Cab 23/53 45 (26); MFGB EC mins, 8 November).

70 D. B. Smith, 'The Struggle Against Company Unionism', *Welsh Hist. Review*, 6, 1973; Griffin, *op. cit.*, pp. 205–8; Williams, *op. cit.*, pp. 737–40; Garside, *op. cit.*, pp. 232–3; Page Arnot, *The Scottish Miners*, pp. 182–95. For further details of the decline of union membership among the miners, see p. 281.

71 Page Arnot, *Miners 1910–26*, pp. 470–71, 505.

72 Garside, *op. cit.*, p. 225.

73 16 and 17 Geo. V., Ch. 28.

74 *Report of the Board of Trade . . . on the Working of Part I of the Mining Industry Act, 1926*, Cmd. 3214, 1928–9; I. Thomas, 'The Coal Mines Reorganization Commission', in W. Robson (ed.), *Public Enterprise* (1937); M. W. Kirby, 'The Control of Competition in the British Coal Mining Industry in the Thirties', *EcHR*, 24, 1973.

75 N. K. Buxton, 'Entrepreneurial Efficiency in the British Coal Industry between the Wars', *EcHR*, 33, 1970; P.E.P., *Report on the British Coal Industry* (1936); *Coal Mining, Report of the Technical Advisory Committee*, Cmd. 6610, 1945; A. Beachem, 'Efficiency and Organisation in the British Coal Industry', *Econ. J.*, 55, 1945.

76 *Report of the Departmental Committee on Co-operative Selling in the Coal Mining Industry* (*Lewis Report*), Cmd. 2770, 1926. The two Labour members of the Committee, Hartshorn and Varley, signed a minority report arguing that the Board of Trade should have power to impose a *national* selling system after two years, in default of voluntary action.

77 Lewis Committee: Report by J. D. R. Bell, D. R. Llewellyn and A. K. McCosh; also Majority Report, p. 23. See, too, Durham Coal Owners' *Ann. Report 1926*, p. 50; A. M. Neuman, *Economic Organisation of the British Coal Industry*, p. 227.

78 Cab 27/319 RCC (26) 99.

79 Neuman, *op. cit.*, pp. 37, 39; Mitchell and Deane, *British Historical Statistics*, p. 116; Page Arnot, *op. cit.*, p. 225. The areas which had carried out the largest effective wage cuts in 1926, the north-east and South Wales, were able to increase exports marginally, but they did so at the expense of Scotland and the other English coalfields.

80 J. H. Jones *et al.*, *The Coal Mining Industry* (1939), pp. 17–18, 25–6; P.E.P. *op. cit.*, pp. 152–3; W. D. Stewart, *Mines, Machines and Men*, p. 92.

81 ILO, *The World Coal Mining Industry*, p. 76. World output rose from an estimated 1237·3 million metric tons in 1925 to 1389·9 millions in 1929 (about 12½ per cent).

82 Board of Trade, *Report on Mining Industry Act*, pp. 7–9; Neuman, *op. cit.*, pp. 227–8; R. Skidelsky, *Politicians and the Slump* (Pelican edn., 1967), pp. 131–2; I. Thomas, *loc. cit.*; M. Kirby, *loc. cit.*

83 Buxton, *loc. cit.*; J. A. Dowie, 'Growth in the Inter-War Years: Some more Arithmetic', *EcHR*, 21, 1968.

NOTES TO CHAPTER XII

1 Citrine, *Men and Work*, p. 198.

2 See Ellen Wilkinson's account of events in Rotherham, *Lansbury's Labour Weekly*, 5 June 1926; and F. Brockway, 'A Diary of the Great Strike', *Socialist Review*, June 1926, on Manchester.

3 *AEU Monthly Journal*, June 1926.

4 For one example of unsuccessful Communist efforts to prolong the stoppage, see B. Davies, *Pages from a Worker's Life*, p. 18.

5 GC 129, 13/7/3 and 13/7/3B.

6 *National Strike, Report of Proceedings of Special Conference of Trade Union Executive, 20–21 January 1927* (henceforth *National Strike*), p. 46. The report prepared for the conference, first approved by the General Council in June 1926, is referred to as *The Mining Dispute*.

7 S. Higenbottam, *Our Society's History* (Manchester 1939), p. 265.

8 For his speeches, see GC Box 131, 13/7/10.

9 The bulk of the miners' financial assistance came from the Soviet Union; but the General Council sent Purcell to the Continent following the strike to seek help from IFTU and other bodies, both for the miners and its own needy affiliates. For the proposal of a general union levy, see above, p. 257.

10 GC mins, 17, 22 June 1926. The most recent charges complained of were allegations that Purcell had criticized the miners' conduct during his European fund-raising mission.

11 *Locomotive Journal*, July 1926: 'It is not leadership to merely stand by whilst thousands of men and their families starve on a slogan. . . . To

many thinking people it is bound to appear to be more sane for some highly-paid men in a disorganized industry to suffer some temporary reduction during a reorganization period than to throw three hundred thousand workers and their families into destitution so that a number of men earning, on the admission of Mr. Cook, the Miners' Secretary, from £5 to £13 per week may retain every penny of their present wages.' Thomas and Cramp, the NUR officials, defended their conduct in the stoppage at some length when their union conference was held in July, but avoided any outspoken attack on the miners.

12 TUC *Report*, 1926, pp. 69–76, 388–92.

13 *National Strike*, pp. 1–3; Labour Party Ann. Conference, 1926, *Report*, pp. 14–17.

14 Klugmann, *Communist Party of Great Britain*, vol. II, p. 246. The miners' *Statement on the General Strike*, submitted to the executives' conference, still bore a marxist imprint, however, thanks probably to the help which the Labour Research Department had given in its drafting.

15 MFGB *Statement*, p. 7, 9; *National Strike*, p. 19.

16 MFGB *Statement*, pp. 10, 13, 15; A. J. Cook, *The Nine Days*, pp. 8, 17, 22–3.

17 *National Strike*, pp. 26, 42–3; *The Mining Dispute*, p. 4.

18 *National Strike*, p. 21.

19 *Ibid.*, pp. 5–6, 27.

20 See especially Bevin's speech, *National Strike*, p. 45.

21 *National Strike*, pp. 23–4.

22 *National Strike*, pp. 4–5; *Mining Dispute*, pp. 8–9.

23 *Mining Dispute*, pp. 16, 21–2.

24 *Sunday Worker*, 13 June 1926.

25 At the Conference of executives in January only one speaker, C. T. Cramp, the railwaymen's Industrial Secretary, suggested that the General Strike raised organizational problems which were intrinsically insoluble, and which rendered its use pointless at any time (*National Strike*, pp. 56–7). J. H. Thomas had, however, argued on similar lines at the NUR General Meeting: 'the more effective you become the more you cripple your own people' (*Report*, p. 12). Other trade unionists had, of course, criticized aspects of the administration of the 1926 stoppage, but they had not regarded these defects as irremediable.

26 *Sunday Worker*, 13 June 1926.

27 TUC 1926, *Report*, pp. 72–3; see also B. Turner, *About Myself*, p. 215.

28 *Mining Dispute*, pp. 15–16.

29 TUC *Report*, 1926, p. 74.

30 NUR AGM 1926, *Report*, p. 12.

31 *Memoirs 1924–37* (1937), pp. 95–6.

32 *Socialist Review*, June 1926, p. 8.

33 CPGB, 8th Party Congress, *Report*, pp. 64–5. The view here expressed was, of course, wholly inconsistent with that held prior to the strike (see

above, p. 191), and significantly different from that expounded in the immediate aftermath (in the *Workers' Weekly* of 4 June), which appeared to accept the possibility of an 'industrial' general strike: 'Nor must the workers accept the argument now being used extensively, that a mass strike of the character which we have recently experienced must end either in revolution or the complete defeat of the working class. This is a travesty of the facts. The General Strike challenging the capitalist system must either go forward to a revolution or down to defeat, but a General Strike for definite concessions, if led with the necessary courage, still holds possibilities for the working class, and the workers cannot throw aside this weapon meantime, for there is no other that can serve them in the struggle against the capitalist offensive.' (Quoted in Klugmann, *op. cit.*, II, p. 216).

34 The nearest approach to such an explanation was offered, though in general terms, by R. Palme Dutt in *The Meaning of the General Strike of 1926* (first published in *International Communist*, vol. 21, June 1926): '[The General Strike was] the extreme point of the development of the old trade unionism and economic struggle, which by the inevitable process of concentration and enlargement had reached the point of automatically passing into a political struggle, i.e. a conflict with the whole forces of the State, whereas the fight was still being endeavoured to be fought by the old means.'

35 Bevin in *T&GW Record*, May–July 1926, p. 243.

36 See 'An Adventure in the Politics of Force,' *Socialist Review*, June 1926, p. 37.

37 See P. Snowden, *An Autobiography*, vol. II, pp. 144–45; Bullock, *op. cit.*, I, pp. 377–9, 636.

38 G. M. Young, *Stanley Baldwin*, p. 124.

39 Barnes and Middlemas, *Baldwin*, p. 449. Their account of the genesis of the measure is marred, however, by the neglect of the activities of the Cabinet Committee and of almost all the negotiations which took place during 1926.

40 A. Anderson, 'The Labour Laws and the Cabinet Legislative Committee of 1926–27', *Bull. Soc. Study of Lab. History*, 23, 1971.

41 CP 204 (26), 17 May; Bald. 22, memo. by T. Inskip, 5 May.

42 The unions principally concerned were the Woodworkers – accounting for one-third of all cases – the Building Trade Workers (16), the Painters and Decorators (14); the ASLEF (18) and the T&GWU (17).

43 CP 204 (26); Anderson, *loc. cit.* The Committee consisted of Cave, Joynson-Hicks, Churchill, Birkenhead, Hogg, Bridgeman, Worthington-Evans, Steel-Maitland and Cunliffe-Lister. Neville Chamberlain was later co-opted.

44 CP 237 (26).

45 See for instance Salisbury's advocacy of co-partnership schemes, CP 365 (26).

46 G. M. Young, *op. cit.*, p. 122.

47 Bald. 11, Steel-Maitland to Baldwin, 11 October 1926; Anderson, loc. cit.

48 Engineering Employers' Federation, *Amendment of the Law relating to Trade Unions and Trade Disputes*, 30 September 1926; National Confederation of Employers' Organizations, *Government proposed amendment to Trade Union Law*, 5 October 1926; Anderson, *loc. cit.*; CP 237, 406 (26).

49 CP 305 (26); Anderson, *loc. cit.*

50 CP 365 (26). Churchill did propose to relieve the financial problems created for the Labour Party by an Exchequer grant towards the election expenses of all parliamentary candidates obtaining a certain proportion of the votes in their constituency.

51 CP 394 (26); reproduced in Anderson, *loc. cit.*

52 CP 406 (26); A. Scheps, 'Trade Unions and the Government 1925–27' (thesis), pp. 404–10.

53 17 and 18 Geo. V c. 22.

54 Lord Birkenhead, *F.E.*, p. 336. For Baldwin's hopes of such support, see Jones, *Whitehall Diary*, vol. II, p. 100.

55 On this see Anderson, *loc. cit.*; Jones, *op. cit.*, II, p. 101; Parl. Proc. (HoC), vol. 205, cs. 1379, 1385; M. C. Shefftz, 'The Trade Disputes and Trade Union Act, 1927', *Review of Politics*, 29, 1967.

56 CP 394 (26).

57 Labour Party Conference 1927, *Report*, p. 27; TUC *Report*, 1927, p. 249.

58 James, *Memoirs of a Conservative*, p. 297. The Conservative Central Office itself issued nine million pamphlets on the subject.

59 Mins of Joint Meeting between Gen. Council and PLP, 17 May 1927; GC mins, 27 July 1927.

NOTES TO CHAPTER XIII

1 H. A. Clegg: 'Some Consequences of the General Strike', *Manchester Statistical Society Papers*, 1954.

2 A. E. Musson, *The Typographical Association*, pp. 399–401; P. Bagwell, *The Railwaymen*, pp. 435–7.

3 Jefferys, *Story of the Engineers*, p. 228; W. S. Hilton, *Foes to Tyranny*, pp. 234–6. The builders' dispute ended in a nominal victory for the unions, but one which failed by some margin to recover the sacrifices of the past two years.

4 Bullock, *Bevin*, I, pp. 236–7.

5 DEP, *British Labour Statistics, 1886–1968*, Table 164.

6 Hyman, *Workers' Union*, pp. 128–30.

7 These figures are not, of course, an accurate indication of union *density* in particular industries. In the case both of general and metal unions the

ratio of actual to potential members is impossible to calculate: the former recruited limited categories of wage-earners in a wide variety of industries, including engineering and shipbuilding. Where approximate estimates of density can be made, the relevant figures are as follows (figures show union membership as a percentage of employees insured under the unemployment insurance acts):

	1923	*1928*	*1932*
Mining and quarrying	68·41	50·20	49·03
Metal manufacturing	27·74	20·70	17·70
Textiles	47·32	45·10	38·84
Paper/printing	53·67	48·31	44·07
Railways	(1922) 65·51	?	(1931) 65·91

8 The funds of the '100 principal unions' were: 1921 £9,452,000; 1924 £9,987,000; 1926 £7,040,000; 1929 £9,631,000. (*Abstract of Lab. Stats.*, vol. 21.)

9 *Min. of Lab. Gazette,* January 1931–4. The total net weekly wage reductions were: 1921 £6,061,000; 1931 £401,150; 1930–3 £772,950. 7,244,000 workers were affected in 1921, just short of six million in 1930–3.

10 Clegg, *loc. cit.*

11 B. Mitchell and P. Deane, *Abstract of British Historical Statistics*, p. 477. For the importance which the General Council attached to wholesale price fluctuations as an explanation of industrial stoppages, see the evidence of the TUC to the Macmillan Committee on Finance and Industry, vol. I, pp. 307–12.

12 R. Martin, *Communism and the British Trade Unions, 1924–33*, p. 82.

13 GC Mins, 24 November 1926, 19 January, 23 February 1927; Citrine, *Men and Work*, pp. 254–6. Martin, *op. cit.*, chap. iv, mentions the NUG&MW, the NUR, the Boot and Shoe Workers, Distributive Workers, Iron and Steel Confederation, Shop Assistants, Painters, Tailors and Garment Workers, the AEU and even the miners. For this subject see also Clinton, 'Trades Councils' (thesis), pp. 252–4.

14 TUC *Report*, 1927, pp. 200–7.

15 Klugmann, *History of the Communist Party*, vol. II, pp. 273–4; J. Lovell and B. C. Roberts, *Short History of the T.U.C.*, p. 96.

16 Lovell and Roberts, *op. cit.*, pp. 96–7; Citrine, *op. cit.*, p. 228; A. Bullock, *Ernest Bevin*, I, pp. 382–3.

17 A. R. Griffin, *The Miners of Nottinghamshire*, p. 161.

18 For the dispute between Bevin and MacDonald, see Bullock, *op. cit.*, I, pp. 348–50; Bev. C Box 6 C2/4/6 and C3/4/30. Professor Bullock's statement that the quarrel was settled appears to rest on slender evidence.

19 MacDonald Papers 5/37 (1) 1926.

20 Middlemas and Barnes, *Baldwin*, p. 453; G. W. McDonald and H. F. Gospel, 'The Mond-Turner Talks, 1927–33: a Study in Industrial Cooperation', *HJ* 18, 1973.

21 *Memorandum on the Causes and Remedies for Labour Unrest*, Cmd. 501, 1919, pp. 12–13; J. B. Seymour, *The Whitley Councils Scheme*, pp. 106–7, 160–1. It is significant that the main opposition to the Mond conversations in 1928 came from the same unions – the miners and the engineers – which had most objected to Whitleyism after the war, though on this occasion the hostility of Cook, the MFGB secretary, was not supported by his executive.

22 GC box 211, f. 262.018, mins of G.C. meeting, 25 January 1928.

23 V. L. Allen, 'Re-organization of the T.U.C.', *BJS*, 11, 1960; TUC *Report*, 1925, pp. 85, 358–69.

24 Bullock, *op. cit.*, I, p. 392.

25 See in particular, Mond's own proposed amendment to the Trade Disputes Bill, referred to in his *Industry and Politics* (1927), pp. 129–30.

26 GC 211 f. 262.063, report on progress of joint committee meetings, 25 June 1928; TUC 1928, *Report*, pp. 224–30.

27 See, for instance, Citrine's letter to Charles Dukes of the NUG&MW, 23 October 1928: 'Part of the scheme I have in mind . . . would be to have a National Industrial Council which would be representative of all the separate Industrial Councils in each industry. However we are probably a long way off that consummation' (GC 235 f. 575).

28 TUC *Report*, 1928, pp. 418, 428–9. Hicks' presidential speech at the 1927 TUC had been suggested by Citrine (*Men and Work*, p. 243). His position in 1928 was difficult to define, and appears to have sprung partly from a personal dislike of Mond. At the end of May Hicks proposed to the Council that the present talks be discontinued, but that a renewed offer be made to meet official representatives of the employers (GC mins, 23 May, 26 June). He then launched an attack on 'capitalist' rationalization in the *Daily Herald* of 21 August. A number of the General Council's members had taken the line that an official conference was preferable to an informal one from the outset, including Bradley (Bleachers and Dyers), Rowan (Electricians) and Bromley (ASLEF).

29 Quoted in W. Milne-Bailey, *Trade Union Documents* (1929), p. 430.

30 For Bevin, see Labour Party Conference, 1930, *Report*, p. 197; for Pugh, *Committee on Finance and Industry*, vol. I, Qs. 4623–4.

31 GC 235 f. 575, Economics Cttee, mins of meeting with certain unions, 16 June 1931.

32 Citrine, *op. cit.*, p. 284–5.

NOTES TO APPENDIX I

1 M. G. Woodhouse, 'Rank and File Movements among the Miners of South Wales, 1910–26' (Oxford University D.Phil. thesis, 1969), p. 140.
2 *Report of a Court of Inquiry concerning the Wages Position in the Coal Industry* (Buckmaster), Cmd. 2129, 1924, pp. 10–15.

NOTES TO APPENDIX II

1 Turner, *op. cit.*, p. 307. For this incident see Citrine, *op. cit.*, pp. 159–60.
2 A. J. P. Taylor, *Beaverbrook* (1972), p. 231.
3 Davidson papers, 'Coal Strike', 26 May; HO 45 12431, Report of Deputy GCC on General Strike.
4 Jones, *op. cit.*, II, p. 33; Cab 23/52 22 (26); Scheps, *op. cit.*, p. 249; James, *op. cit.*, p. 235.
5 Citrine's story that Churchill went to the *Daily Mail* offices presumably confuses the Chancellor's visit, the following day, in the course of launching the *British Gazette* (*op. cit.*, p. 172; see below, p. 178).
6 *The Times*, 4 May 1926. The *Daily News* of 18 May stated that the *Star* had agreed during 3 May to remove some photographs and alter a headline.

Abbreviations used in Notes*

Bald.	Baldwin papers
Bev.	Bevin papers
BJS	British Journal of Sociology
CPGB	Communist Party of Great Britain
D&NCOA	Durham and Northumberland Coal Owners' Association
EcHR	Economic History Review
Econ.J.	Economic Journal
F&ESC	Food and Essential Services Committee
F&GPC	Finance and General Purposes Committee
GC	General Council
IRSH	International Review of Social History
I&STC/GS	Iron and Steel Trades Confederation, General Strike Collection
Intell.Cttee	Intelligence Committee
JCH	Journal of Contemporary History
Labour Party	Labour Party Library
Lon.	Londonderry papers
MAGB	Mining Association of Great Britain
NC	Negotiating Committee
NEC	National Executive Committee
NFBTO	National Federation of Building Trades Operatives
NJC	National Joint Council
NTWF	National Transport Workers' Federation
NUG&MW	National Union of General and Municipal Workers
Pub.Cttee	Publicity Committee
Sam.	Samuel papers
TUC/GS	TUC Library, General Strike collection
W&MC	Ways and Means Committee
WHB	Beveridge papers

* References to government papers in the Public Record Office are given in the Bibliography, section A6.

Biographical Notes (up to 1926)

Trade Unionists

ERNEST BEVIN. Born 1881; National Organizer and Assistant General Secretary of Dock, Wharf, Riverside and General Workers' Union, 1914–21; General Secretary, Transport and General Workers' Union, 1921–; elected to TUC General Council, 1925.

FRED BRAMLEY. 1874–1924; Organizing Secretary, National Amalgamated Furnishing Trades Association, 1912–17; assistant secretary to TUC Parliamentary Committee and General Council, 1917–23; succeeded C. W. Bowerman when the secretaryship became a full-time post in 1923; died October 1924.

JOHN BROMLEY. Born 1876; General Secretary, Associated Society of Locomotive Engineers and Firemen, 1914–; MP for Barrow, 1924–.

WALTER MCLENNAN CITRINE. Born 1887; Mersey District Secretary of Electrical Trades Union, 1914–20; Assistant General Secretary, 1920–3; Assistant General Secretary of TUC, 1924–5; Acting General Secretary from October 1925.

JOHN ROBERT CLYNES. Born 1869; Lancashire District Secretary of Gasworkers and General Labourers (National Union of General Workers); President of National Union of General and Municipal Workers, 1924–; MP (Manchester, Platting) 1906–; Food Controller, 1918; Lord Privy Seal, 1924.

ARTHUR JAMES COOK. Born 1884; miners' agent, Rhondda No. 1 district, 1919–24; member of South Wales Miners' Federation executive, 1919–21; member of Miners' Federation of Great Britain executive, 1921–4; General Secretary, MFGB, 1924–.

CONCEMORE THOMAS CRAMP. Born 1876; President of National Union of Railwaymen, 1918–19; Industrial General Secretary, 1920–.

ARTHUR HAYDAY. Born 1869; District Organizer, Gasworkers and General Labourers (General Workers' Union), 1899–1924; Vice-President and Midlands District Organizer of National Union of General and Municipal Workers, 1924–; MP for Nottingham West, 1918–.

GEORGE HICKS. Born 1879; General Secretary, Operative Bricklayers' Society, 1919–21; General Secretary, Amalgamated Union of Building Trade Workers, 1921–; member of TUC General Council, 1921–.

EDWARD LAWRENCE POULTON. Born 1865; General Secretary, National Union of Boot and Shoe Operatives; member of TUC General Council, 1921–.

ARTHUR PUGH. Born 1870; Assistant General Secretary, British Steel Smelters' Association, 1906–16; General Secretary, Iron and Steel Trades Confederation, 1916–; chairman of TUC General Council, 1925–6.

ALBERT ARTHUR PURCELL. Born 1872; General Secretary, Amalgamated Society of French Polishers, 1898–1910; National Organizer, National Amalgamated Furnishing Trades Association, 1910–; member of TUC General Council, 1921–; chairman, 1923–4; MP Coventry, 1923–4.

TOM RICHARDS. Born 1859; miners' agent, Ebbw Vale, 1888–1901; General Secretary, South Wales Miners' Federation, 1898–; Vice-President, Miners' Federation of Great Britain, 1924–; MP for West Monmouth and Ebbw Vale, 1904–20.

HERBERT SMITH. Born 1862. President, Yorkshire Miners' Association, 1906–; President, Miners' Federation of Great Britain, 1921–.

ALONSO BEAUMONT SWALES. Born 1870; Organizing District Delegate, Amalgamated Society of Engineers, 1912–17; engineering group chairman, ASE and Amalgamated Engineering Union, 1917–; member of TUC General Council, 1921–; chairman, 1924–5.

JAMES HENRY THOMAS. Born 1874; General Secretary, National Union of Railwaymen, 1918– (Political General Secretary, 1920–); member of TUC General Council, 1921–; MP for Derby, 1910–; Secretary of State for Colonies, 1924.

BEN TILLETT. Born 1860; General Secretary, Tea Operatives and General Workers' Union, 1887–9; General Secretary, Dock, Wharf, Riverside and General Workers' Union, 1889–1921; Secretary of Political and International Dept. of Transport and General Workers' Union, 1922–; MP (Salford N.), 1923–4.

BEN TURNER. Born 1863; President, General Union of Weavers and Textile Workers, 1902–22; President, National Union of Textile Workers, 1922–; MP (Batley and Morley), 1922–4; member of TUC General Council, 1921–.

ALEXANDER GEORGE WALKDEN. Born 1876; General Secretary, Railway Clerks' Association, 1906–.

Ministers, employers and public officials

STANLEY BALDWIN. Born 1867; MP for Bewdley, 1908–; Financial Secretary of the Treasury, 1917; President of Board of Trade, 1921–2; Chancellor of the Exchequer, 1922–3; Prime Minister, 1923 and 1924.

SIR WILLIAM HENRY BEVERIDGE. Born 1879; Director of Labour Exchanges, Board of Trade, 1908; Ministry of Munitions, 1915; Director of London School of Economics, 1919–.

WILLIAM CLIVE BRIDGEMAN. Born 1864; MP, 1906–; First Lord of the Admiralty, 1924–9.

GEORGE VISCOUNT CAVE. Born 1856; MP for Kingston, 1906–18; Home Secretary, 1916–19; Lord Chancellor, 1922–4, 1924–8.

NEVILLE CHAMBERLAIN. Born 1869; Director-General of National Service, 1916–17; MP, 1918; Paymaster-General, 1922–3; Chancellor of Exchequer, 1923–4; Minister of Health, 1923, 1924–9.

WINSTON SPENCER CHURCHILL. Born 1874; MP, 1900–22, 1924–; (Liberal) President of Board of Trade, 1908–10; Home Secretary, 1910–11; First Lord of Admiralty, 1911–15; Chancellor of Duchy of Lancaster, 1915; Minister of Munitions, 1917–19; Secretary for War, 1919–21; Colonial Secretary, 1921–2; (Conservative) Chancellor of Exchequer, 1924–9.

SIR IVOR CHURCHILL GUEST, first Viscount Wimborne. Born 1875; Conservative MP, 1900–6; Liberal MP, 1906–10; Paymaster-General, 1910–12; Lord Lieutenant of Ireland, 1915–18.

SIR DOUGLAS HOGG. Born 1872; MP, 1922–; Attorney-General, 1922–4, 1924–8.

THOMAS JONES. Born 1870; student and lecturer, Glasgow University, 1895–1909; Professor of Economics, Queen's University, Belfast, 1909–12; Secretary of Welsh Insurance Commission, 1912; Assistant Secretary and Deputy Secretary to Cabinet, 1917–.

RUFUS DANIEL ISAACS, first Marquess of Reading. Born 1860; Liberal MP, 1904–13; Attorney-General, 1910–13; Lord Chief Justice, 1913–21; Viceroy of India, 1921–6.

WILLIAM JOYNSON-HICKS. Born 1865; MP, 1908– Minister of Health, 1923–4; Home Secretary, 1924–9.

GEORGE RICHARD LANE-FOX. Born 1870; MP, 1906–; Secretary for Mines, 1920–4, 1924–8.

WILLIAM ALEXANDER LEE. Born 1886; civil servant, 1907–; Secretary of Coal Mines Department, 1918–19; Secretary of Mining Association of Great Britain, 1919–.

SIR ALFRED MOND. Born 1868; chairman of Imperial Chemical Industries, Amalgamated Anthracite Collieries Ltd, etc.; MP, 1906–26 (Liberal), 1926– (Conservative); Minister of Works, 1916–21; Minister of Health, 1921–2.

SIR ADAM NIMMO. Chairman, Fife Coal Company, etc.; President, Scottish Coal Owners' Association; Vice-President, Mining Association of Great Britain.

SIR HERBERT SAMUEL. Born 1870; Liberal MP, 1902–18; Chancellor of Duchy of Lancaster, 1909; Postmaster General, 1910; Home Secretary, 1916–18; chairman of Royal Commission on the Coal Industry, 1925–6.

FREDERICK EDWIN SMITH, LORD BIRKENHEAD. Born 1872; MP, 1906–19; Attorney-General, 1915–19; cr. baron 1919, viscount 1921; Lord Chancellor, 1919–22; Secretary for India, 1924–8.

ARTHUR STEEL-MAITLAND. Born 1876; MP, 1910–; junior minister, 1915–19; Minister of Labour, 1924–9.

EVAN WILLIAMS. Born 1871; director, Powell-Duffryn Steam Coal Company, etc.; President of Mining Association of Great Britain, 1919–; President of National Confederation of Employers' Organizations, 1925–6.

HORACE WILSON. Born 1882; Permanent Secretary at Ministry of Labour, 1921–30.

Bibliography

A. Unpublished sources

1. Trade-union reports and minutes cited in footnotes, and held by the TUC Library, together with those belonging to the following organizations:
Iron and Steel Trades Confederation
National Union of Mineworkers (Miners' Federation of Great Britain)
National Union of Railwaymen
Transport and General Workers' Union

2. Minutes of the TUC General Council, together with those of the following subcommittees:
Central (National) Transport Committee
Economic Committee
General Purposes Committee (Finance and General Purposes Committee)
Intelligence Committee
Food and Essential Services Committee
Public Services and Electrical Advisory Committee
Publicity Committee
Special Industrial Committee (Negotiating Committee)
Strike Organization Committee
Ways and Means Committee

3. Labour Party Library: minutes of the National Executive Council, of the Joint Board, and of joint meetings between the NEC and the General Council.

4. Local strike committee reports and proceedings collected by the General Council Intelligence Committee and Strike Organization Committee, and in the case of the Birmingham Transport Committee in the possession of the Library of Political and Economic Science.

5. Private papers:
Baldwin papers (Cambridge University Library)
Beveridge papers (London School of Economics)
Bevin papers (Transport and General Workers' Union)
Davidson papers (Beveridge Library)
Gainford papers (Nuffield College, Oxford)

MacDonald papers (in the possession of David Marquand MP)
Londonderry papers (Durham County Record Office)
Samuel papers (House of Lords Record Office)
Templewood papers (Cambridge University Library)

6. Government documents in the Public Record Office, principally the following series:

Cabinet papers: Cab 23, 24, 27
Home Office: HO45
Ministry of Labour: Lab 27
Ministry of Power: Power 16
Ministry of Transport: MT45
Metropolitan police: Mepol 2

B. Newspapers

Answers
Birmingham Post
British Gazette
British Worker
Colliery Guardian
Daily Chronicle
Daily Herald
Daily Mail
Daily Mail (Hull)
Daily News
Doncaster Gazette
Evening Times and Echo (Bristol)
Forward
Labour Monthly
Lansbury's Labour Weekly
Manchester Guardian
Socialist Review
Sunday Worker
The Times
Western Daily Press
Workers' Weekly
Yorkshire Post

C. Union journals and periodicals

AEU Monthly Journal
Amalgamated Union of Building Trade Workers, *Trade Circular and General Reporter*

Electrical Trades Journal (ETU)
Labour Magazine
Labour Party *Annual Conference Reports*
Locomotive Journal (Locomotive Engineers and Firemen)
Operative Builder (National Federation of Building Trade Operatives)
Railway Pioneer (Cardiff district, National Union of Railwaymen)
Railway Review (NUR)
Trades Union Congress *Reports*
Transport and General Workers' Record
United Society of Boilermakers, *Monthly Report*

D. Official publications

Coal Industry Commission, Report and Evidence, Cmd. 360–1, 1919
Coal Mining: Report of the Technical Advisory Committee, Cmd. 6610, 1945
Department of Employment and Productivity, *British Labour Statistics, 1886–1968* (1973)
Explanatory Memorandum of the Terms of Settlement of the Dispute in the Coal Mining Industry, Cmd. 2488, 1925
Industrial Council, Inquiry into Industrial Agreements, Cd. 6953, 1913
Judicial Statistics of England and Wales, 1926 (Criminal), Cmd. 3055, 1928
Ministry of Labour Gazette
Report of a Court of Inquiry concerning the Coal Mining Industrial Dispute, Cmd. 2748, 1925
Report of a Court of Inquiry concerning the Wage Position in the Coal Industry, Cmd. 2129, 1924
Report of the Board of Trade on the Working of Part I of the Mining Industry Act 1926, Cmd. 3214, 1928–9
Report of the Commissioner of the Police for the Metropolis, 1926, Cmd. 2882, 1927
Reports of His Majesty's Inspectors of Constabulary, 1926, P.P., xi, 1927
Reports of the Departmental Committee on Cooperative Selling in the Coal Mining Industry, Cmd. 2770, 1926
Royal Commission on the Coal Industry, Report, Cmd. 2600, 1926, together with Minutes of Evidence and Appendices, both non-parl.
Statements of Colliery Undertakings, showing Credit Balances and Debit Balances, January 1924–March 1925, Cmd. 2454, 1925

E. Theses

E. BURDICK, 'Syndicalism and Industrial Unionism in England until 1918' (Oxford University D.Phil., 1950)

D. CHEWTER, 'The History of the Socialist Labour Party of Great Britain from 1902 until 1921' (Oxford University B.Litt., 1966)

A. CLINTON, 'A History of Trades Councils from the beginning of the twentieth century to the second world war' (London University Ph.D., 1973)

G. A. PHILLIPS, 'The National Transport Workers' Federation, 1910–27' (Oxford University D.Phil., 1968)

B. PREBICEVIC, 'The Demand for Workers' Control in the Railway, Coal-mining and Engineering Industries, 1910–22' (Oxford University D.Phil., 1957)

A. SCHEPS, 'Trade Unions and the Government, 1925–27, with special reference to the General Strike' (Oxford University D.Phil., 1972)

L. D. THOMSON, 'Relations between Government and the Trade Unions in the General Strike of 1926' (London University Ph.D., 1951)

M. G. WOODHOUSE, 'Rank and File Movements among the Miners of South Wales' (Oxford University D.Phil., 1969)

F. Selected published secondary sources

Works cited are those primarily concerned with the events of the General Strike, and others which have been found particularly useful. (Place of publication London unless otherwise stated.)

'Account of the Proceedings of the Northumberland and Durham General Council and Joint Strike Committee', *Labour Monthly*, June 1926

V. L. ALLEN, 'The Re-organization of the T.U.C.', *British Journal of Sociology*, 11, 1960

A. ANDERSON, 'The Labour Laws and the Cabinet Legislative Committee of 1926–27', *Bull. of Soc. for Study of Labour Hist.*, 23, 1973

S. ARMITAGE, *The Politics of Decontrol of Industry, 1918–21* (1969)

R. PAGE ARNOT, *The Miners: Years of Struggle* (1953)

The General Strike (1926)

'The General Strike in the North East', in L. M. Munby (ed.), *The Luddites and other Essays* (1971)

S. BACKLUND, 'The General Strike in Sweden, 1909', *Labour Magazine*, August 1923

P. BAGWELL, *The Railwaymen* (1963)

'The Triple Industrial Alliance, 1914–22', in A. Briggs and J. Saville (eds.), *Essays in Labour History, 1886–1923* (1971)

D. E. BAINES and R. BEAN, 'The General Strike on Merseyside', in J. R. Harris (ed.), *Liverpool and Merseyside* (1969)

J. BARNES and R. M. MIDDLEMAS, *Baldwin* (1969)

R. BEAN, 'The General Strike in Liverpool', *Bull. of North West Soc. for Study of Labour Hist.*, 1, 1973

R. K. A. BELL, *Randall Davidson, Archbishop of Canterbury* (1938)

W. H. BEVERIDGE, *Power and Influence* (1953)

A. BRIGGS, *The History of Broadcasting in the United Kingdom*, vol. I, (1961)

F. BROCKWAY, 'A Diary of the Strike', *Socialist Review*, June 1926

A. BULLOCK, *Ernest Bevin*, vol. I, (1960)

N. BUXTON, 'Entrepreneurial Efficiency in the British Coal Industry between the Wars', *Economic History Review*, ser. II, 33, 1970

LORD CITRINE, *Men and Work* (1964)

H. A. CLEGG, 'Some Consequences of the General Strike', *Manchester Statistical Society Papers*, 1954

H. A. CLEGG, A. FOX and A. F. THOMPSON, *A History of British Trade Unions since 1889* (Oxford 1964)

G. D. H. COLE, *Labour in the Coal Mining Industry, 1914–21* (Oxford 1923)

A. J. COOK, 'The Coal Crisis and the Way Out', *Labour Monthly*, March 1926

W. H. CROOK, *Communism and the General Strike* (Hamden, Connecticut 1960)

W. H. CROOK, *The General Strike* (Chapel Hill 1931)

Daily News, *Strike Fortnight* (1926)

B. DAVIES, *Pages from a Worker's Life, 1916–26* (1961)

R. H. DESMARAIS, 'Charisma and Conciliation: a sympathetic look at A. J. Cook', *Societas*, 3, 1973

'Strike-breaking and the Labour Government of 1924', *Journal of Contemporary History*, 8, 1973

'The British Government's Strike-breaking Organization and Black Friday', *Journal of Contemporary History*, 6, 1971

W. ELGER, 'The Scottish Worker', *Labour Magazine*, August 1926

E. and R. FROW, 'The General Strike in Manchester', *Bull. of North West Society for Study of Labour Hist.*, 1, 1975

C. FARMAN, *The General Strike* (1972)

H. H. FYFE, *Behind the Scenes of the Great Strike* (1926)

W. R. GARSIDE, *The Durham Miners, 1919–60* (1971)

G. GLASGOW, *General Strikes and Road Transport* (1926)

G. HARDY, *Those Stormy Years* (1936)

R. P. HASTINGS, 'Aspects of the General Strike in Birmingham', *Midland History*, 2, 1974

H. MONTGOMERY HYDE, *Baldwin: The Unexpected Prime Minister* (1973)

R. HYMAN, *Oxford Workers in the Great Strike* (Oxford 1966)

The Workers' Union (Oxford 1971)

A. HURD, 'The Navy on Active Service', *Fortnightly Review*, July 1926

A. HUTT, *The Post-war History of the British Working Class* (1937)

International Labour Organization, *The World Coal Mining Industry* (Geneva 1928)

R. RHODES JAMES (ed.), *Memoirs of a Conservative: J. C. C. Davidson's Memoirs and Papers, 1910–37* (1969)

J. B. JEFFERYS, *The Story of the Engineers* (1945)

J. H. JONES, 'The Report of the Coal Commission', *Economic Journal*, 36, 1926

J. H. JONES, G. CARTWRIGHT and P. GUENAULT, *The Coal Mining Industry* (1939)

T. JONES, *Whitehall Diary*, ed. R. K. Middlemas (2 vols., 1969)

J. M. KEYNES, 'Back to the Coal Problem', *The Nation*, 15 May 1926

M. W. KIRBY, 'The Control of Competition in the British Coal Industry in the Thirties', *Economic History Review*, II, 24, 1973

J. KLUGMANN, *History of the Communist Party of Great Britain*, vol. I, 1919–24 (1968), vol. ii, 1925–7 (1969)

K. C. J. C. KNOWLES, *Strikes* (Oxford 1952)

W. A. LEE, *Thirty Years in Coal* (1954)

D. LLOYD GEORGE (ed.), *Coal and Power* (1924)

L. M. S. RAILWAY, *The General Strike and its Effects on the L. M. & S. Railway* (1926)

J. LOVELL and B. C. ROBERTS, *A Short History of the T.U.C.* (1968)

L. J. MACFARLANE, *The British Communist Party: its origin and development until 1929* (1966)

K. MARTIN, *The British Public and the General Strike* (1926)

R. MARTIN, *Communism and the British Trade Unions, 1924–33* (Oxford 1969)

A. MASON, *The General Strike in the North East* (Hull 1970)

'The Government and the General Strike', *Internat. Rev. of Social Hist.*, 14, 1968

'The Local Press and the General Strike: an Example from the North East', *Durham University Journal*, June 1969

G. W. MCDONALD and H. F. GOSPEL, 'The Mond-Turner Talks, 1927–33: a Study in Industrial Co-operation', *Hist. Journal*, 18, 1973

W. MELLOR, 'The British Worker', *Labour Magazine*, July 1926

L. M. MILLAR, 'The General Strike and the National Council of Labour Colleges', *Bull. of Society for Study of Labour Hist.*, 20, 1970

Miners' Federation of Great Britain, *Statement on the General Strike* (1927)

The Coal Crisis (1925)

Mining Association of Great Britain, *The Case for the Mineowners* (1925)

What Mr. Lloyd George was not Told (1924)

M. MORRIS, *The General Strike* (1973)

A. M. NEUMAN, *Economic Organization of the British Coal Industry* (1934)

R. POSTGATE, E. WILKINSON and J. F. HORRABIN, *A Workers' History of the Great Strike* (1927)

R. A. S. REDMAYNE, *Men, Mines and Memories* (1942)

D. H. ROBERTSON, 'A Narrative of the General Strike of 1926', *Economic Journal*, 36, 1926

VISCOUNT SAMUEL, *Memoirs* (1945)

EARL OF SCARBOROUGH, 'The Organisation for the Maintenance of Supplies', *English Rev.*, 1926

M. C. SHEFFTZ, 'The Trade Union and Trade Disputes Act, 1927', *Review of Politics*, 29, 1967

J. SIMON, *Three Speeches on the General Strike* (1926)

O. SITWELL, *Laughter in the Next Room* (1950)

H. H. SLESSER, *Judgement Reserved* (1941)

D. B. SMITH, 'The Struggle Against Company Unionism in the South Wales Coalfield, 1926–39', *Welsh History Review*, 6, 1973

J. STRACHEY, 'What has the Great Strike Done to us?', *Socialist Review*, July 1926

J. SYMONS, *The General Strike* (1957)

The Times, *Strike Nights at Printing House Square* (1926)

J. H. THOMAS, *My Story* (1937)

Trades Union Congress, *Mining Dispute: National Strike*, Report to a Conference of Executives of Affiliated Trade Unions, 26 June 1926

The Mining Dispute (1925)

B. TURNER, *About Myself* (1930)

S. USHERWOOD, 'The B.B.C. and the General Strike', *History Today*, 22, 1972

A. DE WATTEVILLE, 'The Employment of Troops under the Emergency Regulations', *Army Quarterly*, July 1926

A. R. WILLIAMS, 'The General Strike in Gloucestershire', *Trans. of Bristol and Glos. Archeological Soc.*, 91, 1972

LORD WINTERTON, *Orders of the Day* (1953)

J. WHYMAN, 'The General Strike: its Impact on the Medway Towns', *Cantium*, 3, 1971

P. WYNCOLL, 'The General Strike in Nottingham', *Marxism Today*, June 1972

Yorkshire Post, *The Yorkshire Post and the General Strike* (1926)

Index